The Biographies of Jesus' Apostles

The Biographies of Jesus' Apostles

Ambassadors in Chains

JAMES ALLEN MOSELEY

RESOURCE *Publications* · Eugene, Oregon

THE BIOGRAPHIES OF JESUS' APOSTLES
Ambassadors in Chains

Copyright © 2022 James Allen Moseley. All rights reserved. Except for brief quotations in critical publications or reviews, no part of this book may be reproduced in any manner without prior written permission from the publisher. Write: Permissions, Wipf and Stock Publishers, 199 W. 8th Ave., Suite 3, Eugene, OR 97401.

Resource Publications
An Imprint of Wipf and Stock Publishers
199 W. 8th Ave., Suite 3
Eugene, OR 97401

www.wipfandstock.com

PAPERBACK ISBN: 978-1-6667-3821-6
HARDCOVER ISBN: 978-1-6667-9860-9
EBOOK ISBN: 978-1-6667-9861-6

09/28/22

Unless otherwise noted, Scripture quotations are from *The Holy Bible, English Standard Version*, copyright © 2001 by Crossway Bibles, a publishing ministry of Good News Publishers. Used by permission, in accordance with the "License Agreement for Bible Texts—English Standard Version," http://bibleabc.net/site/translation_esv.htm. All rights reserved or from The Holy Bible: New International Version. © 1996. Grand Rapids: Zondervan. Used in accordance with the publisher.

To Madlene, my wife, and to my children, Natalie, Christopher, Jamie, and Anastasia, and to my grandchildren, James and Mason.

Contents

Who Were the Apostles?	1
What Are Apostles?	12
The Apostles' World	17

BIOGRAPHIES OF THE APOSTLES

Simon Peter, the Rock	33
Andrew, the First Called	65
James, Son of Thunder	75
John, the Apostle of Love	80
Philip, Apostle to Ethiopia	99
Nathanael Bartholomew, Apostle to Armenia	112
Thomas the Twin	115
Matthew Levi, the Tax Collector	123
James, Son of Alphaeus, "the Less"	130
Judas Thaddaeus Lebbaeus, "Dear Heart"	132
Simon the Zealot	136
Judas Iscariot, the Traitor	138
Matthias, the Thirteenth Apostle	150
Saul of Tarsus, or Paul	154
James the Just, the Half-Brother of Jesus	202
Joseph Barnabas, the Encourager	205

OTHERS OF THE APOSTOLIC AGE

John the Baptist	211
Nicodemus and Joseph of Arimathea, Christian Pharisees	238
Stephen, the Martyr	244
John Mark, the Gospel Author	247
Luke, the Beloved Physician	252
Jude, the Half-Brother of Jesus	258

CONTENTS

Timothy, the Bishop of Ephesus	260
Silas or Silvanus, the Colleague of Paul	266
Titus, the Bishop of Crete	269
Aquila and Priscilla, Tentmakers from Rome	272
Apollos, the Eloquent Preacher	275
Minor Characters in the New Testament	278

APPENDICES

Proposed Timeline of Jesus' Life and the Apostolic Age	295
Great Messianic Expectations	339
Pinpointing the Date of Jesus' Birth	347
Pinpointing the Start of Jesus' Ministry	354
Pinpointing the Date of Jesus' Crucifixion	357
Relationships in Jesus' Community	359
The Genealogies of Matthew and Luke	369
Did Matthew Misquote Scripture?	382
Paul's View on Women in Church	385
Calendar Tool	392
Months of the Hebrew Calendar	393
The Hebrew Year	394
The AD-BC Calendar	395
About the Author	397
Bibliography	399

Who Were the Apostles?

"I AM AN AMBASSADOR in chains," wrote Paul (Eph 6:20). He also wrote:

> I think that God has exhibited us apostles as last of all, like men sentenced to death, because we have become a spectacle to the world, to angels, and to men. We are fools for Christ's sake, but you are wise in Christ. We are weak, but you are strong. You are held in honor, but we in disrepute. To the present hour we hunger and thirst, we are poorly dressed and buffeted and homeless, and we labor, working with our own hands. When reviled, we bless; when persecuted, we endure; when slandered, we entreat. We have become, and are still, like the scum of the world, the refuse of all things. (1 Cor 4:9–13)

Who were Jesus' apostles? Were they rich or poor? Educated or illiterate? Related to Jesus and to each other or random strangers? Did they live long and travel far or die young in their hometowns? Did they die as martyrs or in peace?

"Apostle" means "ambassador." These ambassadors did not wear luxurious clothes, travel in style, eat as honored guests at banquets, and retire with government pensions. They bore the cross in pain and joy across the world.

For two centuries, Christians would be a persecuted minority. There was no worldly reward for being Christian. Being a follower of Christ took courage. The twelve apostles, and their first-century coworkers, suffered tribulation and sometimes death as they fulfilled the Great Commission Jesus had given them (Matt 28:19–20). They turned an iron empire upside down and changed our world forever.

In AD 100, about when the apostle John died, there were perhaps one million Christians in the world, probably only 0.3 percent of the global population at that time. Today about 2.5 billion people profess Christianity. So, about 107 times more people, in relative terms, profess Christ today than at the close of the Apostolic Age.[1] These ambassadors in chains fulfilled their mission with surprising effect. This book tells their little-known stories, drawn mainly from the ink on the pages of Scripture, where they have lain in plain sight for over nineteen centuries.

---

1. These statistics are the author's estimate based on the implied growth rate of the nascent church in Acts and on the information available at Pew Research Center, "The Global Religious Landscape," and Kaneda and Haub, "How Many People Have Ever Lived on Earth?"

DISCIPLES AND APOSTLES

All apostles were disciples. Not all disciples were apostles. Disciples (Greek: *mathetes*) were pupils and hence followers. Apostles (Greek: *apostolos*) were ambassadors and hence leaders. Many disciples followed Jesus, witnessing the gospel in the context of their normal lives. The apostles followed Jesus as full-time servants of the Lord and took his word to the world. Jesus had many disciples, but of them he chose only twelve principal apostles (although he also chose Paul, the Holy Spirit chose Matthias to replace Judas, and Scripture calls Barnabas and James the Just apostles).

THE CALLING OF THE APOSTLES

While some of Jesus' twelve disciples followed him part-time from the start of his ministry, they only became full-time followers in phases. On Wednesday, October 17, AD 29, at Bethany by the Jordan River, Andrew and John stopped following John the Baptist and began following Jesus. Andrew called his brother Peter to Jesus that same day. This was during the Feast of Tabernacles in the autumn of AD 29. The next day, Nathanael and Philip were called (John 1:43–45).

These five disciples accompanied Jesus to the wedding at Cana on October 21, after which they all went, with Jesus' whole family, for a lakeshore holiday by the Sea of Galilee (John 2:1–12), probably staying in James's and Peter's capacious homes. They were not, however, yet in full-time ministry.

Not until May 1, AD 30, did Jesus call the four fishermen, Peter, Andrew, James, and John, into full-time ministry. This was 197 days, more than six months, after they first began following him (Matt 4:18–22, Mark 1:16–20). So, Jesus did not appear as a stranger and say, "Follow me, and I will make you fishers of men." Peter, Andrew, James, and John did not rise up and follow someone they did not know. They not only knew him from the previous year, but they probably also had grown up with him from childhood. Jesus of Nazareth was not new to them. Jesus the Messiah was.

Jesus called Matthew toward the end of June AD 30, about two months after calling the four fishermen (Matt 9:9; Mark 2:14). On August 19, AD 30, Jesus selected the full complement of the Twelve. This was 352 days after his baptism in the Jordan and was 111 days after calling the four fishermen (Matt 10:1–4; Mark 3:16–19; Luke 6:13–16).

DUAL NAMES AND LANGUAGES

Why did so many of the apostles have two names, like Simon Peter and Matthew Levi? This was common in ancient Judea, partly because it was a multilingual province. The language spoken in Judean families was Aramaic.[2] The language of worship was

---

2. Aramaic was the language of ancient Assyria, Babylon, and Persia, named after Aram, the son of Shem (son of Noah), whose descendants are the "Shemites" or Semites, including Jews, Arabs,

Hebrew (the primary language of the Old Testament).[3] The language of trade and government was Greek, a legacy of Alexander the Great's conquests.

Judea's Roman rulers from Italy spoke Latin, but few people in the eastern provinces did, so Roman officials had to be educated men, that is, fluent in Greek. Roman soldiers in Judea would have been Greeks, Egyptians, Gauls, Spaniards, Scythians, Armenians, Italians, and others, but if they or Pontius Pilate had spoken Latin, few people would have understood them. Worse, most people would have scorned them, rather as Parisians today disdain tourists who ask directions in English. It was one thing to be a Roman governor in barbarian Britain; one could speak Latin and use an interpreter. Why should a cultured Roman need to speak Celtic or Gallic? But if a Roman were posted to Greece, Asia (Turkey), Syria, Judea, or Egypt, anyone boorish enough not to be schooled in the language of Homer, Sophocles, and Plato would earn pity and contempt. So, in this polyglot society, Jews often had dual names. Matthew had two Hebrew names, Matthew and Levi. Some had one Hebrew and one Greek name, such as John Mark and Saul Paul. And Jesus' followers often had nicknames. Jesus called James and John "the Sons of Thunder." He called Simon "Peter" or "Cephas," which means "the Stone" or "the Rock"—"Rocky." And Andrew and Philip had only one recorded name each, just in Greek.

SCRIPTURAL LISTS OF THE DISCIPLES

All four Gospels record that Jesus chose an inner group of only twelve disciples. The lists of the Twelve in Scripture appear in three groups of four, probably to assist easy memorization in those cultured days when the mind was the library of mankind.

Group One consists of the three men who were always in Jesus' inner circle (Peter, James, and John), plus Andrew, who was one of the only four present for the Olivet Discourse (Matt 24; Mark 13; Luke 21). The names in Group One are consistent, listing the two pairs of brothers (and business partners), the sons of Jonah and the sons of Zebedee. Only the order of the names changes.

Group Two always starts with Philip. The names in Group Two also are consistent, changing only in order. These are the disciples of whom Scripture gives more details; they are the second best-known men after those in Group One.

Assyrians, Babylonians, Carthaginians, Phoenicians, and Ethiopians. ZA Blog, "What Language Did Jesus Speak?"

3. Hebrew may derive its name from Eber, a great-grandson of Shem and ancestor of Abraham. Jewish tradition says that Eber refused to participate in building the Tower of Babel, and so his language, Hebrew, remained pure while God confused the languages of all others. The Jews teach that Hebrew was, therefore, the original language of mankind (Gen 11:1), suggesting that God spoke to Adam in Hebrew and Adam named the animals in Hebrew. This is possible, but as with so much Jewish lore, it lacks biblical support. Moses, who wrote Genesis, was born 2,371 years after Eden. He wrote the Pentateuch in Hebrew but that does not necessarily mean that Hebrew was the language that original humanity spoke. What does seem undeniable is that the Hebrew Bible is the oldest and most reliable complete history of antiquity.

Group Three always starts with James, son of Alphaeus, and concludes with Judas Iscariot (except in Acts, by which time Judas had betrayed Jesus and had committed suicide). Group Three consists of the disciples of whom we know the least. Judas of James has only one "speaking part" in Scripture (John 14:22), while the Bible records no speeches by Simon the Zealot or Jude of James (Judas Thaddaeus Lebbaeus). We know Judas Iscariot only in the context of his treachery.

Group 1

Matt 10:2–4	Mark 3:16–19	Luke 6:14–16	Acts 1:12
Simon Peter	Simon Peter	Simon Peter	Peter
Andrew, his brother	James, son of Zebedee	Andrew, his brother	John
James, son of Zebedee	John, brother of James	James	James
John, his brother	Andrew	John	Andrew

Group 2

Matt 10:2–4	Mark 3:16–19	Luke 6:14–16	Acts 1:12
Philip	Philip	Philip	Philip
Bartholomew	Bartholomew	Bartholomew	Bartholomew
Thomas	Thomas	Thomas	Thomas
Matthew	Matthew	Matthew	Matthew

Group 3

Matt 10:2–4	Mark 3:16–19	Luke 6:14–16	Acts 1:12
James, son of Alphaeus	James, son of Alphaeus	James of Alphaeus	James of Alphaeus
Thaddaeus	Thaddaeus	Simon the Zealot	Simon the Zealot
Simon the Cananean	Simon the Cananean	Judas (Jude) of James	Judas (Jude) of James
Judas Iscariot	Judas Iscariot	Judas Iscariot	

Only Group Three contains apparent inconsistencies. Matthew and Mark list Simon the Cananean, and Luke lists Simon the Zealot. They are the same person. "Zealot" is a translation into Greek (*zelotes*) of the Aramaic word for "zealous" or "jealous" (*qanana*). In English it is rendered as "Cananean." The Zealots were a Jewish faction dedicated to expelling the Romans from Judea by force. They sparked the

Jewish War with Rome (AD 66–73), which ended in the destruction of the Jerusalem Temple in AD 70 and the mass suicide of the last Jewish resistors at Masada in AD 73. Jesus had no difficulty pairing a rebel, Simon the Zealot, with Matthew, the tax collector, a despised collaborator with Roman power. His gospel would embrace the world.

Matthew and Mark list Thaddaeus, where Luke lists Jude of James. Since many of the disciples had more than one name or nickname, there is no reason why Judas Thaddaeus should not have had two names. In fact, he had three: Judas Thaddaeus Lebbaeus. Both Thaddaeus (Greek) and Lebbaeus (Aramaic) translate into "Beloved" or "Dear to the Heart"—"Dear Heart." Since three other disciples had the name Judas (Judas Iscariot, Judas Thomas Didymus, and Judas Simon the Zealot), it is reasonable that Matthew and Mark would distinguish Judas Thaddaeus as Thaddaeus only.

Luke lists the same names in his Gospel as he does in his book of Acts, but in a different order. Possibly he wished to show their later status in the church. In his Gospel, he lists James and John in birth order. In Acts, he lists John, who had become a pillar of the church (Gal 2:9), before James, his older brother, who had died a martyr early in church history (Acts 12:1–2).

THE FULL ROSTER OF THE ORIGINAL TWELVE

1. Simon Peter Cephas bar Jonah
2. Andrew, his brother (no nickname)
3. James, son of Zebedee, son of Thunder, the Elder
4. John, his brother, son of Zebedee, son of Thunder, the disciple Jesus loved
5. Philip (no nickname)
6. Nathanael Bartholomew
7. Judas Thomas Didymus (the Twin)
8. Matthew Levi, son of Alphaeus
9. James, son of Alphaeus, the Younger, the Less
10. Judas Thaddaeus Lebbaeus, son of James
11. Judas Simon the Zealot, the Cananean
12. Judas Iscariot, son of Simon

WHY TWELVE?

Jesus chose the Twelve to correspond to the twelve tribes of Israel. He made this clear when he told the disciples:

> Truly, I say to you, in the new world, when the Son of Man will sit on his glorious throne, you who have followed me will also sit on twelve thrones, judging the twelve tribes of Israel. And everyone who has left houses or brothers or sisters or father or mother or children or lands, for my name's sake, will receive a hundredfold and will inherit eternal life. But many who are first will be last, and the last first. (Matt 19:28–30)

In Revelation, John saw that the New Jerusalem would have twelve foundation stones, and on them would be the names of the twelve apostles of the Lamb (Rev 21:14). John saw his own honorific in this vision. The Twelve would have an eternal place in the new creation. The twelve patriarchs of Israel would also be there. The sons of Jacob (Israel) fathered the chosen people with whom God made the old covenant. The twelve apostles spiritually fathered the church (the *ekklesia* or "people who are called" or the "chosen people") with whom God made the new covenant.

Both sets of twelve give rise to the people of God. The 144,000 witnesses of Revelation (Rev 14:1) are rich in symbolism. Their number possibly reflects the 12 patriarchs x the 12 apostles x 1,000 believers (a multitude) = 144,000. The sense is that Israel multiplied by the gospel multiplied by large numbers of converts (symbolized by 1,000) equals the eternal body of Christ, the kingdom of heaven. Jesus said that the twelve apostles would judge the twelve patriarchs, meaning that the new covenant is superior to the old (Heb 8:13).

Paul explained that faith merges gentile and Jewish Christians into one body, using the metaphor of a cultivated olive tree, Israel, into which God grafts wild olive shoots, gentile Christians (Rom 11:17). The Bible teaches that God has only ever had one chosen people, namely those people who choose God. Israel was the standard bearer, but many non-Israelites, like Ruth, were gentiles whose faith put them in the ancestry of Jesus, the Messiah. Israel was meant to be a light to the gentiles (Isa 49:6; Acts 13:47). The gentiles, by following the Light, Jesus, would join the community of God (John 1:9).

RECORDS OF THE APOSTLES

The written history of the apostles is scanty. The apostles were, for the most part, too busy making history to write it. They also did not consider themselves to be celebrities. Jesus was their whole focus (1 Cor 3:4–11). If the apostles believed that Jesus might return in their lifetimes, they might have felt there was great urgency to convert the world and make new disciples, but little point in writing history for future generations that might never arise to read it.

Luke's Acts of the Apostles is not a history of the apostles but an account of the transformation of the church from an obscure Jewish sect into a worldwide religion. Since Acts tells the story of the emerging church, not of the apostles, it seems almost like a book in two parts: (1) the Acts of Peter and (2) the Acts of Paul. Readers may feel tantalized by the abrupt ending of Acts, wondering what happened to Paul and Peter then. But it never was their story. Acts ends with the arrival of Christianity at the imperial capital of Rome, because that is the tale: the gospel's journey from the Mount of Olives to Vatican Hill.[4]

THE LITERACY OF THE APOSTLES

Sermons frequently refer to the apostles of Christ as poor, uneducated tradesmen. Probably this verse chiefly leads to that conclusion:

> Now when they [the Sanhedrin] saw the boldness of Peter and John, and perceived that they were uneducated, common men, they were astonished. And they recognized that they had been with Jesus. (Acts 4:13)

The Greek word in this passage for "uneducated" means "unlettered." But three of the Twelve, Matthew, John, and Peter, wrote some of the world's all-time best-selling literature. They were thus far more "lettered" than the snobbish Sanhedrin, who felt that only people who had studied under them and accepted the same twisted teachings of Scripture that they professed were educated. In fact, the scholarship of the first-century elite leadership was wobbly at best, false at worst. As just one of many examples, the Jewish elite did not think that any prophet could come from Galilee (John 7:52), whereas Jonah did (2 Kgs 14:25). What affronted the Jewish leaders was that these so-called "unlettered" men were so bold. The apostles were not rabbis, but they had built businesses, had established respectable positions in society, and spoke more persuasively than any group of men in history. They lacked the trappings of the Jewish rulers and yet had more influence. It exasperated the upper class.

SCRIBES IN THE NEW KINGDOM OF HEAVEN

The apostles were more than just literate; Jesus called them scribes "who [had] been trained for the kingdom of heaven . . . like a master of a house, who brings out of his treasure what is new and what is old" (Matt 13:52). It would be surprising if the disciples ignored this and failed to take notes during Jesus' ministry. Consider, for example, that Matthew was not present at the Sermon on the Mount, yet only Matthew recorded it. Either Jesus or the only disciples present, Peter, James, and John (Matt 4:18–22, 5:1), gave Matthew the text. These apostolic scribes would bring out of their

---

4. Christianity reached Rome before Paul first arrived there in AD 57. He wrote his letter to the Roman church from Corinth in AD 54, so there was already a church in Rome by then. Peter probably founded the church in Rome in AD 43. Jewish believers from Rome were present at the birth of the church on Pentecost in Jerusalem (Acts 2:10), and so Christianity reached Rome as early as AD 33. Luke, the author of Acts, used the arrival of the apostle Paul to illustrate the astonishing events that led to the conversion of the empire from within its imperial heart.

treasure what is new, the new covenant, and what is old, the old covenant promises that Jesus fulfilled.

Jesus' ministry lasted 1,350 days, spanning five calendar years (AD 29–33), fifty calendar months, and 44.36 months (calculated as being of 30.5 days' average duration). The Gospels have gaps in their narratives in which Jesus disappears from the pages of history. The gaps total 770 days, which is about two years, representing 57 percent of Jesus' total ministry time. No wonder John wrote, "Jesus did many other signs in the presence of the disciples, which are not written in this book" (John 20:30), and "There are many more things that Jesus did. If all of them were written down, I suppose that not even the world itself would have space for the books that would be written" (John 21:25).

It is plausible that Jesus used these private times to rehearse his disciples in all his teaching and that they, as scribes, wrote their notes and checked them with Jesus for accuracy. In this way, when Jesus ascended and the disciples became apostles, they would have been well equipped with sermon notes that would empower them to take the gospel to all nations, as the Great Commission required. When Matthew, Mark, Luke, and John composed their Gospels, it is also plausible that they would have had access to the sermon notes of all the other apostles, who would doubtless have been happy to share them for the purpose of creating a verified account of Jesus and his ministry. John, therefore, may even have been the first to compose his Gospel, which he may have carried around with him as sermon notes, much as Paul carried notes (2 Tim 4:13). So perhaps John wrote his Gospel before Mark, Matthew, and Luke wrote theirs, but he published his Gospel last of all.

THE ALLEGED POVERTY OF THE APOSTLES

> Peter said [to Jesus], "See, we have left everything and followed you. What then will we have?" (Matt 19:27)

If the disciples had been poor, leaving everything to follow Jesus would have had little merit.

> Peter said, "I have no silver and gold, but what I do have I give to you. In the name of Jesus Christ of Nazareth, rise up and walk!" (Acts 3:6)

Peter might have meant simply that he had no cash on hand, not that he was broke. Or he might have simply been making the point that what he was about to bestow through the power of Christ had "a price above pearls" (Job 28:18).

In the third year of Jesus' ministry (32 AD), a curious event occurred regarding the payment of the tax to support the Jerusalem Temple.

> When they came to Capernaum, the collectors of the two-drachma tax went up to Peter and said, "Does your teacher not pay the tax?" He said, "Yes." And

> when he came into the house, Jesus spoke to him first, saying, "What do you think, Simon? From whom do kings of the earth take toll or tax? From their sons or from others?" And when he said, "From others," Jesus said to him, "Then the sons are free. However, not to give offense to them, go to the sea and cast a hook and take the first fish that comes up, and when you open its mouth, you will find a shekel. Take that and give it to them for me and for yourself." (Matt 17:24–27)

This story does not necessarily imply that Peter lacked the money to pay for himself and Jesus. It does imply that Jesus, as the true King of Creation and Lord of the Temple, was not subject to the tax; nor was Jesus' chosen disciple, Peter. Poignantly, Jesus did not ask Peter to take money out of the disciples' moneybag (John 13:29) to pay the tax. Jesus sent Peter to catch a fish, where he found coins enough to pay for both Jesus and himself. Jesus produced the money from a supernatural source, emphasizing that he was sovereign over all resources.

The apostles all traveled hundreds, and some traveled thousands, of miles proclaiming the gospel. This cost a lot of money. As the gospel spread, they could probably rely on donations from an increasing number of believers. But at the start, they must have relied on their own means. As Margaret Thatcher once said, the good Samaritan could not have been the good Samaritan if he had not had some money in his purse.

The disciples were, most likely, rather well off. Peter and Andrew were business partners of James and John (Luke 5:7, 10). James and John, under the supervision of their father, Zebedee, ran a fishing business wealthy enough to employ multiple hired men (Mark 1:19–20). John apparently had a house in Jerusalem, as well as in Galilee, because when Jesus, from the cross, consigned Mary, his mother, to John's care, the Bible states that John took Mary into his house that same hour (John 19:26–27). That would be impossible if John's only house were in Galilee, since John could not have transported Mary from Jerusalem to Galilee in one hour. It is possible that the Bible was using the word "house" figuratively, meaning that John took Mary into his household that very hour. But there is another piece of evidence suggesting that John owned a house in Jerusalem.

When Nicodemus met Jesus, he came secretly at night to someone's house (John 3:2). Jesus did not have a house. He said that the birds had nests and foxes had dens, but the Son of Man had no place to lay his head (Matt 8:20; Luke 9:58). And since Nicodemus came to Jesus, and not the other way around, the place cannot have been Nicodemus's house. The meeting was private, so presumably Nicodemus and Jesus were alone, except for the only Gospel writer who recorded that meeting: John, the apostle. This does not prove that John owned a house in Jerusalem, but together with the statement about his taking Mary into his house, it does suggest it. If so, he was a man of means, and yet another clue supports this.

When Peter was unable to enter the building where the Jewish leaders were trying Jesus on the night before the Crucifixion, John was able to gain entry for Peter, because John was "known to the High Priest" (John 18:15–16). If John, an ally of Jesus, whom Caiaphas the high priest hated, could still call in a high priestly favor, and, of all favors, that of giving a pass to Jesus' chief disciple, who had just cut off the ear of the high priest's servant, Malchus (Matt 26:51; Mark 14:47; Luke 22:50; John 18:10), John must have been a man of influence. How does one gain influence with a high priest? Be a major donor.

One other clue about the affluence of disciples is that Andrew and John were followers of John the Baptist before they became disciples of Jesus (John 1:35–40). To enroll as disciples of Jesus' radical Nazirite cousin, the Baptist, both John and Andrew must have been young men able to afford some leisure. They cannot have been subsistence fishermen.

Matthew, of course, was a tax collector and as such was flat-out wealthy and educated. Yet the others also were probably not poor. Jesus' statement that it is easier for a camel to pass through the eye of a needle than for a rich man to pass into heaven provoked a yelp from the disciples (Matt 19:24; Mark 10:25; Luke 18:25). They asked who then might be saved? If they had considered themselves poor, they would not have asked that question. Jesus told them that while with men this would be impossible, with God all things are possible.

Paul, who was once one of the Jewish ruling class (Acts 23:6; Phil 3:5), must have been somewhat wealthy to be able to afford to travel from Tarsus to reside in Jerusalem and take up advanced studies under the famous rabbi Gamaliel. His sister also lived in Jerusalem with Paul's nephew, for it was Paul's sister's son who warned Paul of the Jews' intention to ambush and assassinate him (Acts 23:16).

If the disciples were rich or at least comfortable financially when they began to follow Jesus, their faith is more remarkable, not less. They left comfort behind to store up their treasure in heaven.

THE WITNESS OF THE APOSTLES

The testimony of the apostles is some of the most compelling evidence for the truth of the resurrection. That a band of persecuted men would willingly suffer and even go to grisly deaths rather than break down and confess something that every one of them knew to be a lie stretches credulity beyond the breaking point. If Jesus' resurrection had been a fraud, the apostles, of all people, would have known it. While a fanatic might die for a lie he thought to be true, only a lunatic would die for a claim that he knew to be false. Yet even the apostles' enemies knew that they were far from mad; they marveled that such untutored fishermen were so erudite (Acts 4:13).

All the apostles suffered arrest and torture, and most suffered martyrdom for refusing to deny the resurrection of Christ. ("Martyr" is the Greek word for "witness.") Materially and socially, they had everything to lose. There was no rich legacy of money or honor or power for these martyrs to leave to their families if the resurrection was a hoax. Until the Edicts of Toleration in AD 311–337, a Christian in the Roman Empire was a despised outlaw.

From AD 33, on Good Friday[5] through the following Sabbath day,[6] the apostles were whimpering, broken fugitives. After Resurrection Sunday,[7] they were lions who revolutionized the world. What caused this astonishing change? After watching Jesus undeniably die, the apostles saw, touched, and ate with the risen Lord, not once, but many times for over forty days. The fact of the resurrection demonstrated to them (and demonstrates to us) that Jesus is God; and if he is God, his teaching is true. Only the realization of that could have been worth more to the apostles than their lives.

---

5. April 1, AD 33.
6. Saturday, April 2, AD 33.
7. Sunday, April 3, AD 33.

What Are Apostles?

PROOFS OF AN APOSTLE

Many have claimed to be apostles, such as Mohammad and some religious leaders today. Are they? One way to know is to see how many biblical precedents of apostleship they meet. These apply to most of those whom Scripture calls "apostle":

- They saw the Lord Incarnate.
- Jesus called them in person.
- The Holy Spirit worked through them.
- They taught God's word, not their own philosophy.
- God worked miracles through them.

The Apostles Saw the Lord Incarnate

When Peter urged the apostles to choose a replacement for Judas Iscariot after his suicide, he described a direct relationship with Jesus during his earthly mission as an indispensable criterion. He said of the replacement: "One of the men who have accompanied us during all the time that the Lord Jesus went in and out among us, beginning from the baptism of John until the day when he was taken up from us—one of these men must become with us a witness to his Resurrection" (Acts 1:21–22). When Paul defended his status as an apostle, he made this justification: "Am I not an apostle? Have I not seen Jesus our Lord?" (1 Cor 9:1). So, an apostle must have seen Jesus face-to-face.

Jesus Christ Called Them in Person

Jesus personally called the Twelve into a unique, lifelong mission: "And when day came, he called his disciples and chose from them twelve, whom he named apostles"

(Luke 6:13). Jesus told them: "You did not choose me, but I chose you and appointed you that you should go and bear fruit and that your fruit should abide, so that whatever you ask the Father in my name, he may give it to you" (John 15:16). Paul described himself as "an apostle—not from men nor through man, but through Jesus Christ and God the Father, who raised him from the dead" (Gal 1:1). So, an apostle must be someone whom Jesus appointed in person.

The Holy Spirit Worked Through Them

Jesus ordained the apostles to bring the word to the world. God guaranteed the accuracy and success of their mission through the guidance of the Holy Spirit. Jesus told the apostles while he was still with them: "The Helper, the Holy Spirit, whom the Father will send in my name, he will teach you all things and bring to your remembrance all that I have said to you" (John 14:26). The apostles knew that their wisdom and miracles were of God, not the fruit of their own talents. As Paul wrote,

> These things God has revealed to us through the Spirit. For the Spirit searches everything, even the depths of God. For who knows a person's thoughts except the spirit of that person, which is in him? So also no one comprehends the thoughts of God except the Spirit of God. Now we have received not the spirit of the world, but the Spirit who is from God, that we might understand the things freely given us by God. And we impart this in words not taught by human wisdom but taught by the Spirit, interpreting spiritual truths to those who are spiritual. The natural person does not accept the things of the Spirit of God, for they are folly to him, and he is not able to understand them because they are spiritually discerned. The spiritual person judges all things but is himself to be judged by no one. "For who has understood the mind of the Lord so as to instruct him?" But we have the mind of Christ. (1 Cor 2:10–16)

So, the Holy Spirit empowered the apostles.

They Taught God's Word, Not Their Own Philosophy

Paul wrote to the Thessalonians, "And we also thank God constantly for this, that when you received the word of God, which you heard from us, you accepted it not as the word of men but as what it really is, the word of God, which is at work in you believers" (1 Thses 2:13). Peter wrote: "No prophecy of Scripture comes from someone's own interpretation. For no prophecy was ever produced by the will of man, but men spoke from God as they were carried along by the Holy Spirit" (2 Pet 1:20–21). So, apostolic teaching is directly from God, not produced by man.

God Worked Miracles through Them

God endorsed the mission of prophets and apostles through signs and wonders. A true miracle is not merely an inexplicable event. There are many inexplicable events that are so commonplace we hardly notice them. For example, the ability to conceive the thought that your finger should move, to command your finger to move, and to see it move as you intended is fundamentally inexplicable. Physiology can trace some of the mechanisms by which the brain translates an idea into electricity, which traverses the nerves, leaps synapses, and stimulates the finger's muscles to react. But what originally causes the brain to give birth to the idea to set these events in motion is a profound mystery. We can describe why the sun seems to rise and many of the properties of light, but why the sun should exist at all or have the characteristics it does—let alone why its rays should renew hope in a soul which, the night before, lay prostrate in despair—the wise cannot explain. A miracle is an event that God causes to highlight his message to mankind and to inspire faith in his chosen messengers.

Jesus performed miracles that confirmed his identity as Messiah. God worked miracles through the apostles to confirm their authority to preach God's word to the world. After Jesus' ascension, the apostles "went out and preached everywhere, while the Lord worked with them and confirmed the message by accompanying signs" (Mark 16:20). In the early days at Jerusalem, "many signs and wonders were regularly done among the people by the hands of the apostles" (Acts 5:12). Paul assured the church at Corinth that they could trust his message, because "the signs of a true apostle were performed among you with utmost patience, with signs and wonders and mighty works" (2 Cor 12:12). So, the apostles worked verifiable miracles through the power of God.

TESTS OF APOSTLESHIP

There has never been a shortage of false apostles, even in the first century. They fall into two categories: (1) those who deceive others and (2) those who deceive others and themselves. Of those who deceive others, Paul wrote:

> What I do I will continue to do, in order to undermine the claim of those who would like to claim that in their boasted mission they work on the same terms as we do. For such men are false apostles, deceitful workmen, disguising themselves as apostles of Christ. And no wonder, for even Satan disguises himself as an angel of light. So, it is no surprise if his servants, also, disguise themselves as servants of righteousness. Their end will correspond to their deeds. (2 Cor 11:12–15)

Of those who deceive others and themselves, Jesus said:

You will recognize them by their fruits. Not everyone who says to me, "Lord, Lord," will enter the kingdom of heaven, but the one who does the will of my Father who is in heaven. On that day many will say to me, "Lord, Lord, did we not prophesy in your name, and cast out demons in your name, and do many mighty works in your name?" And then will I declare to them, "I never knew you; depart from me, you workers of lawlessness." (Matt 7:20–23)

Discerning Christians should ask these scriptural questions of anyone claiming to be an apostle:

- Has he seen Christ face-to-face?
- Has Jesus personally called him?
- Is the Holy Spirit empowering him?
- Is he teaching God's word and not his own philosophy?
- Is he working confirmed miracles through the Holy Spirit?

Only if these things are true of someone can Christians be quite sure that such a person is an apostle. The likelihood of an apostle, in the original, biblical sense, appearing today is therefore slight. Of course, God can do anything through anyone at any time, but given these criteria, it is probably safe to regard the Apostolic Age as past.

BIBLICAL EXCEPTIONS

Luke calls Barnabas an apostle (Acts 14:14), and Paul calls James the Just an apostle (Gal 1:19). James the Just was the half-brother of Jesus. He certainly knew Jesus face-to-face, and Jesus called him personally. Whether these two criteria were true of Barnabas is unknown. It is, however, possible. Barnabas was a wealthy Jew from Cyprus who was resident in Jerusalem and was a follower of Jesus in the early days of the church. He may have known the incarnate Jesus personally. Perhaps the Holy Spirit called Barnabas in a way that qualified him especially to be called apostle. The inescapable fact is that the Bible calls him an apostle and calls no one else by that title other than the Eleven, Matthias, Paul, and James the Just.

The fact that Scripture never calls Luke, Mark, Timothy, or Titus apostles probably means that we should not bestow the title of apostle on anyone lightly. The office is clearly a special one, for Paul writes, "[Christ] gave the apostles, the prophets, the evangelists, the shepherds and teachers to equip the saints" (Eph 4:11), and "God has appointed in the church first apostles, second prophets, third teachers, then miracles, then gifts of healing, helping, administrating, and various kinds of tongues" (1 Cor 12:28). This latter verse reveals that an apostle ranks even higher in God's kingdom than a prophet, so even higher than Moses or Isaiah. Probably this is because Old Testament prophets foretold the mission of Christ, while Jesus' apostles witnessed and testified to it. Jesus told the Twelve, "for truly, I say to you, many prophets and righteous people longed to see what you see, and did not see it, and to hear what you hear, and did not hear it" (Matt 13:17). The apostles were messengers of Christ especially ordained in the first century to proclaim the gospel to the world. Although many good disciples proclaim the gospel to the world today, to call them apostles is probably a stretch.

The Apostles' World

THEIR FAMILY TIES

God used the twelve patriarchs of Israel, all brothers, to form the old covenant community of God. God used the twelve apostles, all Galileans (except possibly Judas Iscariot), to form the new covenant community of God. Their family ties may have been surprisingly tight. Peter and Andrew were blood brothers (Matt 4:18). James and John were blood brothers (Matt 4:21). Peter, Andrew, James, and John were partners in the fishing industry (Luke 5:7, 10). Matthew Levi and James the Less may have been brothers. James, John, James the Less, Matthew, Judas Thaddaeus, and Simon the Zealot may have been Jesus' cousins, and thus nephews of Jesus' mother, Mary, or stepfather, Joseph. Simon the Zealot may have been the groom at the wedding at Cana. To explore these possibilities, see "Relationships in Jesus' Community" in the Appendices.

In any case, all the apostles came from Galilee, except perhaps Judas Iscariot, whose name means "from Kirioth," a town in Judea. Yet even he may have been a Galilean, for his father, Simon Iscariot (John 6:71, 13:2, 26), may have moved to Galilee and raised Judas there. If so, his identifier, Iscariot, would have made sense, marking him as someone whose family was originally from outside Galilee. Paul was born in Gischala in Galilee. When Quirinius annexed Galilee to the Roman province of Judea in AD 7,[1] Paul's family moved to Tarsus in Cilicia (modern Turkey).[2]

Galilee was a small place, and so all the apostles except Paul undoubtedly knew each other growing up, even if they were not related by blood. They surely traveled together on the yearly family pilgrimages to Jerusalem to celebrate Passover in spring, Pentecost in summer, the High Holy Days in fall, and Chanukah in December.

---

1. Josephus, *Ant.* 18:2:1.
2. Jerome, *On Illustrious Men*.

THEIR APPEARANCE

Paintings of Jesus with long hair and a full beard and of first-century Jews in Persian turbans and Bedouin robes are fantasies of later artists. The Hellenistic world created by Alexander the Great was remarkably homogenous in style. From Britain to North Africa, from Spain to India, people affected Greek manners. The earliest paintings of Jesus depict him as the Good Shepherd with short hair, no beard, and wearing a knee-length tunic.[3] This is probably far more what Jesus looked like than the paintings we know and love. The apostle Paul admonished men not to let their hair grow long (1 Cor 11:14), which he would hardly have done if the other apostles or the Sanhedrin had worn their hair long; he certainly would not have written that if Jesus had worn his hair long.

The caesars all were clean-shaven, until the emperor Hadrian made a short beard fashionable, which he only did to cover his badly blemished skin. The Sadducees, who were the Hellenized rulers of the Jews, and the overtly Romanized Herodians were certainly clean-shaven, in imitation of their Roman overlords. Do not let shaggy medieval and Renaissance portraits of Herod the Great deceive. Look at the smooth ancient busts of Herod; it is hard to distinguish him from a noble Roman. Most of the apostles would have presented themselves in the same way, retaining the services every three days of professional barbers, who used iron razors to keep beards trim. Women wore head coverings and let their hair grow to shoulder length.

People in Jesus' day wore Greek tunics, which were like loose dresses with elbow-length sleeves and a belt. The cloth was wool in winter and linen in summer. The hem of the tunic reached below the knee, although in Greece it often fell above the knee, both for men and women. Over the tunic, men and women wore a cloak, which was a simple, rectangular poncho with a hole for the head and neck. For poor people, the simple cloak might also serve as their only blanket at night. In the eastern empire, people did not wear togas. The toga was the ornamental dress of the nobility in Rome.

GALILEE

Josephus, the first-century Jewish historian, described Galilee in this way:

> Thanks to the rich soil, there is not a plant that does not flourish there, and the inhabitants grow everything . . . walnuts . . . flourish in abundance, as do palms . . . side by side with figs and olives . . . not only does it produce the most surprisingly diverse fruits; it maintains a continuous supply. Those royal fruits the grape and fig it furnishes for ten months on end.[4]

---

3. Caldwell, "Three of the Oldest Images of Jesus."
4. Josephus, *War* 3:10:8.

Galilee was the most fertile and productive part of Israel. Josephus wrote that the region consisted of two hundred villages. It was about the size of Rhode Island, or about one-tenth the size of California. The Sea of Galilee, also called Lake Tiberias, the Sea of Gennesaret,[5] or Lake Kinneret,[6] is only thirteen miles long and eight miles wide with a maximum depth of about 130 feet. It is about one percent the size of Lake Ontario, the smallest of the Great Lakes. At over six hundred feet below sea level, it is the lowest freshwater lake in the world.

Galilee had an important Jewish population, but the majority of its residents were gentile. Other gentile populations also surrounded Galilee—Syrian Phoenicians to the north and west, Samaritans (Assyrian-Hebrew half-castes) to the south, Greeks of the Decapolis, and nomadic Arabs to the east. The Jewish Galileans were independent, resourceful, worldly, and proud of their heritage.

THE IMPORTANCE OF JUDEA

Judea was not a forgotten backwater in the Roman world. Jews represented about ten percent of the population of the western empire and about twenty percent of the population of the eastern empire. By comparison, Jews represent only about two per cent of the population of the United States today. Never since the fall of Judah to Babylon in the sixth century BC until the twentieth century had Jews comprised so large a part of any body politic. The Herods, as faux "kings of the Jews," were on friendly, familiar terms with several Roman emperors, and Roman law initially recognized Judaism as a tolerated religion, despite its frequent friction with the state cult of emperor worship.

Egypt, to the south of Judea, was Rome's breadbasket. Rome relied on the dependable harvests of the Nile Valley for grain to feed its legions. Alexandria in Egypt was the second largest and richest city in the empire, after Rome. Syria, to the north of Judea, was a thriving commercial territory and a bulwark against Rome's only Asian enemy, Parthia (Persia). Antioch in Syria was the third largest and richest city in the empire. Judea was the linchpin between these two vital provinces. The great resources Rome spent defeating the Jewish Revolt of AD 66–73 is a measure of Judea's political, military, and economic importance.

THE JEWISH SECTS

Josephus identified four main Jewish sects.[7] (1) The Sadducees or Zadokis, named after David's priest, Zadok (2 Sam 8:17), meaning "righteous," were the Roman-friendly ruling class who did not believe in an afterlife, angels, or the supernatural. They were the most numerous and powerful Jewish leaders. They believed that only the Torah

---

5. Which means "a garden of riches."
6. Referring to a nearby town, Kinnereth, allotted to the tribe of Naphtali (Josh 19:35).
7. Josephus, *War* 2:8:2–14, 7:8:1; *Ant.* 13:5:9, 18:1:2.

(first five books of the Bible) was canonical. The high priests Ananias (Annas) and Joseph Caiaphas were of their number. (2) The Pharisees, whose name means "set apart," believed in the supernatural, the resurrection of the dead, and angels, and they counted Paul and Gamaliel among their number. (3) The Essenes, "secret or sacred," were a strict, holy order of Jewish ascetics who lived a life of work, prayer, and celibacy in wilderness communities. (4) The Zealots (Hebrew: *kanai*, meaning an ardent follower), objected to Roman emperor worship, Roman taxation, and the Roman-supported Herodian kings. They aimed to drive Rome from the promised land under the leadership of a monarch from the line of Judah (the anticipated Messiah, whom they were prepared to follow, hence their name).

ROME

The Roman Empire extended from Britain to North Africa and from Spain to Russia and Parthia (Persia). It was a somewhat dysfunctional family of nations, forged by military conquest and held together by Roman law and legions. This was the iron part of Daniel's dream statue (Dan 2:40-43). The people of the empire spoke many languages and worshipped diverse gods. The eastern Roman Empire never adopted Latin as its common tongue. Greek was the language of culture and trade. The elite considered Latin vulgar. For this reason, the New Testament was written in Greek and its later translation into Latin by Jerome was called the Vulgate Version, a rendering into the vulgar or common tongue. The empire's cultural diversity was the clay in Daniel's dream statue.

Rome is the city of seven hills (cf. Revelation 17:9). The seven hills are the: (1) Aventine Hill (*Aventinus*), (2) Caelian Hill (*Caelius*), (3) Capitoline Hill (*Capitolinus*),[8] (4) Esquiline Hill (*Esquilinus*), (5) Palatine Hill (*Palatinus*), (6) Quirinal Hill (*Quirinalis*), and (7) Viminal Hill (*Viminalis*). The Vatican Hill was not one of the traditional Seven Hills. It is north of the river Tiber, outside the ancient city walls. The word "Vatican" comes from Latin "*vates*," meaning "seer, soothsayer." Vaticanus was an Etruscan god, and his temple sat on the Vatican Hill. The church of Rome moved its seat to the Vatican Hill in the fourteenth century (after the awkward interlude of the Avignon Papacy, during which, at one point, no fewer than three popes claimed Peter's tiara).

Pagan historians mainly ignored Christianity in its early days. Plutarch's famous history was called *Lives of Noble Greeks and Romans*. The church fathers were neither noble, Greek, nor Roman and therefore little worth noting. The apostles were born in the reign of Caesar Augustus, from 27 BC to AD 14. This was the era of the *Pax*

---

8. The American capitol is spelled with an *-ol* rather than an *-al* in imitation of Rome. The US capital ("head" from Latin, *capus*) city is Washington, DC. The US Congress is on the Capitol (or Capitoline) Hill, because the Founders considered the American Republic a "New Rome." They even pretentiously named Goose Creek, a tiny tributary of the Potomac River, the Tiber, in strained emulation of the Eternal City.

Romana, or Roman Peace. The endless civil wars were over or would be until AD 69. Travel was relatively easy and safe over the Roman network of roads, and the government was tolerant of different religions.

After Augustus, Tiberius reigned from AD 14 to 37.[9] Tiberius was the emperor who appointed Pontius Pilate procurator of Judea. Caligula followed Tiberius, from AD 37 to 41. Caligula started well but went mad. His praetorian guards assassinated him. He attempted to install a statue of himself as a god in the Jerusalem Temple, an abomination that certainly would have caused desolation (Dan 12:11 Matt 24:15; Mark 13:14). The Jews were outraged, but before the ship carrying the statue could reach Caesarea, news of Caligula's death preceded it, and the statue was never installed. Claudius followed Caligula from AD 41 to 54. Although apparently a drooling, stumbling fool, he was savvier than he seemed, and he restored stability to the empire. He had his promiscuous wife, Messalina, executed for plotting against him. He married his niece, Agrippina, and adopted her son, Nero, as his heir. Irritated at the squabbling between Christians and Jews, whom he could probably not bother to distinguish from each other, he expelled all Jews from Rome in AD 49. This caused the Roman church to become gentile-led. When the Jewish Christians returned to Rome as the edict lapsed, they were aghast to find that the church had abandoned Jewish traditions. To bridge this gap between Jewish and gentile Christians, Paul wrote his epistle to the Romans. In AD 54, at the age of sixty-four, Claudius died at a feast, probably from eating mushrooms poisoned by Agrippina so that her son Nero could succeed him. Nero ruled from AD 54 to 68. Like Caligula, he started well, but degenerated into a tyrant of bestial cruelty, persecuting Christians terribly for three and a half years, from mid AD 64 until his suicide in mid-AD 68.

Nero's Persecution of Christians

In AD 64, a great fire destroyed ten of Rome's fourteen districts. Rumors circulated that Nero had started the fire to clear the city of commoners and make space for his planned Golden Palace (*Domus Aureus*). The rumors were dubious, but to deflect the erupting anger of the Roman mob, Nero accused the Christians of arson. He began a persecution of epic proportions, lasting three and a half years, until his death in AD 68. The Roman historian Tacitus wrote this account of what Christians, whom he personally despised, suffered:

> Neither human resources, nor imperial generosity, nor appeasement of the gods, eliminated the sinister suspicion that the fire had been deliberately started. To stop the rumor, Nero made scapegoats—and punished with every refinement the notoriously depraved Christians (as they were popularly called).

---

9. Finegan, *Handbook*, 339. Finegan's chart is a little confusing, but close inspection of it reveals that Finegan means Tiberius's first regnal year was from August 19, AD 14 to August 18, AD 15.

Their originator, Christ, had been executed in Tiberius' reign by the Procurator of Judea, Pontius Pilatus. But in spite of this temporary setback, the deadly superstition had broken out again, not just in Judea (where the mischief had started) but even in Rome. All degraded and shameful practices collect and flourish in the capital. First, Nero had the self-admitted Christians arrested. Then, on their information, large numbers of others were condemned—not so much for starting fires as because of their hatred for the human race. Their deaths were made amusing. Dressed in wild animals' skins, they were torn to pieces by dogs, or crucified, or made into torches to be set on fire after dark as illumination . . . Despite their guilt as Christians, and the ruthless punishment it deserved, the victims were pitied. For it was felt that they were being sacrificed to one man's brutality rather than to the national interest.[10]

Suetonius also wrote, "[after the Great Fire] punishments were also inflicted on the Christians, a sect professing a new and mischievous belief."[11] Ironically, Nero's gardens, where so many Christians suffered, were on the Vatican Hill, the future site of the church of Rome, which would outlive and replace the dynasty of the Caesars. How many Christians died under Nero is unrecorded, but the Neronian persecution was probably not confined to Rome, and throughout the empire it probably claimed the lives of a large number of believers. Christians who were Roman citizens, by law, were exempt from torture. Thus, Paul was beheaded because he was a citizen, while Peter was crucified because he was not. Subsequent emperors (Domitian, Valerian, and Diocletian) imitated Nero's persecution of Christians. They, like the philosopher-king Marcus Aurelius, scorned Christianity. Finally, the emperor Constantine's Edict of Toleration in AD 313 allowed anyone in the empire to observe the Christian religion freely and openly. Under Roman persecution, the church grew through suffering, and it eventually conquered Rome. Under Rome's persecution, the Jewish temple and sacrificial system perished utterly.

The Jewish War

In AD 66, Nero ordered his governor in Judea, Gessius Florus, to confiscate money from the Jerusalem Temple treasury. Some Jews mocked him by passing around a beggar's hat for "that poor procurator, Florus." In retaliation, Florus ordered some random Jews crucified. Judea, where the Jews hated Roman rule, was a powder keg ready for a spark to set it off. In the Old Testament, Balaam had made a Messianic prophecy that said, "a star shall come out of Jacob; a scepter [ruler] shall arise out of Israel" (Num 24:17). Of course, the Messiah, Jesus, had already come, but many Jews had refused to accept him. At the end of AD 64, a comet appeared which some took as the sign that the Messiah would now appear and throw off the Roman yoke.

10. Tacitus, *Annals* 15:47:2–5.
11. Suetonius, *Lives of the Twelve Caesars*, "Nero."

Jewish rebels annihilated one of the Roman garrisons in Jerusalem. An upstart rebel named Menahem raided the great fortress of Masada and seized a cache of weapons. Menahem was the descendant of Judas the Galilean, who had led a revolt against Rome in AD 6 (Acts 5:37).[12] Menahem's followers were the *sicarii*, or "dagger men." They proclaimed Menahem king of the Jews and laid siege to the surviving Roman garrison in Jerusalem. The besieged Romans surrendered, and the *sicarii* lynched them. The Greek inhabitants of Judea in Caesarea, the seat of Roman power, attacked their Jewish neighbors. The Jews responded by attacking Greeks, expelling many of them from Judea and Galilee.

Nero replaced Florus with a new governor, Antonius Julianus. The governor of neighboring Syria, Gaius Cestius Gallus, led the Twelfth Legion (the "Fulminata") into Judea. Gallus liberated the captured city of Sepphoris in Galilee and marched on Jerusalem. He encircled the city, but then, for some mysterious reason, in November, he lifted the siege. Perhaps he was soliciting a bribe. One of the Zealot leaders, Eleazar son of Simon, sortied and destroyed Gallus's legion of five thousand soldiers, even capturing its standards. Gallus fled to Syria in disarray. The loss of a whole legion to Jewish rebels was one of the worst military defeats in Roman history. Knowing that Rome would not leave this disaster unavenged, "many distinguished Jews abandoned the city like swimmers from a sinking ship."[13] As the Roman siege relaxed, the Jewish Christians of Jerusalem remembered the words of Jesus:

> When you see Jerusalem surrounded by armies . . . then let those who are in Judea flee to the mountains, and let those who are inside the city depart, and let not those who are out in the country enter it; for these are days of vengeance, to fulfill all that is written. (Luke 21:20–22)

The Christian residents of Jerusalem fled to the mountain city of Pella in Judea, escaping the coming holocaust.

The rebels elected generals to lead the war against Rome. One of them was Joseph, son of Matthias, the future historian Flavius Josephus. Nero also recalled a new commander, Titus Flavius Vespasianus (Vespasian). After successfully commanding legions in Germany and Britain, Vespasian had committed the unpardonable gaffe of falling asleep during one of Nero's musical performances. Nero had sidelined him. At this critical juncture, however, Nero needed an experienced commander, and he overlooked the affront and appointed Vespasian to take charge in Judea. Nero kept Vespasian's younger son, Domitian, as a hostage to ensure that Vespasian would remain loyal.

The Jews presented a disunified front. A rebel leader named John of Gischala arose and took control of Galilee, the region whose defense had been assigned to Josephus. The factions of John and Menahem now fought each other.

---

12. Josephus, *Ant.* 18:1:1, 20:5:2; *War* 2:8:1.
13. Josephus, *War* 2:20:1.

Meanwhile, Vespasian landed in the port of Ptolemais (Acre, in what was then Phoenicia, although the city is now in modern Israel.). He commanded the Fifth Legion ("Macedonica"). His elder son, Titus, led in the Fifteenth Legion ("Apollinaris"). Vespasian appropriated the Tenth Legion from the Syrian governor Gallus, who, in disgrace, had committed suicide. To these troops were added auxiliaries, so Vespasian had assembled more than fifteen thousand troops.

Vespasian expelled John of Gischala from the town of Gadara and then attacked the town of Jotapata, which Josephus was defending. Vespasian overcame the rebels and captured Josephus, who applied Balaam's Messianic prophecy of Numbers 24:17 to Vespasian. Perhaps Vespasian recognized that Josephus would make a good wartime propagandist, which he did. On the other hand, there were many ominous prophecies swirling about in these times, and Vespasian may have believed them. Suetonius wrote:

> A firm persuasion had long prevailed through all the East that it was fated of the empire of the world, at that time, to devolve on someone who should go forth from Judea. This prediction referred to a Roman emperor, as the event showed; but the Jews, applying it to themselves, broke out into rebellion.[14]

In any case, Vespasian spared Josephus and employed him in the Roman cause.

As Vespasian, Titus, and the other Roman commanders secured the ports of Judea and pacified Galilee, John of Gischala retreated to Jerusalem and set himself up as king. His rivals for rebel leadership were the Sadducees, who ran the temple, and the Zealots under Eleazar. Now three Jewish factions waged civil war within Jerusalem. Jews escaping the city informed Vespasian of the strife within. He decided to bide his time, letting the enemy weaken himself, while he gained control of the Jordan Valley and Peraea.

Finally, as Vespasian was preparing to encircle Jerusalem, news of Nero's suicide arrived. Galba, a senator, had taken the imperial crown. Vespasian sent his son, Titus, to Rome to congratulate the new emperor, but before he arrived, Galba's praetorian guard executed him, and two more contenders for the crown, Vitellius and Otho, prepared for war. Titus returned to Judea, where Vespasian decided to pause his military campaign until the struggle for the empire could be resolved.

In northern Italy in AD 69, when the two contenders for the imperial crown, Vitellius and Otho, were joining battle, an omen appeared. "In the field of Bedriacum, before the battle began, two eagles engaged in the sight of the army; and one of them being beaten, a third came from the east, and drove away the conqueror."[15] The conqueror from the east, the Romans thought, was Vespasian.

Realizing they faced a unique opportunity, Vespasian and Titus began to garner support for themselves. The Roman governor of Egypt and the legions along the

---

14. Suetonius, *Lives of the Twelve Caesars*, "Vespasian."
15. Suetonius, *Lives of the Twelve Caesars*, "Vespasian."

Danube embraced their cause. When, in July AD 69, Vitellius defeated Otho, Vespasian proclaimed himself emperor. He cut off Egypt's supply of grain to Rome. In September, the Danube legions loyal to Vespasian defeated those loyal to Vitellius. The Roman mob murdered Vitellius, and by December, Vespasian was the undisputed emperor. The year AD 69 became known as the Year of the Four Emperors.

Vespasian granted Josephus Roman citizenship and bestowed upon him the emperor's family name, Flavius. Flavius Josephus wrote a book called the *Jewish Wars*, in which he obligingly treated Vespasian and Titus with admiration. Vespasian charged his son with finishing off the Jews. In AD 70, Titus, son of the emperor, prince of Rome, resumed the siege of Jerusalem, as Daniel foretold (Dan 9:26).

The Siege of Jerusalem

The Zealots were the prime movers of the Jewish Revolt, but despite early military successes, they lacked discipline. Titus surrounded Jerusalem with three military formations on the western side and a fourth on the Mount of Olives to the east. He put pressure on food and water supplies by allowing pilgrims to enter the city to celebrate Passover and then refusing to let them out. When Jewish sorties killed a number of Roman soldiers and nearly captured Titus, he sent Josephus to negotiate with the defenders. The Zealots refused to yield.

In May AD 70, Titus breached the city walls with a battering ram. The legions fought from street to street, as the Zealots retreated to the two highest places in the city, the Antonia Fortress and the Temple Mount. Josephus tried a second time to negotiate peace but failed.

After several attempts to breach the fortress, on Saturday, the Sabbath, August 2 (9 Av), AD 70, the Romans launched a night attack, overwhelmed the sleeping Zealot guards, and took the stronghold. With control of the second highest ground in the city, Titus turned to assault the temple. Battering rams failed, but when a Roman soldier threw a torch over the temple walls, flames spread out of control. By the next day, August 3 (10 Av), the temple and residential sectors of the city were in cinders. Jesus had predicted that not one stone would be left standing upon another (Matt 24:2; Mark 13:2; Luke 19:44), and the Romans, after burning the temple, pried the stones apart to recover the temple's ornamental gold and silver that had melted in the fire and drained into the joints. Probably Titus had not intended to destroy the temple. He probably had hoped to capture and dedicate it to his father, the emperor.

After the city was completely under Roman control, Titus returned to Rome, where he and Vespasian celebrated a triumph (victory parade). They erected the magnificent commemorative arch that still stands in the Roman Forum, showing victorious Roman soldiers hauling sacred treasures, including a giant menorah, out of the Jerusalem Temple. Vespasian used the loot from the temple to build a massive arena in Rome, known officially as the Flavian Amphitheater (after Vespasian's family name,

Flavius) and known colloquially as the Colosseum. Back in Judea, Roman officers fiercely pursued the remaining Jewish refugees.

Suicide at Masada

The Zealot leader Eleazar led his *sicarii* to Masada, a nearly impregnable mountain fort built by Herod the Great near the Dead Sea. In AD 72, the governor of Judea, Lucius Flavius Silva, led soldiers to besiege the fortress and its 960 defenders. He built a circumvallation wall and rampart against the western face, using thousands of tons of stones and beaten earth. The Romans finally breached Masada's defenses on April 14, AD 73, 21 Nisan, the seventh or last day of Passover. It was also Friday, a Sabbath eve. Eleazar urged the Zealots to kill their wives and children and then commit suicide. The *sicarii* embraced their spouses, kissed their children, and began their bloody work. Only two women and five children escaped by hiding in a cave.

Jesus' Prophecy Fulfilled

The old covenant ended with the baptism of Christ in AD 29. Rome destroyed Jerusalem and the temple in AD 70. The last vestige of national Israel perished in AD 73. (There would be two second-century revolts, one from AD 115–17 and another from AD 132–36 that would attempt a restoration of Jewish independence, but the Romans would crush them mercilessly.) So, Jesus' generation indeed had not passed away until not one stone of the temple was left standing upon another and until the universal reign of Christ had replaced the rule of Jewish priests (Matt 24).

The Cost and Worth of the Jewish War

The Jewish War cost an estimated one million lives and yielded 97,000 Jewish captives. The death toll represented about 0.43 percent of the total earth's estimated population in the first century.[16] To put this in perspective, World Wars I and II cost about 100 million lives—only about 0.05 percent of the earth's population in the twentieth century, nearly nine times less in relative terms than the Jewish War. That Rome would have waged so bloody a struggle, led personally by the emperor's son, is proof that Judea was not a sleepy province where the Messiah's humble birth went overlooked. On the contrary, Judea trembled in the crosshairs of trade, politics, ambition, and war. God could hardly have chosen a place for the Messiah to appear that would have allowed Christianity to spread so swiftly to the rest of the world, to Italy, Greece, Britain, Spain, Africa, Russia, Persia, and India.

---

16. "Roman Empire Population."

A NEW COVENANT FOR THE WORLD

The missionary labors of the apostles predated the much-prophesied end of the old covenant. Pentecost, Sunday, May 22, AD 33, was an international experience. Hundreds of thousands, if not over two million, visiting Jews came from many nations to Jerusalem.[17] After hearing Peter's sermon, many took the gospel home to Parthia, Media, Elam, Mesopotamia, Cappadocia, Pontus, Phrygia, Pamphylia, Egypt, Libya, and Rome (Acts 2:9–11). In AD 33, Philip witnessed to an Ethiopian eunuch, who brought Christianity to Africa (Acts 8:27–39). In AD 37, God directly told Peter to bring the gospel to a Roman centurion, Cornelius, and his family at Caesarea, proving that Christ's salvation was for gentiles as well as for Jews. Eusebius wrote that the apostles divided the inhabited world into regions of influence for evangelism: Thomas to Parthia (Persia), John to Asia Minor, Peter to Pontus (the south coast of the Black Sea in northern Turkey) and Rome, and Andrew to Scythia (Central Asia).[18] Paul planted churches in Asia Minor (modern Turkey), Macedonia (northern Greece), and Greece from AD 44–54.

Luke finished his book of Acts by AD 59, the year Nero released Paul from his first imprisonment at Rome. The book covered a period of twenty-six years. Probably all the apostles had traveled far by the end of Acts.

THE END OF JUDEA

After the final defeat of the Jews, the Romans posted a garrison of eight hundred men over the temple to prevent any zealous believers from rebuilding it. They hunted down and disposed of anyone who might possibly claim descent from King David, to ensure that there would be no further pretenders to the throne of the twice-conquered nation—no more Messiahs. They renamed Jerusalem Aelia Capitolina, dedicating there a temple to Jupiter. They renamed Judea Philistia after Israel's ancient enemies, thus wiping the name of Judah and Israel off the map until the establishment of the modern state of Israel in 1947.[19] Outside the Roman Empire, in Babylonia, the Jews preserved their religious freedom, but inside the empire, from the first century to modern times, the Jews would experience persecution at the hands of their Latin rulers.

THE CHRISTIAN EMPIRE

The Flavius Valerius Constantinus "Constantine" (AD 285–337) first contended for the title of emperor when fighting his rival, Maxentius, at the Battle of the Milvian Bridge (October AD 312) at Milan, Italy. Before the battle, Constantine had a dream in which

---

17. Josephus, *War* 6:9:3.
18. Eusebius, *Church History* 3:1.
19. "What Was Hadrian's Relationship with His Jewish Subjects?", Encyclopedia Britannica.

he saw the sign of Christ in the sky (the Greek letters X and 'P, equivalent to "Ch" and "R," the first two letters in the title Christ or "Anointed One"). Constantine thought this vision presaged his victory, and he became a Christian. After spending the next twelve years defeating his enemies, he became sole emperor in AD 324. He outlawed pagan sacrifices, and Christianity became Rome's official religion. On November 8, AD 324, (after trying several other sites), he founded the great city of Constantinople[20] ("Constantine's City") and made it the imperial capital. While Rome retained its ancient honors, the population and wealth of the empire was greater in the eastern, Greek-speaking provinces. Italy was now far from the political center of gravity.

Whether Constantine was a true believer is debatable. He built the Church of the Twelve Apostles in Constantinople with the idea of finding and exhuming the bodies of the Twelve, burying them in his church, and choosing a place in their midst for his own tomb as the Thirteenth Apostle. To this end, the emperor set about searching for the remains of the Twelve. He did not get far. He dedicated the church on Easter of AD 337 and died May 22 of the same year. So, he was buried among the apostles' tombs, as planned, but all except his sepulcher were empty.

THE TRAIL OF RELICS

Still, the official search for the remains of the Twelve Apostles continued for centuries, giving rise to the quest for venerable relics. This engendered many stories about where the apostles lived and died. These hagiographies (biographies of saints) were a mixture of truth and legend. In the Middle Ages, Christians were a bit too eager to believe all legends. Possibly today we are a bit too eager to dismiss them. There is, undoubtedly, truth mixed with fantasy in many of them.

Any parts of the apostles' bodies, or pieces of wood or nails from the True Cross, or the cup from which Jesus served the wine of the Last Supper (the Holy Grail)[21] were considered sacred. Superstition attributed holy powers to relics. Churches claiming to house relics became important pilgrim and tourist destinations (raking in donations). Of course, many relics were false. Probably if all the pieces of the "true" cross were put together, one could reconstruct Noah's ark.

FULFILLING THE GREAT COMMISSION

The problem with tracking down the apostles' relics was that the apostles took Jesus' command in Acts 1:8 seriously. The Lord told them to go to Judea, Samaria, and the

---

20. When the Turks conquered Constantinople in AD 1453, they renamed it Istanbul, which is a mispronunciation of the Greek words "*sti poli*" or "to the city." Even today, Greeks refer to this great city as "the City," or "*i poli*." The Turks pronounced "*sti*" as "*istan*" and "*poli*" as "*bul*."

21. Grail is from Old French, *graal*, which is from Latin *gradalis*, which is from Greek, *krateros*, or cup, referring to the Cup of Blessing that Jesus used to drink the wine at the Last Passover Supper.

farthest parts of the world, and off they went. They mostly died in distant mission fields, making recovery of their relics difficult. Nevertheless, the apostles were not aimless wanderers. They had a strategy. They first went to major cities that had a Jewish synagogue (a Greek work that simply means "assembly"). The Jews lived in cities all over the Roman world. There were about 120 synagogues throughout the empire in the first century. In these the new Jewish Christians planted churches. And the apostles did not aim simply to make single converts. They wanted to convert congregations, carry out the Great Commission, and inspire new Christian communities to found other faithful congregations. In this way Christianity spread by the testimony of a few dedicated men who bore astonishing hardships and mainly died as martyrs.

Biographies of the Apostles

Simon Peter, the Rock

PETER WAS THE FIRST in the list of apostles. Peter's original name was Simon (Hebrew: "God has heard"), son of Jonah ("Dove" in Hebrew). Andrew was his brother. He was born in Bethsaida (John 1:44), a small town at the north end of the Sea of Galilee. Bethsaida means "House of Fish," as Bethlehem means "House of Bread." A better English translation of Bethsaida might be Fish Town, and it was probably from life in this fishing village that Peter and Andrew derived their profession. Perhaps fishing was a generational business, accounting for Peter's father's name being Jonah, a wryly appropriate name for a seafaring man.

Philip the apostle also was born in Bethsaida (John 12:21), so Philip, Simon Peter, and Andrew probably knew each other growing up, and perhaps they were friends prior to becoming disciples. Simon Peter and Andrew made their home in Capernaum (Mark 1:29), a larger, nearby town on the northwest shore of the Sea of Galilee. Capernaum means "Town of Nahum." Possibly the town takes its name from the prophet Nahum, although Nahum means "Comfort," so it also is possible that the place name means "Comfort Town."

Peter and Andrew had a fishing business and possessed their own boat (Luke 5:3). Peter lived with his mother-in-law in a house he owned with his brother (Mark 1:29–30; Matt 8:14; Luke 4:38). He was married (obviously), and according to Clement of Alexndria, he had children.[22] Peter took his wife with him on missionary journeys (1 Cor 9:5). Clement wrote that Peter's wife, like her husband, eventually died as a Christian martyr.[23]

PETER'S APPEARANCE

The earliest known portrait of Peter is on a bronze medallion in the Roman catacombs.[24] It dates from the late second or early third century, about 130 years after

---

22. Clement of Alexandria, *Stromata* 3:6:52
23. Clement of Alexandria, *Stromata* 7:11
24. Catacombs are subterranean sepulchral vaults in Rome, of which about forty have been excavated. During the centuries when Christianity was illegal, Roman Christians dug these tunnels out of soft volcanic rock so they could bury their dead and hold funeral services in secret. Pagan Romans

Peter's death. This portrait might have been copied from earlier portraits and might bear a resemblance to Peter. Or it might be just an artist's imagination. In any case, this image of Peter looks resolute, far-seeing, fearless, long-suffering, and distinctive, like a real person who has lived a real life, not like a mere icon.

Painters often portray Peter as burly and old. This is questionable. No doubt Peter was physically fit. All the disciples walked hundreds of miles with Christ, and most walked many thousands more on their missionary journeys after the resurrection. Peter walked on water (until his faith failed). He cut off a man's ear with his sword (he probably missed his main target). And he dove into the Sea of Galilee to swim to Jesus when Jesus called to him from shore. Yet he was not as fast a runner as John, who beat Peter to the empty tomb.

In any case, there is no reason why Peter could not have been younger than Jesus. The only person we can assume Peter was older than is Andrew, since the Bible always lists Andrew second after Peter, suggesting that Andrew was the younger of the two brothers. If Peter were approximately the same age as Jesus, he would have been about thirty-one when Jesus was baptized and about seventy when Nero executed him in AD 68. The dramatic Ford Maddox Brown painting (1856) of Jesus washing an ancient, graying Peter's feet is delightful but probably unrealistic. In that painting, Peter appears to be in his sixties. If he were in his sixties in AD 33, Peter would have been ninety-five or older at his death. This is improbable and not based on scriptural evidence. Peter and all the disciples probably looked very similar—a bunch of Jewish boys from Galilee of about the same age. If they did not all look rather alike, the Sanhedrin might not have needed Judas to point out Jesus at night in the Garden of Gethsemane.

PETER'S HOME

Around Wednesday, May 1, AD 30, Jesus called Peter, Andrew, James, and John to drop their nets and follow him (Matt 4:19–20; Mark 1:16–18; Luke 5:5–11). Jesus made Peter's house his base of operations in Galilee. On the Sabbath of May 18, Jesus taught in the Capernaum synagogue and exorcised a demon-possessed man (Mark 1:23–26). That same day, Jesus found Peter's mother-in-law at home, lying sick with fever (Matt 8:14; Mark 1:30; Luke 4:38). The people spoke to Jesus about her, Jesus raised her up, and the fever left her. Then Jesus healed many who were ill, and he cast out demons, forbidding the demons from saying who he was—for they knew. Jesus did these miracles all through the night, until sunrise. At dawn, on Sunday, he rose and went to a secluded place and prayed (Mark 1:35).

We can deduce from all of this that Peter's house was large, since Jesus spent the night there with two extended families, healing a crowd of people. Also, despite

---

cremated their dead. Christians preferred to entomb their dead, in expectation of the final, bodily resurrection. Some of the catacombs are several kilometers in length and consist of four stories or layers. They are an important source of early Christian art, which adorns their walls.

the house being filled with Peter, his wife, his mother-in-law, Andrew, and two other disciples, Jesus was able to sneak out in the morning without tripping over and waking any of them. However, the house could not have been a palace, because "the whole city was gathered at the door" (Mark 1:33); apparently, they could not all get inside at once. As his Galilean ministry headquarters, Jesus returned to Peter's house often.

WALKING ON WATER

After feeding the five thousand (Matt 14:21; Mark 6:44; Luke 9:14; John 6:10), Jesus told the disciples to coast their boat along the Sea of Galilee shore and shelter at Bethsaida. Disobeying, they instead attempted to make an evening crossing back to Capernaum—where Peter and Andrew had their comfortable house and where Peter's wife and mother-in-law would no doubt serve them a warm meal. After sending them and the crowds away, Jesus went to the hilltop where he had fed the multitude to pray, alone.

A strong wind arose against the disciples in the boat. The sea became rough, they made painfully slow headway, and beaten by waves, the storm blew them far offshore. Against a contrary wind, sailing was useless, so the disciples dropped canvas and took to rowing. The Sea of Galilee is only about five miles wide, and the disciples had rowed about three quarters of the way across. It was now between 3 and 6 a.m.[25] Since the disciples had launched around sunset, they had been toiling at the oars for an exhausting nine to twelve hours.

At this time, Jesus walked across the water to overtake the Twelve in the boat. He had to cross three to four miles of storm-tossed water to catch up to them. When the disciples saw the figure approaching, they were terrified. They cried, "It is a ghost!" But Jesus said, "It is I. Do not be afraid." Peter cried, "If it is you, command me to come to you on the water." Jesus said, "Come!" and Peter got out of the boat and walked to him. But seeing the wind, he lost heart, began to sink, and cried out, "Lord, save me!" Jesus took hold of his hand and said, "You of little faith, why did you doubt?" Jesus brought Peter into the boat, and immediately the storm ceased. The disciples worshipped him and said, "You certainly are God's Son" (Matt 14:22–33).

TRANSFIGURATION

In AD 31, Jesus took his disciples north to Caesarea Philippi near Syria. There he foretold his death. Peter affirmed that Jesus was the Christ. Jesus called Peter blessed. Then Peter wanted to forbid that Jesus should suffer and die. Jesus rebuked Peter, even saying, "Get behind me, Satan!" (Matt 16:23; Mark 8:33) and saying that Peter was a

---

25. The Bible says this was the "fourth watch of the night." Night was considered twelve hours. Dividing it into four watches yielded four three-hour periods: 6 p.m.–9 p.m., 9 p.m.–12 a.m., 12 a.m.–3 a.m., and 3 a.m.–6 a.m.

stumbling block to him, focused on the things of men, not of God. Few have received such high praise and so sharp a rebuke in the course of a few minutes.

On about Tuesday, April 29, Jesus took Peter, James, and John to nearby Mount Hermon, where he was transfigured before them. His face shone like the sun and his clothes became as white as light. Moses and Elijah appeared to them, talking to Jesus. Peter cried out, "Lord, it is good for us to be here. If you wish, I will make three tabernacles here, one for you, one for Moses, and one for Elijah." While Peter was speaking, a bright cloud overshadowed them, and a voice said, "This is My beloved Son, with whom I am well pleased. Listen to him." This was one of three times, Jesus' baptism, the transfiguration, and Palm Sunday, when the Father spoke from heaven with Jesus present (Matt 3:17, 17:5; Mark 1:11, 9:7; Luke 3:22; John 12:28; 2 Pet 1:18), offering a manifestation of the Trinity. The three disciples fell to the ground, terrified. Then Jesus touched them, saying, "Get up. Do not be afraid." And when they arose, they saw no one there but Jesus, who said, "Tell no one about this until the Son of Man has risen from the dead" (Matt 17:1–9). That same day, coming down the slope of Mount Hermon, they met the other nine disciples who were trying, without success, to drive a demon from a boy. Jesus told them that such a demon comes out only with prayer and fasting, and then he exorcised it himself (Matt 17:15–21).

THE TEMPLE TAX

Coming back to Capernaum, the temple tax collectors challenged Peter about Jesus, asking if his rabbi had failed to pay the two-drachma tax. This was not a Roman tax, but a tax imposed on Jews by Jews for the support of the Levitical priesthood that ran the temple. Peter defended Jesus, telling them yes, Jesus did pay it. But when Peter came home, before he could say anything, Jesus told him that kings collect taxes from strangers, not from their sons. Therefore, Jesus, God's Son, was exempt from the temple tax. Jesus could have accessed the disciples' money bag, which Judas Iscariot kept, to pay the tax. Instead, Jesus told Peter, so as not to offend anyone, to go throw a hook into the Sea of Galilee and pull up the first fish he caught. That fish would have a shekel in its mouth. A shekel was worth four drachmas or about four days of a skilled laborer's wages. Peter was to take the money and pay the tax for Jesus and himself (Matt 17:24–27).[26] In all his life of fishing, Peter doubtless found many strange things inside fish, but Jesus surely was amusing both himself and Peter by using this uniquely personal method of prophecy, fulfillment, and teaching.

---

26. Only Matthew, the professional tax collector, recorded this account.

FORGIVENESS AND WEALTH

Peter was the disciple who asked Jesus how many times he should forgive a brother who sinned against him, and Jesus told him not seven times, but seventy times seven times (Matt 18:21–22). When Jesus told the disciples that it was easier for a camel to pass through the eye of a needle than for a rich man to enter the kingdom of God, they were distressed. Peter and Andrew, with their big house, the sons of Zebedee with their fishing fleet, servants, and Jerusalem residence, and Matthew Levi, the tax collector, were certainly not poor. They asked, dismayed, "Who then can be saved?" Jesus replied that with man it would be impossible, but with God all things are possible. Peter pressed the point. "We have left everything and followed you. What then will there be for us?" If they had been poor, leaving everything would probably not have meant as much to them, even though Jesus taught them that the poor woman who gave her little all had given more than the rich who had given only some of their wealth (Mark 12:41–44; Luke 21:1–4). Jesus told him that in the regeneration, when the Son of Man should sit on his glorious throne, they would sit upon twelve thrones, judging the twelve tribes of Israel and would inherit eternal life (Matt 19:28). By this Jesus revealed that the apostles would represent the new covenant, which was superior to the old covenant, represented by the twelve Israelite tribes (Heb 8:13).

PASSION WEEK

On Tuesday, March 29, AD 33, Jesus took only Peter, Andrew, James, and John (the sons of Zebedee) to the Mount of Olives and predicted his death by Friday, as well as the future destruction of the Jerusalem Temple (Matt 24). On Thursday, March 31, Jesus sent only Peter and John from Bethany to Jerusalem to prepare the Last Supper. Normally, preparing Passover would have been a happy task. This year it was grim and foreboding. His disciples already knew Jesus expected this to be his last meal with them; two days ago he had told them he would be dead by Friday. Jesus told Peter and John that they would meet a man carrying a pitcher of water, who would lead them to a house with a large, furnished upper room. They found everything as Jesus foretold (Luke 22:8–13). This must have increased their sense of impending doom. If Jesus were right about these things—as, indeed, he was right about everything—surely tomorrow he would die.

THE LAST SUPPER

When Jesus washed his disciples' feet before the Last Supper, he came first to Peter, who protested that he should be the one to wash Jesus' feet. Jesus declared that if Peter did not accept, Peter would have no part in him. Peter cried, "Lord, not only my feet, but also my hands and my head" (John 13:9). After singing hymns at the end of the meal, Jesus warned that all the disciples would fall away because of him that night, but that Jesus would be struck down, raised, and go ahead of them into Galilee. This must have been thoroughly baffling. How could he die tomorrow and also go ahead of them, back home, safe to Galilee? Peter protested, "Even though all may fall away because of you, I will never fall away." But Jesus told Peter, "This very night, before a rooster crows twice, you will deny me three times." Peter insisted, "Even if I have to die with you, I will not deny you." And all the other disciples said the same (Matt 26:30–35). Peter asked John, who was reclining near Jesus, to ask Jesus who he thought would betray him. Jesus told John that it was the man to whom he would give a morsel of food. Jesus gave that morsel to Judas Iscariot (John 13:24), who then left the room on his treasonous mission.

GETHSEMANE

That night, Jesus went to the Garden of Gethsemane (which means the Garden of the Olive Press) with his disciples. He told eight of them to sit aside, but he took Peter and the sons of Zebedee with him to an isolated place, where he began to grieve and feel great distress. He asked the three disciples to keep watch with him and went to a place a little beyond. After praying in anguish, Jesus returned to find them sleeping. He asked Peter, "Could you not keep watch with me one hour? Keep watching and praying that you might not enter into temptation, for the spirit is willing but the flesh is weak." Then he went and prayed a second time and came back and found them sleeping again. He did not wake them but went and prayed again for the Father's will, not his, to be done. He came back to the three disciples and said, "Are you still sleeping? Get up, let us go. Behold, the one who betrays me is at hand" (Matt 26:36–46).

When the temple soldiers (not Romans) seized Jesus, Peter cut off the ear of Malchus, servant of the high priest. Obviously, Peter had prepared for this abortive attempt to defend Jesus' life. Peter knew from Jesus' rebuke at Caesarea Philippi two years ago that Jesus expected to be killed. Prophecy had to run its course. More than that, Jesus had called Peter Satan for wishing to defend Jesus from death. Peter must have assumed that he could arm himself with a weapon and defend Jesus even against his will. So, Peter procured a sword. In fact, at the Last Supper, the disciples showed Jesus that they had two swords, to which Jesus replied, "it is enough." Jesus would say later that night that he could call on the Father for twelve legions of angels if he wanted to.

When the time came to use his sword, Peter missed. He sliced off Malchus's ear. It is hard to believe that is what Peter was aiming at. He was not trying to warn Malchus off. He was trying to defend Jesus, and that meant killing Malchus, along with anyone else who threatened his rabbi. He was doubtless aiming at Malchus's skull. Jesus told

Peter to put away his sword, saying that those who live by the sword die by it. Then, astonishingly, Jesus healed Malchus's ear (Luke 22:51).[27]

IN THE COURTYARD OF THE HIGH PRIEST

At Jesus' trial, Peter was sitting outside in the courtyard of the home of the high priest. A servant girl eyed Peter closely and said to the people standing by, "This man also was with him." Then she said directly to Peter, "You also were with Jesus, the Nazarene. You are not also one of his disciples, are you?" Peter replied, "I neither know nor understand what you mean. I am not." And the rooster crowed the first time.

When Peter went out to the entrance of the courtyard, another servant girl saw him, and she said to the bystanders, "This man was with Jesus of Nazareth. This man is one of them." Then she said directly to Peter, "You also are one of them." But Peter denied it with an oath, saying, "I do not know the man." Then one of the servants of the high priest, a relative of Malchus, the man whose ear Peter had cut off asked, "Did I not see you in the garden with him?"

The other bystanders crowded around Peter, saying, "Certainly, you too are one of them. Your accent betrays you. You are a Galilean." Peter began to invoke a curse on himself and to swear, "I do not know the man of whom you speak." And the rooster crowed a second time.

Peter then remembered how Jesus had said to him at the Last Supper: "Before the rooster crows twice, you will deny me three times." Peter had done just that. As the mob led Jesus out of the high priest's house, Jesus turned and looked at Peter. Their eyes met. Peter went out and wept bitterly (Matt 26:69–75; Mark 14:66–72; Luke 22:54–62; John 18:15–18).

Judas sold Jesus. Peter denied Jesus three times, cursing and swearing. Both were guilty and felt guilty, but Judas did not seek God's forgiveness. He committed suicide. Peter confessed, repented, sought forgiveness, and received it.

THE ROOSTER

Jesus said to Peter:

> Truly, I tell you, this very night, before the rooster crows, you will deny me three times. (Matt 26:34)
> Truly, I tell you, this very night, before the rooster crows twice, you will deny me three times. (Mark 14:30)
> I tell you, Peter, the rooster will not crow today until you have denied three times that you know me. (Luke 22:34)

---

27. All four Gospel authors recorded Peter's cutting off Malchus's ear; only Luke, the beloved physician, recorded that Jesus healed it.

> Truly, truly, I tell you, before the rooster crows, you will deny me three times. (John 13:38)

These are not contradictory accounts, but various ways of describing the same events. In the courtyard of the high priest, Peter denied Jesus once, and the rooster crowed the first time (Mark 14:68). This should have struck a chord with Peter. It was an omen that Jesus' prediction was about to come true. The rooster's first crowing might have warned him not to deny Jesus two more times. But he did deny Jesus two more times, and the rooster crowed a second time (Matt 26:74; Mark 14:72; Luke 22:60; John 18:27).

So, the statement of Matthew was correct. Before the rooster crowed (albeit for the second time), Peter denied Jesus three times. The statement of Mark was correct. Before the rooster crowed twice, Peter denied Jesus three times. And the statements of Luke and John are correct. Although the rooster did crow once, he stopped crowing and would not crow again until Peter had denied Jesus the second and third time.

THE EMPTY TOMB

On Resurrection Sunday, Mary Magdalene ran to Peter and John with news of the empty tomb. John outran Peter and reached the tomb first. He stooped to look in but did not enter yet. Peter boldly entered first and saw the linen shrouds lying there and Jesus' facecloth rolled up by itself.

This may not mean, as some assert, that Jesus or an angel calmly folded the shrouds after Jesus' resurrection to show that God is in no haste. Jesus' resurrection body, which later that evening would pass through closed doors, probably also passed through these mummy-like winding sheets. They remained folded, that is, wrapped, but empty. This is an additional testimony that Jesus' body was not stolen. Thieves would either have taken the winding sheets with them or torn them off in their haste to escape detection by the guards, whose duty it was to arrest or kill anyone violating their watch.

John then entered the tomb and believed, but what did he believe? The Bible says the disciples did not yet understand that Jesus must rise again from the dead. John believed that the tomb was empty, and that God was somehow at work; but he did not comprehend in what way. Peter and John went back to where they were staying, probably the upper room, leaving Mary Magdalene to be the first to meet the risen Lord (John 20:1–18).

THE RISEN LORD APPEARS TO PETER

Then the risen Jesus met Peter privately, sometime between morning and evening on Resurrection Sunday. Mark, Luke, and Paul all recorded this, but they gave no details of the encounter (Mark 16:7; Luke 24:34; 1 Cor 15:5). This appearance to Peter is significant. Probably Jesus knew how deep Peter's grief was at having denied him three times. The intimate appearance of Jesus to Peter allowed Peter to experience Jesus' kindly mercy, to know that he was forgiven, and to understand that his mission in Christ had only just begun.

EMMAUS AND THE UPPER ROOM

Late in the afternoon on Resurrection Sunday, Jesus appeared to two followers, one named Cleophas and his companion. They broke bread with Jesus at sunset. Only then did they recognize him. Then he vanished from their presence. Cleophas and his companion hurried back to Jerusalem to meet the eleven disciples, only to find them in a state of great excitement, for the risen Lord had already met Peter. Thomas left the room. As Cleophas and everyone else were still speaking, Jesus appeared to the ten disciples, to Cleophas and his companion, and to others assembled in the upper room that Resurrection Sunday evening. The following Monday, Jesus appeared again to the eleven disciples with Thomas present (John 20:26).

BACK TO GALILEE

Then seven disciples (Peter, Thomas, Nathanael, the sons of Zebedee, and two others) went back to Galilee. Peter said, "I am going fishing." His friends went with him. They fished until daybreak but caught nothing. Jesus stood on the beach, but they did not recognize him. He said, "Boys, you do not have any fish, do you?" They said no. Jesus said, "Cast the net on the right side of the boat, and you will have a catch." So they did and could not haul in the net because of the great number of fish they caught. John said to Peter, "It is the Lord." Peter put on his outer garment and plunged into the sea. Why did he get dressed to swim? Because the Bible says he was *gymnos*, or naked. (A gymnasium was a place where athletes exercised naked). The outer garment, an *ependítis* in Greek, is a blouse or a tunic, not a coat, as some Bibles translate it. So, Peter was probably wearing a loincloth, our equivalent of shorts, while fishing. When he saw Jesus, out of respect, he threw on a shirt and went swimming to meet him.

The others followed ashore, bringing the boat and its net full of fish. They found Jesus tending a charcoal fire, with fish and bread already on it. Jesus, who could feed five thousand out of two fishes and five loaves, did not need their catch to make breakfast. But graciously, Jesus said, "Bring some of the fish you caught." Peter, the consummate fisherman, not only brought them, but carefully counted 153 large fish[28] and noted that even with such a big haul, the net was not torn (John 21:1–11). One can imagine Jesus enjoying his friends' very human enthusiasm as they counted the

---

28. Still today a type of tilapia, *Sarotherodon galilaeus galilaeus*, known as St. Peter's Fish, is harvested in the Sea of Galilee and is popular in local markets and restaurants.

fish and inspected the net. This was the third time the resurrected Jesus appeared to the disciples.

In one of the most moving dialogues of Scripture, Jesus compassionately echoed Peter's three denials.

> When they had finished breakfast, Jesus said to Simon Peter, "Simon, son of John, do you love me more than these?" He said to him, "Yes, Lord; you know that I love you." He said to him, "Feed my lambs." He said to him a second time, "Simon, son of John, do you love me?" He said to him, "Yes, Lord; you know that I love you." He said to him, "Tend my sheep." He said to him the third time, "Simon, son of John, do you love me?" Peter was grieved because he said to him the third time, "Do you love me?" and he said to him, "Lord, you know everything; you know that I love you." Jesus said to him, "Feed my sheep." (John 21:15–17)

The Greek words John used to record this conversation add meaning to the passage. Greek commonly uses four words to mean love: *agápe* (love), *philía* (friendship), *storgí* (affection), and *éros* (lust). The first and second times Jesus asked Peter, "Do you love me?" he used the Greek word *agapás*, referring to the noblest form of love. The third time Jesus asked Peter, "Do you love me?" he used the Greek word *phileís*, meaning "Are you my friend?" Jesus' choice of words was touchingly personal, but also echoed what Jesus had said about himself (recorded by John): "Greater love has no one than this, that he lay down his life for his friends" (John 15:13). Jesus was saying, "Do you love me, do you love me, do you really love me enough to give your life for me?" Then Jesus revealed that Peter would give his life as that kind of friend.

> "Truly, truly, I say to you, when you were young, you used to dress yourself and walk wherever you wanted, but when you are old, you will stretch out your hands, and another will dress you and carry you where you do not want to go." (This he said to show by what kind of death he was to glorify God.) And after saying this he said to him, "Follow me." (John 21:18–19)

Realizing Jesus was foretelling a martyr's death, Peter wanted to know how John would end.

> Peter turned and saw the disciple whom Jesus loved [John] following them, the one who had been reclining at table close to him and had said, "Lord, who is it that is going to betray you?" When Peter saw him, he said to Jesus, "Lord, what about this man?" Jesus said to him, "If it is my will that he remain until I come, what is that to you? You follow me!" So the saying spread abroad among the brothers that this disciple was not to die; yet Jesus did not say to him that he was not to die, but "if it is my will that he remain until I come, what is that to you?" This is the disciple who is bearing witness about these things, and who has written these things, and we know that his testimony is true. Now there are also many other things that Jesus did. Were every one of them to be

written, I suppose that the world itself could not contain the books that would be written. (John 21:20–25)

THE GREAT COMMISSION

There were only seven disciples present at the lakeshore breakfast in Galilee. After that, all eleven met in Galilee, reclining at a table with Jesus, probably, as usual, in the house of Peter and Andrew. He rebuked them for their unbelief and hardness of heart because they had not at first believed those who saw him after he had risen. He said to them:

> Go into all the world and proclaim the gospel to the whole creation. Whoever believes and is baptized will be saved, but whoever does not believe will be condemned. And these signs will accompany those who believe: in my name they will cast out demons; they will speak in new tongues; they will pick up serpents with their hands; and if they drink any deadly poison, it will not hurt them; they will lay their hands on the sick, and they will recover. (Mark 16:15–18)[29]

The Eleven also went with Jesus to a mountain in Galilee, possibly Mount Eremos, where Jesus had delivered the Sermon on the Mount. There they worshiped him, but some still doubted. He said to them:

> All authority in heaven and on earth has been given to me. Go therefore and make disciples of all nations, baptizing them in the name of the Father and of the Son and of the Holy Spirit, teaching them to observe all that I have commanded you. And behold, I am with you always, to the end of the age. (Matt 28:16–20)

PETER'S LEADERSHIP

Peter was present at Christ's ascension from Bethany on the Mount of Olives near Jerusalem on Sunday, May 13, AD 33. He, with the other ten apostles, heard the angel say that Jesus would return in the same way that he ascended (Acts 1:9–11). Then Peter assumed leadership of the Eleven in the upper room, where they were praying with Mary, the mother of Jesus, and with Jesus' half-brothers (which surely included at least James and Jude). After Jesus' ascension and before Pentecost, that is, between May 13 and May 21, AD 33, Peter proposed the selection of someone to replace Judas Iscariot. Guided by the Holy Spirit, the apostles chose Matthias (Acts 1:12–26).

---

29. Some manuscripts end the Gospel of Mark at verse 16:8, so possibly this was not part of Mark's original book. That does not necessarily mean, however, that it is not a faithful account of what happened.

PENTECOST

On Sunday, May 22, AD 33, the day of Pentecost, a noise like a rushing wind filled the house where the apostles were gathered, tongues of fire appeared above their heads, and they began speaking in all the tongues of Africa and the Middle East. Visitors from those countries were astonished to hear Galileans speaking their languages. Some mocked them, thinking they were drunk. Peter rose and rebuked the joke. Far from drunk, they were fulfilling prophecy. In a powerful sermon, Peter showed from Scripture how Jesus, whom the Jews had crucified, was Lord and Christ.

Cut to the quick, the congregation asked what they should do. Peter told them to repent and be baptized in the name of Jesus Christ for the forgiveness of their sins, so that they might receive the gift of the Holy Spirit. Three thousand people became followers of Jesus. On that Sunday, the church was born (Acts 2).

When these pilgrims returned to their homes, they brought their faith with them, so that churches were planted all around the empire and in Rome long before the apostles' missionary journeys. The church witnessed the apostles perform many signs and wonders, becoming a community of believers, with others daily added to their numbers. It grew at an astonishing rate. The assembly in the upper room after the ascension was probably about twenty people. The assembly when choosing Matthias was about 120 people (Acts 1:15)—up 600 percent. The assembly at Pentecost was about three thousand people (Acts 2:41)—up 2500 percent!

HEALING THE LAME MAN

One day, at about 3 p.m., Peter and John were going up to the temple for the afternoon prayer[30] when they saw a man lame from birth being carried to the Beautiful Gate where he could beg for alms. He asked Peter and John for money. Peter fixed his gaze on him and said, "Look at me! I do not possess silver and gold, but what I do have I give to you. In the name of Jesus of Nazareth—walk!" The lame man leaped up and entered the temple, praising God. All the people were amazed, and Peter took the opportunity to preach a second sermon about Jesus (Acts 3). About five thousand believed (Acts 4:4).

FIRST ARREST

The priests, the captain of the temple guard, and the Sadducees arrested Peter and John for their public "heresy," keeping them in jail overnight. The next day, Ananias (Annas), the defrocked ex-high priest, Caiaphas, the current high priest (Ananias's son-in-law), and all the Jewish elders placed Peter and John on trial.

---

30. Observant Jews still pray at the time of the morning sacrifice, in the afternoon around 3 p.m., and at sunset.

ANANIAS

Ananias was the first high priest appointed by Rome in AD 6, which made him illegal from the start, since he succeeded to the office by the order of a gentile power, not by being a descendant of Aaron. God had told Moses, "You shall appoint Aaron and his sons, and they shall guard their priesthood. But if any outsider comes near, he shall be put to death" (Num 3:10). Therefore, Ananias, who pushed for Jesus' execution, was himself under a death sentence according to God's law. The Roman procurator Gratus deposed Ananias in AD 15 for subjecting a heretic to capital punishment, which was Rome's sole prerogative. Ananias was presiding when the twelve-year-old Jesus questioned the temple elders in AD 10. Although out of office, Ananias exercised control through his five sons and son-in-law, Joseph Caiaphas, who were his puppet high priests. He presided semi-officially over the trial of Jesus through Caiaphas, who was high priest from AD 18 to 36. Ananias was assassinated in AD 66 for advocating peace with Rome at the outbreak of the tragic Jewish Revolt.

PETER'S DEFENSE

Peter, filled with the Holy Spirit, spoke boldly before Ananias and Caiaphas. He asked if he and John were on trial for healing a sick man. He told them that Jesus, whom they had crucified, God had raised from the dead, and that "there is no other name under heaven that has been given to men by which we must be saved" (Acts 4:12). The council was amazed that these uneducated men could reason so powerfully from the Scriptures. By "uneducated," they did not mean that Peter and John could not read or write; obviously, they could and did. They meant that they had not completed formal religious training. They were not rabbis, like John the Baptist, son of a Levite (John 3:26), Jesus (John 1:38), and Paul (Acts 22:3; Gal 1:14; Phil 3:5).

CIVIL DISOBEDIENCE

The council warned the apostles to speak no more about Jesus. But Peter replied that they would listen to God and not to men and could not keep quiet about the truth. The council threatened them further but released them because they found that the crowd was praising God for the miracle of the lame man healed. Then Peter and John went to the other apostles and told the story. They all rejoiced and prayed to the Lord to give them strength to keep witnessing and performing God's works. They were filled with the Holy Spirit and spoke God's word with boldness (Acts 4). This was around May 27, AD 33.

Writing around AD 59, twenty-six years later, Peter seemed to contradict himself when he said, "Be subject for the Lord's sake to every human institution, whether it be to the emperor, as supreme, or to governors as sent by him to punish those who do evil and to praise those who do good. For this is the will of God" (1 Pet 2:13–15). Paul seems to agree, for he wrote, "let every person be subject to the governing authorities . . . whoever resists the authorities resists what God has appointed" (Rom 13:1–2). Daniel, however, flouted the authority of Babylon's ruler, Belshazzar, saying, "let your gifts be for yourself, and give your rewards to another . . . God has numbered the days of your kingdom . . . you have been weighed in the balances and found wanting" (Dan 5:17–28).

So, should a believer obey civil authorities or not? There is no moral contradiction in these biblical accounts. The abiding principle is that believers should obey civil authorities when they are aligned with the will of God and should disobey them when they oppose God's will.

ANANIAS AND SAPPHIRA

Around May 30, AD 33, Joseph Barnabas, the Levite Cypriot cousin of John Mark, sold a plot of land and gave the proceeds to the church (Acts 4:36–37). Another couple, Ananias and Sapphira, imitated him. They sold a plot of land but kept part of the proceeds for themselves. Ananias, with his wife's full knowledge, pretended to bring all the proceeds, but laid only a portion of it at the apostles' feet. Peter saw through him. He asked Ananias why Satan had filled his heart with the desire to lie. Peter said that the land was his; no one had asked him to sell it or give any part of the money to the church. But now he had lied not to men, but to God. As he heard these words, Ananias breathed his last. The young men present carried him off and buried him. After about three hours, Sapphira came to Peter and told the same lie. Peter replied, "Why have you agreed together to put the Spirit of the Lord to the test? The feet of those who have buried your husband are at the door, and they will carry you out as well." She, too, fell dead, and great fear spread over the whole church as the apostles performed many signs and wonders. People from all around Jerusalem brought the sick and lame and demon-possessed, even laying them on cots along the street, hoping that at least Peter's shadow might fall on some of them. The people brought the afflicted from towns all around Jerusalem, and the apostles healed them all, as the church continued to grow, sharing everything in common (Acts 5:1–16).

SECOND ARREST

The priests and the Sadducees were greatly annoyed that Peter and John continued in their defiant ministry. Around June 6, AD 33, the temple captain threw them in jail a second time. During the night, an angel came and released them, telling them to return to the temple to preach. At daybreak, Peter and John entered the temple and resumed teaching. When the council met again, they called for the prisoners, but the officers reported that, although the prison was still securely locked, they were gone.

Someone came and reported where Peter and John were: in the temple. The authorities dragged the apostles back before the council, but gingerly, as the crowd seemed like it might stone the arresting officers. The council reminded Peter and John that they were not to teach in Jesus' name, but the apostles boldly answered that they must obey God and not men. They then testified that Jesus is the Savior.

The council wanted to put Peter and John to death, but Gamaliel, Paul's mentor, advised letting them alone. "If this plan or action is of men," he said, "it will be overthrown, but if it is of God, you will not be able to overthrow them; or else you even may be found fighting against God." So the council flogged the apostles, warned them once more to stop preaching Jesus, and released them. Peter and John rejoiced that they had been found worthy of suffering for Jesus and continued to preach (Acts 5).

THE MARTYRDOM OF STEPHEN

After this, probably on December 26, AD 33,[31] Stephen was stoned, and Saul began persecuting the church. Possibly in his rampage Saul persecuted Peter and the other apostles personally. Certainly, he persecuted people whom Peter knew and loved. There would be quite a tear to mend between these two men. Yet they became close fellow workers in Christ.

SAMARIA AND SIMON MAGUS

Between December AD 33 and March AD 34, Saul (Paul) was ferociously persecuting Christians in Jerusalem. This may have prompted Philip to go to Samaria and convert Samaritans. Paul's persecution probably did not drive Philip (or Peter or John) out of Jerusalem, because the Bible says that Saul's persecution caused all except the apostles to scatter (Acts 8:1). It also says that those who had been scattered preached the gospel wherever they went (Acts 8:4). Therefore, Paul did not frighten the apostles away. Their evangelistic work in Samaria, on the Gaza Road, and in Antioch was simply obedience to Jesus' statement that the disciples would be his witnesses in Jerusalem, Judea, Samaria, and to the ends of the earth (Acts 1:8).

All this evangelistic outreach right after the stoning of Stephen must have seemed like an epidemic of Christianity to Paul. Like a general seeking to outflank his enemy, he applied for a priestly commission to head the Christian heretics off at Damascus, north of Samaria. Paul, of course, met with an utterly unexpected result, becoming a convert to Christ on the Damascus Road. Meanwhile, Philip reached the city of Samaria (today's Sebastia) and proclaimed Christ. Between January 1 and 15, AD 34, he preached, healed the lame, and cast out unclean spirits. Many believed in Jesus

---

31. This is the Catholic Feast of St. Stephen, which is as good a date as any and which sufficiently fits the chronology of Acts.

and were baptized, including a sorcerer named Simon Magus, who followed Philip's miracles with amazement.

The other apostles in Jerusalem heard that hostile Samaria, of all places, had received the word of God. They sent Peter and John to investigate. John had once asked Jesus for permission to bring heaven's fire down on the Samaritan villages to destroy them (Luke 9:54). Now John and Peter laid hands on the Samaritans, and they received the Holy Spirit. When Simon Magus saw the gift of the Holy Spirit, he offered the apostles money to give him this power. Peter rebuked him, saying:

> May your silver perish with you because you thought you could obtain the gift of God with money! You have neither part nor lot in this matter, for your heart is not right before God. Repent, therefore, of this wickedness of yours, and pray to the Lord that, if possible, the intent of your heart may be forgiven you. For I see that you are in the gall of bitterness and in the bond of iniquity. Simon Magus answered, "Pray for me to the Lord, that nothing of what you have said may come upon me." (Acts 8:20–24)[32]

Simon Magus seemed to be a seeker, but inwardly he was not right with God. Irenaeus recorded that the apostles cast him out and that he went to Rome, where he became a famous magician. The emperor Claudius honored him with a statue. Peter followed him to Rome and overthrew his scam.[33]

FOUNDING THE ANTIOCH CHURCH

Jerome says Peter founded the church in Antioch, Syria.[34] If so, January 15–22, AD 34, was probably the time when Peter did it. Scripture mentions some Jewish Christians from Jerusalem (probably led by Peter) who were preaching the gospel to Jews in Antioch (Acts 11:19). Since Peter was already in Samaria, he could have made the trek to Antioch in about ten hours. It was a convenient time for him to plant a church in the third largest city in the Roman Empire. This came after the stoning of Stephen and the conversion of the Samaritans. The Patriarchate of Antioch confirms this date, saying that AD 34 was the year of the church's founding.[35]

Once the church was established, it became a hotbed of activity. Jews from Cyprus and Cyrene (Libya) descended on Antioch and began preaching and converting many gentiles (Acts 11:20). Then the Jerusalem church sent Barnabas to Antioch between March 29 and April 2, AD 34 (Acts 11:22–24). In Antioch, the followers of Christ were

---

32. Simon's request is the origin of the word "simony," which means attempting to sell grace for money.

33. Irenaeus, *Against Heresies* 1:23.

34. Jerome, *On Illustrious Men*.

35. Antiochian Orthodox Christian Archdiocese of North America, "The Patriarchate of Antioch: Founded by Saints Peter and Paul,"

first called "Christians" (Acts 11:26). Eusebius says that the evangelist Luke was from Antioch,[36] and he may have become a Christian around this time.

MEETING PAUL

In AD 37, after his withdrawal to Arabia, Paul returned to Damascus and preached the gospel fearlessly. The Jews of the city plotted to kill him, so he escaped when friends let him down the city wall in a basket. Full of conviction, Paul went to Jerusalem from about April 22–26, AD 37. Remembering how he had ravaged the church, the Jerusalem Christians feared Paul. Barnabas, however, approached him and mended fences between Paul and the apostles. Paul saw Peter over a period of fifteen days. He also saw James, the half-brother of Jesus. He met no other apostles there at that time (Gal 1:18–19).

Paul preached boldly in Jerusalem. The Jewish leaders, aghast that their agent in Damascus had returned a traitor, plotted to kill him. Paul's friends helped him escape to Caesarea. From there Paul proceeded to his hometown of Tarsus and remained there in obscurity for six years, until about May 19, AD 43. All the while he had a bounty on his head in both Damascus and Jerusalem.

TO LYDDA

In June AD 37, Peter traveled from Jerusalem to Lydda, a journey of thirty miles. There he healed a man called Aeneas, who had been paralyzed and bedridden for eight years. All the people in Lydda and Sharon witnessed this and turned to the Lord (Acts 9:32–35).

RAISING TABITHA IN JOPPA

Then Peter went to nearby Joppa, the same port from which the prophet Jonah sailed away from God's command to preach at Nineveh. Jonah was the name of Peter's father, but this son of Jonah was far more obedient to God's commands than the Jonah of old. Some disciples in Joppa had sent for Peter because a kindly woman named Tabitha (Aramaic for "gazelle") or Dorcas (Greek for "gazelle") had died. Tabitha had done many acts of kindness. When Peter came to where her body lay, he sent all the weeping widows from the room, knelt, prayed, and said, "Tabitha, arise." She opened her eyes, saw Peter, and arose. The miracle became known all over Joppa, and many believed in the Lord (Acts 9:36–43).

---

36. Eusebius, *Church History* 3:4:7.

CORNELIUS

Up the coast toward Syria was the seaport of Caesarea, the seat of Roman power in Judea. Cornelius, who resided there, was a centurion of the Italian cohort, an army unit consisting of about 5,120 soldiers. A centurion commanded about one hundred men and was an important man in the Roman government of Judea. The procurator, Marcellus, who had just replaced Pontius Pilate, would have known Julius personally, met him from time to time, and relied on him as a key subordinate.

The *gens* or tribe of Cornelius was one of the most distinguished patrician family names in Rome. This man was someone important or he was related to someone important. Cornelius and his whole household feared God, gave alms to the Jews, and prayed to God continually. One day at about 3 p.m., Cornelius clearly saw an angel of God, who came to him and called his name. Staring at the angel in terror, Cornelius asked, "What is it, lord?" By calling the angel "lord," Cornelius was showing deference and respect for the heavenly apparition. He was as yet untutored in Christian theology, and so he was not addressing the angel as the risen Jesus. It is unlikely, however, that Cornelius mistook the angel for a pagan Roman god. His prayers to "God," not "the gods," and his almsgiving to Jews suggest that he embraced Jewish monotheism. He was certainly a spiritual seeker, and perhaps he already had a yearning to know about the burgeoning church. The angel replied that God had answered the Roman's prayers and that he should send to Joppa for Simon Peter. Cornelius dispatched a soldier and three servants.

The next day at about noon, Peter was praying on the housetop of his host, a man named Simon the Tanner. Peter grew hungry, and then he saw a vision of the sky opening and a great sheet descending, lowered by four corners to the ground. In it were all kinds of animals and birds. A voice said, "Get up, Peter. Kill and eat!" Peter answered, "By no means, Lord, for I have never eaten anything unholy and unclean." The voice replied, "What God has cleansed, no longer consider unholy." The vision recurred three times. Then Cornelius's messengers arrived, and the Holy Spirit urged Peter to go with them without misgivings, for God was sending him on a mission.

The next day, he and some of the other Christians left Joppa. Since the journey to Caesarea was one of forty-two miles, Peter's party probably spent the night somewhere along the way. Then they entered Caesarea the next day, probably June 11, AD 37. The centurion was waiting for him with all his relatives and close friends. Peter entered the house of Cornelius, who fell at Peter's feet. Peter made him rise, saying, "I too am just a man." Peter told the Roman family that they knew how unlawful it was for him, a Jew, to visit a foreigner, but that God had showed him through visions that he should not call any man unholy or unclean.[37]

---

37. Peter was not referring to Mosaic law, because it nowhere prohibits Jews from visiting gentiles. It does prohibit Jews from adopting gentile pagan practices (Lev 18:24–30) and from marrying gentiles (Deut 7:3; Ezra 9:12), but only because of the risk of foreign wives leading Hebrew men away from the worship of Yahweh (Num 25:1–2; 1 Kgs 11:1–2). The Bible condones the marriage of Boaz

Cornelius told Peter of the angel's visit, and Peter realized that God was sending salvation not only to the Jews but to the gentiles. Peter preached the gospel. The Holy Spirit fell on all who were listening. Peter baptized the entire household in the name of Jesus Christ. He then stayed with his new flock for several days (Acts 10).

Interestingly, Paul had fled from Jerusalem to Caesarea to escape a Jewish death threat a month earlier. Why did God not choose Paul, the apostle to the gentiles, who was available in Caesarea at just the right time, to convert Cornelius and his family? The Bible does not say. It tells us only that God chose Peter instead.

BACK IN JERUSALEM

Around June 19, AD 37, Peter returned to Jerusalem. The other apostles criticized him. "You went to uncircumcised men and ate with them," they said. But Peter told them the whole story, saying that if God gave to the gentiles the same gift he gave to Jews who believed in Jesus Christ, Peter could not stand in God's way. Then the other apostles glorified God, affirming that he had granted to the gentiles the repentance that leads to life (Acts 11:1–18).

PETER IN ASIA MINOR

Peter and Mark preached to Jews in Pontus, Galatia, Cappadocia, Asia, and Bithynia sometime between AD 41 and 43. Reading Acts, one may easily get the impression that Paul was the first to bring the gospel to these parts of the world. In fact, Peter preceded him.

FOUNDING THE CHURCH IN ROME

Jerome wrote that Peter first traveled to Rome in the second year of the reign of the emperor Claudius, AD 43.[38] When Paul first arrived in Rome in AD 57, he found many Christians already there (Acts 28:15), so somebody had to found the Roman church earlier than that. In AD 49, Claudius expelled all the Jews from Rome because of squabbles between non-Christian and Christian Jews (Acts 18:2),[39] so there were Christians in Rome as early as that.[40] This evidence supports the tradition that Peter

---

and Ruth, for example, even though Ruth was a gentile (Ruth 1:4). Moreover, God told the Jews they would be a "light to the Gentiles, and [they would] bring [God's] salvation to the ends of the earth" (Isa 49:6). The Jews of Peter's day had twisted the commands of God into ethnic snobbery.

38. Jerome, *On Illustrious Men*.

39. This caused Aquila and Priscilla to leave Rome and migrate to Corinth, where they ultimately met Paul.

40. Suetonius, *Lives of the Twelve Caesars*, "Tiberius Claudius Drusus Caesar." Cassius Dio, *Roman History* 60:6:6–7.

founded the church in Rome in the year AD 43. Undoubtedly Jews who heard Peter's sermon on Pentecost in Jerusalem in AD 33 brought Christianity back to Rome as early as that (Acts 2:10, 41). The fact that Peter's sermon converted the Roman Jews visiting Jerusalem in AD 33 may qualify Peter as the founder of the Roman church. At any rate, when he visited Rome in AD 43, ten years later, he may have built on that foundation to formally found the church of Rome.

THE BATTLE WITH SIMON MAGUS

Simon Magus, after Peter rebuked him in Samaria in AD 34, traveled to Rome, were he gained such fame as a sorcerer that the emperor Claudius honored him as a god with a statue.[41] Eusebius wrote of this as follows:

> For immediately, during the reign of Claudius, the all-good and gracious Providence, which watches over all things, led Peter, that strongest and greatest of the apostles, and the one who on account of his virtue was the speaker for all the others, to Rome against this great corrupter of life. Clad in divine armor like a noble commander of God, He carried the costly merchandise of the light of the understanding from the East to those who dwelt in the West, proclaiming the light itself, and the word which brings salvation to souls, and preaching the kingdom of heaven.[42]

PETER'S GOSPEL OF MARK

Eusebius quoted Clement of Alexandria as follows: "As Peter had preached the Word publicly at Rome, and declared the Gospel by the Spirit, many who were present requested that Mark, who had followed him for a long time and remembered his sayings, should write them out. And having composed the Gospel he gave it to those who had requested it."[43] John Mark's name is unusual, half Jewish, John, and half Latin, Marcus. Marcus, like Cornelius, is a singularly Latin name. Many Jews in Roman Judea had Jewish and Greek names, like Simon Peter, but having a Latin name was uncommon. Roman officials of the eastern empire spoke Greek, not Latin. John Mark's name suggests that he may have had a Roman father and a Jewish mother. He may have been raised with a western Roman education. Perhaps John Mark spoke Latin, which Peter and the other apostles probably did not. John Mark was thus the perfect assistant to accompany Peter to Rome and translate Peter's Aramaic or Greek into Latin. This fits very well with Eusebius's account that Mark's Gospel evolved because, on this same trip to Rome with Peter, the Romans appealed to Mark to write down Peter's sermons

---

41. Eusebius, *Church History* 2:13:3.
42. Eusebius, *Church History* 2:14:6.
43. Eusebius, *Church History* 6:14:1.

so that "he would leave them a written monument of the doctrine which had been orally communicated to them."[44]

Jerome wrote that Peter held the sacerdotal chair in the Roman church for twenty-five years,[45] which would be until AD 68, the most likely year of Peter's execution by Nero. Since, however, the next time marker in Acts places Peter in Jerusalem in AD 44, when he was arrested by the Jewish leaders for the third time, Peter cannot have remained in Rome without interruption for all twenty-five years. Therefore, Peter arrived in Rome in AD 43,[46] founded the church, opposed and brought down Simon Magus, and returned to Jerusalem by AD 44 (Acts 12:3). He would return to Rome later, and he would remain there until his death.

Peter and John Mark probably remained in Rome for one hundred days, until August 13, AD 43. The ancient sailing season in the Mediterranean "commenced either in March or April and spanned the summer months before drawing to a close in October or November."[47] Because of the dangerous winter sailing weather, they would not have wished to sail after Yom Kippur in AD 43 or before Passover in AD 44. So, they probably set sail for Caesarea around September 1, AD 43, arriving home before Yom Kippur.

AGABUS PREDICTS A FAMINE

While Peter was in Rome, Barnabas went to Tarsus in May AD 43 and brought Paul back to Antioch, where Paul began ministering for one year. A prophet named Agabus traveled from Jerusalem to Antioch. He predicted that a great famine would devastate Judea. The Antioch church sent Barnabas and Saul to Jerusalem with famine relief (Acts 11:30). The prophesied famine occurred between AD 45 and 47.[48] So the famine relief trip had to occur before AD 45, which fits with a date of AD 44.

THIRD ARREST

In AD 44, during Passover, Herod Agrippa I, son of Aristobulus and grandson of Herod the Great, killed James, the son of Zebedee. When he saw that this pleased the Jews, he also arrested Peter on April 1, 16 Nisan, the third day of Passover (Acts 12:3–4). Herod put a guard of sixteen soldiers over Peter, probably remembering

---

44. Eusebius, *Church History* 2:15:1.
45. Jerome, *On Illustrious Men*.
46. Finegan, *Handbook*, 382.
47. Bereford, *The Ancient Sailing Season*, 9.
48. Josephus, *Ant.* 20:2. As foretold by the prophet Agabus and recorded by Josephus, famine raged in Judea under the procurator Cassius Fadus (AD 44–46). Orosius, in his *Histories against the Pagans*, 7:6:9, 12, placed it in the fourth year of Claudius's reign. Claudius began to reign on January 24, AD 41, so his fourth year began on January 24, AD 45. The famine therefore endured from the Passover of AD 45 to the Passover of AD 47, 739 days or slightly over two years.

Peter's former miraculous deliverance from jail and hoping to prevent a repeat of that event. He intended to display Peter to the mob during the Days of Unleavened Bread.

The night before Herod planned to present him, Peter was sleeping chained between two soldiers, with other soldiers also guarding the prison door. An angel of the Lord appeared and illuminated the cell. He struck Peter's side. Peter's chains fell away, and the angel led Peter off, as if in a dream. They passed the first and second guards and came to the outer iron gate, which opened by itself. They went out into the city street, where Peter found himself suddenly alone.

Coming to his senses, Peter went to the house of Mary, the mother of John Mark, cousin of Barnabas and the author of the Gospel of Mark. Many were gathered there, praying. This would have been natural, both because they were concerned for Peter and because it was Passover week. Peter knocked at the gate, and a servant girl named Rhoda came to answer. She recognized Peter's voice, but from joy ran back to tell everyone without letting him in. They said she was out of her mind, but she kept insisting until they thought it must be Peter's angel. Peter kept knocking, and when they opened and saw him, they were amazed. He made a sign for them to keep silent, and then he told them of how the Lord had rescued him. Peter told them to report everything to James, Jesus' half-brother, and the other apostles, and then he went to another place (Acts 12:17). This account is another indicator of the wealth of some of Jesus' followers. First, John Mark's mother had a servant girl, Rhoda. Second, the house was large enough that those within could not hear the voice of Peter beyond the outer door; this was not a modest hovel.

The next day Jerusalem was in an uproar at Peter's escape. With as many as 2.7 million pilgrims in town for the Passover,[49] the miracle could not have occurred at a more dramatic time. Herod executed the guards, and Peter repaired to Caesarea. Shortly afterwards, at the height of his arrogance, Herod died a grisly death by parasitic worms, while the word of the Lord continued to grow and multiply (Acts 12). Then Paul and Barnabas returned to Antioch, taking John Mark with them (Acts 12:25). Paul, Barnabas, and John Mark embarked on their first missionary journey around May 25, AD 44 (Acts 13:1–4). They completed this and returned to Antioch around September 6, AD 44 (Acts 14:26–28). They told the church in Antioch how the Holy Spirit was working among the gentiles.

CONFIRMING PAUL

The predicted famine struck Judea from AD 45 to 47. Then, fourteen years after Paul's conversion, in AD 48. Paul and Barnabas returned to Jerusalem.[50] Paul took the Greek Christian Titus with him. Paul said that this trip was "because of a revelation,"

---

49. Josephus, *War* 6:9:3.

50. This was a logical time for the trip, because it was the third springtime since the famine began, when, if the famine were really over, the signs of fresh growth would be evident.

referring to Agabus's prophecy, meaning that Agabus had prophesied the famine, the famine had occurred, and now Paul, Barnabas, and Titus were traveling to Jerusalem to inspect the aftermath of the famine and the efficacy of the relief funds the church in Antioch had sent.

Since Titus was a Greek Christian, he was uncircumcised. Some "false brothers" spied on Titus and verified the fact. They argued that he must be circumcised. Paul and Barnabas, however, did not submit to this. But some "who seemed to be influential" in the Jerusalem church recognized that Paul "had been entrusted with the Gospel to the uncircumcised, just as Peter had been entrusted with the Gospel to the circumcised." James (Jesus' half-brother), Peter, and John, who seemed to be "pillars" of the church, perceived the grace given to Paul by Jesus, and they agreed with Paul about Titus. They gave Paul and Barnabas the right hand of fellowship and sent them off to the gentiles, while reserving to the other apostles the mission to the circumcised (the Jews). James, Peter, and John only asked them to remember the poor, which Paul said was the very thing he was eager to do (Gal 2:1–10).

This did not mean that Paul was to minister only to gentiles and Peter was to minister only to Jews. Peter had already had experience proclaiming the gospel to gentiles. He had ministered in Samaria (Acts 8:14), to Cornelius and his family (Acts 10:25), to Antioch, and to the Romans. Paul's customary practice was to preach about Jesus in synagogues, and thus to Jews, before preaching to gentiles (Acts 9:20, 14:1, 26:11). Moreover, Jesus had told Peter and the other eleven apostles to "make disciples of all nations" (Matt 28:19), not some, and to be his witnesses in Jerusalem, Judea, Samaria, and to the end of the earth (Acts 1:8). The job of all the disciples was to proclaim the gospel to both Jews and gentiles. Therefore, the meaning of Paul's statement in Galatians 2:7–8 is not absolute but focuses on three things: (1) Paul's authority regarding Titus, (2) Paul's recent first missionary journey (Acts 13–14), and (3) Paul's upcoming second missionary journey (Acts 15–18).

PAUL'S REBUKE OF PETER

Paul, Barnabas, and John Mark returned to Antioch in AD 48. They remained there for some time. Around March AD 49, some Christian Jews came to Antioch from Jerusalem and taught that only those circumcised according to the law of Moses could be saved. Paul and Barnabas had seen God open the door of faith to the gentiles, and they disputed with the Judaizers.

At this time, Peter visited Antioch (Gal 2:11). He probably remained over Passover, which ran from April 3 to 11. Some friends of James, Jesus' half-brother, arrived from Jerusalem and advised Peter to keep aloof from the gentiles, because they were afraid that he would alienate the Jewish Christians. Probably they were thinking that celebration of the Passover meal should be a non-gentile event. Surprisingly, since Peter had ministered to the gentile Cornelius in his house, had already evangelized

Rome, and had agreed with Paul that Titus did not need to be circumcised, Peter did as the Judaizers advised. Other Jewish Christians at Antioch, including Barnabas, followed his lead. Probably Peter and Barnabas, although they both had had experience proclaiming the gospel to gentiles, thought that only Jewish Christians would want to celebrate the Passover anyway.

Paul, however, thought Peter was not being straightforward about the truth of the gospel. He rebuked Peter in the presence of all, saying, "If you, being a Jew, live like the Gentiles and not like the Jews, how is it that you compel the Gentiles to live like Jews? ... A man is not justified by the works of the Law but through faith in Jesus Christ" (Gal 2:14–15). Evidently, Peter accepted this rebuke with humility, and fellowship resumed between Jewish and gentile Christians. Peter returned to Jerusalem.

Paul's words suggest that the Jewish Christians of the first century "lived like Gentiles," perhaps meaning that they did not strictly observe Mosaic law. For example, they probably felt free to travel on the Sabbath and eat food prohibited to Jews (but not food polluted by idol worship). They still observed Jewish holidays (Acts 20:16) and frequented the temple (Acts 21:26), but evidently with a sense of newfound freedom in Christ.

THE JERUSALEM COUNCIL

The vexing question of whether believers had first to become Jews before becoming Christians still burned. The Antioch church decided that Paul and Barnabas should go to Jerusalem and lay the matter before the apostles and elders there. They struck out in May AD 49. At the Council of Jerusalem, which probably convened from June 21 to 23, some Christian Pharisees (Acts 15:5)[51] stood up and stated that gentile Christians should be circumcised and should observe Mosaic law. After much debate, Peter arose and reminded them how he had preached to the gentiles and how God had given them the Holy Spirit, making no distinction between them and Jews and cleansing their hearts by faith. Peter asked why the Pharisees wanted to place a yoke on the necks of the gentiles which the Jews had been unable to bear.[52] Both Jews and gentiles were saved not by obeying the law, but by God's grace. Then the people listened in silence as Paul and Barnabas related the signs and wonders that God had worked through them among the gentiles. Finally, James, the half-brother of Jesus, stood up and agreed with Peter and Paul. He advised that they give Christian gentiles only four prohibitions: (1) to abstain from things sacrificed to idols, (2) to abstain from sexual immorality, (3) to abstain from blood, and (4) to abstain from strangled animals.

These four prohibitions seem to have been designed mainly to separate gentiles from their former pagan practices. Paul wrote that idols were not real gods and so eating animals sacrificed to idols was not really a problem, except that the practice might

---

51. Even Pharisees, who as a group had so vigorously opposed Jesus, were becoming Christians.

52. Despite becoming Christians, these Pharisees still tended to lay burdens on others that they themselves could not bear, as Jesus had told them before (Matt 23:3–4).

lead people without mature theological knowledge to stumble into the trap of idolatry (1 Cor 8:1–13). As for sexual immorality, Leviticus 18 detailed what sexual practices are sinful. In the Ancient Near East temple prostitutes had sex with worshippers to unite the devotee with the spirit of the god. Paul probably had this in mind when he wrote, "Do you not know that he who is joined to a prostitute becomes one body with her? . . . or do you not know that your body is a temple of the Holy Spirit? . . . you are not your own, for you were bought with a price" (1 Cor 6:15–20). Leviticus 17 forbade the Israelites, and the foreigners living among them, to consume blood. This prohibition might be related to the prohibition against strangled animals, for such victims die with their blood still in them, in contrast to animals sacrificed by a knife (the practice of Romans, Greeks, and Jews) whose blood drains out of the carcass. Believers in the Apostolic Age would encounter animals sacrificed by strangulation, for Herodotus wrote that Scythians sacrificed animals in this way.[53] In any case, the main thrust of the apostles' prohibitions cannot have been against eating non-kosher foods, because God had specifically told Peter that it was lawful to eat all kinds of animals (Acts 10:9–16). The point was to prompt new, gentile converts to leave their idolatrous paganism behind. The Jerusalem Council wrote a letter to this effect, entrusting Paul, Barnabas, a certain Judas Justus Barsabbas, and Silas (Silvanus) to bring the welcome news to the gentile converts at Antioch (Acts 15:1–35).

PETER'S TRAVELS

Probably from AD 49 to AD 59, Peter made a wide missionary journey which ended in Rome. Hippolytus, a third-century Christian author, wrote that "Peter preached the Gospel in Pontus, and Galatia, and Cappadocia, and Betania, and Italy, and Asia."[54] He probably also visited Bithynia, on the south shore of the Black Sea, because 1 Peter was written to Christians there. He also visited the church in Corinth,[55] which Paul had planted between January 26, AD 50, and August 24, AD 51. Paul was in Corinth, Ephesus, and Caesarea in this period, returning to Jerusalem in September AD 51. So it is possible that the paths of Peter and Paul crossed. Peter took his wife with him on his travels, as we learn from Paul, who wrote, "Do we not have the right to take along a believing wife, as do the other apostles and the brothers of the Lord and Cephas?" (1 Cor 9:5).

---

53. Herodotus, *History*, IV

54. Hippolytus, "List of the Apostles and Disciples." Hippolytus is an early source, but his facts are not ironclad. For example, by his calculation, Nero would have had to execute Paul in AD 69, a year after Nero died. Hippolytus's information is always worth contemplating, but when comparing it to other biblical and extrabiblical evidence, one should always be prepared to reach for a pinch of salt.

55. Eusebius, *Church History* 2:25:8.

ROME AGAIN

When Peter wrote his first epistle, Mark and Silas were with him. Silas acted as Peter's scribe (1 Pet 5:12–13). This writing probably was from Rome between AD 59 and 68, and not during Peter's first trip to Rome in AD 43, because the letter was to Bithynia (the southern coastline of the Black Sea), and that was too early a date for the establishment of a church in Bithynia, since Paul was planning to evangelize that region in AD 49 (Acts 16:7). The fact that Peter sent Mark's greeting to a number of churches in Bithynia implies that Mark must have been widely known and respected there. Since Mark was with Barnabas in Cyprus in AD 49 (Acts 15:39), was with Paul in Rome during his first incarceration there from AD 57 to 59 (Col 4:10) and was back in Asia Minor in AD 68, when the Romans arrested Paul in Troas (2 Tim 4:11–13), Mark must have joined Peter on his missionary journeys after AD 49 and must have left Rome for the east before Peter's martyrdom in AD 68. Peter was probably on his missionary journeys at the same time that Paul was on his second, third, and fourth missionary journeys, and their paths may have crossed again. Since both Luke and Mark were in Rome during Paul's first imprisonment (Col 4:10, 14), probably Peter and Mark arrived together in Rome prior to Paul's first acquittal in AD 59.

PETER'S DEATH

Eusebius says that Peter and Paul died in Rome.[56] Jerome says that they died on the same day in AD 68.[57] Nero began persecuting Christians after the Great Fire of Rome in July AD 64. Tradition says Nero kept Peter in chains for nine months in the Mamertine dungeon.[58] Possibly Nero's reason for detaining Peter for nine months was that his agents were scouring the empire for that other notorious Christian, Paul, so that Nero could celebrate a double execution.

Nero committed suicide on June 9, AD 68, so Peter and Paul must have died before that date. It is possible that Nero arrested Peter around July AD 67. Probably he arrested Paul in Troas around March AD 68, so Paul would have arrived in Rome by April. Late church tradition says that a spring flowed miraculously up from the depths of the Mamertine prison and that Peter used its water to baptize his jailers and fellow prisoners. Peter's wife was with him, for she also died a martyr's death in Rome. Clement of Alexandria wrote:

> The blessed Peter, on seeing his wife led to death, rejoiced on account of her call and conveyance home, and called very encouragingly and comfortingly,

---

56. Eusebius, *Church History* 3:1:2.
57. Jerome, *On Illustrious Men*.
58. De Montor, *The Lives and Times of the Roman Pontiffs*, 26.

addressing her by name, "Remember thou the Lord." Such was the marriage of the blessed and their perfect disposition towards those dearest to them.[59]

Paul, as a Roman citizen, died in a noble way, by the sword, while Peter, who was not a citizen, died a criminal's death, on a cross.[60] Saying he was unworthy to die in the same way as his Lord, Peter asked his executioners to hang him on the cross upside down, which they did, and so he died. Jesus had foretold the manner of Peter's death:

> Truly, truly, I say to you, when you were young, you used to dress yourself and walk wherever you wanted, but when you are old, you will stretch out your hands, and another will dress you and carry you where you do not want to go." (This he said to show by what kind of death he was to glorify God.) And after saying this he said to him, "Follow me." (John 21:18–19)

These last two words to Peter, "follow me," echoed, movingly, those that the Lord had used in first calling Peter to be a fisher of men.

NERO'S LAST DAYS

Probably Nero's execution of Peter and Paul represented the fierce anger of a cornered animal. The emperor knew he was in fatal danger. In March AD 68, one of Nero's governors in Gaul rebelled against his tax policies. Another loyal governor put down the rebellion at the Battle of Vesontio in May. Support was growing to replace Nero with Galba, a senator and governor of Spain. In a draft speech, Nero considered fleeing to a distant, loyal province, running away to Parthia, throwing himself on Galba's mercy, or begging the people of Rome to forgive him. If they would not consent to let him remain emperor, perhaps they would let him retire as the prefect of Egypt. Nero never delivered that speech for fear that the mob would tear him to pieces before he could reach the forum.

One night, Nero awoke to discover that the palace guard had abandoned him. Terrified and traveling in disguise, Nero and four loyal followers escaped to a villa four miles outside Rome. He ordered his followers to dig a grave for him. Learning that the Senate had declared him a public enemy, he paced back and forth, muttering, "What an artist dies in me!" Lacking the fortitude to kill himself, he asked one of his followers to set the example by committing suicide first. Then the sound of approaching cavalry drove him to beg one of his followers, Epaphroditus, to do the deed. Epaphroditus struck the regicidal blow. When one of the cavalry broke into the villa, he tried to staunch the flow of Nero's blood, but to no avail. Nero's last words were, "Too late! This is loyalty!" If Nero's end had come just a bit sooner, Peter and Paul might have been spared.

---

59. Clement of Alexandra, *Stromata* 7:11; Eusebius, *Church History* 3:30:2.

60. Roman law strictly forbade beating, imprisoning, or crucifying a Roman citizen without due process of law.

Peter was crucified on Vatican Hill, probably around May 5, AD 68. He was originally buried there. His body was then removed to a cemetery along the Appian Way, until the emperor Constantine moved it back to the Vatican and enlarged the Vatican church in the apostle's honor. Peter's head is now supposed to be in the cathedral of Saint John Lateran.

DID JESUS FOUND HIS CHURCH ON PETER?

On this question there are two views: the Catholic view and the Protestant view. The reader must decide which view to embrace. Both views should be considered, as Peter said, with gentleness and respect (1 Pet 3:15).

The Catholic View

The Catholic Church teaches that Jesus gave special authority to Peter. They teach that the pope, the bishop of Rome, derives his authority as leader of the true church from Peter. Peter was the first vicar of Rome, so the pope is Peter's heir.[61] Catholics say that Jesus built his church on the Rock of Peter, and so the papacy is the foundation of Christ's church. Jesus gave Peter the keys to the kingdom of heaven, which means that Peter (and his successors, the popes) exercise unique power over the community of God. This teaching is based on the following verses:

> Now when Jesus came into the district of Caesarea Philippi, he asked his disciples, "Who do people say that the Son of Man is?" And they said, "Some say John the Baptist, others say Elijah, and others Jeremiah or one of the prophets." He said to them, "But who do you say that I am?" Simon Peter replied, "You are the Christ, the Son of the living God." And Jesus answered him, "Blessed are you, Simon Bar-Jonah! For flesh and blood has not revealed this to you, but my Father who is in heaven. And I tell you, you are Peter, and on this rock, I will build my Church, and the gates of hell shall not prevail against it. I will give you the keys of the kingdom of heaven, and whatever you bind on earth shall be bound in heaven, and whatever you loose on earth shall be loosed in heaven." Then he strictly charged the disciples to tell no one that he was the Christ. (Matt 16:13–20)

The title "pope" comes from Latin *papa*, meaning father. The pope's official title is Holy Father, and the correct way to address the Pope is "Your Holiness." Rome, of course, was the capital of the Roman Empire, and the Romans ethnocentrically considered their empire to be the whole world. We read, for example, in Luke that: "In those days a decree went out from Caesar Augustus that all the world should be

---

61. Vicar is from the Latin word *vicarius*, meaning agent or proxy, thus an earthly representative of Christ.

registered" (Luke 2:1). By "all the world," Augustus had Rome in mind. He definitely knew of Persia, Ethiopia, Arabia, India, Russia, and China, but Caesar had no expectation of registering people there. He certainly had no plans to register the Apaches, Aztecs, Incas, Zulus, Maoris, or Eskimos, people who existed but of whom he knew nothing. Rome thought itself to be the only "world" worth considering. Even today, in Italy, Romans smugly say, *"Noi siamo romani. Noi mangiamo, e gli altri lavorano."* ("We are Romans. We eat. Others work.") When Christianity took root in Rome, Romans assumed that Rome's church would lead the world.

The pope first used the title *Vicarius Christi,* meaning the representative of Christ, in the eighth century; before that he used the title Vicar of the Prince of Apostles or *vicarius principis apostolorum.* The Prince of the Apostles was Peter. Since Jesus said he would build his church on Peter the Rock and give Peter the keys to the kingdom of heaven, and since Peter founded the Roman church, died in Rome, and handed his authority to his successor Roman bishops, or popes, the Catholic Church teaches that the pope is the true heir to Christian leadership.

The Protestant View

Jesus' play on words in Scripture is clear in Greek but lost in Latin (and in English). Jesus said that Peter was a *pétros* (stone), but that upon this *pétra* (boulder), Jesus would build his church. In pre-New Testament Greek, Heraclitus coined the phrase "leave no stone (*pétros*) unturned." Since one can turn a *pétros,* it is a rock that can be rolled or thrown. It is a movable stone. The word in Aramaic for a movable stone is *kepha,* which was, in fact, Peter's Aramaic nickname: Cephas. A *pétra* is a foundation stone, a boulder, or a cliff. It is a large, unmovable rock. The corresponding Aramaic word for *pétra* is *shua.* Where Jesus is called a rock elsewhere in the New Testament, the Greek word is *pétra,* an immovable rock. For example, Paul wrote, "all drank the same spiritual drink. For they drank from the spiritual Rock that followed them, and the Rock (*pétras*) was Christ" (1 Cor 10:4).[62] In Matthew 7:24, the reference to the man who built his house upon a rock rather than upon sand uses the word *pétra* for that immovable rock. In Matthew 27:60, Joseph of Arimathea's tomb was hewn out of rock (*pétra*); the large stone that was rolled over the entrance was a *lithos* in Greek, a movable marker stone.

Catholic scholars say that Jesus had to call Peter a *pétros* because that is the masculine form of *pétra,* and Peter was a man. In Greek, adjectives must agree with the gender of the noun they modify, but when one makes a simile, likening one noun to another, the gender of each side of the simile need not conform. To use an

---

62. The image of drinking from a rock refers to the story of how Moses, at God's command, twice struck a rock, causing water to gush from it to slake the thirst of the Israelites in the wilderness (Exod 17:1–6; Num 20:10–11).

approximation in English, if one calls call a man an "old woman," he means he is effeminate in behavior, not that his gender is female.

Catholics also say that if Jesus made his declaration in Aramaic, he would not have made a distinction between *pétros* and *pétras*, since he would have used *kepha* in both parts of the statement, i.e., "you are *kepha*, and on this *kepha* I will found my Church." The problem is no one can guess what words Jesus might have used in Aramaic. The only Gospel manuscripts we have are in Greek. Furthermore, Aramaic does have two distinct words, like Greek, for a moveable stone (*kepha*) and an immovable rock (*shua*). Since the Gospel writers chose Greek as their language of communication (not Aramaic), they must have been comfortable in either language. In a multilingual society, such as Judea was and Israel still is, there is no reason why Jesus may not have chosen to make this statement originally in Greek, especially if he wanted to employ the pun which the Greek preserves for us. In multilingual countries and families, it is normal for people to intermix phrases from whichever language makes the point best. This is especially true of dramatic or humorous remarks.

If Jesus had not meant to make a distinction between himself, the foundation of the church, and Simon, a tile in the church's mosaic, he could have used the same word: "Simon, you are a *pétra*, and on this *pétra* I will build my Church." Yet Matthew takes pains to retain the exact emphasis Jesus made: "You are *pétros* and on this *pétra* I will build my Church." Jesus basically was saying, "Simon, you are a pebble, but I am the rock on which I will build my Church. You are a chip off the old block." Peter echoed this interpretation of his own and Christ's roles when he wrote:

> As you come to him, a living stone rejected by men but in the sight of God chosen and precious, you yourselves like living stones are being built up as a spiritual house, to be a holy priesthood, to offer spiritual sacrifices acceptable to God through Jesus Christ. For it stands in Scripture: "Behold, I am laying in Zion a stone, a cornerstone chosen and precious, and whoever believes in him will not be put to shame." So, the honor is for you who believe, but for those who do not believe, "The stone that the builders rejected has become the cornerstone," and "A stone of stumbling, and a rock of offense." They stumble because they disobey the word, as they were destined to do. But you are a chosen race, a royal priesthood, a holy nation, a people for his own possession, that you may proclaim the excellencies of him who called you out of darkness into his marvelous light. (1 Pet 2:4–9)

Paul removed any doubt about who is the church's one foundation when he wrote, "for no one can lay a foundation other than that which is laid, which is Jesus Christ" (1 Cor 3:11). Moreover, Jesus did not give exclusive control over the keys to the kingdom of heaven to Peter (which is the basis of making Peter, and his successor popes, uniquely authoritative). Speaking to all his disciples, Jesus said:

> Truly, I say to you [ὑμῖν, you, plural], whatever you [ὑμῖν, you, plural] bind on earth shall be bound in heaven, and whatever you [ὑμῖν, you, plural] loose on earth shall be loosed in heaven. Again I say to you [ὑμῖν, you plural], if two of you [ὑμῖν, you, plural] agree on earth about anything they ask, it will be done for them by my Father in heaven. For where two or three are gathered in my name, there am I among them. (Matt 18:18–20)

Peter was a prominent apostle, but not uniquely powerful. Peter did use the keys Christ gave him to open the door to heaven in some special ways, namely, (1) through the first great sermon at Pentecost, (2) by leading Cornelius and his gentile household to Christ, (3) by preaching in Samaria, Antioch, Bithynia, and Rome, and (4) by his many other inspired and miraculous acts. His leadership was remarkable. But the other apostles did similar work for the Lord, and the Protestant view is that there is no scriptural basis for the apostolic transmission of unique authority from Peter down through the popes.

PETER'S PERSONALITY

Peter was impetuous, emotional, and assertive. When Jesus invited Peter to follow him, he decisively dropped his net. When Jesus walked on water, Peter stepped over the side of the boat and did so, too. Jesus spoke more to Peter than to any other disciple. Jesus praised Peter more than any other disciple. "Blessed are you, Peter son of Jonah" (Matt 16:17). Peter was the only disciple who dared to rebuke Jesus. When Jesus said he would go to Jerusalem and be killed, Peter cried, "God forbid it, Lord! This shall never happen to you" (Matt 16:22). Jesus rebuked Peter more sharply than any other disciple. "Get behind me, Satan! You are a stumbling block to me; for you are not setting your mind on God's interest, but man's" (Matt 16:23). In the Garden of Gethsemane, Jesus rebuked Peter for sleeping while Jesus suffered fatal anguish (Mark 14:37). Peter was the loudest in vowing loyalty to Jesus before his arrest; he even armed himself with a sword and cut off Malchus's ear. Yet he abandoned Jesus, cursing and swearing. When Jesus looked at Peter during his trial, Peter wept bitterly. After the resurrection, Peter charged first into the empty tomb and later leapt into the Sea of Galilee to join Jesus on shore. Peter rebuked Simon the Magician. Peter worked miracles, including raising the dead. Peter led Romans to Christ. Peter graciously accepted a rebuke from Paul. Peter defended the rights of gentile Christians at the Jerusalem Council. And Peter demanded to die on an upside-down cross because he refused to believe he was worthy to die in the way his friend, Savior, and Lord had died.

PETER'S EPISTLES

Peter wrote 1 and 2 Peter, two inspired letters that are part of the New Testament. A minority of scholars disputes Peter's authorship, but the majority, dating from the earliest church fathers, affirms it. Peter's first letter aimed to encourage Christians who were suffering for Christ. It promised that suffering is not eternal; heaven is the real home of Christians because of God's grace. He seems to have written the letter from Rome, since he wrote that he was in "Babylon" (1 Pet 5:13). He might really have been in Babylon, but more likely Babylon was code for one of two apostate cities: Jerusalem or Rome. Peter addressed the letter to Christians who were "elect exiles of the dispersion in Pontus, Galatia, Cappadocia, Asia, and Bithynia" (1 Pet 1:1); he also mentioned that Silvanus and Mark were with him at the time of writing. Silvanus appears to have acted as Peter's scribe on this occasion (1 Pet 5:12–13). There were probably few, if any, churches in Asia Minor prior to Paul's first missionary journey of AD 44. So, Peter probably did not write this letter on his first trip to Rome with Mark in AD 43. He probably composed 1 Peter around AD 59.

The book of Jude and 2 Peter are similar in content. In his second letter, Peter urged his readers to be stronger Christians, to shun false teachers, to hold fast to sound doctrine, and to be ready for Christ's return and for the final judgment of the wicked. He probably also wrote this from Rome between AD 59 and 68. Probably he wrote it toward the end of this period, when the Neronian persecution of Christians (AD 64–68) and the Roman-Jewish War (AD 66–73) were raging. That would explain Peter's emphasis on the truth of the gospel (2 Pet 1:16), his warning against false teachers, who were abundant in Judea during the Roman-Jewish conflict (2 Pet 2), and his apocalyptic vision of the Day of the Lord in 2 Peter 3:1–13.

Andrew, the First Called

ANDREW WAS VARIOUSLY THE second or the fourth in the list of apostles. His name, Andreas, means "manly" in Greek. The Bible records no Hebrew or Aramaic name for him. He was born in Bethsaida, "Fish Town," at the north end of the Sea of Galilee. Later, he lived with his brother, Simon Peter, in Capernaum. The fact that Scripture lists him after Peter suggests that he was Peter's younger brother; but given Peter's prominence as the leader of the apostles, it is also possible that Peter was younger, but more important, as in the cases of Isaac and Ishmael and Jacob and Esau.

The father of Peter and Andrew was Jonah ("Dove" in Hebrew)—the same name as that of Jonah, the prophet to Nineveh, who came from the village of Gath-hepher ("Wine Press"), two miles from Nazareth. Jonah, perhaps with intentional irony, was a common name for men in the fishing trade. The sons of Jonah started out in the little fishing village of Bethsaida. As their fishing business prospered, they moved to the larger town of Capernaum, bought a big house, and formed a partnership with Zebedee and his sons, James and John (Luke 5:7, 10).

EARLY SPIRITUAL QUEST

The Eastern Orthodox Church honors Andrew with the title *protókletos*—the first-called of Jesus' disciples (John 1:40).[1] Andrew and his business partner, John the son of Zebedee, first went to hear the message of John the Baptist in the High Holy Days of AD 29, which ran from Rosh Hashanah Eve (Monday, September 24) through the last day of the Feast of Tabernacles (Thursday, October 18). In that year, crowds of people from Jerusalem went to Bethany on the Jordan, about twenty miles east of Jerusalem, to hear the Baptist preach.

The Baptist began his ministry at the age of thirty-two in the fifteenth year of Tiberius Caesar on or before Saturday, August 18, AD 29, the last day of Tiberius's

---

1. This passage mentions two disciples. It positively identifies one as Andrew. The other remains anonymous. However, since all the other disciples first called by Jesus are named at the wedding of Cana except one, and since only John's Gospel records the wedding (making John a probable eyewitness), it is likely that the unnamed disciple is John, consistent with John's literary technique of not explicitly naming himself.

fifteenth year (Luke 3:1).² Pharisees and Sadducees from Jerusalem went to question him. In those days, John preached: "Repent, for the kingdom of heaven is at hand." Isaiah referred to John when he described a "voice of one crying in the wilderness," saying "make ready the way of the Lord, make his paths straight" (Matt 3:1–3).

John baptized his thirty-one-year-old cousin, Jesus, around Sunday, September 2, AD 29.³ Jesus would not have been baptized the day before, on the Sabbath, not necessarily because it would have been a problem for Jesus, but because there would have been few, if any, Jews abroad to witness the event. After being baptized, Jesus ventured into the wilderness and fasted for forty days. The Feast of Tabernacles began on October 9, the thirty-seventh day of Jesus' fasting. On the Sabbath, October 13, Satan tempted Jesus, and on Monday, October 15, after the Sabbath, priests and Levites again traveled out from Jerusalem to question John the Baptist about his identity (John 1:19). The next day, Tuesday, October 16, Jesus returned from his sojourn in the wilderness to the banks of the Jordan, where the Baptist first proclaimed him the Lamb of God (John 1:29). The next day, Wednesday, October 17, the Baptist proclaimed for a second time, as he saw Jesus passing by, "behold, the Lamb of God" (John 1:36). On this day, Andrew and John were present.

Hearing this, Andrew and John followed Jesus, who turned to them and said, "What do you seek?" They asked, "Rabbi, where are you staying?" Jesus said, "Come, and you will see." This was a very natural conversation during the Feast of Tabernacles. During this feast, God commanded the Jews to come before him (make a pilgrimage to Jerusalem) and to construct booths, tents, or huts (tabernacles; Hebrew: *sukkot*) and live in them for a week to commemorate Israel's wandering in the desert during the Exodus. One can infer from Josephus that as many as 2.7 million Jews descended upon Jerusalem for pilgrimage feasts during the first century,⁴ so there was not enough room in the city to house everyone. People stayed in the homes of relatives and friends and even strangers in the surrounding countryside. During the Passover week of AD 33, Jesus and his disciples stayed either in Bethany or on the Mount of Olives. So, during the Feast of Tabernacles in this year of AD 29, it was logical for Andrew and John to ask Jesus where he was staying. It might have been in a makeshift booth almost anywhere.

Andrew and John spent the day until about 4 p.m. in Jesus' company. Then Andrew went and found his brother Peter and told him, "We have found the Messiah" (John 1:41). Although Andrew immediately followed the Lord, Jesus had not yet chosen him as a full-time disciple. He was still a casual follower. In fact, Andrew may still have considered himself a disciple of John the Baptist and may have remained so until Jesus called him personally around May 1 of AD 30, over seven months later. The next

---

2. Finegan, *Handbook*, 339.
3. See "Pinpointing the Start of Jesus' Ministry" in the Appendices. No other date works.
4. Josephus, *War* 6:9:3.

day, Thursday, October 18, Jesus called Philip and Nathanael and started back toward Galilee with these two disciples, plus Andrew, Peter, and John, in tow.

THE WEDDING AT CANA

On the third day, Sunday, October 21, 17 Tishri, there was a wedding at Cana in Galilee, and the mother of Jesus was there. "On the third day" means on the third day since calling Philip and Nathanael. The day Jesus called them was the last day of the Feast of Tabernacles, so it was natural that it would be the right day to return to Galilee, as the fall pilgrimage to Jerusalem for the High Holy Days ended. Jesus also was invited to the wedding with his disciples.

The walk from Bethany on the Jordan to Cana, following the eastern route along the Jordan River to avoid Samaria, was a journey of about eighty-two miles. In Jesus' day, people walked everywhere, every day, so unless they were very old or young, they were fit and would probably average a pace of about 3.7 miles per hour. So, this journey would take a total of about twenty-two hours. When traveling, Jesus and his disciples probably would have walked about ten hours on each non-Sabbath day. On Thursday, aware that a Sabbath was coming the next day, they probably pushed it. Sunrise was at 5:45 a.m. and sunset was at 5:06 p.m. in Israel on that day, giving about eleven daylight hours. They probably managed ten hours' walking, covering thirty-seven miles. They spent the night somewhere in the Jordan Valley, probably in a village with friends.

The next day was Friday, and so they would have wanted to start early—again around 6 a.m.—and finish early, around 3 p.m., so that they might find a house to stay in an hour before sunset to observe the Sabbath. They might have walked only nine hours on that day, about thirty-three miles. That would leave only about twelve miles to cover on the final day, Sunday, the day of the wedding. If they rose with the sun and started out at 6 a.m. again, they would reach Cana in three hours, at about 9 a.m., plenty of time to wash from their journey and prepare to join the wedding party.

Jesus' mother was already there. Mary likely had walked from Nazareth, not from Jerusalem. As a woman, she was not required to make the pilgrimages. From Nazareth to Cana was about a two-hour walk. Possibly Jesus met Mary in Nazareth and accompanied her north to Cana. Possibly Mary had already gone to Cana before the Sabbath to help prepare for the wedding. Since the end of the story says that Jesus left the wedding with his mother, his brothers, and his disciples, obviously, his brothers also were there. The word "brothers" in Greek probably means brothers and sisters, since is unlikely that Mary's daughters would have missed a family wedding. Jesus' brothers may have been in Jerusalem for the High Holy Days and may also have just arrived from Judea, perhaps in the company of Jesus and his five new disciples. His sisters may have been in Nazareth with Mary and may have come with her directly from there. In any case, Jesus' family was all at the wedding, which suggests, along with Mary's taking command of events, that the bridegroom was a relative of Jesus. In fact, the bridegroom may have been Simon the Zealot, who would later become one of the twelve disciples, and who may have been the brother of Matthew Levi and James the Less and may have been, like them, Jesus' cousin.[5] Nathanael Bartholomew, who was also present, was a resident of Cana.

When the wine at the feast ran out, Jesus' mother said to him, "They have no wine." Jesus said to her, "Woman, what does this have to do with me? My hour has not yet come." Mary said to the servants, "Do whatever he tells you." There were six stone water jars there for the Jewish rites of purification, each holding twenty or thirty gallons. Jesus said to the servants, "Fill the jars with water." They filled them to the brim. And he said to them, "Now draw some out and take it to the master of the feast." So, they took it. When the master of the feast tasted the water now become wine and did not know where it came from (though the servants who had drawn the water knew), the master of the feast called the bridegroom and said to him, "Everyone serves the good wine first, and when people have drunk freely, then the poor wine. But you have kept the good wine until now" (John 2:1-11).

Jesus' reply to Mary's request was brusque—not disrespectful, but firm. He was telling Mary that his role had changed. A mere fifty-five days ago, he had left Galilee as the head of his family's household, her eldest son. Now, baptized, triumphant over Satan, and with five disciples, his agenda was God's agenda, no longer that of his earthly family. Jesus complied with Mary's request, but he redefined the purpose of the event. Jesus would not let his earthly family run his ministry. He and the Father were one, and God was running it. Mary told the servants, perhaps with some asperity, to do whatever Jesus told them. But she yielded authority to him, where it belonged.

That the wine ran out and that Mary wanted there to be more suggests that Jesus and his family were attending a feast that was not abstemious. The six stone jars held 120 to 180 gallons of water, the equivalent of 600 to 900 of our modern 750-mL bottles of wine. This does not mean that the wedding party drank all of them in one day. The abundance of the miracle reflected the wonderful power of God. Jesus produced more than the necessary amount of food to feed the five thousand (Matt 14:20) and the four thousand (Matt 15:37), as Elijah produced more flour and oil than the widow of Zarephath could consume in one day (1 Kgs 17:15) and Elisha produced more oil for the wife of one of the prophets than she could consume in one day (2 Kgs 4:3–7). The Bible prohibits addictive and uncontrolled drunkenness, not the drinking of alcohol and enjoying the pleasure it gives in moderation.

In John 15:1–5, Jesus said, "I am the true vine, and my Father is the gardener . . . you are the branches." The function of a grapevine is to turn water into wine. Jesus' miracle at Cana had great symbolic significance. Jesus transformed people. He turned fishermen into fishers of men. He turned water into wine. He turns sinners into saints.

---

5. See "Relationships in Jesus' Community" in the Appendices.

This, the first of his signs, Jesus did at Cana in Galilee and manifested his glory. And his disciples believed in him. Jesus would later do at least one other miracle at Cana—healing the official's son, but that would be on Sunday, April 28, AD 30, about five months later.

HOLIDAY ON THE SEA OF GALILEE

After this Jesus went down to Capernaum, with his mother, his brothers, his sisters, and his disciples, and they stayed there for a few days. Capernaum was about an eight-hour walk from Cana. We know that Jesus had four half-brothers—James, Joses, Simon, and Judas (Matt 13:55–56; Mark 6:3). Of these at least James and Judas would come to believe that their resurrected half-brother was the Christ. They would write the New Testament books of James and Jude. Jesus also had at least three half-sisters whose names the Bible does not record. So, there were at least eight children in Mary's home. Mary and the seven children lived in Nazareth (Mark 6:3), where her husband, Joseph (probably now deceased), established their home after he, Mary, and Jesus returned from Egypt.

Going to Capernaum to stay a few days on the shores of Lake Galilee in autumn sounds rather like a holiday. Since James and John, the sons of Zebedee, were likely Jesus' first cousins,[6] and since Zebedee was rich, he probably had a big house. So, Mary and the seven children may have stayed there, at the home of her sister, Salome, the wife of Zebedee. The disciples may have stayed in Peter's house, which was also large. So this seems to have been an intimate time of relaxation at the shore for the greater family of Jesus after the miracle in Cana.

Scripture makes no further mention of Jesus and the disciples until the Passover of next year, AD 30, when Jesus first cleansed the temple. Presumably, the same disciples were obediently on pilgrimage to Jerusalem (John 2:13) and witnessed the event. At that time, Jesus instructed Nicodemus secretly in someone's house, probably that of John (John 3:2). On Sunday, April 14, following the first Sabbath after Passover, Jesus left Jerusalem, and his disciples began baptizing in the Judean countryside. Despite Jesus' growing fame, John the Baptist was free from jealousy about him (John 3:30).

THE SAMARITAN WOMAN AT THE WELL

Then John the Baptist was taken into custody by Herod, and Jesus decided to leave Judea for Galilee. Rather than follow the Jordan route, Jesus took the unusual step of traveling straight through Samaria. Jews avoided hostile Samaria whenever possible, but John wrote that Jesus had to pass through Samaria. Perhaps, after arresting John the Baptist, the authorities were looking for Jesus, too, and this may have compelled him

---

6. See "Relationships in Jesus' Community" in the Appendices.

to take an unconventional route. In fact, Jesus traveled overnight, suggesting a hasty flight, and arrived at a well in the town of Sychar (Shechem, modern Nablus) at 6 a.m.

While his disciples went into the town of Sychar for food, he met and conversed with a Samaritan woman at Jacob's well (John 4:5–7). Impressed by Jesus' wisdom, the woman brought people from the town, and all of them agreed that Jesus must be the Christ. Jesus commented that this proved that a prophet was without honor in his hometown. He stayed for two more days over the Sabbath among these traditional enemies of the Jews. Then he returned to Galilee, where the Galileans welcomed him. They, too, had been to Jerusalem on pilgrimage and had witnessed what he had done there (John 4:45). We do not really know which disciples traveled with Jesus for this Passover and which simply attended the feast in Jerusalem and saw him more casually. It is probable that the inner circle, Peter, Andrew, James, and John, were with him all the way.

CALLING THE FOUR FISHERMEN

Around May 1, AD 30, 242 days (nearly eight months) after his baptism, Jesus returned to the lakeshore at Capernaum. He saw the two brothers, Peter and Andrew, casting a net into the sea. He said to them, "Follow me, and I will make you fishers of men." They left their nets at once and followed him. Shortly after, they saw the business partners of Peter and Andrew, the sons of Zebedee, James and John. He called them, and immediately they left mending their nets, abandoning their father and servants in their fishing boat, and followed him (Matt 4:22). At last, Andrew, Peter, James, and John were full-time disciples. Andrew followed Jesus throughout the rest of his earthly ministry.

ANDREW'S ROLE

Andrew was a people person. He went searching for John the Baptist and found Jesus and then went to tell his brother Peter. At the feeding of the five thousand, in March AD 31, Andrew was not shy, but was out among the crowd. He was the one who introduced the boy with loaves and fishes to Jesus. He appears to have convinced the boy to sacrifice his lunch and, considering that there were five thousand hungry people and not much food, Andrew must have been persuasive (John 6:8–9). Perhaps because both Andrew and the boy were from Bethsaida, they knew each other.

When Greeks—non-Jews—desired to meet Jesus on Palm Sunday, AD 33, they approached Philip, a disciple with a Greek name. "Sir," they said, "we wish to see Jesus." Philip told Andrew (another disciple with a Greek name), and Andrew took Philip to tell Jesus (John 12:20–22).

Andrew was present at some of Jesus' most intimate teachings. He, along with Peter, James, and John, were the only disciples present at the Sermon on the Mount. On Tuesday, March 29, AD 33, on the Mount of Olives, opposite the temple, Peter,

Andrew, James, and John privately asked the Lord about the times of the end, saying, "Tell us, when will these things be, and what will be the sign when all these things are going to be fulfilled?" Jesus told them not to be deceived by false teachers, by wars and rumors of wars, by nation rising against nation, by earthquakes or famines, for these were all the birth pangs of the end (Mark 13:3–8).

Andrew witnessed Jesus' ascension. He was present in the upper room on the evening of Resurrection Sunday with Thomas absent and was there a week later when Jesus again appeared to the Eleven with Thomas present. Andrew was among the Eleven when his brother Peter led them to choose Matthias to replace Judas. Andrew witnessed the birth of the church on Pentecost, Sunday, May 22, AD 33, and attended the Jerusalem Council in AD 49.

ANDREW'S MISSIONS

When Andrew left Jerusalem to spread the gospel is unknown. It may have been about the same time his brother Peter went to Rome in AD 43. The Bible fixes Andrew back in Judea at the Jerusalem Council in AD 49 because "the apostles," presumably all of them, attended (except James, the son of Zebedee, who had died in AD 44). So Andrew may have traveled for about six years, from AD 43 to 49, returned to Jerusalem, and then may have set out on missionary journeys again.

Hippolytus says that he "preached to the Scythians and Thracians."[7] Eusebius confirms his mission to Scythia.[8] The Scythians were a nomadic people who lived in what is now southern Russia, Ukraine, Romania, and Bulgaria. Thrace was a Hellenic territory in part of what is now Bulgaria and along the western shore of the Black Sea. So Andrew's missionary trips, which are not recorded in Scripture, seem to describe a large arc across Central Asia, Eastern Europe, northern Anatolia, and Greece. There would have been ample time in six years to accomplish these journeys. He may have founded churches as far north as the Volga and Kiev. Andrew is thus the patron saint of Russia and Romania.

The apocryphal *Acts of Andrew and Matthias*[9] says that Andrew saw in a dream that Matthias, the apostle who replaced Judas Iscariot, had been imprisoned in a savage land inhabited by cannibals. They blinded Matthias, but when the risen Christ sent Andrew to save him, Andrew miraculously restored his sight. Andrew triumphed over the cannibals through prayer and freed Matthias. The *Acts of Andrew* further says that Andrew continued to Byzantium (which three hundred years later would become the Christian

---

7. Hippolytus, "List of the Apostles and Disciples."
8. Eusebius, *Church History* 3:1:1.
9. "The Acts of Andrew and Matthias." This is a highly fanciful account, and while it may contain a grain of truth, swallowing the entire narrative requires a liberal pinch of salt.

city of Constantinople) and founded this great see, becoming its patron saint.[10] Andrew then continued to Greece, traveling to Thrace, Macedonia, Corinth, and finally Patras.[11]

ANDREW'S DEATH

The *Acts of Andrew* and Tertullian[12] say that in Patras, the Roman proconsul of Achaia (Greece), Aegeates, heard Andrew's preaching and demanded that he and his Christian brethren worship the Hellenic gods. Andrew refused. He explained that these "gods" were in fact demons who lured men to destruction. He carried out an extensive public debate with Aegeates, inviting him to become a disciple of Christ. Aegeates said that it was absurd and obscene for anyone to follow a man who had been executed on a cross and threatened that he would rather extract God's secrets from Andrew by torture than by debating him. Andrew replied that salvation came through faith, not violence, and that Jesus' death on the cross was God's victory, not a disgrace. Aegeates threw Andrew in prison with this ultimatum: either worship the Hellenic gods or die on a cross himself.

Aegeates' wife, Maximilla, moved by Andrew's preaching, took a vow of celibacy. Aegeates was outraged. He told Maximilla that if she renounced this vow, he would forgive her and even release Andrew. If she did not, he would execute Andrew. Maximilla visited Andrew in prison and told him of her dilemma. She said she wanted to hold fast to her celibate vow. Andrew praised her and encouraged her to do so, even if it cost his life. Note that this teaching is at odds with biblical doctrine, suggesting that this narrative may be fanciful, even though it may contain a germ of truth.

From the entire province, an angry crowd of twenty thousand gathered and threatened to storm the prison, to release Andrew, and to kill Aegeates. Andrew asked them to keep the peace. The next day, Aegeates had Andrew hauled before him and asked if he were ready to pour a libation to the pagan gods. Andrew replied that up till then he had spoken kindly to Aegeates. Now he told the proconsul that he was headed for hell if he did not repent and that no threat of execution could deter Andrew from speaking plainly. Andrew added that the proconsul had no power to punish any Christian, since to die was to enter eternal life with Christ, which was a reward.

Enraged, Aegeates ordered Andrew's execution. Calmly, Andrew took off his clothes and presented himself to be tied to a cross.[13] Sadistically, Aegeates tied Andrew to a sideways cross. This was so that, as he hung dying, he would be within reach of wild dogs who might ravenously tear at his limbs and increase his suffering and humiliation. Aegeates also ordered his soldiers not to break any of Andrew's joints,

10. "The Acts of Andrew." "See" derives from the Latin word *sedes* or "seat."
11. Hippolytus, "List of the Apostles and Disciples."
12. Tertullian, *Acts and Martyrdom of the Holy Apostle Andrew*.
13. Usually, the Romans tied victims to a cross. Nailing Jesus' forearms and ankles to the cross was an act of extra cruelty.

so that he might suffer prolonged agony as he hung. (Death on a cross comes from becoming too weak to expel air from the lungs and take a fresh breath; the victim dies of asphyxiation. If the joints are intact, the victim has some leverage to continue to push air from his lungs; when the joints or limbs are broken, that leverage is gone.)

Twenty thousand protestors crowded around the cross. Smiling, Andrew preached to them with eloquence and lucidity for three days and nights. Astonished at the wisdom of his words and the undimmed light of his intellect while he suffered, the crowd became furious at Aegeates's injustice and, on the fourth day, demanded that Aegeates set Andrew free. Seeing that the crowd was dangerous, Aegeates agreed. Maximilla rejoiced with the others at Andrew's liberation.

When Aegeates approached the cross to untie the apostle, however, Andrew persisted in confronting the proconsul, saying that he did not believe Aegeates was doing this because he repented, but merely from fear of the mob. Andrew prayed that God should not let an adversary of Christ free him. A bright light suffused the cross, so dazzling that the people could not look upon it. It shimmered for about half an hour, and then Andrew died. Maximilla, with no regard for her nobility, personally removed Andrew's body from the cross, anointed it with costly spices, and buried him in her own tomb.

Aegeates implored his wife to disassociate herself from these Christians. He offered to leave her all his wealth if she would agree. But she separated from him and devoted herself to a celibate life in the Christian community. Furious, Aegeates decided to lodge an official accusation with Nero Caesar against Maximilla and the rebels in Achaia. Before he could do so, in the dead of night he rose up, and, tormented by the devil, he fell down from a great height. He rolled into the middle of the city marketplace and breathed his last. By tradition, he died on the last day of November.

We do not know when this all was supposed to happen, exactly, but we can make an educated guess. The emperor Claudius designated Achaia a proconsular province in AD 44. Lucius Junius Gallio, the brother of the Roman philosopher Seneca, served as proconsul in this same province of Achaia, probably from AD 51 to 53. Acts 18 reports that Gallio refused to punish Paul, who was in Corinth around AD 50–51, when the Jews requested that Gallio silence him. Aegeates was, therefore, probably proconsul sometime after AD 53.

After the death of Claudius, Nero became emperor in AD 54. He ruled normally at first. After the Great Fire of Rome in AD 64, popular rumors placed the blame for the fire on Nero. The gossip was that he had purposely torched Rome to clear ground for his new, magnificent, golden palace. Seeking a scapegoat, Nero began persecuting Christians on a massive scale. This tribulation, probably from about August 25, AD 64, thirty-one days after the Great Fire, to August 25, AD 68, twenty-four days before Nero's suicide,[14] was a time when Aegeates's stance could have found favor with his boss in Rome. Nero killed Peter probably in May AD 68. We do not know certainly

---

14. John mentions period of 1,260 days of tribulation twice in Revelation 11:3 and 12:6.

when Andrew died, but it seems reasonable that he died after AD 64, when the Neronian persecution of Christians had begun. If so, he may have pre-deceased his brother Peter by as many as four years.

SCOTLAND AND ELSEWHERE

No ancient tradition suggests that Andrew ever visited Scotland, but a Christian named Saint Regulus took a few bones thought to be relics of Andrew to Scotland in the fourth or fifth century. He buried them at a place he named "Saint Andrew's," and Andrew became Scotland's patron saint. The flag of Scotland displays Saint Andrew's sideways cross. When England forged a union of England, Scotland, and Protestant Ireland and called it the United Kingdom, it superimposed the vertical Cross of Saint George on a sideways Saint Andrew's Cross to create a double-cross flag, the Union Jack.

Saint Andrews, Scotland, is the place where golf was invented in the fifteenth century, without, however, any known apostolic endorsement. The winners of tournaments at the Royal and Ancient Golf Club are listed with a Saint Andrew's Cross marking their names.

Andrew became the patron saint of several other places, which, like Scotland, he may never have visited, including Amalfi, Prussia, Sicily, and Malta. Andrew was a seeker of truth, an outgoing ambassador of the gospel, a follower always introducing others to the Messiah, a persuasive speaker, a loyal friend, a brave and hard-working evangelist, and faithful even to death.

James, Son of Thunder

JAMES WAS VARIOUSLY THE second or the third in the lists of the apostles. James and John were brothers, the sons of Zebedee and of Mary Salome. The fact that James's name almost always appears before John's (except in Luke 8:51, 9:28, and Acts 1:13) suggests that James was John's elder brother, but we have no firmer proof of their ages than that. James is Yaakov or Jacob ("one who laughs") in Hebrew. James in Greek became Iakovos, Jacobus in Latin, Jacques in French, Iago (Santiago—Saint James) or Jaime in Spanish, Giacomo in Italian, Jakob in German, and James in English.

Three prominent people bear the name of James in the New Testament: (1) James the Great (or Elder), the son of Zebedee and brother of the apostle John, (2) James the Less (or Younger), the son of Alphaeus, another of the original twelve apostles, and (3) James the Just, half-brother of Jesus, leader of the Jerusalem church. Archeological finds reveal many artifacts bearing the extremely common names of James, Judas, and Jesus (Joshua) in first-century Judea. They were almost the equivalents of our "Tom, Dick, and Harry."

James and John were probably first cousins of Jesus and probably knew him from boyhood.[1] The sons of Zebedee were apparently well-to-do. Mark tells us that when Jesus called James and John, they left their father Zebedee in the boat with hired servants (Mark 1:20). If they could afford to hire servants, their fishing business must have had some substance. A further hint of the wealth of Zebedee's family is found in Matthew 27:56, which depicts Zebedee's wife counted among the many women of Galilee who were following and ministering "of their substance" to the Lord. In the first century this presumably required masculine permission, leisure, and means. James's brother, John, had connections with the high priest in Jerusalem, evidence that the family was prominent and respected (John 18:15–16). And James, John, Peter, and Andrew were business partners (Luke 5:7, 10).

When John the Baptist revealed that his cousin, Jesus, was the Lamb of God, Andrew went and found his brother Peter and told him (John 1:41). John does not mention going to tell James about Jesus at the same time that Andrew told Peter. Perhaps James was back in Galilee tending the family business. Perhaps he was in

---

1. See the section "Were the Sons of Zebedee Jesus' Cousins?" in the Appendices.

Jerusalem observing the Feast of Tabernacles. Did James meet Jesus and recognize him as the Messiah at this time? Did James join the others on the return trip to Galilee and attend the wedding at Cana? Scripture makes no mention of it.

In all four Gospels, in the lists of the apostles, Peter, Andrew, James, and John form the first group. They are a prominent and chosen team, especially Peter, James, and John. Jesus allowed these three alone to witness the miracle of raising Jairus's daughter (Luke 8:51). Only Peter, James, and John were present at the transfiguration (Matt 17:1–2). Only Peter, James, and John witnessed Jesus' agony in the Garden of Gethsemane—and failed him by falling asleep (Mark 14:33–41). Jesus surely knew that James would be the first apostle to die in AD 44. So, his inclusion of James in these events equipped him for a post-resurrection ministry of only eleven years.

John never mentioned his brother James in his Gospel. This is in keeping with John's humble reserve when writing about himself and his family. But humility was not always a family trait. Jesus had a special nickname for James and John. "He appointed the twelve: Simon (to whom he gave the name Peter); James the son of Zebedee and John the brother of James, to whom he gave the name Boanerges, that is, Sons of Thunder" (Mark 3:17). The Sons of Thunder argued with the other disciples, told outsiders not to cast out demons in Jesus' name, and asked Jesus if they, like Elijah, could bring fire from heaven on Samaritans who had refused Jesus hospitality. They wanted to be Jesus' "enforcers." On Jesus' last journey to Jerusalem, the Zebedee brothers asked Jesus to give them special preferment.

> James and John, the sons of Zebedee, came up to him and said to him, "Teacher, we want you to do for us whatever we ask of you." And he said to them, "What do you want me to do for you?" And they said to him, "Grant us to sit, one at your right hand and one at your left, in your glory." Jesus said to them, "You do not know what you are asking. Are you able to drink the cup that I drink, or to be baptized with the baptism with which I am baptized?" And they said to him, "We are able." And Jesus said to them, "The cup that I drink you will drink, and with the baptism with which I am baptized, you will be baptized, but to sit at my right hand or at my left is not mine to grant, but it is for those for whom it has been prepared." And when the Ten heard it, they began to be indignant at James and John. And Jesus called them to him and said to them, "You know that those who are considered rulers of the Gentiles lord it over them, and their great ones exercise authority over them. But it shall not be so among you. But whoever would be great among you must be your servant, and whoever would be first among you must be slave of all. For even the Son of Man came not to be served but to serve, and to give his life as a ransom for many." (Mark 10:35–45)

The Sons of Thunder probably still expected Jesus' kingdom to be an earthly restoration of the Maccabean monarchy.[2] Jesus fit the required profile for a new

---

2. The Maccabees were a family of Levites who led a revolt against the Greek-Syrian kings of the

Messianic king. He was of the tribe of Judah, a descendant of David, and a charismatic leader. He was alive at exactly the right time in history—in fact, prophetically, Jesus was in history's last window of opportunity for the Messiah to appear (Dan 9:24–27). He was foreshadowed by his namesake, Joshua, who had first conquered the promised land with God's help. And his miracles endorsed him.

James and John were sure they were fit to be King Jesus' chief ministers once a triumphant Judah had ejected Rome. Their request adds some weight to the argument that James and John were Jesus' first cousins; in a dynasty, family members would receive royal preferment. "Thunder" is a good name for them—a big noise that follows lightning, but which, unlike lightning, has no power. And Jesus did not even call them "thunder." He called them "sons of thunder." How proud they must have been of this impressive nickname until its ironic insignificance sank in. Perhaps this is why John, the beloved disciple, learned to be so modest about references to himself in his Gospel, in his letters, and in Revelation. His relationship with Jesus taught him humility very different from the character with which he and James were born.

As one of the Twelve, James was present in the upper room on Resurrection Sunday. He was in the upper room with Thomas present on the following Monday. He was at Jesus' ascension. He helped to choose Matthias. And he as at the birth of the church on the day of Pentecost in AD 33. He died, however, before the Jerusalem Council in AD 49.

JAMES'S DEATH

Jesus asked James and John if they were able to drink the cup that Jesus would drink, that of martyrdom. They replied that they were able, and James died a martyr a few short years later, in the Passover week of March 30–April 7, AD 44.

Herod Agrippa I, son of Aristobulus and grandson of Herod the Great, reigned at that time over a dominion greater than that of his grandfather. The Herodian kings were Idumeans, that is, Edomites, descendants of Esau and rivals and enemies of Jacob's descendants, the Jews. They ruled at the pleasure of Rome, and Rome wanted only three things from them: (1) to keep Judea in order, (2) to act as a buffer state against enemy Parthia, and (3) to keep the tax revenues flowing. So, Herod Agrippa I desired to pacify the Jews in every way, which meant showing great regard for the law of Moses and Jewish customs. Since Christians, especially Jewish Christians, offended

---

Seleucid empire. They ruled in Judea from 140 BC until 37 BC, when Rome installed Herod the Great as King of the Jews in their place. The patriarch of the Maccabee dynasty was Mattathias, who was a high priest and a Levite. The name Maccabee means "hammer" and was the nickname of Judas Maccabaeus, who hammered the rulers of the Seleucid Empire in battle and forged a new independent Jewish state. The Maccabees assumed the titles of both king and high priest. As Levites, they could legitimately claim only the latter, for the kings of Judah were all of the tribe of Judah, not Levi. Thus, they were a flawed model of the promised Messianic kingdom. Jesus, who had true royal and priestly credentials, was the perfect fit.

the Jews, Herod Agrippa I perpetrated gratuitous cruelties on the Jerusalem church during the Passover of AD 44. James was Herod Agrippa's first celebrity victim.

> About that time Herod the king laid violent hands on some who belonged to the Church. He killed James the brother of John with the sword, and when he saw that it pleased the Jews, he proceeded to arrest Peter also. This was during the days of Unleavened Bread. (Acts 12:1–3)

According to Eusebius,

> The one who led James to the judgment-seat, when he saw him bearing his testimony, was moved, and confessed that he was himself also a Christian. They were both therefore . . . led away together; and on the way he begged James to forgive him. And he, after considering a little, said, 'Peace be with you,' and kissed him. And thus, they were both beheaded at the same time.[3]

James the Less may have been the son of James, the son of Zebedee.[4] So, James's son and his brother John, both fellow apostles, may have seen his martyrdom. The word "martyr" is Greek for "witness."

JAMES AND SPAIN

According to tradition, James preached Christianity in Spain.[5] The Bible says that in the Jewish persecution of Christians by Paul, which began in late AD 33 and continued until Paul's conversion in April AD 34, all believers "except the apostles" scattered throughout Judea and Samaria (Acts 8:1). Those who scattered preached the gospel wherever they went (Acts 8:4). This scattering lasted until about June AD 37 (Acts 11:19–22). If the apostles did not scatter in this interval when all the others scattered, one might conclude that James did not leave Jerusalem until the summer of AD 37. Since, however, Philip, Peter, and John preached outside of Jerusalem during the period of scattering, the meaning of Acts 8:1 is not necessarily that the apostles remained confined to Jerusalem but that they did not scurry away in fear. They proclaimed the gospel abroad confidently and intentionally. James could, therefore, have traveled to Spain in the spring of AD 34, the same year when Peter founded the church in Antioch. If so, he must have returned before the fall Holy Days of AD 43 (sailing after Yom Kippur was dangerous), since this would have placed him in Jerusalem for the Passover of AD 44, when he met his death. James would thus have had plenty of time, about ten years, to bring the gospel to Spain.

Tradition, for which there is no ancient attestation, says that the remains of James the Elder were taken to Compostela in Spain. The medieval legend is that a mystical

---

3. Eusebius, *Church History* 2:9:2–3.
4. See "Relationships in Jesus' Community" in the Appendices.
5. O'Kane, *Little Lives of the Great Saints*, 28.

ship with a crew of angels took his relics across the sea. While the heavenly ship is fanciful, someone may nevertheless have taken James's relics to Spain. James's presumptive burial place in Spain was a major site of pilgrimage in the Middle Ages, and the Spaniards, fighting to drive the Moors out of Iberia, adopted the battle cry, "*Santiago de Compostela,*" meaning "Saint James of Compostela!" The papal bull (decree, from the same Latin word that gives us the English word "bulletin") of Leo XIII in 1884 affirmed the authenticity of James's relics in Spain.

James was the first apostle to die. His brother John was the last. James was a martyr. John died a natural death.

John, the Apostle of Love

JAMES AND JOHN WERE brothers, the sons of Zebedee and Mary Salome. John is Yochanan in Hebrew, meaning "God is gracious." John in Greek became Ioannis, Iohannes in Latin, Jean in French, Juan in Spanish, Giovanni in Italian, and Johann in German.

There are two prominent Johns in the New Testament: (1) John the Baptist, the son of Zacharias, a Levite, and Elizabeth, second cousin of Jesus, and (2) John the apostle, first cousin of Jesus. If Mary Salome was the wife of Zebedee and was the sister of Jesus' mother, Mary, then James and John were first cousins of Jesus and probably knew Jesus from boyhood.[1]

JOHN'S WEALTH

The sons of Zebedee were apparently well-off. John was known to the high priest in Jerusalem, as the following passage, suggesting wealth and respect, shows:

> Simon Peter followed Jesus, and so did another disciple. Since that disciple was known to the High Priest, he entered with Jesus into the court of the High Priest, but Peter stood outside at the door. So the other disciple, who was known to the High Priest, went out and spoke to the servant girl who kept watch at the door, and brought Peter in. (John 18:15–16)

The "other disciple" is, most scholars agree, John, the author of John's Gospel. John also appeared to have had a home in Jerusalem, implied in John 3, because although Jesus' nocturnal interview with Nicodemus was secret, John probably was there, as he is the only Gospel writer to record it. Since Nicodemus went to Jesus, and since Jesus did not have a home (Matt 8:20; Luke 9:58), the event probably occurred in John's house.

There is another clue that John had a Jerusalem house. When Jesus on the cross put his mother (probably John's aunt) into John's care, John took Mary into his household "from that hour" (John 19:26–27). If John was staying at a rented room in

---

1. See "Relationships in Jesus' Community" in the Appendices.

Jerusalem, he might not have been able to take Mary into his household "from that hour." A household in Jerusalem as well as in Galilee implies some wealth. Of course, Jesus might have been using the word "household" figuratively, meaning John took Mary into his "care." But this, together with the Nicodemus clue, is more suggestive of having a Jerusalem home.

The fact that John had the leisure to leave his business, observe the fall pilgrimage to Jerusalem, and to enroll as the Baptist's disciple in AD 29 further suggests that John had means. Of course, every faithful Jew should have observed the pilgrimage feasts, and each year millions did; but the Jewish population represented ten percent of the Roman Empire at that time. If all of them had come on pilgrimage to Jerusalem, their numbers would have been about 4.5 million,[2] not the 2.7 million that Josephus recorded on one Passover.[3] And if we include the Jewish population outside the Roman Empire, in Babylon, Parthia, Ethiopia, and India, the number would have been even greater. So, clearly, many Jews lacked the means or the will to observe the pilgrimages as John did.

JOHN'S HUMILITY

John mentioned two disciples following John the Baptist in his Gospel, specified one of them, Andrew, and left the other unnamed (John 1:40). This literary technique of referring to himself obliquely is consistent in John's accounts, so he is almost certainly the unnamed other disciple. John's reticence to refer to himself overtly is strikingly modest because John was a business partner of Peter and Andrew and was almost certainly the cousin of John the Baptist and of Jesus.[4] Even if he was not related, John probably knew most of Jesus' disciples from childhood. As a further demonstration of modesty, John did not give himself or his brother, James, any speaking part in his Gospel; only the Synoptic Gospel authors recorded speeches by the sons of Zebedee.

Peter, Andrew, James, and John were Jesus' inmost circle, especially Peter, James, and John. These three alone were allowed to witness the miracle of raising Jairus's daughter. They alone were present at the transfiguration. They witnessed Jesus' agony in the Garden of Gethsemane and failed him by falling asleep. Jesus sent only John and Peter into Jerusalem to prepare the Last Supper (Luke 22:8). At the Last Supper, the place of John, the disciple Jesus loved, was next to Jesus. "One of his disciples, whom Jesus loved, was reclining at table close to Jesus, so Simon Peter motioned to him to ask Jesus of whom he was speaking. So, that disciple, leaning back against Jesus, said to him, 'Lord, who is it?'" (John 13:25). John was probably also that "other disciple" who with Peter followed Christ after his arrest into the palace of the high priest (John

---

2. Using ten percent of the estimated total population of the empire, "Roman Empire Population."
3. Josephus, *War* 6:9:3.
4. See "Relationships in Jesus' Community" in the Appendices.

18:15–16). Modest as he was, perhaps John's referring to himself as the disciple that Jesus loved was a bit of veiled self-praise.

The world-shaking phenomena of Christ's ministry were arising out of John's small family and business circle. He had connections to brag about. Yet he and all the other the apostles made no attempt (after the resurrection) to establish a "Jesus elite" with themselves as celebrities. They never claimed Jesus' legacy as a family dynasty, as the leaders of other prominent families, like that of the high priest Ananias (Annas), promoted their legacies. Daniel foretold four worldly empires that a fifth eternal empire would succeed (Dan 2:44, 7:27). This was the kingdom of God that Jesus said was at hand (Matt 4:17; Mark 1:15) and which the apostles labored to serve. The apostles grasped the divine meaning of Christ's work. They served, suffered, and died not to aggrandize themselves, but to bring the word to the world.

AT THE CROSS

John alone remained near his Master at the foot of the cross with the mother of Jesus and the other women from Galilee (John 19:25–26). Peter had denied Jesus and had run away. All the other disciples had also abandoned him (Matt 26:56; Mark 14:50). Jesus' Roman executioners gambled for his clothes, physically tormented him, and jeered as he hung in indescribable agony for hours. Yet when Jesus looked down from the cross, he could take comfort in the sight of one man courageous and affectionate enough to be there, "the disciple that Jesus loved." No wonder Peter felt so troubled when Jesus asked him three times after the resurrection if Peter loved him. Only one man and four named women had braved the wrath of Rome and the high priest to kneel in devotion at the cross. No wonder Jesus said to his grieving mother, "Woman, behold your son!" and then to John, "Behold your mother!" In Mary's household were at least seven other children, four boys and (at least) three unnamed girls (Matt 13:55–56; Mark 6:3). Two of the boys, James and Judas, would become prominent disciples of their half-brother Jesus, the Messiah. They would each write a book in the New Testament (James and Jude). But it was to the faithful and beloved John that Jesus consigned his precious mother. From that hour, John took this helpless, shattered widow into his household (John 19:27).

Jesus' choice for Mary's protector was logical since John was probably Mary's nephew, was probably Jesus' cousin, probably had a household in Jerusalem, was probably wealthy, and was destined to outlive most of the other apostles. There are two traditions: (1) that John took Mary with him to Ephesus when he became bishop there, and that she died in Ephesus, and (2) that Mary lived in John's household in Jerusalem until her death there. Since neither tradition is certain, two locations, one at Ephesus and one at Jerusalem, are venerated today as the place of Mary's death.

AFTER THE RESURRECTION

John with Peter was the first of the disciples to hasten to Jesus' tomb, and he was the first to believe that Christ truly had risen.

> Now on the first day of the week Mary Magdalene came to the tomb early, while it was still dark, and saw that the stone had been taken away from the tomb. So she ran and went to Simon Peter and the other disciple, the one whom Jesus loved, and said to them, "They have taken the Lord out of the tomb, and we do not know where they have laid him." So Peter went out with the other disciple, and they were going toward the tomb. Both of them were running together, but the other disciple outran Peter and reached the tomb first. And stooping to look in, he saw the linen cloths lying there, but he did not go in. Then Simon Peter came, following him, and went into the tomb. He saw the linen cloths lying there, and the face cloth, which had been on Jesus' head, not lying with the linen cloths but folded up in a place by itself. Then the other disciple, who had reached the tomb first, also went in, and he saw and believed. (John 20:1–8)

John reveals an amusing competitiveness by reporting that he beat Peter to the tomb. This bravado recalls his asking, along with his brother James, to sit at Jesus' right and left hand when Christ should come into his kingdom. But John's recording of Peter's courage to enter the tomb first, while John held back, shows this Son of Thunder had learned some humility. Yet John stated that he believed at once, perhaps suggesting that Peter did not yet believe the evidence of his eyes.

When later Christ appeared at the Sea of Galilee, John was the first of the seven present disciples to recognize the Master he loved standing on the shore.

> After this Jesus revealed himself again to the disciples by the Sea of Tiberias, and he revealed himself in this way. Simon Peter, Thomas (called the Twin), Nathanael of Cana in Galilee, the sons of Zebedee, and two others of his disciples were together. Simon Peter said to them, "I am going fishing." They said to him, "We will go with you." They went out and got into the boat, but that night they caught nothing. Just as day was breaking, Jesus stood on the shore; yet the disciples did not know that it was Jesus. Jesus said to them, "Children, do you have any fish?" They answered him, "No." He said to them, "Cast the net on the right side of the boat, and you will find some." So they cast it, and now they were not able to haul it in, because of the quantity of fish. That disciple whom Jesus loved therefore said to Peter, "It is the Lord!" When Simon Peter heard that it was the Lord, he put on his outer garment, for he was stripped for work, and threw himself into the sea. The other disciples came in the boat, dragging the net full of fish, for they were not far from the land, but about a hundred yards off. When they got out on land, they saw a charcoal fire in place, with fish laid out on it, and bread. Jesus said to them, "Bring some of the

> fish that you have just caught." So Simon Peter went aboard and hauled the net ashore, full of large fish, 153 of them. And although there were so many, the net was not torn. Jesus said to them, "Come and have breakfast." Now none of the disciples dared ask him, "Who are you?" They knew it was the Lord. Jesus came and took the bread and gave it to them, and so with the fish. This was now the third time that Jesus was revealed to the disciples after he was raised from the dead. (John 21:1-14)

John showed how close his relationship was to his Lord and Master by the title with which he was accustomed to indicating himself: "the disciple whom Jesus loved." John the apostle and Lazarus (John 11:11, 33, 35, 13:23, 20:2, 21:7, 20) were probably Jesus' best friends during his earthly ministry.

JOHN'S LEADERSHIP

John was, with Andrew, the first of the disciples to follow Jesus (John 1:35-37). He was present in the upper room on Resurrection Sunday, was in the upper room with Thomas present on the following Monday, was at Jesus' ascension, was at the choosing of Matthias, was at the birth of the church on the day of Pentecost in AD 33, helped Peter evangelize Samaria, was, with Peter and James (Jesus' half-brother) in Jerusalem to give Paul the right hand of fellowship in AD 48 and was at the Jerusalem Council in AD 49.

ARREST

After Christ's ascension and the descent of the Holy Spirit on Pentecost, John, together with Peter, took a prominent role in leading the church. He was with Peter when Peter healed the lame beggar at the Beautiful Gate (Acts 3:1-10). The Sadducees threw Peter and John into prison for "teaching the people and proclaiming in Jesus the Resurrection from the dead" (Acts 4:2). John, with Peter, defied them and continued to preach with authority and courage.

> Now when they saw the boldness of Peter and John, and perceived that they were uneducated, common men, they were astonished. And they recognized that they had been with Jesus. But seeing the man who was healed standing beside them, they had nothing to say in opposition. But when they had commanded them to leave the council, they conferred with one another, saying, "What shall we do with these men? For that a notable sign has been performed through them is evident to all the inhabitants of Jerusalem, and we cannot deny it. But in order that it may spread no further among the people, let us warn them to speak no more to anyone in this name." So they called them and charged them not to speak or teach at all in the name of Jesus. But Peter and John answered them, "Whether it is right in the sight of God to listen to you

rather than to God, you must judge, for we cannot but speak of what we have seen and heard." And when they had further threatened them, they let them go, finding no way to punish them, because of the people, for all were praising God for what had happened. For the man on whom this sign of healing was performed was more than forty years old. When they were released, they went to their friends and reported what the Chief Priests and the elders had said to them. (Acts 4:13–23)

SAMARIA

The apostles sent John with Peter to investigate Philip's astonishing conversion of the despised Samaritans to Christ. This was ironic, since James and John, the Sons of Thunder, had asked Jesus to let them call fire from heaven down upon the Samaritan villages that rejected Jesus (Luke 9:54).

Now when the apostles at Jerusalem heard that Samaria had received the word of God, they sent to them Peter and John, who came down and prayed for them that they might receive the Holy Spirit, for he had not yet fallen on any of them, but they had only been baptized in the name of the Lord Jesus. Then they laid their hands on them and they received the Holy Spirit. (Acts 8:14–17)

IN THE JERUSALEM CHURCH

We have no positive information about how long John remained in Judea. He was in Jerusalem in AD 48 when Paul met him there and called John, along with Peter and James (the half-brother of Jesus) a pillar of the church (Gal 2:7–10). John agreed with Paul at this time that the Greek Christian Titus did not need to be circumcised. He also agreed that Paul was a true apostle, and he gave him the right hand of fellowship. John was almost certainly at the Jerusalem Council, AD 49, because Scripture tells us that the apostles and elders presided, and the term "apostles" probably included all Eleven, minus John's deceased brother, James (Acts 15:4).

THE GREAT COMMISSION

It is unlikely that John disobeyed Jesus' Great Commission (Matt 28:19), and therefore he probably left Judea and evangelized somewhere. Eventually John ended up as the leader of the church in Ephesus.[5] Since Paul planted the first seeds of the Ephesian church in AD 51 (Acts 18:19) and last met with the Ephesian leaders in AD 54 (Acts 20:17), and since Scripture makes no mention of John's presence there while Paul

---

5. Eusebius, *Church History* 3:1:1, 20:11, 23:4, 6.

was there, John probably went to Ephesus after AD 54. That leaves at least five years of John's life, from the Jerusalem Council in AD 49 until AD 54, unaccounted for. He probably went somewhere to evangelize. His three epistles and Revelation suggest that John was well acquainted with conditions in the various Christian communities around Ephesus, and Eusebius says he governed churches all across that region.[6] From Ephesus, later in life, John probably went to Rome, because Jerome says the emperor Domitian banished him to the island of Patmos in AD 94, which suggests he was exiled from Rome.[7]

DOMITIAN'S PERSECUTION OF JOHN

The apocryphal *Acts of John* says that the Roman emperor Domitian (the younger son of Vespasian), who reigned from AD 81 to 96, persecuted the Jews.[8] The Jews wrote a letter to Domitian complaining of the Christians, and, accordingly, Domitian persecuted them, too. Hearing of John's teaching in Ephesus, the emperor summoned John to Rome. On his voyage to Italy, John's ascetic habits impressed his captors.

When John appeared before Domitian, the emperor commanded him to drink poison. John drank some of it. It had no effect on him. Jesus had said that his when his followers would "drink any deadly poison, it [would] not hurt them" (Mark 16:18). Suspecting that the drink did not contain enough poison, Domitian experimentally forced a criminal to drink the rest of the cup. The criminal died, but John revived him. This is why the early church used the symbol of a chalice with a snake sliding out of it as John's emblem. The snake represented the satanic power of poison receding from the cup. After this, John also raised a Roman girl to life who had been slain by an unclean spirit.

Domitian then tried to kill John by immersing him in boiling oil. The church of *San Giovanni in Oleo* (Saint John in Oil) in Rome commemorates the event. The apostle survived lengthy immersion in the boiling oil without being burned, preaching all the while to his would-be executioners. The Romans concluded that they were dealing with some powerful magician. Frustrated, Domitian banished John to the island of Patmos, not far from John's hometown of Ephesus.[9] Tertullian, the third-century church father, confirmed this, writing, "the apostle John was first plunged, unhurt, into boiling oil, and thence remitted to his island exile."[10] Jerome claims that John's exile was in AD 94.[11]

---

6. Eusebius, *Church History* 3:23:1
7. Jerome, *On Illustrious Men*.
8. "The Acts of John."
9. De Voragine, *The Golden Legend*, "9: On St. John the Apostle and Evangelist."
10. Tertullian, *Prescription against Heresies*, ch. 36.
11. Jerome, *On Illustrious Men*.

SHIPWRECK

Eusebius wrote that Tertullian confirmed the cruel, general persecution of Christians under Domitian.[12] After Domitian's death, his successor, the emperor Nerva, freed John from Patmos.[13] On his homeward journey, John was shipwrecked. He survived by floating on a piece of cork. He made landfall at Miletus[14] and then returned to Ephesus.[15]

CERINTHUS

Polycarp, John's disciple and successor as bishop of Ephesus, recorded that John once entered a public bath, where he learned that a notorious glutton, sexual pervert, and pagan, Cerinthus, was within.

> John sprang from the place and rushed out of the door, for he could not bear to remain under the same roof with him. And he advised those that were with him to do the same, saying, "Let us flee, lest the bath fall; for Cerinthus, the enemy of the truth, is within."[16]

JOHN'S LAST DAYS

Jerome recorded that John, as an old man, had to be carried to church in Ephesus by the elders. At these meetings, he used to say nothing more than, "Little children, love each other." After a while, the disciples were tired of always hearing the same words and asked, "Master, why do you always say this?" John replied, "It is the Lord's command. And if this alone be done, it is enough."[17]

JOHN'S DEATH

Jerome wrote that in Ephesus John continued to found and build churches across Asia Minor, until, worn out by old age, he died in AD 98.[18] He must have been in his nineties. Jesus had foretold that John would live a long life and die a natural death (John

---

12. Eusebius, *Church History* 3:17.
13. Eusebius, *Church History* 3:20:9–10
14. "The Acts of John."
15. Orosius, *Histories against the Pagans*, 7:11
16. Eusebius, *Church History* 3:28:6.
17. Jerome, *Commentary on Galatians*, 3:6:10.
18. Jerome, *On Illustrious Men*. Jerome calculates this date assuming that it was sixty-eight years after Jesus' crucifixion. Jerome consistently makes the erroneous assumption that the crucifixion was in AD 30. It was definitely in AD 33, because in all the years from AD 29 to 33, Passover fell on a Friday only in AD 33, and Jesus was crucified on Passover Friday. Correcting for Jerome's error yields the date of AD 98.

21:22–23). He lived into the reign of the emperor Trajan, AD 98–117.[19] Hippolytus wrote that Simon the Zealot died at the age of 120 years.[20] If so, he, and not John, was probably the longest-lived apostle.

THE GOSPEL OF JOHN

It is said that Matthew wrote his Gospel to the Jews, Luke to the gentiles, and John to the world. Eusebius wrote:

> When Mark and Luke had already published their gospels, they say that John, who had employed all his time in proclaiming the Gospel orally, finally proceeded to write for the following reason. The three gospels already mentioned having come into the hands of all and into his own too, they say that he accepted them and bore witness to their truthfulness; but that there was lacking in them an account of the deeds done by Christ at the beginning of his ministry... John, accordingly, in his gospel, records the deeds of Christ which were performed before the Baptist was cast into prison, but the other three evangelists mention the events which happened after that time.[21]

According to the third-century Christian writer Gaius, John's fellow disciples and bishops entreated him to write his Gospel. John replied, "Fast with me for three days. What may be revealed to any of us, let us reveal it to each other." That same night, Andrew had a revelation that John was to write an account of Christ under his own name, and so he did.[22] If this is correct, and if Andrew died in the Neronian persecution of AD 64, this event occurred no later than that year. Mark wrote his Gospel in AD 43, the year Peter founded the church in Rome. Matthew wrote his Gospel around AD 49. Luke composed his Gospel between AD 49 and 59. John may have published his Gospel between AD 59 and 64, a mere twenty-six to thirty-one years after the resurrection. Certainly, John composed it before AD 70, since it, like Revelation, makes no mention of Rome destroying the temple.

This would explain why John's Gospel contains different material than the others and takes a different point of view and tone. For this reason, the Gospels of Matthew, Mark, and Luke are called "Synoptic," that is, "seeing with a single eye," while the Fourth Gospel looks at Jesus' ministry through another lens. For example, only John records Jesus' first miracle, turning water into wine at the wedding in Cana (John 2:11). Only John records Jesus' first cleansing of the temple (John 2:15). Only John tells the story of Nicodemus's secret, nocturnal interview with Jesus (John 3:1–2),

---

19. Eusebius, *Church History* 3:23:3.
20. Hippolytus, "List of the Apostles and Disciples."
21. Eusebius, *Church History* 3:24:7–13.
22. "Muratorian Canon, Fragment III."

which probably occurred in John's house. This is the sort of material the other Gospel writers would not have possessed and which John would have wanted to hand down.

John's Gospel is rich in time markers with respect to Jesus' early ministry. This suggests a book written soon after the events, because it would be difficult to recall all the dates and make no mistakes many years afterwards.

THE PERICOPE OF ADULTERY

Only John's Gospel narrates the story of the adulterous woman whom the Jewish leaders dragged before Jesus for stoning (John 7:53—8:11). In this story, as Jesus listened to her accusers, he bent down and wrote something in the dust. Then he stood up and delivered his verdict: "Let him who is without sin among you be the first to throw a stone at her." Once more he bent down and wrote in the dust. The woman's accusers melted away. Jesus asked the woman where her accusers had gone. "Has no one condemned you?" he asked. She said, "No one, Lord." And Jesus said, "Neither do I condemn you; go, and from now on sin no more." There are many fanciful conjectures about what Jesus wrote in the dust, but the Bible simply does not say.

This passage is known as the "Pericope of Adultery" or the passage on adultery. The earliest surviving Greek manuscripts do not contain the pericope. However, in 1941 a large collection of the writings of Didymus the Blind (ca. AD 313–398) was discovered in Egypt. These refer to the pericope's being found in several copies of John's Gospel. It is now considered established that the pericope was present in its usual place in some Greek manuscripts known in Alexandria and elsewhere from the fourth century onwards. The fourth-century Codex Vaticanus, written in Egypt, marks the end of John chapter 7 with an umlaut (¨), indicating that an alternative reading was known at this point.

Jerome reported that the pericope was to be found in its usual place in "many Greek and Latin manuscripts" in Rome and the Latin West in the late fourth century. He included it in his Vulgate (Latin) translation of the Bible, which the Council of Trent pronounced authentic. Some Latin fathers of the fourth and fifth centuries, including Ambrose and Augustine, confirmed this view. Augustine claimed that the passage may have been wrongly excluded from some manuscripts to avoid the impression that Jesus sanctioned adultery.

> Certain persons of little faith, or rather enemies of the true faith, fearing, I suppose, lest their wives should be given impunity in sinning, removed from their manuscripts the Lord's act of forgiveness toward the adulteress, as if he who had said, "Sin no more," had granted permission to sin.[23]

---

23. Augustine, "De Adulterinis Conjugiis" 2:6–7.

Several early church fathers quoted parts of this passage, apparently receiving it as genuine. C. S. Lewis noted that the detail of Jesus writing in the dust has the distinct feeling of an eyewitness account.[24]

The pericope fits well into John's Gospel. Its message is consistent with the rest of Scripture and the stylistic touches are consistent with the character of Jesus, his enemies, and those whom he touched with love. The story also fits well with events in John's Gospel that surround it. The pericope occurred at the end of the Feast of Tabernacles in AD 31. On the last day of the feast, many people believed in him, wondering aloud, "when the Christ appears, will he do more signs than this man has done?" (John 7:31). The temple officers reported to the Pharisees that they had tried but were unable to seize Jesus. Jesus proclaimed in the temple that he was the source of living water. Nicodemus defended Jesus. The other Pharisees rebuked Nicodemus, stating that no prophet comes from Galilee. In this the Pharisees displayed their faulty knowledge of Scripture, for Jonah came from Gath-hepher, two miles from Nazareth, and Nahum may have given his name to Capernaum ("Town of Nahum"). The scribes and Pharisees were frustrated and angry and itching to find a way to trap Jesus once and for all.

Everyone went to their homes, but Jesus went to the Mount of Olives (John 8:1). Jesus returned to the temple early the next morning to teach. The scribes and Pharisees had apparently been conspiring all night, a night in which, somehow, some of them had managed to capture the adulterous woman in the act (John 8:3). Perhaps one of their number had committed that act.

The argument against the authenticity of this passage is that it is not in the earliest and most reliable manuscripts. The arguments for the authenticity of the passage are (1) it is in some early manuscripts, (2) early church fathers quoted verses from this passage as genuine, (3) some highly respected church fathers defended the whole passage as genuine, (4) the passage contains no contradiction of the rest of Scripture, (5) the passage is consistent with the character of Jesus, his critics, and with the reaction of other sinners to whom he showed mercy, (6) the passage fits neatly into the surrounding narrative in John's Gospel, and (7) the passage seems stylistically genuine. The arguments for the authenticity of the pericope therefore outweigh the arguments against.

It may be that the pericope was part of John's original sermon notes. He may have preached the story often. He may have excluded it from the first edition of his published Gospel, thinking the story a bit too racy. Others may have reassured him of the story's theological value and persuaded him to add it back in.

THE HARMONY OF THE FOUR GOSPELS

We call Matthew, Mark, and Luke the Synoptic Gospels. "Synoptic" is from Greek, meaning "with agreeing eyes," or "from the same point of view." This does not mean

---

24. Keller, *The Reason for God*, 107.

that John's Gospel contradicts the others. The four Gospels contain no contradictions. They offer supplementary details. For example, Matthew recorded one angel at Jesus' tomb. Luke recorded two, of which only one spoke. This is not a contradiction, but additional supporting detail. If two angels were there, of course, there had to be one. Additive and non-contradictory detail strengthens the Gospels' reliability. If all four Gospels were identical, they would simply be copies. Since the Gospels contain differences, but no contradictions, they act as independent, corroborating witnesses. While the whole Bible is provably true, we have only one witness of the Torah, Moses, whereas we have multiple witnesses of Jesus' life: Matthew, Mark, Luke, and John, not to mention the contents of Acts and the Epistles.

If the evangelists had decided to invent the story of Jesus and devise clever lies about his miracles, it would have been difficult to keep all the accounts in perfect accord. In today's electronic media different reports of current events not only disagree in many facts but also often miss the basic truth. This happens both accidentally and on account of deliberate bias. It is also true about non-inspired books from the ancient world. The miraculous integrity of Scripture is one of the reasons that we can know the Bible is divine, rather than only human, in origin. Its reliability is more than remarkable; it is unique in the record of human achievement. Billions of written words throughout history prove amply that human authors simply cannot achieve a comparably harmonious testimony, however hard they try.

Ancient writers, especially Hebrew writers, felt no need to write chronologically. They habitually grouped thoughts together topically. This is clear in the clustering of parables in Matthew 13. Did Jesus tell all these parables in one sitting? Maybe. But the writing feels very much like Matthew decided to draw together many parables with complimentary meanings in one place. Jesus may have said them over several years, and he probably repeated them many times over the years, as a way to help his disciples remember his message.

Skeptics attack the Gospels and especially the Gospel of John. But their criticisms are, without exception, straw men. One example of an apparent contradiction in John's Gospel is the telling of Jesus ejecting the money changers from the temple. John places this event early in Jesus' ministry, while Matthew and Luke place it on Jesus' triumphal entry to Jerusalem, and Mark places it on the Monday after Palm Sunday. Is this a contradiction? Not at all. Jesus cleansed the temple three times, first during the first Passover of Jesus' ministry, Thursday, April 4, AD 30 (John 2:15), second on Palm Sunday, March 27, AD 33 (Matt 21:12; Luke 19:45), and third on the Monday following Palm Sunday, March 28, AD 33 (Mark 11:15). No wonder the Jewish leaders were upset with him! The temple money-changing business was largely in the hands of the family of Ananias (Annas), the defrocked high priest, and Joseph Caiaphas, the high priest who was Ananias's son-in-law. Jesus repeatedly wrecked their affairs, and they lobbied Pilate to kill Jesus.

John inserted detailed time markers into his Gospel. The Synoptic evangelists include time markers, too, but to a lesser extent. Today we can use computer programs to compare the Gospel time markers to Jewish festival dates, astronomical events, and the Roman calendar of the first century. This makes it possible to fix many events in time and check for contradictions. But it is not always simple. Sometimes careful and laborious analysis is required to understand how the various calendars and events coincide. Yet in the Gospels they always do coincide. This is nothing short of miraculous when one considers that the Gospel writers had none of the sophisticated computer tools we use today. They had memory, honesty, and the inspiration of the Holy Spirit, and they never, not even once, got a date wrong. If we can rely on John's accuracy with respect to ordinary events, we can rely on his reporting Jesus' supernatural works, like the raising of Lazarus from the dead. By the way, the other Gospels record Jesus raising Jairus's daughter (Matt 9:25; Mark 5:42; Luke 8:55) and raising the widow's son (Luke 7:15), but only John records the raising of Lazarus (John 11:44).

THE APOSTLE OF LOVE AND THE NEW COMMANDMENT

John has earned the title "the Apostle of Love" because so much of his writing emphasizes God's love (John 3:16, 14:21, 23, 15:9, 12, 21:17; 1 John 4:7, 11, 12, 18, 19, 20, 5:2). In the Gospel of John, Jesus said, "A new commandment I give to you, that you love one another: just as I have loved you, you also are to love one another. By this all people will know that you are my disciples if you have love for one another" (John 13:34–35). John also recorded this statement by Jesus: "Greater love has no one than this, that someone lay down his life for his friends" (John 15:13). Finally, John took the concept of love to its apotheosis when he wrote that "God is love" (1 John 4:16).

REVELATION: AUTHORSHIP

Some controversy exists about whether John wrote Revelation and, if so, when. One reason for doubting that the apostle John was its author is the uneven style of the Greek writing in Revelation, compared to the smooth simplicity of John's Gospel and Epistles. Revelation seems grammatically loose, whereas the other writings of John are polished. One German scholar, Ludwig Radermacher, wrote that Revelation is "the most uncultured literary production that has come down to us from antiquity."[25] Of course, if we consider book sales, John's "uncultured" work has swamped the demand for Radermacher's *Neuetestamentliche Grammatik* (in German, 1925, now out of print) by billions of copies in over two thousand languages. Most modern critics did not grow up from childhood speaking, reading, and writing Greek, whereas most of the writers of the Apostolic and Patristic Eras did. If those Greek speakers did not find

---

25. Gregg, *Revelation*, 13.

the style of Revelation and of John's other writings too different to have come from the same pen, the sensibilities of modern scholars may be too delicate. Nevertheless, the Greek in Revelation and even its style in English strain common literary form. The Fourth Gospel and John's Epistles display a simple poise very different from Revelation's breathless, reckless style. But this is not a conclusive argument for authorship other than John's. John may not have been a very good Greek writer. His first language may have been Aramaic, not Greek. He may have used a scribe to take down and edit his Gospel and Letters, while perhaps no such help was available to him when he composed Revelation. Or perhaps the wild intensity of the visions in Revelation caused John to create a veritable grammar of his own.

Revelation's author reveals himself simply as "John" (Rev 1:1, 4, 9, 22:1). Who else, in the early days of the church, could expect everyone to recognize him simply by calling himself "John?" The early church fathers, Justin Martyr, Irenaeus, Clement of Alexandria, and Tertullian unanimously identified the author of Revelation as John, the son of Zebedee, the apostle. And the only books in the New Testament that refer to Jesus as the Word and the Lamb of God are the Gospel of John and Revelation, further evidence of singular authorship.

THE DATE OF REVELATION

The two main theories about when John wrote the Book of Revelation (also called the Apocalypse or the "Unveiling") are that John wrote it in the reign of the emperor Domitian, around AD 96,[26] or that he wrote it during Nero's persecution of Christians, from AD 64 to 68.[27] If the first theory is true, John wrote Revelation after the fall of the Second Temple in AD 70. If the second theory is true, John wrote Revelation before the temple's fall. John stated that he saw the Revelation in the following circumstances:

> I, John, your brother and partner in the tribulation and the kingdom and the patient endurance that are in Jesus, was on the island called Patmos on account of the word of God and the testimony of Jesus. I was in the Spirit on the Lord's Day, and I heard behind me a loud voice like a trumpet. (Rev 1:9–10)

The question is, did John see the Revelation on Patmos earlier than his exile there or during his exile? Irenaeus was a Greek bishop who lived in the south of France in the second century. He wrote about John and the composition of Revelation in his book *Against Heresies*, 5:30:3.[28] The original passage from Irenaeus does not survive, but Eusebius, the fourth-century church historian (died AD 339), quoted *Against Heresies*, writing:

---

26. Schnabel et al., *Revelation*, 17.
27. Schnabel et al., *Revelation*, 14.
28. Schnabel et al., *Revelation*, 13.

[Roman Emperor] Domitian, having shown great cruelty toward many, and having unjustly put to death no small number of well-born and notable men at Rome, and having without cause exiled and confiscated the property of a great many other illustrious men, finally became a successor of Nero in his hatred and enmity toward God. He was in fact the second that stirred up a persecution against us, although his father Vespasian had undertaken nothing prejudicial to us. It is said that in this persecution the apostle and evangelist John, who was still alive, was condemned to dwell on the island of Patmos in consequence of his testimony to the divine word. Irenaeus, in the fifth book of his work *Against Heresies,* where he discusses the number of the name of Antichrist, which is given in the so-called Apocalypse of John, speaks as follows concerning him: if it were necessary for his name to be proclaimed openly at the present time, it would have been declared by him who saw the Revelation. For it was seen not long ago, but almost in our own generation, at the end of the reign of Domitian. To such a degree, indeed, did the teaching of our faith flourish at that time that even those writers who were far from our religion did not hesitate to mention in their histories the persecution and the martyrdoms which took place during it. And they, indeed, accurately indicated the time. For they recorded that in the fifteenth year of Domitian Flavia Domitilla, daughter of a sister of Flavius Clement, who at that time was one of the consuls of Rome, was exiled with many others to the island of Pontia in consequence of testimony borne to Christ.[29]

John said he saw the Revelation on Patmos but did not say when he was there. He did, however, say why he was there. It was "on account of the word of God and the testimony of Jesus." He does not say is that he was in exile or imprisoned on Patmos. Since Patmos is an island in the Aegean Sea a mere 120 miles from John's home church of Ephesus, it is easy to imagine that John visited the island more than once. Spreading the word of God and testifying about Jesus was John's vocation as an apostle. He did not need to be exiled to Patmos to evangelize the island. If John did live into the reign of the emperor Domitian, who was assassinated in AD 96, John had perhaps sixty-three years from the year of the cross, AD 33, till Domitian's death to visit Patmos. John, therefore, could have been on Patmos earlier than AD 96 and could have seen the Revelation then. His exile to Patmos, which occurred at a later date, may have been long after he wrote Revelation.[30]

Eusebius quotes Irenaeus (above) as referring to "him who saw the Revelation. For it was seen not long ago, but almost in our own generation, at the end of the reign of Domitian." A possible assumption is that when Irenaeus wrote, "it was seen not long ago," he meant "the Revelation was seen not long ago." This, however, is not the only possible translation of Eusebius's Greek: οὐδὲ γὰρ πρὸ πολλοῦ χρόνου ἑωράθη,

---

29. Eusebius, *Church History* 3:17–18.
30. Elwell, *Encountering the New Testament*, 358.

ἀλλὰ σχεδὸν ἐπὶ τῆς ἡμετέρας γενεᾶς, πρὸς τῷ τέλει τῆς Δομετιανοῦ ἀρχῆς. The word ἑωράθη (*heoráthi*) means something "was seen," but grammatically the phrase may mean that "it" (the Revelation) was seen or that "he" (John) was seen. If the latter translation is correct, Irenaeus was simply saying "if it were necessary to proclaim who the Antichrist was, John, whom we saw not long ago, in Domitian's reign, would have told us." If this is the correct translation, the only thing it says about the date of Revelation's composition is that it was before Irenaeus's companions last saw John. The phrase is at best ambiguous and cannot be used to prove conclusively that John saw the Revelation in the reign of Domitian.

In the excerpt above, Eusebius says that Irenaeus "discusses the number of the name of Antichrist, which is given in the so-called Apocalypse of John." Possibly Irenaeus did discuss this, but John did not declare in Revelation who the antichrist was, because John never mentioned the antichrist in Revelation. The number 666 (Rev 13:18) pertained to the name of a man who was symbolically portrayed as a beast. That may qualify him to fit John's definition of an antichrist (1 John 2:18, 22, 4:3, 2 John 1:7), but John neither said so in Revelation nor did he ever teach that there was only one antichrist. While he said that there was an antichrist coming, he said that there were already many antichrists and that they were not future individuals but were then currently in the world (1 John 2:18).

Eusebius quotes Irenaeus elsewhere about Revelation, as follows:

> He speaks as follows concerning the Apocalypse of John, and the number of the name of Antichrist: as these things are so, and this number is found in all the approved and ancient copies, and those who saw John face-to-face confirm it, and reason teaches us that the number of the name of the beast, according to the mode of calculation among the Greeks, appears in its letter... we are not bold enough to speak confidently of the name of Antichrist. For if it were necessary that his name should be declared clearly at the present time, it would have been announced by him who saw the revelation. For it was seen, not long ago, but almost in our generation, toward the end of the reign of Domitian.[31]

The first point that leaps from this passage is the phrase "those who saw John face-to-face." This statement tends to support the interpretation of the first quotation from Irenaeus, above, that what "was seen" not long ago "in the reign of Domitian" was John, not John's vision, the Revelation. Irenaeus lived from about AD 130 to 202. If he were writing this second passage at the midpoint of his life, around AD 170, and was referring to "ancient" copies of Revelation composed toward the end of the reign of Domitian, AD 96, his definition of "ancient" would have meant a copy only seventy-four years old, within the living memory of men. In the same passage, Irenaeus says that the end of the reign of Domitian was "not long ago." How could a

---

31. Eusebius, *Church History* 5:8:5–6.

copy of Revelation be ancient if it were composed "not long ago?" If, by contrast, John wrote Revelation in AD 68, its oldest copies would have been about 102 years old if Irenaeus wrote this in AD 170. Any copy older than a century is better described as "ancient" than a copy that is less than a century old. Therefore, the phrase "it was seen not long ago" probably means "John was seen not long ago" not that "the Revelation was seen not long ago." John did not, therefore, necessarily write Revelation in the reign of Domitian.

There is another reason why it is likely that John wrote Revelation before AD 70, the date when the Roman general Titus destroyed Jerusalem and the Second Temple. This is the same overriding reason why probably every New Testament book was written before this event. The destruction of the temple was not only a cataclysm for all Jews, but it was also an event specifically prophesied by Jesus.

> And as he came out of the temple, one of his disciples said to him, "Look, Teacher, what wonderful stones and what wonderful buildings!" And Jesus said to him, "Do you see these great buildings? There will not be left here one stone upon another that will not be thrown down." (Mark 13:1–2)

False witnesses at Jesus' trial used this prophecy (although twisting it) as a charge against him.

> Now the chief priests and the whole Council were seeking false testimony against Jesus that they might put him to death, but they found none, though many false witnesses came forward. At last, two came forward and said, "This man said, 'I am able to destroy the temple of God, and to rebuild it in three days.'" And the high priest stood up and said, "Have you no answer to make? What is it that these men testify against you?" (Matt 26:59–62)

Onlookers at the cross mocked Jesus about this prophecy. "Those who passed by derided him, wagging their heads, and saying, 'You who would destroy the temple and rebuild it in three days, save yourself! If you are the Son of God, come down from the cross'" (Matt 27:40).

If any inspired Christian author had written any of the New Testament books after Jesus' prophecy was fulfilled in AD 70, that author surely would have pointed out that Jesus' prophecy had come true. They would have seized upon this fact as powerful proof of Christ's authority. And failing to mention the destruction of Jerusalem and the temple in any book about Judea after AD 70 would be like writing a history of World War II without mentioning Pearl Harbor or writing a history of New York City without mentioning 9/11.

The view that John wrote Revelation before or during Nero's persecution of Christians between AD 64 and 68 helps explain the extraordinary symbolism of the book. John knew that many were dying at the hands of Nero simply for being Christians. John called himself "your brother and partner in the tribulation" (Rev 1:9).

John, the Apostle of Love

He was indeed a partaker of the tribulation, if that tribulation meant the Neronian persecution. To be caught with a Christian text at such times was a mortal risk. Like Christians in Mao's China, the only way Christians in Nero's Rome could safely communicate their faith was in code. Revelation is rich in symbols that readers of the Old Testament could interpret but that pagan Roman officers, untutored in Jewish lore, could not. This is especially true of the code name 666.

"This calls for wisdom: let the one who has understanding calculate the number of the Beast, for it is the number of a man, and his number is 666" (Rev 13:18). The number of the Beast equals the name of a man. The man is Nero Caesar, emperor of Rome.

In ancient languages, including Hebrew, Greek, and Latin, letters of the alphabet have numerical equivalents. This number-letter equivalency is called gematria. If, for example, we assign letters to the English alphabet as follows: A=1, B=2, C=3, etc., then my name, JIM, would have these numerical equivalents: J= 10, I = 9, M = 13. My gematria code name may be rendered 10+9+13 = 32.

John wrote Revelation in Greek, but he spoke Aramaic and probably Hebrew, too. The Greek version of Nero Caesar transliterates into Hebrew as *Nron Qsr*, נרון קסר, and yields a numerical value of 666, as shown (read right to left):

Sum	Resh (ר)	Samekh (ס)	Qoph (ק)	Nun (נ)	Vav (ו)	Resh (ר)	Nun (נ)
666	200	60	100	50	6	200	50

Some ancient manuscripts of Revelation say, "the number of a man, and his number is 616." This is probably a scribal error, but even the error proves the identity of Nero, because Nero's name in Latin is transliterated into Hebrew by dropping the second Nun (נ), so it becomes *Nro Qsr*, transliterating into Hebrew as נרו קסר. This yields 616, as follows (reading right to left):

Sum	Resh (ר)	Samekh (ס)	Qoph (ק)	Vav (ו)	Resh (ר)	Nun (נ)
616	200	60	100	6	200	50

Evidently some earlier copyists, assuming the Latin name of the Roman Emperor was preferable to his name in Greek, used 616 instead of 666; but they were still aware that the man in view was Nero. John warned his readers that decoding the name would call for wisdom, by which he meant knowing Hebrew, the language of the wise Torah. John encoded Nero's name and wrote Revelation in a symbolic, apocalyptic style to protect Christians who would read and be blessed by the book's message of hope in tribulational times. If Roman officials could not understand Revelation's full meaning, they would have had a harder time convicting those who possessed it. Nero was alive until June 9, AD 68, so John may have written Revelation between AD 64, the start of Nero's persecution, and mid-AD 68.

In conclusion, the preponderance of evidence seems to favor AD 64–68 as the date of Revelation's composition, but whether the date was AD 68 or 96 must remain open to debate, because there is no absolute proof either way.

ANTICHRISTS

John never mentions an antichrist or indeed any antichrists in Revelation. The only mention of antichrists anywhere in Scripture are in John's First and Second Epistles, in which he writes that it is the last hour, and that although his readers had heard that the antichrist was coming, many antichrists had already come. By that fact they should know that it was indeed the last hour. The last hour of what? The world? Probably of the old covenant, for the destruction of the temple in AD 70 would render the observance of Mosaic law with its many, mandatory sacrifices impossible.

John also wrote that these antichrists were originally part of the church but that they left, making it plain that they were not real Christians. He wrote that anyone who denies the Father and the Son is the antichrist (1 John 2:22). He further warned his readers to test every spirit to see if they are from God, because many false prophets had gone out into the world. Every spirit that confesses that Jesus Christ has come in the flesh, he taught, comes from God, and every spirit that does not do so is not from God. This, he wrote, is the spirit of antichrist, which his readers heard was coming into the world but was in the world already.

He encouraged his readers, saying, "Little children, you are from God and have overcome them [the antichrists], for he who is in you is greater than he who is in the world" (1 John 4:4). He further wrote that "many deceivers have gone out into the world, those who do not confess the coming of Jesus Christ in the flesh. Such a one is the deceiver and the antichrist. Watch yourselves, so that you may not lose what we have worked for but may win a full reward" (2 John 1:7–8).

Philip, Apostle to Ethiopia

PHILIP WAS THE FIFTH disciple whom Jesus called, and that is the order in which he always appears in the lists of the Twelve. Philip's name is classically Greek. It means "Lover of Horses:" *philos* (friend) and *hippos* (horse). The most famous Philip of ancient times was Philip II, king of Macedon, father of Alexander the Great. No Hebrew or Aramaic name is recorded for this apostle, which does not necessarily mean that he was only part Jewish. Andrew, Peter's brother, is known only by his Greek name, and he was thoroughly Jewish. Philip was a Jew, but with a name like Philip, he may have had a Greek father or mother who may have converted to Judaism. Or it is possible that Philip was his Greek-equivalent name, as Paul was the Greek name that Saul used among the gentiles.

John the Baptist introduced Andrew and John to Jesus. Andrew called Simon Peter, and then Jesus found Philip. At the end of the Feast of Tabernacles in AD 29,

> The next day [Jesus] purposed to go into Galilee, and he found Philip. And Jesus said to him, "Follow me." Now Philip was from Bethsaida, of the city of Andrew and Peter. Philip found Nathanael and said to him, "We have found him of whom Moses in the Law and also the Prophets wrote—Jesus of Nazareth, the son of Joseph." (John 1:43–45)

Like Peter and Andrew, Philip was born in Bethsaida on the northern shore of Lake Galilee. Very likely, Philip knew Peter and Andrew from boyhood. Since Capernaum is not far from Bethsaida, and since the sons of Jonah lived there and conducted a fishing business with the sons of Zebedee, it is easy to imagine that Peter, Andrew, James, John, and Philip all knew each other from an early age. And since Philip immediately called Nathanael (of Cana), it is likely those two were friends and that all six of these young men had been acquainted from childhood. It is also probable that Philip, like his Galilean friends, may have known and despised Matthew, the tax collector in Capernaum and possible black sheep cousin of Jesus.

Apart from the lists of disciples, all Gospel references to Philip are in the book of John. Mark and Luke did not belong to this group of childhood friends and families, and Matthew's career as a tax collector put him outside the pale until Jesus called him. John's accounts of Philip, therefore, may be an additional hint that Philip was a long-time friend of John, and therefore of James, Peter, and Andrew. Moreover, since James and John may have been first cousins of Jesus and since John the Baptist was a second cousin of Jesus,[1] it is reasonable to imagine that all these boys may have known Jesus and traveled with each other every year to Jerusalem on the four pilgrimage feasts, which were like grand family outings. Of course, we cannot know for sure that Jesus' apostles were his childhood friends. But it is difficult to imagine, in so small a place as Galilee, in a family-centric Middle Eastern culture, that Jewish clans would fail to gather often, marking births, celebrating weddings, mourning deaths, and worshiping God.

FOLLOW ME

Philip was the fifth apostle to whom Jesus spoke the momentous words, whose power and love echo down the corridor of time: "follow me." The Bible was not written to us, but for us. Jesus said, "follow me" to Philip and others, and through them he also invited every human being to follow him. How do we know? He said to them, "This is My blood of the covenant, which is poured out for many" (Mark 14:24), and "as many as received him, to them he gave the right to become children of God, even to those who believe in his name" (John 1:12). Every human being on earth is called. Yet only a minority is bound for heaven. God's call, his grace, is conditional upon each individual accepting the free gift of salvation. Without acceptance, forgiveness is an incomplete transaction, a one-sided handshake.

FEEDING THE FIVE THOUSAND

John recorded three episodes in his Gospel about Philip which occurred during Jesus' earthly ministry. At the first, the feeding of the five thousand, Jesus tested Philip.

> Jesus went up on the mountain, and there he sat down with his disciples. Now the Passover, the feast of the Jews, was at hand. Lifting up his eyes, then, and seeing that a large crowd was coming toward him, Jesus said to Philip, "Where are we to buy bread, so that these people may eat?" He said this to test him, for he himself knew what he would do. Philip answered him, "Two hundred *denarii* would not buy enough bread for each of them to get a little." One of his disciples, Andrew, Simon Peter's brother, said to him, "There is a boy here who has five barley loaves and two fish, but what are they for so many?" Jesus said, "Have the people sit down." Now there was much grass in the place. So the men sat down, about five thousand in number. Jesus then took the loaves, and when he had given thanks, he distributed them to those who were seated. So also the fish, as much as they wanted. And when they had eaten their fill, he told his disciples, "Gather up the leftover fragments, that nothing may be lost." So they gathered

---

1. See "Relationships in Jesus' Community" in the Appendices.

them up and filled twelve baskets with fragments from the five barley loaves left
by those who had eaten. When the people saw the sign that he had done, they
said, "This is indeed the Prophet who is to come into the world." (John 6:3–14)

The passage refers to five thousand men and does not take into account the women and children present. Even so, there were probably not so many more than five thousand present because the feeding occurred on a grassy knoll east of Bethsaida, along the north coast of the Sea of Galilee. It was not a great population center, and the crowds who were following Jesus in boats to that place, and who sailed the next day back across the lake to the western shore, were probably mostly men. It would be unlikely that men, women, and children in equal numbers would have braved the rigors of these lake crossings in pursuit of the Nazarene rabbi. After all, that very night the disciples nearly perished in a storm on the lake. They were saved only by Jesus' walking out on the water.

When Jesus asked Philip where they were to buy bread to feed so many people, Philip skipped over the question of where they might obtain the bread and pointed to an even greater problem: even if they were near a market, they would need two hundred *denarii* to feed this many people even for one day.

The buying power of the Roman *denarius* cannot be translated exactly into the buying power of precious metal today. Two hundred *denarii* are equal to 95.2 troy ounces of silver, which is worth about $1,677 in 2022 US dollars. But a *denarius* was also an average day's wages. In the United States, the average wages for a day are about $214. So, Philip's cost estimate might be something more like $32,000 in modern terms. This makes sense, because if one were feeding fish tacos to five thousand people today, assuming that one would pay $2.82 per taco or about $5.64 per person, that would cost about $28,200.

Philip flunked Jesus' test, because Jesus asked, "Where can we buy bread?" and Philip, failing to realize that Jesus was the bread of life, instead calculated the cost. The bread motif in Jesus' ministry recurred to illustrate what the real source of our sustenance is. Jesus was, after all, born in Bethlehem, which means "House of Bread." Key verses speaking of bread include:

> And the tempter came and said to him, "If you are the Son of God, command these stones to become loaves of bread." But he answered, "It is written, "Man shall not live by bread alone, but by every word that comes from the mouth of God." (Matt 4:3–4)

> Give us this day our daily bread. (Matt 6:11)

> Jesus then said to them, "Truly, truly, I say to you, it was not Moses who gave you the bread from heaven, but my Father gives you the true bread from heaven. For the bread of God is he who comes down from heaven and gives life to the world." They said to him, "Sir, give us this bread always." Jesus said

> to them, "I am the bread of life; whoever comes to me shall not hunger, and whoever believes in me shall never thirst." (John 6:32–35)

> Now they had forgotten to bring bread, and they had only one loaf with them in the boat. And he cautioned them, saying, "Watch out; beware of the leaven of the Pharisees and the leaven of Herod." And they began discussing with one another the fact that they had no bread. And Jesus, aware of this, said to them, "Why are you discussing the fact that you have no bread? Do you not yet perceive or understand? Are your hearts hardened? Having eyes do you not see, and having ears do you not hear? And do you not remember? When I broke the five loaves for the five thousand, how many baskets full of broken pieces did you take up?" They said to him, "Twelve." "And the seven for the four thousand, how many baskets full of broken pieces did you take up?" And they said to him, "Seven." And he said to them, "Do you not yet understand?" (Mark 8:14–21)

> Now as they were eating, Jesus took bread, and after blessing it broke it and gave it to the disciples, and said, "Take, eat; this is my body." (Matt 26:26)

> When he was at table with them, he took the bread and blessed and broke it and gave it to them. And their eyes were opened, and they recognized him. And he vanished from their sight. (Luke 24:30–31)

This was the message Jesus wanted to give Philip: not the cost of bread, but the priceless value of the bread of heaven.

JESUS AND THE GREEKS

The next episode that John recorded about Philip was the request of certain Greeks to meet Jesus. This occurred on Monday, March 28, AD 33, five days before the crucifixion.

> Now among those who went up to worship at the feast were some Greeks. So, these came to Philip, who was from Bethsaida in Galilee, and asked him, "Sir, we wish to see Jesus." Philip went and told Andrew; Andrew and Philip went and told Jesus. And Jesus answered them, "The hour has come for the Son of Man to be glorified. Truly, truly, I say to you, unless a grain of wheat falls into the earth and dies, it remains alone; but if it dies, it bears much fruit. Whoever loves his life loses it, and whoever hates his life in this world will keep it for eternal life. If anyone serves me, he must follow me; and where I am, there will my servant be also. If anyone serves me, the Father will honor him." (John 12:20–26)

The Greeks seeking to meet Jesus seemed to gravitate toward the disciple who had a Greek name. Yet Philip did not take the Greeks straight to Jesus. First, he consulted Andrew, the disciple who loved to introduce people to Jesus (and who also had a Greek name). Andrew took the Greeks to the Master. Were the Greeks going up to worship at the Passover Feast? Were they converts to Judaism? Were they thinking of conversion? Or were they simply visitors to Jerusalem who were curious about the customs of the Jews and even more curious about Jesus, of whom so many stories were circulating? Whatever the answers to these questions, Jesus told the Greeks these things: (1) the hour of his glorification had come, (2) through death a seed bears fruit, (3) this life is worthless without eternal life, and (4) following Jesus is the pathway to God. In these brief statements, Jesus imparted the whole gospel to the Greeks by saying, in paraphrase, "Observe what is about to happen in the next few days. You will see me killed, raised, and exalted. Understand and follow me to life eternal."

If the Greeks remained in Jerusalem till Friday, they would have witnessed Jesus' crucifixion. If they remained till Sunday, they would have witnessed his resurrection. Since John wrote his Gospel to the world, this is a meaningful foreshadowing of how the apostles, and notably Peter and Paul, would carry the good news to the gentiles. But the first to do this was Philip, who, after the resurrection, preached in despised, half-pagan Samaria and proselytized a eunuch from Ethiopia. Possibly observing Jesus' witness to the Greeks helped equip Philip for these opportunities.

SEEING THE FATHER

In the final Gospel reference to Philip, at the Last Supper, he seemed to struggle with Jesus' teaching and asked to see the Father so that he might believe Jesus' extraordinary claims. Jesus marveled at Philip's failure, after witnessing so many miracles, to grasp that Jesus was God incarnate.

> "If you had known me, you would have known my Father also. From now on you do know him and have seen him." Philip said to him, "Lord, show us the Father, and it is enough for us." Jesus said to him, "Have I been with you so long, and you still do not know me, Philip? Whoever has seen me has seen the Father. How can you say, 'Show us the Father'? Do you not believe that I am in the Father and the Father is in me? The words that I say to you I do not speak on my own authority, but the Father who dwells in me does his works. Believe me that I am in the Father and the Father is in me, or else believe on account of the works themselves. Truly, truly, I say to you, whoever believes in me will also do the works that I do; and greater works than these will he do, because I am going to the Father. Whatever you ask in my name, this I will do, that the Father may be glorified in the Son. If you ask me anything in my name, I will do it. If you love me, you will keep my commandments." (John 14:7–15)

As one of the Twelve, Philip was present in the upper room on Resurrection Sunday, in the upper room with Thomas present on the following Monday, at Jesus' ascension, at the meeting to choose Matthias to replace Judas, at the birth of the church on the day of Pentecost in AD 33, and at the Jerusalem Council in AD 49.

THE HISTORY OF SAMARIA

The next Bible reference to Philip, in Acts, shows him preaching among the Samaritans.[2] Samaria was the remnant of Ephraim, the ancient Northern Kingdom of Israel. Israel was originally one kingdom under King Saul. As Saul's power waned, two tribes of Israel's twelve tribes, Judah and Benjamin, gave their allegiance to King David. When Saul died, the ten other tribes also went over to David. When David died, his son Solomon became king and held all twelve tribes together for most of his reign. As Solomon strayed away from God, however, Jeroboam, the son of Nabat, of the tribe of Ephraim, conspired to become king. When Solomon discovered the plot, Jeroboam fled to Egypt under the protection of Pharaoh Shishak.

When Solomon died, Jeroboam returned from exile. Solomon's son, Rehoboam, tried to hold the kingdom together, but he attempted it through cruel dictatorship. The northern ten tribes resented such treatment. In 931 BC Jeroboam successfully made himself king of the ten tribes, which became a separate Northern Kingdom. It went under the nicknames of Ephraim and Samaria. Ephraim referred to the son of Joseph who had ruled in Egypt, and this was Jeroboam's tribe. Samaria referred to the region's capital city. Omri, father of King Ahab, had bought a hill site from someone named Shemer for two talents of silver and named the place Samaria ("Shomron" in Hebrew) after Shemer.

The Southern Kingdom, commonly called Judah, consisted of two tribes, Judah and Benjamin (and some Levites, who served in the temple). When the single Kingdom of Israel split, Judah remained loyal to David's grandson, Rehoboam. Jerusalem was the capital of Judah, and so Solomon's Temple was under Judah's control. To ensure that his subjects did not drift back into allegiance with Rehoboam, Jeroboam

---

2. Many scholars aver that Luke here refers to Philip the Evangelist (Acts 6:5, 21:8), not to Philip the apostle. This seems improbable. By simply mentioning "Philip" without further identifying the person, Luke seems to imply that his reference is to the most famous and prominent Philip, the apostle. The argument in favor of Philip the Evangelist is that the Samaritans received the baptism of the Holy Spirit only when the apostles Peter and John prayed over them and laid hands on them (Acts 8:15–17). The inference is that Philip lacked the authority or power to confer the Holy Spirit, and therefore he cannot have been Philip the apostle, because all the apostles would have had equal authority and power. But both Philip the apostle and Philip the evangelist were full of the Holy Spirit (Acts 1:2, 5, 8, 6:5), and thus both had the power to introduce the Samaritans to the Holy Spirit. The overriding point of the passage is not to compare the power of the apostles to that of other evangelists, but to illustrate the stepwise progress toward salvation. The Samaritans initially believed (Acts 8:12). Simon Magus also initially believed and was amazed (Acts 8:13). However, mere belief in the gospel is not the same as salvation, for "even the demons believe and shudder" (James 2:19). This episode is not about the power of the apostles, but about the developing stages of salvation in new converts. The Samaritans were open to belief and subsequently open to the Holy Spirit, and so they received the Holy Spirit and were saved. The arrival of Peter and John in Samaria was the tipping point in fully developing their faith. Simon Magus was open to belief but not open to the Holy Spirit; he was only interested in using the Holy Spirit to enhance his prestige, and so he remained unsaved. Apollos (Acts 18:25) and the twelve disciples in Ephesus (Acts 19:1–7) experienced the same gradual progress toward salvation: first they believed, then they repented (received the baptism of John), and finally they opened their hearts to the indwelling of the Holy Spirit.

established a rival place of worship on Mount Gerizim in Samaria. Eventually, both kingdoms turned away from God and followed pagan practices.

The prophets Elijah, Elisha, Hosea, and Amos warned the Northern Kingdom of God's wrath, but all nineteen of the northern kings persisted in evil. From 722–718 BC, God used Assyria to destroy the Northern Kingdom (and engulf the rest of the Middle East) while miraculously sparing a tiny oasis of freedom, Judah. Assyria deported and scattered the ten tribes into what became known as the diaspora (Greek for dispersion). The ten tribes were then mostly lost to history, hence "the lost tribes of Israel." The Assyrians populated the Northern Kingdom with Aramaic-speaking settlers, who brought pagan religious practices into the territory. Yet there was always some remnant of the original Hebrews, and these intermarried with the settlers, mixing the worship of Yahweh with Assyrian cults, thus creating a syncretistic religion.

The prophets Isaiah, Jeremiah, Joel, Micah, Habakkuk, and Zephaniah warned the Southern Kingdom of God's wrath, but only eight of their nineteen rulers did good in the eyes of God. King Josiah brought about godly reforms in Jerusalem in the early days of Jeremiah, Daniel, and Ezekiel, but the last four kings of Judah were all evil, and in 586 BC, God used Nebuchadnezzar, King of Babylon, to destroy Judah, Jerusalem, and Solomon's Temple. God preserved a Jewish remnant, as Nebuchadnezzar deported about 14,000–18,000 Jews to Babylon in exile.[3] Jeremiah prophesied, with amazing accuracy, that the captivity would last seventy years (Jer 25:12). When Cyrus the Great conquered Babylon and added it to his Persian empire in 539 BC, he permitted the Jews to return to Judah. Under Zerubbabel (an ancestor of Jesus) and Jeshua (the high priest), and encouraged by the prophets Zechariah and Haggai, the Jews rebuilt the temple by 515 BC, seventy years after its destruction.[4] After Esther and Mordecai saved the Jews from Persian genocide in 475 BC, Ezra led a second return of Jewish survivors to Jerusalem, followed by Nehemiah, who governed Judah and rebuilt Jerusalem's walls. The last Old Testament prophet, Malachi ministered in their time.

PHILIP'S FIRST MISSIONARY JOURNEY

So, because of all this history, the Jews despised the Samaritans as half-breeds and pagans. The Messiah, however, had come to save not just the Jews but everyone, including Samaritans, not because any particular nation or race deserved salvation, but because God so loved the world. In the tale of the good Samaritan, the Samaritan showed more charity to a wounded Jew than did a priest or a Levite (Luke 10:33). The narrative of Jesus' encounter with the Samaritan woman at the well (John 4:7–42) shows that: (1) the Samaritans yearned for God and the Messiah, (2) the Jews despised them, and (3)

---

3. Gottheil et al., "Captivity, or Exile, Babylonian."

4. This interval was from the day that Nebuchadnezzar's captain, Nebuzaradan, burned the first temple (9 Av, 586 BC) until the day when the Jews completed the second temple (3 Adar, 515 BC), which was 25,774 days or 70.6 years.

Jesus had come to save them. The Samaritan woman quickly recognized the Messiah while even Jesus' half-brothers and the learned Pharisees and scribes had failed to do so. Not only that, when she told the town of Sychar (Shechem) about Jesus, they all recognized him as the Messiah, and he spent two days with them, over the Sabbath.

When we see Philip preaching to the Samaritans in Acts, we can appreciate what prejudices he was up against. Philip was the first apostle to bring the gospel to the non-Jewish world. The age-old strife between Samaria and Judah was resolved forever in Jesus Christ. Jesus was the fulfillment of all the types and shadows of the Old Covenant and the eternal replacement of the temple that the Romans would finally demolish in AD 70.

In AD 33, Saul (Paul) began ferociously to persecute Christians, which may have prompted Philip to evangelize outside Jerusalem. Paul's persecution probably did not drive Philip out of Jerusalem, because the Bible says that Saul's persecution scattered all except the apostles (Acts 8:1). It also says that those who had been scattered preached the gospel wherever they went (Acts 8:4). Therefore, Philip's evangelistic work was simply obedience to Jesus' statement that the disciples would be his witnesses in Jerusalem, Judea, Samaria, and to the ends of the earth (Acts 1:8). Nevertheless, the evangelistic outreach of Philip to Samaria, Gaza, and Caesarea, right after the stoning of Stephen must have seemed like an epidemic of Christianity to Paul. So, like a general seeking to outflank his enemy, he applied for priestly permission to head the Christian heretics off at Damascus, north of Samaria. Philip's zig-zag ministry evaded Paul, and Paul met with unexpected results, becoming a convert to Christ on the Damascus Road. Meanwhile, Philip reached the city of Samaria (today's Sebastia) and proclaimed Christ. He performed miracles, casting out demons and healing the paralyzed and the lame. The citizens of Samaria were overjoyed, and they listened attentively to Philip's preaching.

There was, however, a man in Samaria named Simon Magus or Simon the Magician. He impressed the Samaritans with his magic and made himself out to be someone great. The Samaritans thought Simon wielded the power of God. But when they heard Philip's message about the kingdom of God and Jesus Christ, they were baptized, both men and women. When Simon saw Philip's miracles, he was amazed. He believed, got baptized, and began following Philip.

When the apostles in Jerusalem heard that Samaria had received the gospel, they sent Peter and John to investigate. When they saw that the reports were true, they prayed for the Samaritans, laid hands on them, and the Samaritans received the Holy Spirit. When Simon saw this, he said, "Give me this power also, so that anyone on whom I lay my hands may receive the Holy Spirit" (Acts 8:19). But Peter said to him, "May your silver perish with you, because you thought you could obtain the gift of God with money! You have neither part nor lot in this matter, for your heart is not right before God. Repent, therefore, of this wickedness of yours, and pray to the Lord that, if possible, the intent of your heart may be forgiven you. For I see that you are in the gall of bitterness and in the bond of iniquity." Simon answered, "Pray for me to the Lord, that nothing of what you have said may come upon me" (Acts 8:20-24).

This sounds like Simon was truly a seeker, but in reality his heart was not right with God. He went to Rome and resumed his practice of magic arts there. Invoking the power of demons, he claimed to be a god. He won many followers and so impressed Claudius that the emperor erected a statue on the island in the Tiber River in Simon's honor.[5] Peter pursued Simon to Rome and defeated his chicanery once and for all.

Peter and John preached the word of the Lord in many Samaritan villages. This is ironic, because John and his brother James had once asked Jesus if he would permit them to call down fire from heaven on the Samaritan villages who had rejected him. After ministering in Samaria, Peter, John, and Philip returned to Jerusalem.

PHILIP'S SECOND MISSIONARY JOURNEY

Back in Jerusalem, an angel of the Lord came to Philip and told him to take the road south to Gaza. As he walked along the desert road, he met an Ethiopian eunuch, a court official of Candace, queen of the Ethiopians. The eunuch was in charge of all her treasure. He had come to Jerusalem to worship and was returning home, riding in a chariot, and reading the book of Isaiah. Since he was riding and reading, there must have been a charioteer with the eunuch, and so the chariot was like a coach. The Holy Spirit spoke to Philip, saying, "Go over and join this chariot." So, Philip ran to him and heard him reading aloud. He asked, "Do you understand what you are reading?" The Ethiopian said, "How can I, unless someone guides me?" And he invited Philip to come up and sit with him.

The passage of Scripture that the eunuch was reading was this: "Like a sheep he was led to the slaughter and like a lamb before its shearer is silent, so he opens not his mouth. In his humiliation justice was denied him. Who can describe his generation? For his life is taken away from the earth" (Acts 8:32-33; Isa 53:7-8). The eunuch asked Philip whether the prophet was speaking of himself or of someone else. Using the Messianic passages of Isaiah 53, Philip told the eunuch the whole gospel. As they traveled, they came to a place with water, and the eunuch asked, "What prevents me from being baptized?" He commanded the chariot to stop, and both he and Philip went down to the water, where Philip baptized him. When they came out of the water, the Spirit of the Lord carried Philip away. The eunuch saw him no more, but he went along his way, rejoicing. This perhaps means that the Holy Spirit carried Philip away miraculously. It may also simply mean that, inspired by God, Philip departed for Azotus and that he and the eunuch never met again.

---

5. Justin Martyr, "First Apology," 26; "Dialogue with Trypho," 120.

ETHIOPIA

Why had an Ethiopian come to Jerusalem to worship? Why, of all people, the treasurer of Queen Candace? There was an ancient community of Jews in Ethiopia. There was also an early community of Christians. According to the *Kebre Negast*, an Ethiopian holy book, Menelik I, an Ethiopian ruler who was supposedly the son of King Solomon and the Queen of Sheba, took the Ark of the Covenant to Ethiopia.[6] From AD 1320 to 1620, Ethiopian Jews and Christians waged war until the Christians conquered the Jews. The Christians placed what they claim was the original Ark of the Covenant in the Church of Saint Mary of Zion, in the mountain city of Axum. To this day, they jealously guard the ark, and only their patriarch may view it once a year.

This tradition is questionable. Jeremiah mentioned the ark (Jer 3:16) in a way suggestive of its presence in the temple in his day (three centuries after Solomon). When Nebuchadnezzar looted the temple in 586 BC, he took all the cups and plates to Babylon, the very plates that Belshazzar would insultingly use to drink toasts to Babylonian gods on the night when God's finger wrote his doom on a wall (2 Kgs 24:13; 2 Chron 36:7, 18; Dan 5:2). Nebuchadnezzar may have taken the ark with him. Or the ark may have perished when Nebuchadnezzar burned the temple down (2 Kgs 25:9; Jer 52:13).

Whatever the truth, the existence of an ancient community of Jews and Christians in Ethiopia is certain. And the Old Testament shows that Ethiopia was part of God's plan, as David said: "Nobles shall come from Egypt; Cush [Ethiopia] shall hasten to stretch out her hands to God" (Ps 68:31). In describing a time when God would reject unbelieving Israel and accept the worship of other people, the prophet Zephaniah, fifty years before Nebuchadnezzar's destruction of Jerusalem, wrote:

> For at that time I will change the speech of the peoples to a pure speech, that all of them may call upon the name of the Lord and serve him with one accord. From beyond the rivers of Cush [Ethiopia] my worshipers, the daughter of my dispersed ones, shall bring my offering. On that day you shall not be put to shame because of the deeds by which you have rebelled against me; for then I will remove from your midst your proudly exultant ones, and you shall no longer be haughty in my holy mountain. (Zeph 3:9–11)

Isaiah also prophesied this event.

> Ah, land of whirring wings that is beyond the rivers of Cush, which sends ambassadors by the sea, in vessels of papyrus on the waters! Go, you swift messengers, to a nation tall and smooth, to a people feared near and far, a nation mighty and conquering, whose land the rivers divide ... At that time tribute will be brought to the LORD of hosts from a people tall and smooth, from a people feared near and far, a nation mighty and conquering, whose land the rivers divide, to Mount Zion, the place of the name of the LORD of hosts. (Isa 18:1–7)

---

4. Encyclopedia Britannica, "Aksum."

The land of whirring wings is evocative of the fact that locust hordes in the Middle East often arose out of Ethiopia. The vessels of papyrus refer to the boats on which the Ethiopians plied the many rivers dividing their land, especially the Blue Nile, whose source is in Lake Tana. The phrase "a people tall and smooth" aptly describes the typical physique of Ethiopians, whose bodies are tall, slender, and not very hairy compared to Middle Easterners.

The Ethiopians were a formidable military nation in antiquity. The Twenty-Fifth Dynasty of Egypt (747–656 BC) was ruled by Ethiopian pharaohs. Isaiah prophesied that Ethiopia would bring tribute to Jerusalem, which is exactly what the eunuch was doing, and that God's people should send swift messengers to Ethiopia, which is the evangelistic mission Philip was fulfilling.

In the context of these passages, here is what was going on at the time when Philip met the Ethiopian. The Pharisees and scribes had rejected the Messiah and felt no shame about it. Other people—Greeks, Romans, and Samaritans—were accepting Christ and joining the community of God. The treasurer of the queen of Ethiopia was returning from a journey of worship and offerings to Jerusalem, searching the Messianic passages in Isaiah 53 for the truth. In thirty-seven years, Rome would destroy the Second Temple and end the rule of the proud, exulting Jewish heretics upon the holy mountain of Zion. So, the eunuch and Philip were meeting at a crossroads in history prophesied by David one thousand years before, by Isaiah about 775 years before, and by Zephaniah about 670 years before.

CONCLUSION OF PHILIP'S SECOND MISSIONARY JOURNEY

After arriving in Azotus (Ashdod), Philip went north to the seaport of Caesarea, preaching the gospel in all the towns along the way. In sum, Philip's travels in AD 33 were as follows: (1) from Jerusalem to Samaria, forty-five miles or a fifteen-hour walk to the north, (2) back to Jerusalem, (3) from Jerusalem to Gaza, eighty-five miles or a seventeen-hour walk to the southwest, (4) from Gaza to Azotus, twenty-five miles or an eight-hour walk north along the Mediterranean coast, and (5) from Azotus to Caesarea, sixty-two miles north or a twenty-hour walk along the costal road, a total of 262 miles.

PHILIP THE APOSTLE AND PHILIP THE DEACON

Some traditions confuse Philip the apostle with Philip the evangelist, who was one of the seven chosen to serve the widows of the church. A clear reading of the text precludes this.

> Now in these days when the disciples were increasing in number, a complaint by the Hellenists arose against the Hebrews because their widows were being neglected in the daily distribution. And the twelve summoned the full number

of the disciples and said, "It is not right that we should give up preaching the word of God to serve tables. Therefore, brothers, pick out from among you seven men of good repute, full of the Spirit and of wisdom, whom we will appoint to this duty. But we will devote ourselves to prayer and to the ministry of the word." And what they said pleased the whole gathering, and they chose Stephen, a man full of faith and of the Holy Spirit, and Philip, and Prochorus, and Nicanor, and Timon, and Parmenas, and Nicolaus, a proselyte of Antioch. These they set before the apostles, and they prayed and laid their hands on them." (Acts 6:1–6)

Since these seven men, including Philip, were brought before the twelve apostles, including Philip the apostle, the two Philips must have been two different men. If the Twelve appointed seven to do work unsuitable for the Twelve, the Philip of the seven cannot have been the Philip of the Twelve. The deacon Philip, one of the seven, appeared again in Acts.

"On the next day we departed and came to Caesarea, and we entered the house of Philip the evangelist, who was one of the seven, and stayed with him. He had four unmarried daughters, who prophesied" (Acts 21:8–9). Eusebius seems to have confused the two Philips,[7] demonstrating that the early church fathers, while valuable sources, are sometimes wrong. The canon of Scripture never is. (Canon, by the way, comes from the Greek word *kanon*, "measuring stick.")

FRANCE

There is a tradition in France that Philip evangelized Gaul (ancient France). Philip appears in French art as an especially revered saint. There may be a grain of truth in this. Galatia was a province of Turkey invaded and settled by Gauls (ancient inhabitants of France) during the reign of Alexander the Great (the late fourth century BC). They displaced the native Hittites and called the region they conquered Galatia, Gallia of the East, or, if we were to make it sound more modern, "Asian France." That Philip, like Paul on his second missionary journey, should have preached in Galatia seems credible. If he preached among the Gauls of Galatia, it is easy to see how tradition might stretch the point to say that Philip preached among the Gauls, the French. Of course, it is also possible that preaching among the Gauls of Galatia inspired Philip to carry the gospel to their brethren in France. Or Galatian converts may have carried Philip's message from Galatia home to France. All of this simply is unknown. In any case, Philip is the only apostle anciently associated with France.

---

7. Eusebius, *Church History* 3:31:4.

PHILIP'S DEATH

Hippolytus wrote: "Philip preached in Phrygia and was crucified in Hierapolis [modern Pamukkale, Turkey, near Colossae, Laodicea, and Galatia] with his head downward in the time of Domitian [AD 81–96] and was buried there."[8] If this is so, he shared the same form of crucifixion that Peter suffered back in AD 68. Perhaps Philip agreed with Peter that he was unworthy to die in the manner of his Lord. Eusebius quoted Polycrates of Ephesus as also affirming that Philip died in Hierapolis, although this is the same dubious passage in Eusebius that erroneously confuses Philip the apostle with Philip of the seven servants.[9]

In Hierapolis, a spring of chemical-rich lukewarm water sparkles over a giant, crystallized waterfall. In ancient times, invalids from afar visited this famous spa, making it an ideal crossroads where Philip could meet travelers and spread the gospel. Since John and Philip were friends, apparently from childhood, they may have enjoyed ministering in provinces that were fairly near to each other, Ephesus and Hierapolis.

The apocryphal book *The Acts of Philip*[10] gives an account of Philip's martyrdom. In this story, Philip, Bartholomew, and Philip's sister, Mariamne, were ministering in Hierapolis, when Philip miraculously healed and converted the wife if the city's proconsul. The proconsul was enraged at this challenge to his pagan cult. He tortured Philip, Bartholomew, and Mariamne. Then he crucified Philip and Bartholomew upside down. The dying Philip preached from his cross. As a result of Philip's preaching, the crowd released Bartholomew from his cross, but Philip suffered a martyr's death. This book is unreliable, so its account of Philip's death may have a grain of truth or may be pure fable.

Pope John III (AD 560–72) moved the remains of Philip from Hierapolis to the Church of the Holy Apostles of Saint Philip and Saint James at Rome. Today visitors can see a large marble sarcophagus said to contain the bones of Philip and James.

PHILIP'S NATURE

Philip was a man who eagerly responded to Christ's call, willingly asked and answered questions in his search for truth, even at the risk of getting it wrong, and boldly took the Good News to the world. The brief sketch of him in Acts suggests that his missionary work was daring, joyful, untiring, and especially blessed by miraculous acts of the Holy Spirit.

---

8. Hippolytus, "List of the Apostles and Disciples."
9. Eusebius, *Church History* 3:31:4.
10. "Acts of Philip."

Nathanael Bartholomew, Apostle to Armenia

NATHANAEL BARTHOLOMEW WAS THE sixth in the lists of the apostles. Matthew, Mark, and Luke mentioned Bartholomew, but never Nathanael, whereas John mentioned Nathanael, but never Bartholomew. Since all four evangelists recorded only twelve main disciples, the conclusion that Bartholomew and Nathanael were the same man is inescapable. Nathanael means "gift of God," and Bartholomew means Bar Tolmai or "son of Tolmai."

The most extensive record of Nathanael is in the Gospel of John, whose author may have been a longtime friend. Nathanael clearly was a friend of Philip, who led him to Jesus during the Feast of Tabernacles in AD 29.

> Now Philip was from Bethsaida, the city of Andrew and Peter. Philip found Nathanael and said to him, "We have found him of whom Moses in the Law and also the prophets wrote, Jesus of Nazareth, the son of Joseph." Nathanael said to him, "Can anything good come out of Nazareth?" Philip said to him, "Come and see." Jesus saw Nathanael coming toward him and said of him, "Behold, an Israelite indeed, in whom there is no deceit!" Nathanael said to him, "How do you know me?" Jesus answered him, "Before Philip called you, when you were under the fig tree, I saw you." Nathanael answered him, "Rabbi, you are the Son of God! You are the King of Israel!" Jesus answered him, "Because I said to you, 'I saw you under the fig tree,' do you believe? You will see greater things than these." And he said to him, "Truly, truly, I say to you, you will see heaven opened, and the angels of God ascending and descending on the Son of Man." (John 1:44–51)

This promised vision of heaven opening was consciously reminiscent of Jacob's ladder. At Bethel, Jacob had a dream about a "ladder set up on the earth, and the top of it reached heaven. And the angels of God were ascending and descending on it. And the LORD stood above it" and blessed the promised land for Jacob (Gen 28:12–14). This image is of a bridge between God and man, and, of course, Jesus was that ultimate bridge.

Jesus' promised vision could not have referred to the transfiguration on Mount Hermon when Jesus appeared with Moses and Elijah. This occurred around April 29 of AD 31, 559 days or little more than eighteen months later, and Nathanael was not one of the three disciples Jesus invited to the top of the mountain. He brought only Peter, James, and John. Nathanael was one of the other nine disciples at the foot of Mount Hermon, trying unsuccessfully to exorcise a demon that could only come out with prayer and fasting. But Nathanael did witness Jesus' ascension from the Bethany side (east side) of the Mount of Olives. Two angels spoke to the apostles then (Acts 1:10–11), and Nathanael saw them with the rest. This occurred on Friday, Sabbath Eve, May 13, AD 33, the forty-first day after Resurrection Sunday (the Feast of Firstfruits). It was about forty-three months or more than three and a half years after Nathanael's first conversation with Jesus at Bethany beyond the Jordan. Of course, Jesus may just have been speaking figuratively, meaning that Nathanael would witness miraculous things, allowing him to peer into the kingdom of heaven.

Nathanael was a Galilean from Cana (John 21:2), the village where he witnessed Jesus at a wedding five days after their first encounter turn water into wine. If he was startled at his first encounter with Jesus when Jesus saw him under a fig tree from afar, he must have been further amazed to learn that Jesus was heading to a wedding in Cana, the very place he called home. When Nathanael asked if anything good could come from Nazareth, he probably did not especially despise the town. Since Nahum and Jonah both likely came from Galilee, he must have understood that good things could come from there. But since he, along with the priests of Jerusalem, expected the Messiah to come from Bethlehem, what he may have meant was that "the great good" Israel was expecting at this time (according to the prophecy of Daniel 9:24–27) would come not from Nazareth in Galilee but from Bethlehem in Judea (Mic 5:2). It is also possible that Nathanael was speaking in a humble sense, basically astonished that the Messiah would come from his neighborhood. He may essentially have been saying, "Is he really one of us?"

Nathanael was quick to identify Jesus with the Son of God, a remarkable insight in so short a time. This supports the idea that all Israel was in the grip of great Messianic expectations in the first century. Old Testament prophesies, especially Genesis 49:10 and Daniel 9:24–27, fixed the time for the Messiah's appearance in a tight window around the time of Jesus. Nathanael was on a hair trigger.

The Bible says no more of Nathanael Bartholomew except that he was one of the Twelve. It is evident that, with them, he was present in the upper room on Resurrection Sunday, was in the upper room with Thomas present on the following Monday, saw Jesus' ascension, helped choose Matthias to replace Judas, witnessed the birth of the church on the day of Pentecost in AD 33, and attended the Jerusalem Council in AD 49.

NATHANAEL BARTHOLOMEW'S MISSIONARY JOURNEYS

The apocryphal *Acts of Philip*[1] holds that Nathanael Bartholomew traveled to Hierapolis in Turkey with Philip. The two preached the gospel and healed and converted the wife of a Roman proconsul. The proconsul ordered the execution of the two apostles. Philip was crucified. Nathanael Bartholomew was crucified but was released. Hippolytus wrote: "Bartholomew, again, preached to the Indians, to whom he also gave the Gospel according to Matthew, and was crucified with his head downward, and was buried in Allanum [or Albanum], a town of the great Armenia."[2] So, the story is that Nathanael preached in India and then came back west to Armenia, carrying a copy of Matthew's Gospel. He arrived in Armenia about AD 66[3] and converted many Armenians.

NATHANAEL BARTHOLOMEW'S DEATH

The Armenian King Astyages, angry that Bartholomew converted his brother and that he refused to worship pagan gods, had him skinned alive. He then beheaded him, or crucified him, or perhaps both, in the city of Albanopolis (Derbent) on the western shore of the Caspian Sea in what is now Russia but in ancient times was known as Greater Armenia. Michelangelo portrayed Bartholomew in the *Last Judgment* in the Sistine Chapel with his skin hanging over his arm. He became the patron saint of tanners.

Bartholomew's tomb is in that part of Iran which once was Greater Armenia. He, along with Judas Thaddaeus, is a national patron saint of Armenia. Bartholomew's relics were allegedly transported to Lipari, near Sicily, in the seventh century, to Benevento, Italy, in AD 809, and to Rome in AD 983. Today they repose in the *Basilica di San Bartolomeo all'Isola* on the island in the River Tiber. Fragments of Bartholomew's skull were supposedly transferred to Frankfurt, Germany, while an arm is venerated in Canterbury Cathedral in England today.

---

1. "Acts of Philip."
2. Hippolytus, "List of the Apostles and Disciples."
3. "Saints Thaddaeus and Bartholomew," *The Armenian Prelacy*.

Thomas the Twin

THOMAS IS THE SEVENTH in the lists of the disciples. Although the Bible records little of Thomas, John's depiction of him in the Fourth Gospel delineates his character vividly. His name in Aramaic, Tauma, means twin, which is Didymos in Greek. Whose twin he was Scripture never reveals. Later apocryphal writings, in which Thomas figures prominently, say that Jesus was Thomas's twin, which is, of course, impossible.

The fourth-century church historian Eusebius refers to this apostle as Judas Thomas,[1] so his full name was Judas Thomas Didymus. There were five men named Judas among Jesus' disciples: (1) Judas Thomas Didymus (the Twin), (2) Judas Thaddaeus Lebbaeus, son of James, (3) Simon Judas, the Zealot, (4), Judas Iscariot, son of Simon, and (5) Jesus' half-brother Judas, who wrote the biblical book of Jude. Since there were four prominent contemporary men named Judas, this is probably why Thomas was called by a distinguishing nickname, "the Twin."

DEVOTED TO JESUS

Matthew, Mark, and Luke named Thomas as one of the Twelve, but only John recorded Thomas's role in the account of Lazarus, which occurred a mere three months before the Crucifixion.

> Now Jesus loved Martha and her sister and Lazarus. So, when he heard that Lazarus was ill, he stayed two days longer in the place where he was. Then after this he said to the disciples, "Let us go to Judea again." The disciples said to him, "Rabbi, the Jews were just now seeking to stone you, and are you going there again?" Jesus answered, "Are there not twelve hours in the day? If anyone walks in the day, he does not stumble, because he sees the light of this world. But if anyone walks in the night, he stumbles, because the light is not in him." After saying these things, he said to them, "Our friend Lazarus has fallen asleep, but I go to awaken him." The disciples said to him, "Lord, if he has fallen asleep, he will recover." Now Jesus had spoken of his death, but they thought that he meant taking rest in sleep. Then Jesus told them plainly,

---

1. Eusebius, *Church History* 1:13:10

"Lazarus has died, and for your sake I am glad that I was not there, so that you may believe. But let us go to him." So, Thomas, called the Twin, said to his fellow disciples, "Let us also go, that we may die with him." (John 11:5–16)

Was Thomas a fatalist? A pessimist? Or was he so zealous for Jesus that he would rather have died with the Master than to have lived without him? The ensuing passages show that Thomas was passionately devoted to his Lord. This dialogue occurred at the Last Supper:

[Jesus said], "Let not your hearts be troubled. Believe in God; believe also in me. In my Father's house are many rooms. If it were not so, would I have told you that I go to prepare a place for you? And if I go and prepare a place for you, I will come again and will take you to myself, that where I am you may be also. And you know the way to where I am going." Thomas said to him, "Lord, we do not know where you are going. How can we know the way?" Jesus said to him, "I am the way, and the truth, and the life. No one comes to the Father except through me. If you had known me, you would have known my Father also. From now on you do know him and have seen him." (John 14:1–7)

Thomas was ready to ask Jesus the bluntest of questions. But just as three months before Thomas was prepared to follow Jesus to Judea and probable death, here again Thomas implied that he wanted to know where Jesus was going so that he could follow him at any cost. Jesus' response to Thomas is one of the Lord's most quoted and beautiful sayings: Jesus is the way, and the truth, and the life, and no one comes to the Father but through him.

JESUS' POST-RESURRECTION APPEARANCE TO PETER

After his appearance to the women at the tomb, the next person Jesus appeared to after his resurrection was Peter (Mark 16:7; Luke 24:34; 1 Cor 15:5). Mark, Luke, and Paul all recorded that Jesus appeared singularly to Peter, but they gave no details of the encounter. Perhaps Peter kept the details private. Possibly this was because it was an emotional encounter, following Peter's triple denial of Jesus, Jesus' rebuking Peter silently with a piercing glance, and Peter's bitter weeping over his failure, all only two days before.

JESUS ON THE EMMAUS ROAD

Jesus next appeared to two followers, one named Cleophas, probably Jesus' uncle,[2] on the road the Emmaus, seven miles northwest of Jerusalem, in the late afternoon of Resurrection Sunday. As Cleophas and his companion broke bread with Jesus at sunset, they recognized him, and he vanished from their presence. They hurried back

2. See "Relationships in Jesus' Community" in the Appendix.

to Jerusalem to meet the disciples, only to find them in a state of great excitement, for the risen Lord had already appeared to Peter.

JESUS' FIRST APPEARANCE IN THE UPPER ROOM

As they were speaking, Jesus appeared to the ten disciples, to Cleophas and his companion, and to others assembled in the upper room that Resurrection Sunday evening. Thomas must have just left the room after the arrival of Cleophas and his companion but before the appearance of Jesus because Luke recorded that (1) Cleophas and his companion met the Eleven including Thomas (Luke 24:33) and others assembled with them in the upper room, and John recorded that (2) when Jesus appeared, Thomas was absent, and there were only the Ten (John 20:24). Why did Thomas leave the upper room after hearing Jesus had appeared to Peter but before Jesus arrived? Reading between the lines, it sounds like Thomas was overcome with emotion and either needed time alone or went to look for Jesus. Here are the passages of Scripture describing this momentous post-resurrection appearance of Jesus.

> On the evening of that day, the first day of the week, the doors being locked where the disciples were for fear of the Jews, Jesus came and stood among them and said to them, "Peace be with you." When he had said this, he showed them his hands and his side. Then the disciples were glad when they saw the Lord. (John 20:19–20)

> As they were talking about these things, Jesus himself stood among them, and said to them, "Peace to you!" But they were startled and frightened and thought they saw a spirit. And he said to them, "Why are you troubled, and why do doubts arise in your hearts? See my hands and my feet, that it is I myself. Touch me and see. For a spirit does not have flesh and bones as you see that I have." And when he had said this, he showed them his hands and his feet. And while they still disbelieved for joy and were marveling, he said to them, "Have you anything here to eat?" They gave him a piece of broiled fish, and he took it and ate before them. (Luke 24:36–43)

Notice that, just like Thomas, the ten disciples doubted. Only after Jesus showed them his hands and his side were they glad to see the Lord. Yet even then they disbelieved until Jesus proved his physical reality by eating a piece of broiled fish.

JESUS' SECOND APPEARANCE IN THE UPPER ROOM

The following Monday, Jesus appeared again to the Eleven Disciples in the upper room with Thomas present (John 20:26). The most famous account of Thomas is this, which earned him the nickname "Doubting Thomas." It occurred eight days after Resurrection Sunday, on Monday, April 11, AD 33, in the upper room.

> Now Thomas, one of the Twelve, called the Twin, was not with them when Jesus came. So the other disciples told him, "We have seen the Lord." But he said to them, "Unless I see in his hands the mark of the nails and place my finger into the mark of the nails, and place my hand into his side, I will never believe." Eight days later, his disciples were inside again, and Thomas was with them. Although the doors were locked, Jesus came and stood among them and said, "Peace be with you." Then he said to Thomas, "Put your finger here, and see my hands; and put out your hand and place it in my side. Do not disbelieve but believe." Thomas answered him, "My Lord and my God!" Jesus said to him, "Have you believed because you have seen me? Blessed are those who have not seen and yet have believed." (John 20:24–29)

Although this account has earned Thomas the reputation of a skeptic, really the passage affirms that Thomas was a profound believer. The other disciples were glad only after Jesus showed them his hands and his side. Thomas's request to see these proofs of Jesus' resurrection was no different than the proofs the other disciples had required. They were just as doubtful as Thomas was. Furthermore, Thomas, the man of passionate impulse, made the greatest possible theological statement in response to these proofs. He cried, "My Lord and my God!" Thomas grasped the miraculous fact that Jesus was both the Messiah and *theanthropos*, the God-Man.

Jesus not only accepted the title of Lord and God, but he also commended Thomas for believing and commended even more those who would believe in his deity without seeing the physical proofs of it. Jesus could only have accepted worship as God if he were God; if he were not, accepting honor due to God alone would make Jesus a blasphemer or insane. In other passages of Scripture, we see that God-fearing men and angels never accepted worship due only to their Creator.

> When Peter entered, Cornelius met him and fell down at his feet and worshiped him. But Peter lifted him up, saying, "Stand up; I too am a man." (Acts 10:25–26)

> Then I fell down at his feet to worship him, but he said to me, "You must not do that! I am a fellow servant with you and your brothers who hold to the testimony of Jesus. Worship God." (Rev 19:10)

> I, John, am the one who heard and saw these things. And when I heard and saw them, I fell down to worship at the feet of the angel who showed them to me, but he said to me, "You must not do that! I am a fellow servant with you and your brothers the prophets, and with those who keep the words of this book. Worship God." (Rev 22:8–9)

FINAL APPEARANCES IN SCRIPTURE

John mentioned Thomas in the Fourth Gospel one more time, when Jesus met seven of the Twelve on the shore of the Sea of Galilee after his resurrection.

> After this Jesus revealed himself again to the disciples by the Sea of Tiberias, and he revealed himself in this way. Simon Peter, Thomas (called the Twin), Nathanael of Cana in Galilee, the sons of Zebedee, and two others of his disciples were together. Simon Peter said to them, "I am going fishing." They said to him, "We will go with you." They went out and got into the boat, but that night they caught nothing. Just as day was breaking, Jesus stood on the shore; yet the disciples did not know that it was Jesus. Jesus said to them, "Children, do you have any fish?" They answered him, "No." He said to them, "Cast the net on the right side of the boat, and you will find some." So, they cast it, and now they were not able to haul it in, because of the quantity of fish. (John 21:1–6)

The final direct biblical reference to Thomas, by Luke, depicts him present once again in the upper room at Jerusalem, with the surviving Eleven of the Twelve, along with Mary, the mother of Jesus, as well as with Jesus' brothers (probably James and Judas and possibly the two unnamed others). This was the day of the ascension, Sunday, May 13, AD 33.

> Then they returned to Jerusalem from the mount called Olivet, which is near Jerusalem, a Sabbath day's journey away. And when they had entered, they went up to the Upper Room, where they were staying, Peter and John and James and Andrew, Philip and Thomas, Bartholomew and Matthew, James the son of Alphaeus and Simon the Zealot and Judas the son of James. All these with one accord were devoting themselves to prayer, together with the women and Mary the mother of Jesus, and his brothers. (Acts 1:12–14)

Scripture tells us no more of Thomas, directly. But, as one of the original Twelve, he was at the meeting to choose Matthias as a replacement for Judas, he witnessed the birth of the church on the day of Pentecost in AD 33, and he participated in the Jerusalem Council in AD 49.

GNOSTICS

There is a body of apocryphal literature about Thomas. The gnostics wrote much of it. The gnostics were people who believed that, in order to free oneself from the material world, one needed *gnosis*, or special knowledge. The gnostics fraudulently used Thomas's name as the supposed author of books that handed down secret teachings, allowing only the elect to know the truths of God. What worse representative could the gnostics possibly have chosen? Thomas was the man who was ready to let the Jews stone him with Jesus; wanted to follow Jesus wherever he was going; wanted physical proof that Jesus was alive after seeing him die; and confidently proclaimed that Jesus was Lord and God. Thomas, like Peter, was one of the most outspoken, blunt apostles. In fact, none of the apostles was especially secretive or esoteric. They were not gnostics.

GNOSTICS, AGNOSTICS, ATHEISTS, AND THE PROOF OF GOD

What is the difference between gnostics, agnostics, and atheists? An atheist says that God does not exist. He is sure about that. An agnostic says that he has insufficient knowledge to tell whether God exists or not. He not only thinks that he does not know, but he also thinks nobody can know. If either theism or atheism is true, that is, if it is possible to know whether God does or does not exist, then agnosticism cannot be true.

Agnostics try to challenge atheists by asking them to prove the non-existence of God. They know that proving the non-existence of anything is philosophically impossible. There is no such thing as nothing, for nothing, to be something, would need to exist and therefore could not be nothing. It is, however, possible to solve the atheistic and agnostic puzzles by proving the existence of God on the basis of pure logic.

GOD IS A FACT

The existence of God can be proven by considering four ontological theses. Of the origin of the universe, only four things can be true: (1) it does not really exist. It is an illusion; (2) it always existed from eternity past; (3) it created itself; or (4) it was created.

If the universe is an illusion, then you do not exist, since you are part of the universe. But if you are thinking that you do not exist, you are thinking. Since to think you must exist, you exist. René Descartes summarized this by saying, "*Cogito ergo sum*—I think, therefore I am."

Isaac Newton's second law of thermodynamics and all scientific observations tell us that the universe is "winding down." If the universe existed from eternity past, it would have gone extinct an eternity ago.

To create itself, the universe would have to exist before it existed to bring itself into existence. Nothing comes from nothing, as Parmenides observed.[3]

The only remaining possibility is that the universe was created, and if it was created, it necessarily had a Creator. The Creator, like the universe, cannot: (1) be an illusion, since an illusion cannot create a reality; (2) be created, because then the Creator would need a Creator, who would then need a Creator, who would then need a Creator, *ad infinitum*, posing the problem of infinite regression; or (3) have created

---

3. Parmenides of Elea was a fifth-century-BC pre-Socratic Greek philosopher. This dictum later became famous in Latin, articulated by Lucretius in *De Rerum Natura*: "*Ex nihilo nihil fit.*"

itself, because nothing comes from nothing. Therefore, the Creator must be eternally self-existent and un-created.

The Creator is the unmoved prime mover, the uncaused first cause. All effects have causes, but not all causes are the effects of some other cause. The first cause (the Creator) has no cause. All effects emanate from him. The first cause is God, the Necessary Being: if anything exists, God must exist. Since this is logically demonstrable, it is possible to know this, so agnosticism is invalid.

Since this logically proves the necessary existence of God, atheism is invalid. Since all that is required to know this is logic, not some secret knowledge, Gnosticism is invalid. Since logic alone produces this conclusion, neither faith nor Scripture are needed to prove that God is a fact.

THOMAS'S MARTYRDOM IN INDIA

While gnostic books, like the *Gospel of Thomas*[4] and the *Acts of Thomas*[5], are obviously late forgeries (one has only to read a few pages to see how weak they are compared to the majestic style of the Bible), they may contain germs of truth: one or two germs, but not an epidemic. According to the *Acts of Thomas*, a book possibly written in Edessa, Syria, around AD 200, the apostles divided the world between them so that each might evangelize a region. India fell to Thomas.

According to this tale, after AD 49 (the Council of Jerusalem) an Indian envoy named Abban took Thomas to the wedding feast of king named Gundafor who reigned in India at that time. Gundafor supposedly entrusted money to Thomas to build a palace, but the apostle spent it on the poor instead. Gundafor imprisoned Thomas, but he escaped by a miracle (reminiscent of Peter's and Paul's escapes from jail), which inspired Gundafor to become a Christian.

Thomas then preached throughout the subcontinent until he came to the city of a certain King Mazdai. He converted Mazdai's queen, Tertia, and their son, Vazan. Supposedly Tertia's (mis)understanding of the Christian faith led her to take a vow of celibacy, which infuriated her husband. Mazdai condemned Thomas to death. Four of the king's soldiers led him to a hill outside the city, where they pierced him with spears. They buried Thomas in the tomb of their kings, but later his remains were moved to the West.

There is another tradition, still believed in India today, that Thomas made missionary journeys as far south as Mylapore, near Madras, and suffered martyrdom there. Hippolytus wrote: "Thomas preached to the Parthians, Medes, Persians, Hyrcanians, Bactrians, and Margians, and was thrust through in the four members of his body with a pine spear at Calamene, the city of India, and was buried there."[6]

4. Mark M. Mattison, ed., "Gospel of Thomas."
5. M. R. James, trans., "The Acts of Thomas."
6. Hippolytus, "List of the Apostles and Disciples."

Biographies of the Apostles

The story behind the story may simply be that Thomas preached in Persia and India and, being an apostle, did what apostles did, namely, converted many, healed the sick and lame, raised the dead, and suffered martyrdom for his politically incorrect testimony. If so, he traveled an astonishing four thousand miles. When Portuguese explorers first discovered the Malabar Coast of India in the 1500s, they found, to their amazement, communities of Christians.

THOMAS'S RELICS

The relics of Thomas purportedly reached Edessa (in modern Turkey) in the fourth century. As the Muslim Turks conquered more and more of the Byzantine Empire, Thomas's bones were taken to the Greek island of Chios in 1258 and finally to Ortona, in Italy, where they allegedly rest today.

This fourth-century hymn by Saint Ephraim[7] of Syria commemorated the missionary work of Thomas in India and the eventual transfer of his relics to the city of Edessa in Greater Armenia:

On Thomas the Apostle

Blessed are you, Thomas, the Twin, in your deeds . . .
Renowned is your name among the apostles . . .
A land of people dark fell to your lot that these in white robes
You should clothe and cleanse by baptism.
A tainted land Thomas has purified . . .
The solar ray from the great orb,
Your grateful dawn India's painful darkness dispels.
You, the great lamp, one among the Twelve,
With oil from the Cross replenished,
You flood India's dark night with light.
Blessed are you whom the Great King has sent,
That India to his One-Begotten you should espouse . . .
Blessed are you, O Thrice-Blessed City [Edessa]
That has acquired this pearl.[8]

Keeping the tradition alive, a 1972 an Indian postage stamp commemorated Thomas's mission to India.

---

7. Saint Ephraim was born around AD 306 in Syria. When his home came under Persian rule in AD 363, Ephraim and many Christians moved to Edessa in Asia Minor (Greater Armenia). Ephraim died there in AD 373 while ministering to plague victims. He wrote over one thousand poems. His descriptions of heaven and hell may have inspired Dante.

8. Ephraim, "On Thomas the Apostle."

Matthew Levi, the Tax Collector

MATTHEW IS THE EIGHTH in the list of the apostles. Matthew means "Gift of God" in Hebrew. Levi and Matthew are the same man, a tax collector. Jesus may have conferred the affectionate nickname of Matthew, "gift of God," on Levi, because even though he was a despised tax collector, he would leave all to follow only the Lord and would write an inspired and beautiful Gospel. This may explain why only Mark and Luke called him Levi, his real name, while Matthew enjoyed referring to himself by the nickname which Jesus probably gave him.

Matthew was a tax collector at Capernaum under Herod Antipas, tetrarch over Galilee and Peraea. This king was the second husband of Herodias and was the stepfather of Salome, who demanded the head of John the Baptist on a platter. Since Matthew lived in Capernaum, he probably was Galilean. He was a Hebrew, but the Pharisees despised him, as they despised all tax collectors. Matthew's friends were reprobates like himself, as indicated by the guests he invited to the party after being called by Jesus. If Jesus had been running for public office, he could hardly have done worse than to consort with the people he so often did: gentiles, adulterous women, lepers, paralytics, and tax collectors.

The account of Matthew's calling in Matthew, Mark, and Luke are harmonized as follows.

CALLING MATTHEW

After casting demons into the swine in Gadara, on the eastern shore of the Sea of Galilee, Jesus entered a boat and crossed back over to his own city, Capernaum. After healing a paralytic, he went to Peter's house. When he next left the house, he passed by the tax booth and saw the tax collector, Matthew Levi, the son of Alphaeus. Jesus said to him, "Follow me." Leaving everything, Matthew rose and followed him. Jesus called Matthew after calling the four fisherman, sometime between June and July AD 30, 288 days or more than nine months after his baptism in the Jordan.

MATTHEW'S FEAST

Levi hosted a great feast for Jesus at his house. There was a large company of tax collectors, sinners, and others reclining at table with Jesus and his disciples. The Pharisees and their scribes grumbled at Jesus' disciples, saying "Why do you eat and drink with tax collectors and sinners?" Jesus answered them, "Those who are well have no need of a physician, but those who are sick. I have not come to call the righteous but sinners to repentance" (Mark 2:17; Matt 9:12–13; Luke 5:31–32). Apparently, the scribes and the Pharisees were not sufficiently offended to refrain from attending Matthew's sumptuous feast; they simply complained that tax collectors and sinners were also invited.

MATTHEW'S RELATIONSHIPS

Since Matthew and James the Less were both sons of a man named Alphaeus, Matthew may have been the brother of James the Less and thus may have been Jesus' cousin. Also, Simon the Zealot may have been Jesus' cousin, the brother of Matthew Levi and of James the Less, and the bridegroom of the wedding at Cana.[1] If so, Matthew certainly would have been a black sheep. That might have made Matthew's prompt response to Jesus' call even more understandable. Matthew may have been inwardly grieving for some time at his sinful life. He was a Levite serving the temple of Rome rather than the temple of God. He may have yearned to be reconciled with his family. If Simon the Zealot were the bridegroom at the wedding of Cana, he may also have been related to Matthew,[2] who, as the outcast of the family, would not have been invited. If Matthew were Simon's brother, this would have been especially painful. In any event, in so small a community as Galilee, Matthew would have heard of the miracle of Jesus turning water into wine.

ROMAN TAXES

Rome's method of collecting taxes was to engage locals who knew which people had money and where they kept it. Rome divided each province into tax districts. Local entrepreneurs bid for the office of tax collector. The winner made a contract to collect a certain sum of money for Rome, and whatever he collected above and beyond that was his commission. Rome did not care how much it was. A chief tax collector, like Zacchaeus in Luke 19, owned the contract for his region, Jericho. He employed others, like Matthew, to collect taxes in the villages. Matthew was not a chief tax collector, so in his district, Galilee, he would have been subordinate to someone like Zacchaeus.

Rome exacted three kinds of tax: a land tax, a head tax, and a customs tax of 2 to 5 percent on the value of goods imported to or exported from a province. Tax

---

1. See "Were Matthew and James the Less Cousins?" in the Appendices.
2. See "Relationships in Jesus' Community" in the Appendices.

collectors set up booths at city gates to assess merchandise coming to market. Fishermen, like Peter, Andrew, James, and John, would pay a customs tax on exports of dried fish from the Sea of Galilee to Syria, which was an important local revenue stream. In fact, they likely paid such taxes directly to Matthew, who was a collector in their tax district. Matthew likely had wrenched money from them unjustly for years. So they probably knew and disliked Matthew personally. While following Jesus the disciples might often have reminisced about those bad old days.

The people hated tax collectors as they hated thieves. Under Roman law, a subject of the empire was guilty until proven innocent. All a tax collector had to do was report a person for tax fraud to Herod or Rome, and the police state would allow or even help the tax collectors to take almost anything they liked by extortion. They could rape wives or daughters, sell children into slavery, and seize property or money. From a distance of twenty centuries, we tend to romanticize ancient Rome. Even the word "romanticize," a word that comes from the name Rome, reveals how we gild Rome's lily. A romance is "a Roman story." But in Jesus' day, Rome was a giant, heartless mafia. If Caesar Augustus decided that all the world should be taxed, he could not care less if it meant uprooting a simple carpenter and his pregnant wife and forcing them to journey three days to Bethlehem to be registered and pay up. Jesus reflected the popular loathing of tax collectors when he said:

> If your brother sins against you, go, and tell him his fault, between you and him alone. If he listens to you, you have gained your brother. But if he does not listen, take one or two others along with you, that every charge may be established by the evidence of two or three witnesses. If he refuses to listen to them, tell it to the Church. And if he refuses to listen even to the Church, let him be to you as a Gentile and a tax collector. (Matt 18:15–17)

Matthew, the tax collector, in an act of faithful humility, recorded this teaching of Jesus. He might have omitted it if he had been more defensive and less humble. The Pharisees thought uncleanness was conveyed by touch or association. To enter the houses of tax collectors, sinners, and gentiles was therefore taboo. "Now the tax collectors and sinners were all drawing near to hear him. And the Pharisees and the scribes grumbled, saying, 'This man receives sinners and eats with them'" (Luke 15:1–2). We can learn something about Matthew's profession through Luke's account of the tax collector Zacchaeus.

> He entered Jericho and was passing through. And there was a man named Zacchaeus. He was a chief tax collector and was rich. And he was seeking to see who Jesus was, but on account of the crowd he could not, because he was small of stature. So, he ran on ahead and climbed up into a sycamore tree to see him, for he was about to pass that way. And when Jesus came to the place, he looked up and said to him, "Zacchaeus, hurry and come down, for I must stay at your house today." So he hurried and came down and received him

joyfully. And when they saw it, they all grumbled, "he has gone in to be the guest of a man who is a sinner." And Zacchaeus stood and said to the Lord, "Behold, Lord, the half of my goods I give to the poor. And if I have defrauded anyone of anything, I restore it fourfold." And Jesus said to him, "Today salvation has come to this house, since he also is a son of Abraham. For the Son of Man came to seek and to save the lost." (Luke 19:1–10)

Note that Zacchaeus said, "If I have defrauded anyone of anything, I will give him back four times as much." Jesus must have smiled. There really can have been no "if" about it, or Zacchaeus would not have said this. Zacchaeus had defrauded many of much. And since Jesus pronounced Zacchaeus was saved, it is likely that Zacchaeus, a man of numbers, was using an exact formula.

The legal restitution for theft under Mosaic law was to pay back double. "If a man gives to his neighbor money or goods to keep safe, and it is stolen from the man's house, then, if the thief is found, he shall pay double" (Exod 22:7). So, we may deduce that Zacchaeus, as a tax collector, was particularly rapacious. If Zacchaeus realized that to repent properly of his theft, he would have had to pay back four times what he had stolen, that means his customary practice must have been to seize twice as much as he should have, because the basis for repayment was only his illegitimate gains, not his legitimate collection. For example: if a taxpayer owed Rome $100, and it would have been normal for the tax collector to exact $150, keeping $50 for himself, what Zacchaeus is implying is that his practice was to collect twice a customary commission of $50, that is, an extra $50. So, Zacchaeus's tax burden on the taxpayer would have been $200. Rome would have received $100, and Zacchaeus would have kept $100 for himself. Now, if Zacchaeus was offering to pay back fourfold his excess charge, he was offering to pay back 4 x $50 = $200. Zacchaeus was actually offering to go "in the hole."

Paying back fourfold meant that Zacchaeus was sincere in his desire to gain the approval and forgiveness of Jesus and of the grumbling Pharisees. No wonder Jesus said that salvation had come that day to Zacchaeus's house. Zacchaeus really was not counting on earthly treasure but laying up treasure in heaven. He was ready to stop serving two masters, God and Mammon, and to begin serving God alone. Jesus' approval, of course, was based on Zacchaeus's heart and on the free gift of grace, not on a legalistic formula, but Zacchaeus could not have comprehended that yet.

THE TEMPLE TAX

Matthew, keenly interested in taxes and finance, is the only Gospel writer to record this unusual account:

When they came to Capernaum, the collectors of the two-drachma tax went up to Peter and said, "Does your teacher not pay the tax?" He said, "Yes." And when he came into the house, Jesus spoke to him first, saying, "What do you think, Simon? From whom do kings of the earth take toll or tax? From their sons or from others?" And when he said, "From others," Jesus said to him, "Then the sons are free. However, not to give offense to them, go to the sea and cast a hook and take the first fish that comes up, and when you open its mouth, you will find a shekel. Take that and give it to them for me and for yourself." (Matt 17:24–27)

MATTHEW'S MINISTRY

So, Matthew was probably a rank below Zacchaeus and spent his days in a tax booth in Capernaum, near Peter's big house, waiting to collect a toll on any goods transported past him as they entered or left the region ruled by Herod Antipas. Jesus' words "Follow me!" must have pierced Matthew's soul, for he chose to leave wealth for poverty in an instant. This must have been complicated. His boss, the chief tax collector of the district, must have been apoplectic. From Luke's words, it sounds as though he left his booth, records, and cash without a backward glance.

Without his official role as tax collector, Matthew had no protection but that of Jesus. He could no longer appeal to Rome's or Herod's henchmen to shield him from the hatred of the populace. There must have been many neighbors and relatives who would have loved to settle scores with Matthew in a dark alley. Jesus' protection would prove eternally effective, but how could Matthew have known that in an instant? Yet such was the power of Jesus' call.

When Matthew invited Jesus to a great feast, he invited Pharisees and scribes as well as his tax collector friends. He wanted reconciliation. And he was evangelizing already. The religious leaders went. The food and wine were free and probably good. But they grumbled about the sinful company to the disciples, who apparently did not know what to say.

At this stage, the only disciples Jesus had called to full-time ministry were Peter, Andrew, James, and John. Probably they felt awkward and embarrassed about the inclusion of Matthew. Even though James and John may have been cousins of Matthew, as men in the fishing business, they doubtless knew and had hated Matthew as the obnoxious collector of customs duties in the past. But Jesus was perfectly comfortable. He replied on behalf of the disciples to the Pharisees in his usual, incontrovertible way, saying, "Those who are well have no need of a physician, but those who are sick. I have not come to call the righteous but sinners to repentance" (Mark 2:17; Matt 9:12–13; Luke 5:31–32). Jesus' elegant answer rebuked the Pharisees while at the same time embracing the sinners. He did not care about a person's reputation. He had come to save the outcast and the unloved. This is what the Pharisees and scribes should have done.

Matthew must have felt proud, but also chagrined. By inviting Jesus to his house, he had exposed the Lord to the criticism of the Pharisees and scribes. He had shamed a guest, something deeply wounding to any host in the Middle East. The disciples must gradually have felt drawn to Matthew as they saw the Master eat with him, laugh with him, and touch him kindly.

Matthew followed Jesus throughout his earthly ministry, witnessing the crucifixion and the resurrection. He was in prayer in the upper room on the evening of Resurrection Sunday, on April 3, AD 33.

> Then they returned to Jerusalem from the mount called Olivet, which is near Jerusalem, a Sabbath day's journey away. And when they had entered, they went up to the Upper Room, where they were staying, Peter and John and James and Andrew, Philip and Thomas, Bartholomew and Matthew, James the son of Alphaeus and Simon the Zealot and Judas the son of James. All these with one accord were devoting themselves to prayer, together with the women and Mary the mother of Jesus, and his brothers. (Acts 1:12–14)

As one of the Twelve, Matthew was in the upper room with Thomas present on the Monday after Resurrection Sunday; he helped choose Matthias, witnessed Jesus' ascension, and saw the birth of the church on the day of Pentecost in AD 33.

Irenaeus states that Matthew preached the gospel among the Jews. Clement of Alexandria claims he did this for fifteen years after the resurrection, or until AD 48. Matthew, with the surviving eleven apostles, was at the Council of Jerusalem in AD 49. After the Council, Matthew would heed the call of the Great Commission to evangelize other nations, which Eusebius says he did, but not before giving his Gospel in Hebrew to the Jews, thus compensating "those whom he was obliged to leave for the loss of his presence."[3] Thus, Matthew probably composed his Gospel before or in AD 49.

MATTHEW'S DEATH

Matthew may have evangelized an area south of the Caspian Sea called Ethiopia (not the Ethiopia in Africa).[4] Some writers claim that he evangelized in Macedonia and Parthia (Persia).[5] Ancient tradition suggests that Matthew died a martyr; however, there is disagreement as to whether he was burned, stoned, or beheaded. Hippolytus says he died in Hierees, in Parthia, near the Caspian Sea.[6]

MATTHEW'S GOSPEL

The Gospel of Matthew is inspired, that is, written through the Holy Spirit. Jerome says that he wrote it in Hebrew for the benefit of the Jews in Judea and that afterward

---

3. Eusebius, *Church History* 3:24:6.
4. Jerome, *On Illustrious Men*.
5. Davies and Allen, *Matthew 1-7*.
6. Hippolytus, "List of the Apostles and Disciples."

it was translated into Greek. He also says that up to Jerome's day a copy of Matthew was preserved in the library of Caesarea. He cites, as evidence of its composition in Hebrew, that whenever Matthew quotes the Old Testament, he follows the Hebrew Bible, not the Septuagint, which was the popular Greek translation of the Bible in Matthew's day.[7] Matthew quoted the Old Testament ninety-nine times, more than the other three Gospels put together.

Matthew opened his Gospel with a genealogy of Jesus, meaning to prove that Jesus is the Christ. Luke's Gospel contains a different genealogy of Jesus. Critics often contend that this represents a contradiction in Scripture and proves that the Bible contains errors. This is untrue. The two genealogies are both legitimate and accurate ancestries of Jesus. There is no contradiction whatever.

Skeptics claim that Matthew's genealogy is incomplete. In fact, his genealogy deliberately omits certain people for both biblical and symbolic reasons. Another critique is that Jesus cannot be King of the Jews because Matthew wrote that Jesus was descended from King Jeconiah, whom God had cursed. In fact, Jesus was not descended from King Jeconiah, but from another Jeconiah, the eldest son of King Josiah, and that Jeconiah was not cursed. One last challenge is that Jesus cannot be both king and priest, since kings of Judah were always of the tribe of Judah, and priests were always of the tribe of Levi. However, as the legal son of Joseph, son of David (Matt 1:20), Jesus was also a son of David. The sons of David were not only kings, but they were also priests (2 Sam 8:18). Since Mary was related to Zechariah and Elizabeth, who were both Levites (Luke 1:5), Jesus also descended from Levi on his mother's side. (Mary may have had one parent who was of Levi and another who was of Judah, or she may have been a pure Levite). Therefore, Jesus was qualified to be both king (Matt 2:2; Rev 19:16) and priest, on the order of Melchizedek (Heb 7:17).[8]

If one had to spend the rest of one's life on a desert island and could choose only one book to take along, the Gospel of Matthew would be a wonderful choice. Matthew's words adorn God's message with inspired beauty in many passages. One of the loveliest, surely, is this: "Go therefore and make disciples of all nations, baptizing them in the name of the Father and of the Son and of the Holy Spirit, teaching them to observe all that I have commanded you. And behold, I am with you always, to the end of the age" (Matt 28:19–20).

---

7. Jerome, *On Illustrious Men*.

8. For a full resolution of these critiques, see "The Genealogies of Matthew and Luke" in the Appendices.

James, Son of Alphaeus, "the Less"

JAMES WAS THE NINTH in the lists of the apostles. There are three prominent men named James in the New Testament: (1) James, the son of Zebedee, known as James the Great or Elder, possibly the father of Judas Thaddaeus Lebbaeus; (2) James, the son of Alphaeus, the Less or the Younger, of the original Twelve, possibly the brother of Matthew Levi; and (3) James, the half-brother of Jesus, named "James the Just," leader of the Jerusalem church after Christ's resurrection and author of the New Testament book of James.[1]

No one really knows why James was called "the Less." Theories are that he was: (1) younger than James, the son of Zebedee; (2) shorter than James, the son of Zebedee; or (3) less famous than James, the son of Zebedee. An extrabiblical tradition holds that James the Less resembled Jesus, and that for this reason Judas Iscariot promised to kiss Jesus to identify him in the Garden of Gethsemane, so the soldiers would be sure to arrest the right man. If Jesus and James the Less were cousins, there may well have been a family resemblance. Anyway, Jesus' entire group, apart possibly from Judas Iscariot, was composed of young Galileans of similar age, accents, customs, and appearance. This, and the dark of night, in an age before the invention of eyeglasses, make it easy to see why Judas would need to help the soldiers to recognize Jesus.

RELATIONSHIPS

Since Matthew and James the Less were both sons of a man named Alphaeus, Matthew may have been the brother of James the Less and thus may have been Jesus' cousin. Also, Simon the Zealot may have been Jesus' cousin, the brother of Matthew Levi and of James the Less, and the bridegroom at the wedding at Cana.[2]

---

1. See "Relationships in Jesus' Community" in the Appendices.
2. See "Were Matthew and James the Less Cousins?" in the Appendices.

JAMES'S MISSION

As one of the Twelve, James the Less was present in the upper room on Resurrection Sunday evening and in the upper room with Thomas present on the following Monday; he witnessed Jesus' ascension; he was at the meeting to choose Matthias as a replacement for Judas; he saw the birth of the church on the day of Pentecost in AD 33; and he attended the Jerusalem Council in AD 49. Nothing else is known for certain about his life and ministry. Tradition holds that he brought the gospel to Judea, Armenia, Greece, and Egypt.

THE DEATH OF JAMES THE LESS

Reportedly James died a martyr in Ostrakine, in Lower (northern) Egypt, where he was preaching. His symbol is a carpenter's saw because his body supposedly was sawed to pieces to verify his death after his crucifixion. Alternatively, Hippolytus wrote: "And James the son of Alphaeus, when preaching in Jerusalem, was stoned to death by the Jews, and was buried there beside the Temple."[3]

---

3. Hippolytus, "List of the Apostles and Disciples."

Judas Thaddaeus Lebbaeus, "Dear Heart"

JUDAS THADDAEUS LEBBAEUS is variously the tenth or the eleventh in the lists of the disciples. There were five men named Judas among Jesus' disciples: (1) Judas Thomas Didymus (the Twin), (2) Judas Thaddaeus Lebbaeus, son of James, (3) Simon Judas, the Zealot, (4) Judas Iscariot, son of Simon, and (5) Jesus' half-brother Judas, who wrote the biblical book of Jude. Since no Christian writer would wish to confuse Judas, the betrayer of Jesus, with a faithful apostle, it is not surprising that the other two Judases were better known by their nicknames, Thaddaeus, Thomas, and Simon. Thaddaeus and Lebbaeus both mean "beloved" or "near to the heart"—"dear heart"— in Greek and Aramaic, respectively.

Luke identified Judas Thaddaeus as Judas of James (Luke 6:16), so he was possibly the son of James, the son of Zebedee, and thus perhaps Jesus' second cousin.[1] Apart from the lists of disciples, John's is the only Gospel to give an account of Judas Thaddaeus in Scripture:

> [Jesus said], "Whoever has my commandments and keeps them, he it is who loves me. And he who loves me will be loved by my Father, and I will love him and manifest myself to him." Judas (not Iscariot) said to him, "Lord, how is it that you will manifest yourself to us, and not to the world?" Jesus answered him, "If anyone loves me, he will keep my word, and my Father will love him, and we will come to him and make our home with him. Whoever does not love me does not keep my words. And the word that you hear is not mine but the Father's who sent me. These things I have spoken to you while I am still with you. But the Helper, the Holy Spirit, whom the Father will send in my name, he will teach you all things and bring to your remembrance all that I have said to you." (John 14:21–26)

This is the only speaking part in Scripture ascribed to Judas Thaddaeus Lebbaeus, and it is the last question any disciple asked Jesus before his arrest in Gethsemane. As one of the eleven surviving apostles, Judas Thaddaeus was present in the upper room on Resurrection Sunday, was in the upper room with Thomas present on the following Monday, witnessed Jesus' ascension, helped choose Matthias as a replacement for

---

1. See "Relationships in Jesus' Community" in the Appendices.

Judas, saw the birth of the church on the day of Pentecost in AD 33, and attended the Jerusalem Council in AD 49. Tradition holds that he brought the gospel to Armenia in AD 43.[2] Eusebius, the fourth-century church historian, describes his Armenian mission as follows.

JESUS' LETTER AND THADDAEUS'S MISSION TO EDESSA

The miracles and divinity of Christ were reported in countries far away from Judea. King Abgarus, who ruled Greater Armenia beyond the Euphrates, was afflicted with a terrible disease that no physician could cure. He sent a message to Jesus, begging him to come heal him. Eusebius, who claimed that the letter was preserved in the archives of Edessa, the capital of Greater Armenia, down to his day, cites the entire letter, translated from the Syriac language.

> Abgarus, ruler of Edessa, to Jesus the excellent Savior who has appeared in the country of Jerusalem, greeting. I have heard the reports of you and of your cures as performed by you without medicines or herbs. For it is said that you make the blind to see and the lame to walk, that you cleanse lepers and cast out impure spirits and demons, and that you heal those afflicted with lingering disease, and raise the dead. And having heard all these things concerning you, I have concluded that one of two things must be true: either you are God and having come down from heaven you do these things, or else you, who does these things, are the Son of God. I have therefore written to you to ask you if you would take the trouble to come to me and heal the disease which I have. For I have heard that the Jews are murmuring against you and are plotting to injure you. But I have a very small yet noble city which is great enough for us both." The answer of Jesus to the ruler Abgarus by the courier Ananias: "Blessed are you who have believed in me without having seen me. For it is written concerning me, that they who have seen me will not believe in me, and that they who have not seen me will believe and be saved. But in regard to what you have written me, that I should come to you, it is necessary for me to fulfill all things here for which I have been sent, and after I have fulfilled them thus to be taken up again to him that sent me. But after I have been taken up, I will send to you one of my disciples, that he may heal your disease and give life to you and yours."[3]

MISSION TO ARMENIA

After the resurrection and ascension, Thomas urged Thaddaeus to go to Edessa. There Thaddaeus began, in the power of God, to heal every disease and infirmity, causing

2. "Saints Thaddaeus and Bartholomew," *The Armenian Prelacy*.
3. Eusebius, *Church History* 1:13:1–20.

all to wonder. When Abgarus heard of this, he suspected that this was the disciple Jesus had promised him. Abgarus summoned Thaddaeus, and as soon as he appeared before the king, Abgarus saw a vision and prostrated himself before the apostle. Everyone at court was astonished, because they could not see the vision, which appeared to Abgarus alone. The king asked Thaddaeus, "Are you in truth a disciple of Jesus, the Son of God?" Thaddaeus replied, "Because you believed in him who sent me, the petitions of your heart shall be granted." Abgarus said, "I believed in him so much that I wanted to take my army and destroy those Jews who crucified him. I was deterred only by the power of the Romans." Thaddaeus said, "Our Lord has fulfilled his Father's will and has been taken up to his Father." Abgarus said, "I, too, believe in him and his Father." With that, Thaddaeus placed his hand upon the king, and immediately Abgarus was cured of his disease. Then a certain Abdus, afflicted with gout, came and fell at Thaddaeus's feet. Thaddaeus laid hands on him, blessed him, and he, too, was healed. And so Thaddaeus cured many other citizens of Edessa, worked signs and wonders, and preached the word of God.

King Abgarus thanked Thaddaeus for the healing, but he wanted more. He wanted to know all about Jesus, how he was born and of the marvelous deeds he did. Thaddaeus asked the king to assemble all the citizens of Edessa the next day. Then Thaddaeus publicly declared how Jesus was born, the details of his mission, the reason he was sent by the Father, the power of his works, the mysteries he proclaimed in the world, the humiliation of his death, his resurrection, and his ascension to the Father. Hearing this, the king offered Thaddaeus gold and silver, but the apostle refused it, saying that since he had forsaken his own possessions to follow Christ it would not be right for him to take the possessions of another. These things were all done in the three hundred and fortieth year of the founding of Edessa or AD 33.[4]

THE CHURCH OF SAINT THADDAEUS THE APOSTLE

This author's wife, Madlene, was baptized at the age of thirteen at the Church of Saint Thaddaeus the Apostle in Dedmashen, near Tabriz, in the West Azerbaijan Province of Iran, which was once in Greater Armenia. She says:

"The church is one of the oldest in the world. It is typical of ancient Armenian church architecture. It stands on a hill overlooking a wide valley through which the Tigris River flows. Beyond the rim of the valley, the snowclad peaks of Mount Ararat and Massis arise. Every year, many Christians make a pilgrimage to this shrine. First, they arrive at Tabriz and spend the night. Then they drive out to the church in the morning. They do not drive there by night because there are bandits and vandals on

---

4. This date refers to the 340th year of the Kingdom of Edessa, whose founding was in the Third Year of the 117th Olympiad, 308 BC. From 308 BC to AD 33, the year of the cross, are in fact 341 years, but just as a child is only one year old after the first twelve months of life, so with a kingdom. Thus, in 307 BC the Edessene Kingdom was one year old and in AD 33 it was 340 years old.

the rural roads. Since the church is really in the middle of nowhere, the local Armenian diocese pitches hundreds of tents on the hillside around the church where the pilgrims stay for the night before the ceremony.

"The next morning, the *Catholicos*, or head of the Armenian church in the Iranian prelacy, conducts a mass and performs many baptisms. There are so many pilgrims, the church is open for two or three days. On my day, I was the last person in a long line. The priest made the sign of the cross on my forehead with myrrh-infused oil and then baptized me. Since the church is in a desert place and since there are so many pilgrims, there is not enough water for immersion, so they baptize by sprinkling."

THADDAEUS'S DEATH

According to tradition, after preaching in Armenia and Mesopotamia, Thaddaeus suffered martyrdom in Berytus (modern Beirut, Lebanon) around AD 65. If so, he died three years before the presumed date of Peter's and Paul's executions in Rome. Judas Thaddaeus supposedly was killed with a halberd (a long-handled war axe).

His relics were preserved in the Church of Saint Thaddaeus in Armenia (now in Iran) until Mongol invasions prompted moving them for safekeeping to Saint Peter's Basilica in Rome. The Armenian Apostolic Church honors Thaddaeus and Bartholomew as its patron saints.

Simon the Zealot

SIMON IS VARIOUSLY THE tenth or the eleventh in the lists of the disciples. There are nine Simons in the New Testament: (1) Simon Peter, (2) Simon Judas the Zealot, (3) Simon the half-brother of Jesus (Matt 6:3), (4) Simon the Leper (Matt 14:3), (5) Simon the Pharisee (Luke 7:4), (6) Simon the father of Judas Iscariot (John 6:7), (7) Simon of Cyrene (Luke 23:2), (8) Simon Magus or the Magician (Acts 8:8–24), and (9) Simon the Tanner (Acts 9:4). According to Hippolytus, the full name of the eleventh apostle was Simon Judas,[1] making him the fifth disciple to bear the name of Judas, along with (1) Judas Thomas Didymus, the Twin, (2) Judas Thaddaeus Lebbaeus, (3) Judas Iscariot, and (4) Judas, the half-brother of Jesus. Jesus' half-brother, who wrote the book of Jude, was also named Judas.

Scripture calls Simon "the Zealot" or "the Cananean" to distinguish him from the other Simon in the Twelve, Simon Peter. Simon the Cananean and Simon the Zealot are the same person, "zealot" being a translation into Greek (*zelotes*) of the Aramaic word for "zealous" or "jealous" (*ganana*) represented by the English transliteration "Cananean." Simon means "he who hears."

ZEALOTS

Josephus identifies four main first-century Jewish sects: (1) the Pharisees, (2) the Sadducees, (3) the Essenes, and (4) the Zealots.[2] The Zealots objected to Roman emperor worship and taxation. They wanted a Jewish king descended from David. As a Zealot, probably Simon's first interest in Jesus' ministry was as a means to expel Rome by force of arms.

---

1. Hippolytus, "List of the Apostles and Disciples."
2. Josephus, *War*, 2:8:2–14, 7:8:1; *Ant*. 13:5:9, 18:1:2.

RELATIONSHIPS

Simon may have been Jesus' cousin, the brother of Matthew Levi and of James the Less, and he may have been the bridegroom at the wedding at Cana. Given Mary's dominant role in the wedding, she may have been Simon's aunt.[3]

SIMON'S MINISTRY

In the lists of disciples, Simon always comes before Judas Iscariot, perhaps because they may have shared Zealot politics. Because of their being listed as "teammates," Simon and Judas Iscariot possibly went together when Jesus sent the disciples out in pairs (Matt 10:4). In this case, Simon may have been the performer of miracles empowered by the Holy Spirit if Judas Iscariot was never a true believer. On the other hand, if Judas was a believer at that time, he may have performed miracles together with Simon and may have lost his faith later.

Unlike Judas Iscariot, Simon the Zealot came to understand and embrace Jesus' teaching. He abandoned the Zealots' policy and accepted Christ's Great Commission. As one of eleven survivors of the original twelve apostles, Simon was present in the upper room on Resurrection Sunday, was in the upper room with Thomas present on the following Monday, saw Jesus' ascension, helped choose Matthias as the replacement for Judas Iscariot, witnessed the birth of the church on the day of Pentecost in AD 33, and attended the Jerusalem Council of AD 49.

THE DEATH OF SIMON THE ZEALOT

The Golden Legend says that under the emperor Hadrian Simon died by crucifixion in Jerusalem.[4] Hippolytus wrote that Simon the Zealot became bishop of Jerusalem after James the Just, and that he died at the age of 120 years.[5] If so, he, and not John the son of Zebedee, was probably the longest-lived apostle. If one assumes that Simon was about thirty years old, like Jesus, at the Wedding of Cana, he would thus have died around AD 123.

---

3. See "Relationships in Jesus' Community" in the Appendices.
4. De Voragine, *The Golden Legend*, "159: Saints Simon and Jude."
5. Hippolytus, "List of the Apostles and Disciples."

Judas Iscariot, the Traitor

JUDAS IS THE TWELFTH in the list of the disciples. Judas in Greek is Ioudas and in Hebrew is Judah, meaning "praised." In his Gospel, John called him "son of Simon Iscariot" (John 6:71, 13:2, 26). There were five men named Judas among Jesus' disciples: (1) Judas Thomas Didymus (the Twin), (2) Judas Thaddaeus Lebbaeus, son of James, (3) Simon Judas, the Zealot, (4) Judas Iscariot, son of Simon, and (5) Jesus' half-brother Judas, who wrote the biblical book of Jude. Since no Christian writer would wish to confuse Judas, the betrayer of Jesus, with a faithful apostle, it is not surprising that the other two Judases were better known by their alternate names, Thaddaeus and Thomas. The traitorous disciple was known as Judas Iscariot. Iscariot means "from Kerioth," a city in Judea.

Jesus called Judas to discipleship along with the other Twelve. He was the only one of the Twelve possibly not from Galilee, although perhaps his father, Simon, moved from Kerioth to Galilee and raised Judas there. Judas probably walked with Jesus during his entire earthly ministry, from the baptism of John to the crucifixion. This is logical, since those were the credentials Peter wanted Judas's replacement to have. Anyway, Judas certainly followed Jesus for most of his ministry. Yet Scripture never mentions him without some reference to his betrayal.

Objective contemporary observers of Judas would have considered him a role model. They might have wished to be just like him, a loyal and specially chosen servant of Jesus. The reality was that Judas was indwelt by Satan. And Jesus knew all along that Judas would betray him. In March AD 31, two years before Judas's betrayal, Jesus said, "'Did I not choose you, the Twelve? And yet one of you is a devil.' He spoke of Judas the son of Simon Iscariot, for he, one of the Twelve, was going to betray him" (John 6:70–71).

AT THE HOME OF MARY OF BETHANY

John reported that Judas acted as treasurer for the disciples, though he was always a thief (John 12:6). He revealed this in the context of the account of Mary of Bethany, who poured expensive perfume on Jesus' feet on Friday, March 25, AD 33, one week before the Crucifixion.

> Six days before the Passover, Jesus therefore came to Bethany, where Lazarus was, whom Jesus had raised from the dead. So, they gave a dinner for him there. Martha served, and Lazarus was one of those reclining with him at table. Mary therefore took a pound of expensive ointment made from pure nard and anointed the feet of Jesus and wiped his feet with her hair. The house was filled with the fragrance of the perfume. But Judas Iscariot, one of his disciples (he who was about to betray him), said, "Why was this ointment not sold for three hundred *denarii* and given to the poor?" He said this, not because he cared about the poor, but because he was a thief, and having charge of the moneybag he used to help himself to what was put into it. Jesus said, "Leave her alone, so that she may keep it for the day of my burial. For the poor you always have with you, but you do not always have me." (John 12:1–8)

Three hundred *denarii* were about three hundred days' wages in the first century. The silver value in 2022 would be a little more than US$1,183, but the purchasing power of money then was far greater then than it is today. Using the average daily wage in the US of $214 in 2022, the current equivalent purchasing power of three hundred *denarii* would be about $64,200.

Of course, if Jesus said that he knew that Judas would betray him a year before it happened, Jesus obviously also knew that Judas was a thief and a liar at this supper in Bethany, which was just six days before the Last Supper. Ironically, Jesus gave Judas, the dishonest disciple, the job of treasurer. Jesus had no difficulty in producing money out of nowhere; he told Peter to find a shekel in the mouth of a fish. Jesus put Judas in a position where he might confront and overcome his most personal temptation if he were willing.

SATAN ENTERS JUDAS

Scripture states that Satan entered into Judas on Wednesday of the passion week.

> Then Satan entered into Judas called Iscariot, who was of the number of the twelve. He went away and conferred with the Chief Priests and officers how he might betray him to them. And they were glad and agreed to give him money. So, he consented and sought an opportunity to betray him to them in the absence of a crowd. (Luke 22:3–6)

Judas was not seduced into betraying Jesus. Judas took the initiative and carried out his betrayal with premeditated conviction.

THIRTY PIECES OF SILVER

Only Matthew, the accountable tax collector, recorded the amount of money Judas took in his bargain to betray Christ.

> Then one of the twelve, whose name was Judas Iscariot, went to the Chief Priests and said, "What will you give me if I deliver him over to you?" And they paid him thirty pieces of silver. And from that moment he sought an opportunity to betray him. (Matt 26:14–16)

Thirty pieces of silver are the equivalent of only about $250 in silver in 2022; but again, the relative purchasing power in the first century probably was the equivalent of $5,340 in 2022 US dollars—not much considering that Mary of Bethany had just squandered ointment worth ten times that amount. Exodus established thirty shekels of silver as the price of a slave (Exod 21:32). So, the chief priests put a deliberately insulting price on Jesus' head, equating Jesus to a slave. Yet through Jesus' grace, there is neither Jew nor Greek, slave nor free, male nor female, for all are one in Jesus Christ (Gal 3:28).

BETRAYAL AT THE LAST SUPPER

Splicing together these passages from the four Gospels paints a complete picture of the Last Supper and the arrest in Gethsemane (Matt 26:20–27:10; Mark 14:17–50; Luke 22:14–53; John 13:1–30, 18:1–11).

Before the Feast of the Passover, when Jesus knew that his hour had come to depart out of this world to the Father, having loved his own who were in the world, he loved them to the end. When it was evening and the hour came, he reclined at table, and the twelve apostles were with him. During supper, when the devil had already put it into the heart of Judas Iscariot, Simon's son, to betray him, Jesus, knowing that the Father had given all things into his hands and that he had come from God and was going back to God, rose from supper. He laid aside his outer garments, and taking a towel, tied it around his waist. Then he poured water into a basin and began to wash the disciples' feet and to wipe them with the towel that was wrapped around him. He came to Simon Peter, who said to him, "Lord, do you wash my feet?" Jesus answered him, "What I am doing you do not understand now, but afterward you will understand." Peter said to him, "You shall never wash my feet." Jesus answered him, "If I do not wash you, you have no share with me." Simon Peter said to him, "Lord, not my feet only but also my hands and my head!" Jesus said to him, "The one who has bathed does not need to wash, except for his feet, but is completely clean. And you are clean, but not every one of you." For he knew who was to betray him; that was why he said, "Not all of you are clean."

And he said to them, "I have earnestly desired to eat this Passover with you before I suffer. For I tell you, I will not eat it until it is fulfilled in the kingdom of God." And he took a cup, and when he had given thanks he said, "Take this, and divide it among yourselves. For I tell you that from now on I will not drink of the fruit of the vine until the kingdom of God comes." And he took bread, and when he had given thanks, he broke it and gave it to them, saying, "This is my body, which is given for you. Do this in remembrance of me." And likewise the cup after they had eaten, saying, "This cup that is poured out for you is the new covenant in my blood, which is poured out for many for the forgiveness of sins. But behold, the hand of him who betrays me is with me on the table. For the Son of Man goes as it has been determined, but woe to that man by whom he is betrayed!" And they began to question one another, which of them it could be who was going to do this.

A dispute also arose among them, as to which of them was to be regarded as the greatest. And he said to them, "The kings of the Gentiles exercise lordship over them, and those in authority over them are called benefactors. But not so with you. Rather, let the greatest among you become as the least, and the leader as one who serves. For who is the greater, one who reclines at table or one who serves? Is it not the one who reclines at table? But I am among you as the one who serves. You are those who have stayed with me in my trials, and I assign to you, as my Father assigned to me, a kingdom, that you may eat and drink at my table in my kingdom and sit on thrones judging the twelve tribes of Israel. Simon, Simon, behold, Satan demanded to have you, that he might sift you like wheat, but I have prayed for you that your faith may not fail. And when you have turned again, strengthen your brothers." Peter said to him, "Lord, I am ready to go with you both to prison and to death." Jesus said, "I tell you, Peter, the rooster will not crow this day, and before the rooster crows twice, you will deny three times that you know me."

After saying these things, Jesus was troubled in his spirit, and testified, "Truly, truly, I say to you, one of you will betray me." The disciples looked at one another, uncertain of whom he spoke. And they were very sorrowful and began to say to him one after another, "Is it I, Lord?" Jesus said, "He who has dipped his hand in the dish with me will betray me." Although there may have been more followers of Jesus in the upper room for the Last Supper, Jesus was reclining at table with only the Twelve (Matt 26:20; Luke 22:14). This means that all of them would have dipped their hand in the dish of bitter herbs with him as a required part of the Passover ceremony. Consequently, Jesus' answer at this point left the disciples still in the dark. Then Judas, who would betray him, said, "Is it I, Rabbi?" He said to him, "You have said so." Now this made the answer to the question clear to Jesus and Judas, but the others were still uncertain.

One of his disciples, the one whom Jesus loved (John), was reclining at table close to Jesus, so Simon Peter motioned to him to ask Jesus of whom he was speaking. So that disciple, leaning back against Jesus, said to him, "Lord, who is it?" Jesus answered, "It is he to whom I will give this morsel of bread when I have dipped it. The Son of

Man goes as it is written of him, but woe to that man by whom the Son of Man is betrayed! It would have been better for that man if he had not been born." So when he had dipped the morsel, he gave it to Judas, the son of Simon Iscariot. Then after Judas had taken the morsel, Satan entered into him. Jesus said to him, "What you are going to do, do quickly."

This should have made the situation perfectly clear, but none of the disciples at the table knew why Jesus said this to Judas. This shows how incredible it was to the disciples that one of them would betray the Christ. Some thought that, because Judas had the moneybag, Jesus was telling him, "Buy what we need for the feast," or that he should give something to the poor. So, after receiving the morsel of bread, Judas immediately went out. And it was night.

And Jesus said to them, "When I sent you out with no moneybag or knapsack or sandals, did you lack anything?" They said, "Nothing." He said to them, "But now let the one who has a moneybag take it, and likewise a knapsack. And let the one who has no sword sell his cloak and buy one. For I tell you that this Scripture must be fulfilled in me: 'And he was numbered with the transgressors.' For what is written about me has its fulfillment." They said, "Look, Lord, here are two swords." And he said to them, "It is enough."

IN GETHSEMANE

When they had sung a hymn, he came out and went, as was his custom, to the Mount of Olives. The disciples followed him. They went to a place called Gethsemane. And when he came to the place, he said to them, "Pray that you may not enter into temptation."

Jesus said to them, "You will all fall away, for it is written, 'I will strike the shepherd, and the sheep will be scattered.' But after I am raised up, I will go before you to Galilee." Peter said to him, "Even though they all fall away, I will not." And Jesus said to him, "Truly, I tell you, this very night, before the rooster crows twice, you will deny me three times." But he said emphatically, "If I must die with you, I will not deny you." And they all said the same.

He said to his disciples, "Sit here while I pray." He took with him Peter, James, and John and began to be greatly distressed and troubled. He said to them, "My soul is very sorrowful, even to death. Remain here and watch." And going a little farther, about a stone's throw, he fell to the ground and prayed that if possible the hour might pass from him. He said, "Abba, Father, all things are possible for you. Father, if you are willing, remove this cup from me. Nevertheless, not my will, but yours, be done."

And he came and found them sleeping, and he said to Peter, "Simon, are you asleep? Could you not watch with me one hour? Watch and pray that you may not enter into temptation. The spirit indeed is willing, but the flesh is weak."

And again he went away and prayed, saying the same words. And there appeared to him an angel from heaven, strengthening him. And being in agony he prayed more earnestly; and his sweat became like great drops of blood falling down to the ground. And when he rose from prayer, he came to the disciples and found them sleeping for sorrow, for their eyes were very heavy. He said to them, "Why are you sleeping? Rise and pray that you may not enter into temptation." And they did not know how to answer him.

Leaving them again, he went and prayed a third time, and a third time he came back and said to them, "Are you still sleeping and taking your rest? Sleep and take your rest later on. It is enough; see, the hour has come and is at hand. The Son of Man is betrayed into the hands of sinners . . . rise, let us be going; see, my betrayer is at hand."

JESUS' ARREST

Now Judas, who betrayed him, also knew the garden where Jesus was, for Jesus often met there with his disciples. Judas came, one of the twelve, and with him a great crowd with swords and clubs, from the chief priests and the elders of the people. Now the betrayer had given them a sign, saying, "The one I will kiss is the man; seize him." Since all Jesus' disciples were young men from Galilee, they would be difficult to distinguish from one another in the dark and in an age before the invention of eyeglasses. Judas came up to Jesus at once and said, "Greetings, Rabbi!" And he kissed him. Jesus said to him, "Friend, do what you came to do."

Jesus, knowing all that would happen to him, came forward and said to them, "Whom do you seek?" They answered him, "Jesus of Nazareth." Jesus said to them, "I am he." Judas, who betrayed him, was standing with them. When Jesus said to them, "I am he," they drew back and fell to the ground. So he asked them again, "Whom do you seek?" And they said, "Jesus of Nazareth.'" Jesus answered, "I told you that I am he. So, if you seek me, let these men go." This was to fulfill the word that he had spoken: "Of those whom you gave me I have lost not one." Then Simon Peter, having a sword, drew it, struck the high priest's servant, and cut off his right ear. (The servant's name was Malchus.) Jesus said to Peter, "Put your sword into its sheath; shall I not drink the cup that the Father has given me?"

JUDAS'S SUICIDE

Later, when Judas, his betrayer, saw that Jesus was condemned, he changed his mind and brought back the thirty pieces of silver to the chief priests and the elders, saying, "I have sinned by betraying innocent blood." They said, "What is that to us? See to it yourself." And throwing down the pieces of silver into the temple, he departed, and he went and hanged himself.

But the chief priests, taking the pieces of silver, said, "It is not lawful to put them into the treasury, since it is blood money." So they took counsel and bought with them the potter's field as a burial place for strangers. Therefore, that field has been called the Field of Blood to this day. Then was fulfilled what had been spoken by the prophet Jeremiah, saying, "And they took the thirty pieces of silver, the price of him on whom a price had been set by some of the sons of Israel, and they gave them for the potter's field, as the Lord directed me" (Matt 27:9–10).

Judas acquired the field with the reward of his wickedness and falling headlong he burst open in the middle and all his bowels gushed out. And it became known to all the inhabitants of Jerusalem, so that the field was called in their own language Akeldama, that is, Field of Blood.

WHO BOUGHT THE FIELD OF BLOOD?

Matthew wrote that the Chief Priests and elders bought the potter's field (Matt 27:9–10). Luke wrote in Acts that Judas bought this field, which the inhabitants of Jerusalem called the Field of Blood (Acts 1:18–19). This is not a contradiction. The chief priests bought the field in the name of Judas. They used the silver belonging to Judas, because it was cursed and they did not wish to spend it in their own names. Therefore, they said, "he bought it," although they executed the purchase on his behalf.

DID MATTHEW AND LUKE CONTRADICT EACH OTHER?

Is there a contradiction in Scripture between the account of Judas's death in Matthew and Acts? Matthew wrote that Judas hanged himself (Matt 27:5). Luke wrote in Acts that "he burst open in the middle and all his bowels gushed out" (Acts 1:18). These accounts are not mutually exclusive. If Judas hanged himself from a tree over the edge of a cliff or gully, and if his body fell on sharp rocks below, then his entrails would gush out just as Luke vividly described.

Judas hanged himself on Friday, April 1, AD 33, the eve of both Passover and the Sabbath. No righteous Jew would defile himself and the holy day by cutting down a corpse during the feast of Unleavened Bread, which lasted until Friday, April 8, because "whoever touches the dead body of any person shall be unclean for seven days" (Num 19:11). But April 8 was also a Sabbath eve, so no one would have cut Judas down until the end of Passover, Sunday, April 10. Judas therefore hung, unattended, for ten days, decomposing and finally falling and bursting open.

Luke adds accurate detail to Matthew's account without introducing a contradiction. His account fits the calendar of that year with astonishing precision. The day after Judas's cadaver burst, Monday, April 11, the resurrected Jesus again appeared to the disciples in the upper room, this time with Thomas present. What Judas missed!

WERE THE BETRAYALS OF JUDAS AND PETER DIFFERENT?

If both Judas and Peter felt remorse about betraying Jesus, why was Peter forgiven and Judas condemned? All who earnestly seek God find him, "for whoever would draw near to God must believe that he exists and that he rewards those who seek him" (Heb 11:6). In fact, God "is patient toward you, not wishing that any should perish, but that all should reach repentance" (2 Pet 3:9).

However, those who seek God on their own terms will not be saved, since he "saved us, not because of works done by us in righteousness, but according to his own mercy, by the washing of regeneration and renewal of the Holy Spirit" (Titus 3:5). The Bible says, "There is a way which seems right to a man, but its end is the way to death" (Prov 14:12). Further, there are those who seek too late, namely, after they die, for "it is appointed for man to die once, and after that comes judgment" (Heb 9:27). (See also the rich man and Lazarus in Luke 16:19–31.)

All who come to God in this life in penitence, falling upon his mercy, receive his gracious gift of salvation. Judas felt remorse, but not repentance. This is evident because Judas did not seek forgiveness from God, but from his co-conspirators, the Jewish elite. He wanted them to take back the money and remove his guilt. But only God could remove his guilt. Had Judas freely repented, God would have granted him grace. Judas regretted his sin (Matt 27:4) but did not repent. Peter regretted his sin and repented. Hence, Judas was lost (John 17:12), and Peter was saved.

DID GOD FORCE JUDAS TO BETRAY JESUS?

If God foreknew that Judas would betray Jesus, was Judas to blame? If Judas had to fulfill this prophecy because God had predestined him to do so, should it not have been God's fault? If Judas could have chosen freely not to fulfill the prophecy, could he have falsified the prophecy and put God in error?

This misconception of predestination arises when we try to understand time from a human, rather than a divine, perspective. The human mind is trapped in time, just as a word is trapped on a page. The word on a page cannot see what is on the page before, the page after, the end of the chapter, or the beginning of the chapter, much less the front and back cover of the book. But just as a reader can do all those things, and even put the whole book on a shelf and choose to read a different book, so God can contemplate, pick up, and set aside time.

God is a super-temporal (eternal) Being. Time is a created thing. The Creator created time. The Creator is greater than the creation. Thus, the Creator is not subject to time. Time is subject to the Creator. The Creator transcends time. It is therefore incorrect to speak of God as knowing "in advance." If God is above and beyond time, then he knows everything in one "eternal now." He does not really foreknow; he simply knows.

God can know for sure what will happen freely. But just because God is certain about a future event does not mean that it will not freely occur. The same event can be necessary from the vantage point of God and free from the standpoint of human choice. For example, if we see a child running on a wet pool deck, we may say, "That child is going to trip and fall." That does not mean we caused the child to trip and fall; we simply predicted it. God in his omniscience sees the future with the same certainty with which he sees the past. He knew that Judas would betray Christ. That does not mean Judas was coerced. God knew certainly that Judas would betray Christ freely.

You may say, "This is nonsense. It is impossible for something to be both mandatory and merely probable." But why? Possibility and impossibility are also God's creations. God is not subject to universal laws within which he has to operate. God created all universal laws. The creator of anything is always greater than his creation. When we say something is impossible, it is only because God chose to make it impossible. Had he wished to design the universe otherwise, with, for example, square circles, it would have been possible with him, because with God all things are possible (Matt 19:26).

A good example of this relates back to time. "With the Lord one day is as a thousand years, and a thousand years as one day" (2 Pet 3:8). Is it possible for a day and one thousand days to pass in the same interval? On earth it is impossible. But Einstein's theory of relativity says that the faster an object travels through space the slower it travels through time. An object that travels through space at the speed of light will experience time that is very nearly at a standstill, as almost all its motion through time has been converted into its motion through space. So, in the instant of creation, a million years at the stationary epicenter of a cosmic Big Bang might transpire in one day for an object speeding through space at the rapidly expanding edge of the universe. The apostle Peter articulated this concept perfectly.

DID JUDAS LOSE HIS SALVATION?

Judas's case raises the question of eternal security: is a believer forever saved? Sincere Christians have various views about eternal security, but the Bible does promise that once we are saved, we are forever saved. Jesus said we need to be born again, not born again and again and again. The Bible does not teach believers to live in eternal insecurity. But the question is: Can a believer choose to become a non-believer?

Some say that if one is truly born again, one can no more become un-born again than one can undo his physical birth. But this is not a persuasive analogy, because one can, of course, commit suicide. Suicide does not undo one's physical birth, but it terminates physical life. How about spiritual suicide? What about the person who once was saved but who then consciously chooses to reject an ongoing relationship with God? Is there eternal security for a former believer? Will God override the unbeliever's free choice and force him into salvation?

Paul wrote, "I am sure that neither death nor life, nor angels nor rulers, nor things present nor things to come, nor powers, nor height nor depth, nor anything else in all creation, will be able to separate us from the love of God in Christ Jesus our Lord" (Rom 8:38–39). So, these are ten things that cannot separate us from Christ: (1) death, (2) life, (3) angels, (4) rulers, (5) things present, (6) things to come, (7) powers, (8) height, (9) depth, or (10) anything else in creation. All these things cannot separate us, but Paul does not include one thing: our own choice. We can separate ourselves.

John 10:27–29 says that the Lord's sheep know his voice, he knows them, they follow him, they receive eternal life, and no one can snatch them from his hand. True, no one else can snatch them from the Lord's hand. But what if a former believer chooses to stop listening to the Lord's voice and elects to stop following him? Has he not jumped out of the Lord's hand? The sheep has himself chosen to become a goat.

The simple biblical reality is that one has the choice to be a sheep or a goat. If one chooses to be a goat or makes no choice, he will be a goat. But if one chooses to be a sheep, he becomes a new creature in Christ (2 Cor 5:17; Eph 4:24; Col 3:10). One can go back to living with the goats if he wants, but most people, having experienced life as a goat and as a sheep, will want to stick with the flock.

WAS JUDAS EVER SAVED?

Jesus sent Judas out with the Twelve (Matt 10:1–4; Luke 9:1–2) and the seventy-two (Luke 10:1). If he was never saved, did Judas, like the others, preach the good news, heal the lame, give sight to the blind, and perform the same miracles to the glory of God that the other disciples did? The Bible says that Jesus gave to the Twelve, not to the Eleven, the authority to cast out demons and heal diseases. This must have therefore included Judas.

Perhaps Judas received the offer of this authority, but never accepted it, just as God offers salvation to all as a free gift but not all accept it. If so, Judas may not have performed signs and wonders; he may merely have witnessed his companion (probably Simon the Zealot) do so when Jesus sent the disciples out in pairs. This seems unlikely, however, because Simon would surely have commented upon it. Rather, when the disciples returned to Jesus, they were all excited at the wonders they had performed. If, however, the argument is true that a believer may become a former believer, possibly Judas did perform signs and wonders and once was saved but ultimately he rejected salvation. Or, as one more possibility, Jesus testified that even non-believers may sometimes perform miracles:

> "Not everyone who says to me, 'Lord, Lord,' will enter the kingdom of heaven, but the one who does the will of my Father who is in heaven. On that day many will say to me, 'Lord, Lord, did we not prophesy in your name, and cast out demons in your name, and do many mighty works in your name?' And

then will I declare to them, 'I never knew you; depart from me, you workers of lawlessness.'" (Matt 7:21–23)

Deuteronomy 13 also says that a false prophet may perform miracles, but his false teaching demands that those who love God not follow him. This means that God may use anyone, even Judas or a false prophet, for his purposes. God causes all things work together for good to those who love God, to those who are called according to his purpose (Rom 8:28).

Satan entered Judas at the Last Supper (John 13:27). This suggests that Satan had not entered Judas until then, even though Judas was previously dishonest (John 12:6). A saved believer cannot be indwelt by Satan or a demon, "for he who is in you is greater than he who is in the world" (1 John 4:4). Jesus confirmed this when he said, "How can someone enter a strong man's house and plunder his goods, unless he first binds the strong man? Then indeed he may plunder his house" (Matt 12:29). When the Jews accused Jesus of being demon-possessed, he responded, "I do not have a demon, but I honor my Father, and you dishonor me" (John 8:49). Being demon-possessed and being indwelt by the Holy Spirit are therefore mutually exclusive states. When Judas betrayed Jesus, he was indwelt by Satan, and thus was not at that time saved. Before he was indwelt by Satan, although a sinner, he may have been saved. Jesus' comment about Judas, that it would have been better if he never had been born, is evidence of hell's reality. Jesus would never have said that if Judas's fate after death were annihilation, soul sleep, or anything other than extended conscious torment apart from God.

APOCRYPHA

Muslims cite the *Gospel of Barnabas*,[1] which says that Jesus never died on the cross. They say Allah substituted Judas for Jesus at the last moment. This is how Jesus was able to appear to be dead and also manage "post-resurrection" appearances. Serious scholars agree that a first-century disciple of Christ did not write the *Gospel of Barnabas*. The first mention of this book is from the fifth century, and there is no evidence to support its authenticity. The *Gospel of Judas* is another apocryphal work, purporting to record conversations between Jesus and Judas Iscariot.[2] Its gnostic author does not even pretend that Judas wrote the book. It is inauthentic.

WAS JUDAS WELL-MEANING?

Many have tried to justify Judas by making him a Zealot, like his fellow disciple, Simon. The argument is that Judas was a member of the *sicarii*, Zealots dedicated to expelling the Romans forcefully from Judea. The idea is that he wished to promote Jesus

---

1. *Gospel of Barnabas*, 215-217.
2. Mattison, trans., *Gospel of Judas*.

as a leader of this movement and that when Jesus refused to accept the role of rebel chief, Judas betrayed him to the high priest, hoping to goad Jesus into action. When the plan tragically misfired and Jesus died, Judas's remorse drove him to suicide.

The problem with this tale is that it lacks evidence. Simon, although a Zealot, understood Jesus' message and chose loyalty to the Master over devotion to a political party. The *sicarii* emerged as a political movement in AD 40–68, seven to thirty-five years after Judas's death. Scripture portrays Judas as a man voluntarily given to greed and sin, not as a misguided idealist. Lacking contemporary testimony to the contrary, the burden of proof is on the thesis that whitewashes Judas.

The tragedy of Judas's betrayal is similar to the Sanhedrin's rejection of Jesus. As trained rabbis, they had all the evidence they needed to know that Jesus was, as he claimed, the expected Messiah. Theirs was the unforgivable sin: the conscious, deliberate, persistent rejection of the Holy Spirit (Mark 3:29; Luke 12:10). Judas's sin led to suicide and hell. The Sanhedrin's sin led to the annihilation of Israel in AD 70, the end of the old covenant, the diaspora of the Jews, and to hell. Judas personally heard Jesus say, "I am the way, and the truth, and the life; no one comes to the Father but through me" (John 14:6). Judas consciously chose to reject that truth.

> A man's own worth by himself is priced.
> Judas, for silver, sold himself, not Christ.[3]

---

3. A paraphrase of Cholmondeley, "Betrayal."

Matthias, the Thirteenth Apostle

AFTER JUDAS ISCARIOT'S BETRAYAL and suicide, Peter understood that God wanted the Eleven to choose someone to take Judas's place. After Jesus' ascension on May 13, AD 33, he said:

> "So one of the men who have accompanied us during all the time that the Lord Jesus went in and out among us, beginning from the baptism of John until the day when he was taken up from us—one of these men must become with us a witness to his Resurrection." And they put forward two, Joseph called Barsabbas, who was also called Justus, and Matthias. And they prayed and said, "You, Lord, who know the hearts of all, show which one of these two you have chosen to take the place in this ministry and apostleship from which Judas turned aside to go to his own place." And they cast lots for them, and the lot fell on Matthias, and he was numbered with the eleven apostles. (Acts 1:21–26)

This is Scripture's only mention of Matthias. Since Peter wanted a candidate who had witnessed Jesus' ministry from his baptism by John all the way to his ascension, Matthias and Joseph Justus Barsabbas must have been very early followers of Jesus, earlier than most of the other disciples. Perhaps the distinction between those who were qualified to be among the Twelve was not length of service, but that Jesus called the original Twelve personally and specifically. There were many others who witnessed the ministry of Jesus from the baptism to the Ascension of whom the Gospels said nothing specific. It is likely, for example, that there were more people than the twelve apostles at the Last Supper, because Jesus said that the traitor was one of the Twelve who had dipped his bread in the dish with Jesus. Since everyone at the Passover meal would have done that, by specifying that the traitor was one of the Twelve who did it, Jesus implied there were others there—probably at least John Mark, for the upper room was likely in his house. We also know that there were others beside the Eleven Apostles present in the upper room after the ascension (Acts 1:13–14). So, we should probably imagine many unnamed people accompanying Jesus throughout his ministry, and, indeed, the Gospels frequently refer to immense crowds following him. Thus, Matthias might well have been an early, but initially unmentioned, follower of Jesus. Eusebius wrote that Matthias was one the seventy-two disciples Jesus sent out (Luke

10:1).[1] At any rate, Matthias was at the birth of the church on Pentecost, Sunday, May 22, AD 33 and at the Jerusalem Council in AD 49.

SHOULD CHRISTIANS CAST LOTS?

Were the Eleven gambling or practicing superstition by drawing lots when they chose Matthias? Should Christians follow this apostolic example and make major decisions by casting lots? Is this biblical? Proverbs says, "The lot is cast into the lap, but its every decision is from the Lord" (Prov 16:33). The proverb does not advocate casting lots; it merely states that God, not random chance, guides events. God may make his will known through casting lots but casting lots will not necessarily reveal the will of God.

In Jonah we see another example of casting lots: "And they said to one another, 'Come, let us cast lots, that we may know on whose account this evil has come upon us.' So, they cast lots, and the lot fell on Jonah" (Jon 1:7). The sailors in Jonah's ship were anxious to know God's will, but they did not care which god told them the truth. Their piety may have been the kind found in foxholes. The Bible does not say that the sailors always discovered or followed God's will by casting lots, only that in this case God chose to use their casting of lots to steer events according to his plan. Neither of these passages makes a clear case advocating the use of lots by believers today. But the apostles were not arbitrarily playing dice.

First, they were under the guidance of the Holy Spirit. The fact that miracles attended their ministries shows that they were uniquely under God's hand. The apostles may have been common human beings, but God used them for uncommon missions in uncommon ways. Believers may take lessons from the behavior of the apostles, but we cannot slavishly imitate everything the apostles did. We are called, like them, to preach to Jerusalem, Judea, Samaria, and the world, because other verses make evident that Jesus' Great Commission is for all believers. But we are not called to replace Judas Iscariot. That was a task unique in type and in time. Second, the Eleven did more than merely cast lots. They took counsel of each other and put forward two men who demonstrably met the standards of an apostle of Christ. Third, they prayed for God's selection and believed that God would answer their prayers. Fourth, they cast lots between two good choices, two godly men, chosen by godly men, selected in a godly way. So, in this case, casting lots was not like choosing between good or evil, but between good and good.

All of this suggests that it would be risky to adopt casting lots as a Christian means of making decisions. If we were to follow the Eleven and cast lots to determine God's will in our lives, we would need to ensure that: (1) like the Eleven, we are taking counsel of godly companions and are under the clear guidance of the Holy Spirit, (2) we are seeking God's will in prayer, and (3) we are casting lots between two equally

---

1. Some manuscripts say seventy, some seventy-two. Eusebius, *Church History* 1:12:3.

good options. The risks of using lots are that we might: (1) persuade ourselves that we are under God's guidance when we really are not, (2) fail to have the good advice of many godly companions, as the Eleven had, (3) put more emphasis on casting lots than on prayer, and (4) persuade ourselves that we are casting lots between two good choices, when, really, the choices might not be equally good. In the election of Matthias, the Eleven were devoted to God, not superstition. Their casting lots was appropriate for the task God gave them. But casting lots is unlikely to be an appropriate decision tool for believers of all times.

MATTHIAS'S IMPORTANCE

Was Matthias an apostle of secondary importance? No. Scripture shows that the full number of twelve tribes and twelve apostles remains important in God's eternal plan. Revelation 21:14 showed that the new Jerusalem has twelve gates to honor Israel's twelve tribes and twelve foundation stones named after the twelve apostles, even though ten of the twelve tribes were lost to apostasy in the Assyrian conquest of Israel in 722–718 BC and the other two were lost after rejecting Christ and in the Roman desolation of Judea in AD 66–73. Judas Iscariot, the twelfth disciple, betrayed Christ and committed suicide. In the end, God says he makes all things new (Rev 21:5), including a full restoration of the twelve tribes and of the twelve apostles as witnesses for God.

MATTHIAS IN ARMENIA AND CUSH

Armenian tradition holds that Matthias, along with Andrew, Nathanael Bartholomew, Judas Thaddaeus, and Simon the Zealot, was among the five apostles who evangelized Armenia. Supposedly cannibals from Cush (not the Cush in Africa, Ethiopia, but an ancient province near Armenia on the Caspian Sea) imprisoned Matthias and blinded him. The risen Christ appeared to Andrew and sent him to save Matthias. Andrew went and miraculously restored Matthias's sight. Andrew triumphed over the cannibals through prayer and freed Matthias.[2]

ARMENIA'S CHRISTIAN HERITAGE

In the fourth century, Armenia's King Tiridates persecuted Christians. He tortured an evangelist, Gregory, and threw him into a pit full of serpents and corpses, where he languished for thirteen years. During Gregory's imprisonment, Tiridates fell in love with Hripsima, a virgin under the care of a Christian abbess named Gayane. Hripsima rejected Tiridates's love, so the king put to the sword all the young girls under the

---

2. The apocryphal "Acts of Andrew and Matthias."

abbess's care. Then Tiridates fell desperately ill. His Christian sister, Khosroviducht, had a dream in which she perceived that only Gregory could cure the king. She urged him to free Gregory. The king finally did so, and Gregory miraculously healed him. Tiridates became a Christian and destroyed all the pagan temples in Armenia, except for that at Garni, which even today is one of the most beautiful ancient Greek temples still standing. Gregory invented the Armenian alphabet so that he could translate the Bible into the Armenian tongue. He composed one of the oldest translations of Scripture in the world.[3] Armenians ever after called him Gregory the Illuminator. Armenia became the first nation to embrace Christianity in AD 301, twelve years before the emperor Constantine made Rome a Christian empire by his Edict of Milan in AD 313.

THE DEATH OF MATTHIAS

According to tradition, Matthias returned to Jerusalem, where hostile Jews stoned him to death. If so, this would have been some time in the twenty-year interval between AD 49, the Jerusalem Council, and AD 70, when the Roman general Titus burned Jerusalem to the ground. It might have been in or after AD 66, when the Roman-Jewish war began, because at that time Jerusalem was in the hands of angry Jewish factions. Helena, the mother of Constantine the Great, allegedly brought Matthias's relics to Constantinople. Later they were taken to Rome.

---

3. When this author's wife, Madlene, organized relief to Armenia after the 1988 earthquake, one aspect of the mission was to bring Bibles to the people of that then-atheist Soviet regime. Some American major donors called Madlene for assurance that their funds would be used to bring only the King James Version to Armenia. Madlene explained that the Bibles would be in the Eastern Armenian language and that the Armenian translation from Greek predated the KJV by nearly thirteen centuries.

Saul of Tarsus, or Paul

He approved of the cold-blooded stoning of an innocent man. He ravaged the church, going from house to house and throwing both men and women into prison. He breathed threats and murder against believers in Christ and obtained a license to hunt them down in another country and drag them back to Jerusalem in chains. Violent mobs rioted against him, threatened him with death, or threw him out of at least eight cities. Forty of his co-religionists vowed to fast until they saw him dead. He did four stints in jail. The authorities whipped him five times with thirty-nine lashes. He was beaten with rods three times. Once he was stoned and left for dead. He was shipwrecked four times.[1] He argued publicly with the foremost leaders of the church two times. So far, how would this minister fare if he were applying to your church for a pastoral post?

But Jesus called him personally and spoke to him directly seven times. He paid his own way and raised funds for other believers in about 22,500 miles and thirty-five years of ministry on two continents. He founded at least thirteen churches and probably many more. He worked healing miracles and raised a dead man to life. He assertively bridged the gap between two hostile religions. He advocated the rights of all people and both genders with world-changing effect. He led opposition to slavery, misogyny, and racism. He trained and empowered a team of talented and effective leaders who influenced thousands. And he wrote half of the books of the New Testament. How would this applicant for a pastoral post at your church fare now?

This was the apostle Paul, a passionate man who began his career on the wrong track, made a breathtaking reversal, influenced the world as few ever have, and did so with bold confidence in his beliefs but with total personal humility.

Other apostles may have traveled as far and endured as much as Paul, but Acts focuses on Paul exceptionally. This is not because the labors of the other apostles were less worthy or effective. It is because the book of Acts aimed not to record every act of every apostle, but to show how the Way evolved from a local sect of Messianic Jews to a worldwide call for all humanity into a restored relationship with God. The two men who most contributed to this event in the Roman world were Peter and

---

1. His shipwreck in Malta was his fourth, occurring after he wrote 2 Corinthians 11:24–27.

Paul. Paul was probably twenty-nine years old when Jesus called him on the Damascus Road and sixty-three years old when he died in AD 68. He spent thirty-five years in Christian ministry.

PAUL'S SEVENTEEN LETTERS

Paul's surviving writings comprise fourteen of the twenty-seven books of the New Testament. Three of his letters, two to Corinth and one to Laodicea, have been lost. He may also have written the epistle to the Hebrews, although some attribute it to Barnabas, Apollos, or Luke. The following is the list of these epistles.

1. Galatians, May AD 49, from Antioch to the churches in Galatia (modern Turkey)
2. First Thessalonians, February AD 50, from Corinth to the church in Thessalonica (Macedonia, modern Greece)
3. Second Thessalonians, April AD 50, from Corinth to the church in Thessalonica
4. A lost letter of warning (1 Cor 5:9), November AD 51, from Ephesus (modern Turkey) to the church in Corinth (Greece)
5. First Corinthians, March AD 52, from Ephesus to the church in Corinth
6. A lost, severe letter of tears (2 Cor 2:3, 4 and 7:8), May AD 52, from Ephesus to the church in Corinth
7. Second Corinthians, November AD 53, from Macedonia to the church in Corinth
8. Romans, March AD 54, from Corinth to the church in Rome
9. First Timothy, around April AD 54, from Caesarea to Timothy in Ephesus
10. Ephesians, AD 57–69, from Rome to the church in Ephesus
11. Philippians, AD 57–59, from Rome to the church in Philippi (Macedonia, modern Greece)
12. Colossians, AD 57–59, from Rome to the church in Colossae (modern Turkey)
13. A lost letter (Col 4:16), AD 57–59, from Rome to the church in Laodicea (modern Turkey)
14. Philemon, AD 57–59, from Rome to Philemon, the head of the church in Colossae (modern Turkey)
15. Hebrews, January AD 59, from Rome to the Jewish Christians in Jerusalem
16. Titus, AD 66, from Corinth to Titus in Crete
17. Second Timothy, around April AD 68, from Rome to Timothy in Ephesus

Biographies of the Apostles

PAUL'S JOURNEYS

1. Jerusalem–Damascus–Arabia–Damascus–Jerusalem–Tarsus
   a. Purpose: conversion and retreat
   b. From 2 April AD 34 to 24 May AD 37
   c. 1,148 days or a little over 3 years
   d. 1,372 miles
   e. 1.2 miles per day

2. Tarsus–Antioch–Jerusalem–Antioch
   a. Purpose: coming out of retirement and bringing famine relief
   b. 24 May AD 43 to 19 April AD 44
   c. 331 days
   d. 1,028 miles
   e. 3 miles per day

3. Antioch–Cyprus–Perga–Pisidian Antioch–Iconium–Lystra–Derbe–Attalia–Antioch
   a. Purpose: "First Missionary Journey"
   b. 25 May AD 44 to 6 September AD 44
   c. 103 days
   d. 1,319 miles
   e. 13 miles per day

4. Antioch–Caesarea–Jerusalem–Antioch
   a. Purpose: following up on famine relief results
   b. AD 47
   c. 926 miles

5. Antioch–Jerusalem–Antioch
   a. Purpose: the Jerusalem Council
   b. AD 49
   c. 977 miles

6. Antioch–Lystra–Troas–Philippi–Thessalonica–Berea–Athens–Corinth–Illyricum–Cenchreae–Ephesus–Caesarea–Jerusalem–Antioch
   a. Purpose: "Second Missionary Journey"
   b. 29 July AD 49 to 25 September AD 51

c. 788 days or a little over 2 years

d. 4,396 miles

e. 5.6 miles per day

7. Antioch–Ephesus–Corinth–Ephesus–Troas–Corinth–Philippi–Troas–Assos–Chios–Samos–Miletus–Cos–Rhodes–Patara–Tyre–Acre–Caesarea–Jerusalem

    a. Purpose: "Third Missionary Journey"

    b. 25 September AD 51 to 28 May AD 54

    c. 926 days or 2.7 years

    d. 3,155 miles

    e. 3.4 miles per day

8. Jerusalem–Antipatris–Caesarea–Sidon–Cyprus–Myra–Cnidus–Crete–Fair Havens–Cauda–Malta–Syracuse–Rhegium–Puteoli–Rome

    a. Purpose: escape from Jerusalem to Caesarea and first trip to Rome and imprisonment there

    b. 6 June AD 54 to 8 March AD 57

    c. 1,006 days or 2.8 years

    d. 2,596 miles

    e. 2.6 miles per day

9. Rome–Spain–Illyricum–Greece–Macedonia–Crete–Ephesus–Greece–Nicapolis–Troas–Rome

    a. Purpose: release from first Roman incarceration, unrecorded missionary journeys, arrest and return to Rome and execution

    b. 17 March AD 59 to 5 May AD 68

    c. 3,336 days or a little more than 9 years

    d. About 7,000 miles

    e. About 2 miles per day

PAUL'S PERSONAL LIFE

Paul was supposed to be short, broad-shouldered, and somewhat bald, with closely-knit eyebrows, an aquiline nose, a thick, gray beard, and a pleasing, friendly manner. Jerome says that Paul was of the tribe of Benjamin and the town of Giscalis (Gischala) in Galilee. When the Romans claimed this region (in AD 7)[2] he moved with

---

2. Josephus, *Ant.* 18:2:1.

his parents to Tarsus in Cilicia. So, Paul was of Galilean origin. Assuming Paul was at least two years old when his family made the move to Tarsus, he may have been born in AD 5.

His parents sent him around AD 33 to Jerusalem to study law. He would have been about twenty-nine years old. Paul says that he was brought up in Jerusalem (Acts 22:3), but since he grew up in Tarsus, by "brought up" he means educated, studying under Gamaliel, a rabbi and "a most learned man,"[3] who was a leading authority among the Sanhedrin (Acts 22:3). Paul's sister and nephew lived in Jerusalem; when he was imprisoned there, his sister's son brought him news of the Jewish plot to ambush him (Acts 23:16).

As was common in the bilingual culture of Roman Judea, he probably used the name Saul in Jewish circles and Paul in Greek (and Roman) society. Every respectable Jewish young man learned a trade. A Jewish proverb says, "He who does not teach his son a trade teaches him to steal." Saul's parents trained him in the trade of making tents (Acts 18:3).

Paul's father was a Roman citizen, and so was Paul. Paul described himself as a man who was duly circumcised on the eighth day after his birth (as Moses prescribed), of the nation of Israel, of the tribe of Benjamin, a Hebrew of Hebrews, and, as to the law, a Pharisee (Phil 3:5). As a Pharisee, he was a religious conservative and believed in the resurrection of the dead, angels, and spirits. The Sadducees, who were the more numerous members of the Sanhedrin, believed in none of these things. They were Hellenizers, imitators of the dominant Greek culture. The Pharisees were purists, conservative adherents to Jewish tradition.

THE THORN IN PAUL'S FLESH

Paul suffered from a mysterious "thorn in his flesh," a messenger from Satan meant to keep him humble, which he prayed three times for the Lord to remove. Jesus declined to do so, saying, "My grace is sufficient for you, for my power is made perfect in weakness" (2 Cor 12:7–9). There are many conjectures about what this thorn was. It may have been a physical malady. Paul's parents may have rejected him after he began following Jesus. He may have had a never-mentioned wife who rejected him for becoming Christian. He may have been a widower and may have struggled with the desire to remarry and settle down, as opposed to following God's call on seemingly endless missionary journeys. Or he may have struggled with some other temptation or grief. Scripture simply does not say.

---

3. Jerome, *On Illustrious Men*.

STONING STEPHEN

Saul first appeared in Scripture at the stoning of Stephen, in AD 33, the year of the cross. Luke described him as a young man who guarded the robes of those who executed the first martyr, Stephen. Saul was in hearty agreement with putting Stephen to death (Acts 8:1). But this was not enough for this zealous young Pharisee. In fact, Stephen's death made things worse, because it caused all Christians in Jerusalem except the apostles to scatter, preaching the gospel wherever they went (Acts 8:4).

The apostle Philip did not scatter, that is, retreat in fear, but he did leave Jerusalem and evangelize in Samaria. Peter and John joined him in that effort. Then Philip converted an Ethiopian eunuch in Gaza and preached all along the Mediterranean coast as far north as Caesarea. Saul was alarmed that the Christian sect was spreading so quickly. Like a general, he thought to outflank the enemy. Breathing threats and murder against the disciples of the Lord, Saul went to the high priest and asked for letters from him to the synagogues in Damascus giving him authority so that if he found any followers of the Way, whether men or women, he might bring them in chains to Jerusalem. If Saul could cause havoc among the Christians in Damascus, he might stop the progress of the cult and hammer it back down.

THE DAMASCUS ROAD: JESUS SPOKE TO PAUL THE FIRST TIME

The following is a synthesis of the three accounts of Paul's Damascus Road experience in Acts (Acts 9:3–9, 22:6–11, 26:12–18). There is no contradiction between them. Luke simply changed emphasis and details in each telling, but the three accounts have total integrity.

Saul was convinced that he ought to do many things in opposing the name of Jesus of Nazareth. He did so in Jerusalem. He not only locked up many of the saints in prison after receiving authority from the chief priests, but when they were put to death he cast his vote against them. He punished them often in all the synagogues and tried to make them blaspheme, and in raging fury against them he persecuted them even to foreign cities.

Now as Saul went on his way, with the authority and commission of the chief priests,[4] he journeyed and drew near to Damascus. And suddenly, about noon,[5] he saw on the way a great light from heaven, brighter than the sun, that shone around

---

4. Paul carried a letter to the ethnarch under Aretas, who was king of Arabia Petraea, (modern Jordan) and of Damascus, although there, like Herod Antipas in Galilee and Peraea, he was a puppet king under Rome. An ethnarch was the ruler of an ethnic group within a kingdom or province, in this case, Syria. This ethnarch was the representative of the Jews. His job was to present Jewish petitions to the rulers of Damascus and help the rulers keep the Jews in line. Damascus was a rich target for Paul because the Jewish population of the city was very numerous. Within this large, Jewish population were some, and perhaps many, who called upon the name of Jesus (Acts 9:14).

5. Sunday, April 2, AD 34.

him and those who journeyed with him. And when they had all fallen to the ground, he heard a voice saying to him in the Hebrew language, "Saul, Saul, why are you persecuting me? It is hard for you to kick against the goads." And he answered and said, "Who are you, Lord?" And he said to him, "I am Jesus of Nazareth, whom you are persecuting."

Now the men who were traveling with him stood speechless, hearing the voice, but seeing no one. Those who were with him saw the light but did not understand the voice of the one who was speaking to him. And he said, "What shall I do?" And the Lord said to him:

> Rise and stand upon your feet, for I have appeared to you for this purpose, to appoint you as a servant and witness to the things in which you have seen me and to those in which I will appear to you, delivering you from your people and from the Gentiles—to whom I am sending you to open their eyes, so that they may turn from darkness to light and from the power of Satan to God, that they may receive forgiveness of sins and a place among those who are sanctified by faith in me. Go into Damascus, and there you will be told all that is appointed for you. (Acts 9:5–9, 22:10–21, 26:16–18)

And because of the brightness of that light, although his eyes were opened, he saw nothing. So, those who were with him led him by the hand and brought him into Damascus. For three days he was without sight and neither ate nor drank.

The Lord appeared in a vision to a Damascus disciple named Ananias and told him, "Get up and go to the street called Straight and inquire at the house of Judas for a man from Tarsus named Saul, for he is praying, and he has seen in a vision a man named Ananias come in and lay his hands on him, so that he might regain his sight." Ananias answered, "Lord, I have heard from many about this man, how much harm he did to your saints at Jerusalem. And here he has authority from the chief priests to bind all who call on your name." But the Lord said to him, "Go, for he is a chosen instrument of mine, to bear my name before the gentiles and kings and the sons of Israel; for I will show him how much he must suffer for my name's sake."

So Ananias went and laid hands on Saul, and immediately something like scales fell from Saul's eyes. He regained his sight, got up, and was baptized. Then he took food and regained his strength. Saul joined the other Christians in Damascus and at once began proclaiming Jesus in the synagogues, saying, "He is the Son of God." The people were amazed that this former persecutor of Christians was now preaching Christ.

ARABIA: AD 34–37

In Galatians 1, Paul said that after his conversion on the Damascus Road, he did not go immediately to Jerusalem, but went to Arabia. As Paul journeyed from Damascus to Arabia, he must have passed the place on the Damascus Road where Jesus had first called him. He must have paused to reflect on that miraculous encounter. After a sojourn in Arabia, Paul returned to Damascus, and then after three years went to Jerusalem. Those three years mark a span from AD 34 to 37.

Possibly Paul went to Arabia to meditate on the Scriptures and on how Jesus fulfilled their Messianic prophecies. Saul had a great deal of theological re-thinking to do. Perhaps Paul retreated to the Mountain of God, consciously following in the footsteps of Elijah. It is not likely that by "Arabia" Paul meant Arabia Petraea (modern Jordan), the realm of King Aretas, because Paul's original mission was endorsed by a letter from the Jewish leaders in Jerusalem to King Aretas's ethnarch in Damascus. Moreover, Aretas's governor in Damascus was the official who ordered Paul's arrest (2 Cor 11:32). By "Arabia," Paul meant the deep and vast Arabian Peninsula, the very place where Paul specified Mount Sinai stood (Gal 4:25).

THE MOUNTAIN OF GOD

When King Ahab told his wife Jezebel how Elijah had killed the prophets of Baal with the sword (1 Kgs 19:1), Jezebel threatened to kill Elijah. Terrified, Elijah fled to Beersheba and left his servant there. He then went a day's journey into the desert. An angel gave him food and drink and he traveled another forty days and forty nights to Horeb, the Mountain of God, where Moses received the Ten Commandments. It is improbable that this mountain, also known as Mount Sinai, was in the Sinai Peninsula in Egypt. Rather, it was probably what is now called Jebel al-Lawz in Saudi Arabia.

There are two mountains that are candidates for being the Mountain of Moses. Mount Saint Catherine in Sinai, Egypt, rises 4,353 feet above Beersheba (850 feet above sea level), from which it is 259 miles distant. To walk from Beersheba without taking a break, would take 4.5 days.[6] Jebel al-Lawz rises 7,615 feet from Beersheba and is 309 miles distant. To make that trek with no break would take 5.3 days. The hike to either mountain from Beersheba would take about forty days if the traveler were walking for four hours per day and pausing for twenty hours per day. This might be the case if the traveler were walking only in the cool of the morning and conserving his strength for the rest of the day while fasting.

Jebel al-Lawz was more likely Elijah's destination. Elijah lodged in a cave on Mount Horeb (1 Kgs 19:9). There is no cave on Mount Saint Catherine in Egypt, while there is a sizable cave on Jebel al-Lawz. Furthermore, Paul stated that "Mount Sinai is in Arabia" (Gal 4:25). Paul would not have confused Sinai with Arabia, since from at least the third millennium BC the Sinai Peninsula was under Egyptian rule. The Egyptians called Sinai *Mafkat*, meaning the "country of turquoise," which, along with copper, the pharaohs mined there from great antiquity. Therefore, Paul's retreat to

---

6. "Walking Englishman's Walk Time Calculator."

Arabia, although he never states the destination, may have been to Jebel al-Lawz. But why go there?

Paul's realization that Jesus was the Messiah required him to go back to the Scriptures. Similarly, on the road to Emmaus Jesus took Cleophus (Clopas) and his companion through this same scriptural review to explain his role as Messiah (Luke 24:45). Paul may have journeyed to Mount Horeb, the sacred ground where God gave Moses the law, to seek understanding from God about Christ. Perhaps he saw himself as a second Elijah. He would, like Elijah, perform miracles through the Holy Spirit. For example, Elijah restored a child to life (1 Kgs 17:22), and Paul resurrected a young man named Eutychus (Acts 20:9–12).

Unlike Elijah, Paul stayed in Arabia for about three years. It is impossible to know what he did there or with whom he stayed. Perhaps there was a community of religious recluses, similar to the community at Qumran, who congregated near the holy site of Mount Horeb. Perhaps Paul searched the Scriptures with them. Or perhaps he studied alone. This side of heaven, barring some stunning archaeological find, we may never know.

One other intriguing speculation is that perhaps Jesus, when he went for forty days and forty nights into the wilderness, also journeyed to Mount Horeb in Arabia. One clue to this is that during that desert sojourn, "the devil took him up to a high mountain" (Matt 4:8; Luke 4:5). Jebel al-Lawz, with an elevation of 8,465 feet above sea level, would fit. Of course, the devil also took Jesus to the pinnacle of the Jerusalem temple (Matt 4:5; Luke 4:9), which must surely have been either an imaginative or a supernatural event; therefore, the ascent of the high mountain might also have been imaginative or supernatural and is not proof positive that Jesus was at Mount Horeb.

After Jesus' temptation, angels from heaven came and strengthened and attended him, and he was with the wild animals (Matt 4:11; Mark 1:13; Luke 22:43). Similarly, at the start of Elijah's journey into the wilderness, an angel appeared to the prophet and gave him nourishment sufficient for forty days and nights (1 Kgs 19:5). So, both Elijah and Jesus fasted for forty days and nights and both were nourished by an angel, one at the beginning and one at the end of his desert sojourn. Since the Holy Spirit "drove" Jesus into the wilderness (Mark 1:12), if the inspired destination was Mount Horeb, perhaps the Holy Spirit also led Paul to the same place.

BACK IN DAMASCUS: AD 37

Paul returned from Arabia to Damascus after three years, that is, three years after his conversion (Gal 1:18). Once again, as he traveled the Damascus Road, he must have paused at the spot where Jesus had first appeared to him. As he meditated on the last three years, no doubt the deep meaning of Christ's call was more moving than ever.

Everyone in Damascus hearing Saul was amazed, saying, "Is this not he who in Jerusalem destroyed those who called on this name and who had come here for the purpose of bringing them bound before the chief priests?" But Saul kept growing in strength and confounding the Damascus Jews by proving that Jesus was the Christ (Acts 9:21–22).

ESCAPE FROM DAMASCUS

Luke wrote that "when many days had elapsed, the Jews plotted to kill him" (Acts 9:23). The ethnarch under Aretas, the Syrian king, threatened to seize him (2 Cor 11:32). An ethnarch was a national ruler, from the Greek words "*ethnos*" (nation) and "*archon*" (leader). This ethnarch was the Jewish liaison officer whom Aretas appointed to govern the Jewish community in his kingdom. The Jewish ethnarch was just as violently opposed to Saul's Christianizing as Saul had been against Stephen. Probably the letters Paul obtained from the priests in Jerusalem, authorizing him to arrest Christian Jews in Damascus, were addressed to King Aretas and this ethnarch, asking them to give Paul official permission and assistance.

This unnamed ethnarch served under King Aretas IV, who ruled Jordan, Arabia, and Damascus from 9 BC to AD 49. His daughter married Herod Antipas, who put her away in favor of Herodias, his niece (who had previously incestuously married and divorced another uncle, Herod Philip). In AD 36, Aretas made war on Herod Antipas. Rome took Antipas's side. The death of the emperor Tiberius in AD 37 saved Aretas from Rome's retribution.

Meanwhile, Paul's would-be assassins were watching the city gates day and night so that Saul would not escape. Saul's friends took him by night and let him down through an opening in the wall, lowering him in a large basket (Acts 9:25, 2 Cor 11:33). It was a less-than-triumphal exit.

FIRST RETURN TO JERUSALEM: AD 37

After escaping from Damascus, Saul went to Jerusalem to associate with the disciples, but they were all afraid of him. This was three years after his conversion on the Damascus Road (Gal 1:11). The disciples suspected that he had not really become a believer, but Barnabas took hold of Saul and brought him to the apostles and described to them how Paul had seen the Lord on the Damascus Road and had preached in the synagogues of Syria. Then they accepted him, and he began loudly speaking out in the name of the Lord. At this time, Saul saw Peter, but stayed with him for only fifteen days. While in Jerusalem he did not see any of the other apostles, except for James, the half-brother of Jesus (Gal 1:18–19). Probably by this time, the other apostles were already exploring various mission fields.

In Jerusalem, Saul debated vigorously with the Hellenistic Jews (the Sadducees), who plotted to put him to death. Paul must have been very persuasive in arguing that Jesus was the Messiah, since his opponents almost always had one of two responses:

to believe him or attempt to kill him. No adversaries ever seem to have felt that they could defeat Paul in debate.

JESUS SPOKE TO PAUL A SECOND TIME

For the second recorded time, around May 9, AD 37, Jesus spoke directly to Paul. Luke gave Paul's account:

> When I had returned to Jerusalem and was praying in the temple, I fell into a trance and saw him saying to me, "Make haste and get out of Jerusalem quickly, because they will not accept your testimony about me." And I said, "Lord, they themselves know that in one synagogue after another I imprisoned and beat those who believed in you. And when the blood of Stephen your witness was being shed, I myself was standing by and approving and watching over the garments of those who killed him." And he said to me, "Go, for I will send you far away to the Gentiles." (Acts 22:17–21)

OBSCURITY IN TARSUS: AD 37–43

When the Jerusalem Christians heard of this latest Jewish plot against Paul, they took him to Caesarea. It was not the last time he would escape a death threat by being escorted there. They sent him away to his hometown of Tarsus (Acts 9:30). Paul disappeared from history for six years.

JOURNEY TO PARADISE: AD 39

In 2 Corinthians 12:1–5, Paul wrote this enigmatic testimony:

> I must go on boasting. Though there is nothing to be gained by it, I will go on to visions and revelations of the Lord. I know a man in Christ who fourteen years ago was caught up to the third heaven—whether in the body or out of the body I do not know, God knows. And I know that this man was caught up into paradise—whether in the body or out of the body I do not know, God knows—and he heard things that cannot be told, which man may not utter. On behalf of this man I will boast, but on my own behalf I will not boast, except of my weaknesses.

Who was this man? Since Paul wrote "I know," rather than "I knew," the man was still alive when Paul wrote this letter, which he composed in the year AD 53. Since the event occurred fourteen years before writing the letter, it happened in AD 39. Most commentators think that Paul was referring to himself in the third person. The plain language of the text suggests that Paul was speaking of someone other than himself, although who that might be remains a mystery.

PAUL'S MINISTRY BEGINS AGAIN: AD 43–44

Around AD 43, Barnabas, who must have been impressed with him from their Jerusalem meeting, went and found Paul and encouraged him to enter ministry at Antioch, where they worked together for a year. Antioch was the third largest and richest city in the empire, after Rome and Alexandria. Believers were first called Christians in the Antioch church, which tradition says Peter founded (Acts 11:26).

SECOND RETURN TO JERUSALEM: AD 44

In AD 44, Agabus, a prophet, journeyed from Jerusalem to Antioch and predicted that a great famine would devastate Judea. The Antioch church sent Barnabas and Saul to Jerusalem with famine relief funds one year in advance of the disaster (Acts 11:27–30). Meanwhile, between Tuesday, March 29, and Thursday, April 7 (the Passover and Feast of Unleavened Bread), of AD 44, Herod Agrippa I, son of Aristobulus and grandson of Herod the Great, killed James the son of Zebedee and then arrested Peter.[7] An angel released Peter from prison, and he went to the house of Mary, mother of John Mark (Acts 12:6–17). When Jerusalem broke into an uproar at the news of Peter's escape, Herod executed the prison guards, and Peter fled. Then Herod died a grisly death from parasitic worms (Acts 12:20–23). But the word of God increased and multiplied (Acts 12:24). After that, Paul and Barnabas returned to Antioch, taking John Mark with them (Acts 12:2). In AD 45–47 the great famine predicted by Agabus and recorded by the Roman historian Paulus Orosius struck Judea.[8]

FIRST MISSIONARY JOURNEY: AD 44

The years of Paul's three great missionary journeys were the most active of his life. His achievements were astonishing. He was probably about thirty-nine years old when he embarked upon his first missionary journey in May AD 44. After serving in the Antioch church for one year, Lucius of Cyrene, Paul, Barnabas, Simeon Niger, and Manaen were praying and fasting. All five men were teachers and prophets in Antioch. The Holy Spirit called for the appointment of Barnabas and Paul for a special

---

7. Eusebius, *Church History* 2:9.

8. Josephus, *Ant.* 20:2. As foretold by the prophet Agabus and recorded by Josephus, famine raged in Judea under the procurator Cassius Fadus (AD 44–46). Orosius, in his *Histories against Pagans* 7:6:9, 12, placed it in the fourth year of Claudius's reign. Claudius began to reign on January 24, AD 41, so his fourth year began on January 24, AD 45. The famine therefore endured from the Passover of AD 45 to the Passover of AD 47, 739 days or slightly over two years.

assignment. Lucius, Simeon, and Manaen laid hands on Barnabas and Paul and sent them on Paul's first missionary journey to evangelize among the gentiles (Acts 13:1–3). They left Antioch and embarked at Seleucia, Antioch's seaport in Syria, with Barnabas's cousin, John Mark. They sailed for Cyprus, the birthplace of Barnabas, and preached in the synagogue of Salamis.

This was not John Mark's first missionary journey; Peter and Mark preached to Jews in Pontus, Galatia, Cappadocia, Asia, and Bithynia, sometime between AD 41 and 43. Then they pushed on to Rome, founding the church there in AD 43.[9] Reading Acts, one may easily get the impression that Paul was the first to bring the gospel to these parts of the world. In fact, Peter and Mark preceded him. Mark had already composed his Gospel in Rome in AD 43. Doubtless, he brought it with him on this missionary journey so that he, Paul, and Barnabas could refer to it.

CYPRUS

They crossed the island from east to west and reached Paphos, the residence of the Roman proconsul, Sergius Paulus. Opposed by a Jewish false prophet named Bar Jesus Elymas, Saul, who then began using his Hellenic name of Paul, fixed his gaze on him, condemned him, and caused him temporarily to go blind. Witnessing this miracle, the Roman proconsul converted, and Luke thereafter wrote of Paul as the leader of the mission, with Barnabas following.

From Paphos they sailed to Perga in Pamphylia (Asia Minor), near Paul's birthplace, Tarsus. There, to Paul's disappointment, John Mark deserted them and returned to Jerusalem. Why did Mark go back to Judea? Scripture is silent. Although it is conjecture, perhaps Mark felt called to disseminate his Gospel rather than to pursue this missionary trip with Paul and Barnabas. After all, he had been through this line of country with Peter the year before. Maybe he felt that by leaving them a copy of his Gospel, he was not deserting them at all, but managing to cover more ground by splitting up. At this time, Mark probably went to Jerusalem and then on to Alexandria, where he founded the Egyptian church. Perhaps that is where Mark thought his real calling led.

PISIDIAN ANTIOCH

Paul and Barnabas carried on through the wild and bandit-infested mountains of Pisidia toward Antioch (not the great city in Syria), seven days' journey from Perga on the coast. Paul preached the gospel in the synagogue, and many Jews accepted Christ. But on the following Sabbath, a large crowd of angry Jews rejected and persecuted Paul and Barnabas. Shaking the dust of Pisidian Antioch off their feet, they turned to the gentiles, and the gospel went out to the whole region of Antioch.

---

9. Eusebius, *Church History* 2:14–15.

ICONIUM AND LYSTRA

They proceeded to Iconium (modern Konya), four days' journey to the east, where they met with hostility from the native Jews. Then they walked eighteen miles south to Lystra. In Lystra, Paul healed a man lame from birth, and the citizens proclaimed Barnabas and Paul gods: Zeus and Hermes. They assumed that since Paul was the more talkative one, he must be Hermes, the messenger of the gods, and that Barnabas, the strong, silent one, must be Zeus, the king of gods. The priest of Zeus brought oxen to sacrifice to them, but Paul and Barnabas tore their robes and refused to accept blasphemous worship. They preached the gospel, but the Jews from Antioch and Iconium caught up with them and incited the crowd, who stoned Paul and left him outside the city for dead. Surrounded by Christian disciples, he rose and staggered back into the city.

DERBE AND HOME

The next day he and Barnabas set out for Derbe, forty miles to the east. They made many converts there. Paul must have had great fortitude to travel forty miles and preach the day after having been stoned nearly to death. Then they returned to Lystra, Iconium, and Antioch, strengthening the new churches and appointing elders. They returned to Perga, where they preached, and then went to Attalia, another coastal town, from which they took ship to Syrian Antioch. Home again, they reported to their church how the door of faith had opened to the gentiles. They remained with the disciples there "no little time" (Acts 14:28).

THIRD RETURN TO JERUSALEM: AD 48

Fourteen years after his conversion, that is, in AD 48, Paul took the Greek (gentile) Christian, Titus, on a journey to Jerusalem "because of a revelation" (Gal 2:1–2). This could not have been the trip in Acts 11:28–30, because Luke placed that trip before Herod Agrippa's murder of James in AD 44. Paul said in Galatians that this journey was "after" fourteen years, probably meaning after his conversion, which would put it in AD 48. The "revelation" referred to the prophecy of Agabus. One year before the famine, in March AD 44, the Antioch church had sent Paul and Barnabas to Jerusalem with famine relief. The famine occurred in AD 45–47 (probably from Passover to Passover, since the first expected crop harvest in Israel, "Firstfruits," was right after Passover). On the trip in AD 48, probably Paul and his team wanted to see how the revelation had panned out and how effective their famine relief had been.

Some commentators believe this trip to Jerusalem is the same as the trip to attend the Jerusalem Council one year later, but this not possible for several reasons. Paul wrote Galatians to show that gentile Christians need not be circumcised, that is, need not become Jews to become Christians. The Jerusalem Council officially settled this issue, siding with Paul. If the Jerusalem Council had already occurred, Paul would not have needed to write Galatians at all. He could simply have forwarded the decree of the Jerusalem Council to the Galatians and said, "Read it and weep." Paul says he took this trip to Jerusalem "because of a revelation" (Gal 2:2). Paul went to the Jerusalem Council not because of a revelation, but because of dissent in the Antioch church (Acts 15:2). The famine relief mission occurred because of the revelation of Agabus, the prophet, before the famine occurred, and the follow-up mission occurred after the famine to see how the survivors had fared. Also, Paul's meeting with Peter, John, James, and Barnabas was private on this trip (Gal 2:2). The debates of the Jerusalem Council were public (Acts 15:5).

ECUMENICAL CHRISTIAN THEOLOGY

This trip of Paul to Jerusalem marked a significant step in the development of Christian theology. The whole matter is covered in Galatians 2. The trip was motivated by "a revelation," namely the prophecy of Agabus, prompting Paul, Barnabas, and Titus to bring famine relief funds from the rich church in Antioch to the poor church in Jerusalem. Paul, however, took advantage of this opportunity to set before Peter, John, and James (the half-brother of Jesus) the gospel that he was presenting to gentiles in Antioch and that he had presented to gentiles on his first missionary journey. Paul wanted to make sure that he was "not running or had not run in vain."

Paul had no doubt that he understood the gospel correctly. He stated that he had received it directly from Christ, that he did not have to consult with anyone about its interpretation, and that he did not need to ratify it with those who were apostles before him (Gal 1:15–17). So, why did Paul, when he did not feel the need to get advice from the other apostles in AD 37, during his trip back to Jerusalem in AD 44, want to set his presentation of the gospel before Peter, John, and James? It was because Paul had affirmed a discovery that Peter had first made when Peter presented the gospel to the gentile household of Cornelius, namely that the gospel did not require gentiles to become Jews to be Christians, and it did not require Jews to become gentiles to become Christians. Each group of people could remain in their cultural nest and still be brothers and sisters in Christ, because "[they had] been crucified with Christ. It is no longer [they] who live, but Christ who lives in [them]. And the life [they] now live in the flesh [they] live by faith in the Son of God" (Gal 2:20). Peter, James, and John entirely agreed with Paul. They felt no need to add anything to his message (Gal 2:6), and they gave Paul and Barnabas the right hand of fellowship. This theological issue was further tested on that same trip to Jerusalem when some Judaizers spied on Titus, who was a gentile Christian from Antioch. They saw that he was uncircumcised. They tried to compel his circumcision, but Paul and Barnabas refused to submit to their demand, and James, Peter, and John agreed with them.

Paul and Barnabas had proven themselves in many ways, not the least of which had been their bringing funds to the Jerusalem church before the famine. James, Peter, and John only asked Paul to remember to help the poor of Jerusalem, which was the very thing he wished to continue doing (Gal 2:10). Paul never forgot the poor of Jerusalem. Several times he encouraged his gentile flocks to raise money for their support. No doubt Paul felt a deep sense of guilt for his early, fierce persecution of those people who now were his brothers in Christ. He wrote, "for I am the least of the apostles, and not fit to be called an apostle, because I persecuted the Church of God" (1 Cor 15:9).

Paul's commission to preach to gentiles and Peter's commission to preach to Jews were primary, not exclusive, assignments. Paul was not actually the first missionary to the gentiles. Philip, Peter, and John were, in Samaria, to the Ethiopian eunuch, and to the household of Cornelius, the Roman centurion. Probably by the time of this trip to Jerusalem the other apostles had already been on missionary journeys, probably making gentile converts, too. Paul's commission was to preach primarily to the gentiles, as that of Peter and the other apostles was to preach primarily to the Jews (Gal 2:9), but all the apostles preached with great effect to both gentiles and Jews. The main lesson from this trip to Jerusalem was that "there is neither Jew nor Greek [gentile], there is neither slave nor free, there is no male and female, for you are all one in Christ Jesus" (Gal 3:28). And, importantly, it was not necessary for gentiles to become Jews or Jews to become gentiles for all to become Christians.

DEBATE WITH JUDAIZERS AND OPPOSITION TO PETER: AD 49

Paul and his companions returned to Antioch sometime in AD 48, where he remained "no little time," until around May of AD 49. Judaizers from Jerusalem arrived in Antioch and tried to persuade the gentiles there that they had to become Jewish to be Christian. Paul and Barnabas debated this with them. After seeing the door of faith opened to the gentiles during their first missionary journey and having settled the matter in Jerusalem with Peter, John, and James with regard to Titus, Paul must have been astonished that the Judaizing argument could still carry on.

Probably between March 30 and April 15, AD 49 (Passover), Peter visited Antioch, and a dispute arose between him and Paul. Peter agreed that Christian Jews were free of the law, but he refrained from eating with gentiles because he thought it unwise to offend the Judaizers, who were associates of James, the Lord's half-brother. Peter probably thought it was not a big issue, because the gentile Christians would probably not care about eating the Passover meal with Peter anyway. Only the Jewish Christians would be eager to do so. He possibly also thought that what he, Paul, John, and James had agreed upon in Jerusalem was that Paul's department was the gentiles and Peter's department was the Jews. But Paul's argument went far beyond that. He meant that when evangelizing the apostles did not need to persuade converts to abandon their cultural heritage; they could become Christians just as they were (so long as they did not drag idolatrous or sinful baggage into the church). Peter's example in Antioch would have influenced gentiles and Jews to reach the opposite conclusion and either create opposing camps within the church or repel many from the church altogether. Paul opposed Peter's actions publicly and to his face. Peter humbly accepted Paul's rebuke. Then Peter sailed back to Caesarea and from there returned to Jerusalem, probably between April 15 and 20.

THE EPISTLE TO THE GALATIANS

The Judaizers seem not to have accepted the matter as settled, because the Antioch church decided to send Paul and Barnabas to Jerusalem to confer with the apostles and the elders there on this question. At this time, Paul wrote his fiery letter to the Galatians, affirming that gentiles were free of the law in Christ. The passionate arguments of Paul in this epistle probably reflect the emotion he displayed in his debates with the Judaizers. Galatians tracks theologically with the book of Romans, but it almost seems that Galatians is Romans written in a bad mood. It is evident that Paul wrote Galatians before, not after, the Jerusalem Council because after the council the letter to the Galatians would have been unnecessary. Paul would only have needed to refer the Galatian churches to the apostles' decree. The fact that Paul wrote Galatians before the council further illustrates that Paul knew his position was right. He received his guidance, as he said in Galatians, from Jesus directly, not from being an understudy to other apostles. And the apostles at the council would agree with him. Paul was one of the most influential authors of all time. His writing career began with this epistle.

The book of Acts does not explicitly record Paul and Barnabas visiting Galatia. Galatia was named after a tribe of Gauls (Celts), who, in the third century BC, migrated from what is now France, invaded the Balkans and Asia Minor, and eventually settled in what is now central Turkey. By the first century BC, these Gauls had become so Hellenized that the Greeks and Romans called them "Greek Galatians," or, modernizing the epithet, "Greek Frenchmen." In 25 BC, the emperor Augustus turned Galatia into a Roman province, including in Galatia proper the regions of Pamphylia,[10] "Lycaonia, Isauria, and portions of Phrygia and Pisidia."[11] The first missionary journey of Paul and Barnabas took them to the island of Cyprus and then across the Mediterranean Sea to Perga in Pamphylia (Acts 13:13), to Antioch in Pisidia (not Syria, Acts 13:14), to Iconium (modern Konya) in Phrygia (Acts 13:51), to Lystra and Derbe in Lycaonia (Acts 14:6), back along the same route to Antioch in Pisidia (Acts 14:21), back to Perga (Acts 14:25), and from Attalia by ship back to their home church of Antioch in Syria (Acts 14:26). When Paul wrote Galatians, therefore, he was addressing all the churches (except those in Cyprus) that he and Barnabas founded on this journey, all of which were located in what Paul's contemporaries would have recognized as

10. Smith, *Dictionary of Greek and Roman Geography*, 316.
11. Cheetham, "The Province of Galatia," 396.

"greater Galatia." The term "Galatian church," therefore, is shorthand for the cluster of churches in the Galatian region founded by Paul and Barnabas.

Paul and Barnabas traveled south from Antioch to Jerusalem, through Phoenicia and Samaria. They told Christians all along the way how gentiles were coming to Christ, and the brothers rejoiced. Evidently Paul was in no doubt about how this question would be settled. He had no intention of waiting for the apostles in Jerusalem to affirm his position. He freely gave out his views along the way.

THE JERUSALEM COUNCIL: AD 49

When the council convened, some Christian Pharisees continued to insist that circumcision was required for believers. It is important not to let the phrase "Christian Pharisees" slip by unnoticed. First, it is amazing that many Pharisees, formerly the implacable enemies of Jesus, had become Christians, just as Nicodemus, Joseph of Arimathea, and Paul had done. Luke also records that many priests became Christians (Acts 6:7). But even after becoming Christians, Pharisees still had a tendency toward legalism. Old habits die hard.

Paul and Barnabas argued against the Judaizing Christian Pharisees. After much debate, Peter sided with Paul and Barnabas. James, the half-brother of Jesus, agreed. (James, the son of Zebedee, was not present, for Herod Agrippa I had murdered him in AD 44.) The Jerusalem Council officially recognized that Christianity was more than a Jewish sect; it was a universal religion, embracing Jews and gentiles.

The council decided that gentiles were acceptable as Christians without circumcision, but that they should refrain from eating meat offered to idols, from eating blood and strangled animals, and from fornication. All these rituals were associated with the worship of pagan gods. The council further affirmed that Christian Jews were free to continue observing the law of Moses, but that, like Christian gentiles, they might also consider themselves free from the law and under the new covenant of grace. The council wrote a letter to this effect and charged a certain Judas Justus Barsabbas and Silas (Silvanus) to go to the gentile brethren in Syria and Asia Minor, promulgating the council's decree.

SECOND MISSIONARY JOURNEY: AD 49-51

With the letter from the Jerusalem Council in hand, and, no doubt, with copies of his epistle to the Galatians, Paul asked Barnabas to return with him to all the young churches they had planted in Asia Minor to see how they were. They had been on their own for five years. Doubtless he wanted to ensure that the Judaizers had not also shaken their faith. Barnabas wanted to bring his cousin, John Mark, but Paul sharply disagreed to take the one who had deserted them in Pamphylia. Mark may seem in this account to be an inexperienced boy, not up to the rigors of evangelism. But Mark had already accompanied Peter to Rome by this date and had composed his Gospel.[12] He may also already have founded the church in Egypt. At any rate, Barnabas returned with Mark to Cyprus, and Paul took Silas back to Asia Minor. Silas was a Roman citizen, like Paul, a fact that would become relevant when they crossed over to Europe.

Paul and Silas walked from Antioch in Syria to Derbe and Lystra. On the way, the two apostles would have had to pass by Saul's hometown of Tarsus. Whether they stopped to greet Paul's family or whether, knowing Paul's family shunned him for becoming a Christian, they passed silently by can only be imagined. In Derbe and Lystra, a few years before, Paul had healed a man lame from birth. The people had tried to worship Barnabas and Paul as Zeus and Hermes, and the Jews of Iconium had stoned Paul and left him for dead.

ENLISTING TIMOTHY

This time in Lystra, they met a disciple named Timothy, son of a Jewish Christian mother and Greek father. This Christian family must have remembered the ignominious treatment Paul had suffered before, but rather than despise him for it, they admired him.

Paul wanted to take Timothy on their missionary journey, so Paul had Timothy circumcised. This was not because Timothy's salvation depended on it, but because Timothy wanted to evangelize among the Jews. This was not a reversal of the council's decision about Judaizing. As the son of a Greek gentile, Timothy could not have entered synagogues for missionary purposes without being circumcised, and in the living conditions of the first century, sooner or later his physical state would have been observed. This willing self-sacrifice by Timothy shows how devoted he was to the cause.

As the missionaries visited the young churches, they shared the decree of the Jerusalem Council, and the churches grew. Then the Holy Spirit forbade them from preaching any more in Asia Minor (Turkey). As they passed through Galatia and Phrygia and reached Mysia, on the coast of the Aegean Sea, they wanted to go north, to the populous and prosperous province of Bithynia on the Black Sea, but the Spirit of Jesus prevented them, so they came to Troas, near the ancient city of Troy. There Paul dreamed of a man from Macedonia urging him to come over to Europe and help them. At this point in the narrative (Acts 16:10), Luke changed from the pronouns "he" or "they" to the pronoun "we." Evidently Luke joined Paul's mission at Troy. It may be that Luke had completed and published his Gospel in AD 49 and brought a copy with him when he joined Paul, at which point he began composing the book of Acts.

---

12. Eusebius, *Church History* 2:14–15.

PHILIPPI

Around October AD 49,[13] they sailed from Troy to the Greek island of Samothrace, and then to Neapolis in Thrace. From Neapolis they walked to Philippi, a leading Roman city in Macedonia. Philip II, father of Alexander the Great, founded Philippi in 356 BC. In 42 BC at the Battle of Philippi, Marc Antony and Octavian (the future emperor Augustus) defeated Brutus and Cassius, the assassins of Julius Caesar and defenders of the Roman Republic. This was an important city.

On their first Sabbath in Philippi, as there was no synagogue, they went to the banks of the Krenides River, which they thought might be a place of prayer. There they met Lydia, a seller of purple fabrics from Thyatira, a city in Asia Minor. Lydia became Paul's first convert in Europe.[14] She and all her household were baptized, and they gave lodging to Paul and his followers. Since this household of new believers is denoted as Lydia's household, Lydia seems to have been the first leader of the Philippian church. This undermines the frequent claim that Paul was a misogynist.

In Philippi, Paul commanded a demon to come out of a slave girl whose masters had profited from her fortunetelling. Angered, the girl's masters dragged Paul and Silas in front of the city authorities and accused them of teaching unlawful doctrines. The city magistrates had them stripped, beaten, and jailed. They then warned the jailer to guard them well. The jailer threw them into the innermost cells and locked their feet in stocks.

About midnight, despite painful injuries, Paul and Silas were singing hymns. The other prisoners were listening to them. Then an earthquake struck, broke open the prison doors, and ruptured the prisoners' bonds.[15] At this, the jailer nearly committed suicide, knowing that the penalty for losing his prisoners would be death. If he had tried to escape his fate by running away, the authorities would have killed his family. Suicide would be an honorable remedy that would spare him a lingering death and save his loved ones. However, Paul called out loudly for the jailer not to harm himself, for all his prisoners were there. Paul witnessed to the jailer. He and his whole household believed and were baptized that night.

In the morning, the magistrates ordered the prisoners released. Paul indignantly informed them that he and Silas were Roman citizens and that the magistrates had punished them without a trial. For this, the magistrates might have faced severe

---

13. Navigation between September and March was perilous in the Mediterranean (Acts 27:9), but this trip was a short one across the Aegean Sea. The travelers could have timed it to avoid bad weather, and this may have been why they stopped at the island of Samothrace along the way.

14. If the Roman Christians were present at the birth of the church on Pentecost, AD 33, brought their faith back to Rome, and if Peter and Mark had evangelized Rome in AD 43, Lydia would not have been the first convert in Europe, just Paul's first convert there. She may have been the first convert in Greece.

15. The bonds were probably stocks, not chains, as an earthquake would probably not have broken chains.

punishment.[16] Terrified, they begged Paul and Silas to leave Philippi. Haughtily taking their time, Paul and Silas went to stay with Lydia, and then departed for Amphipolis, Apollonia, and Thessalonica, where they found a synagogue of Jews.

THESSALONICA

They preached in Thessalonica, and a number of Jews, Greeks, and prominent women in the city believed. But other Jews became angry, and they dragged Jason, who was hosting Paul and Silas, before the authorities, complaining that he was helping these renegades to proclaim another king, Jesus, in place of Caesar. They stirred up a crowd and extorted a pledge from Jason not to support the preaching of Paul and Silas anymore. The Christians of Thessalonica smuggled Paul and Silas out of the city by night. They made their way to Berea, further south, near Mount Olympus.

BEREA

In Berea, around January of AD 50, they preached in the synagogue again. The Berean Jews were more noble-minded than those of Thessalonica, and they eagerly searched the Scriptures to check if what Paul was teaching about Jesus fit Messianic prophecies. Many Jews and Greeks believed. But the Jews from Thessalonica pursued them to Berea and incited a mob. The brethren sent Paul, Luke, and some others to Athens. Silas and Timothy remained in Berea, but Paul left Timothy instructions to return to the church in Thessalonica to encourage them after all the trouble the Thessalonian Jews had made in their own city and in Berea (1 Thess 3:2). After that, Silas and Timothy were to join Paul in Corinth as soon as they could.

ATHENS

Paul and Luke were alone in Athens.[17] The city was full of idols, including one to the "unknown god." Paul preached in the Athenian synagogue and marketplace, and

16. Roman law strictly forbade beating, imprisoning, or crucifying a Roman citizen without due process of law. Cicero, *Against Verres*, 2:5:161-163.

17. Some assume that because Luke stopped using the pronoun "we," which he adopted in Acts 16:10, and reverted to the pronoun "they" at this time, that Luke did not accompany Paul to Thessalonica and beyond. Luke resumed using the pronoun "we" in Acts 20:5, when Paul sailed back to Macedonia after his third visit to Corinth. This begs the question of who recorded Paul's eloquent speech in Athens. Paul may have recited the details from memory to Luke later as he composed the book of Acts, but Luke's vivid account of the Athenian episode in Acts 17:20–34 seems like an eyewitness account. If Luke was in Athens, he may have made an insignificant pronoun shift between Act 17:1 and 20:5, purely as a literary decision. In that case, he may have accompanied Paul all the way from Philippi to Thessalonica to Berea to Athens to Corinth to Ephesus to Jerusalem, back to Ephesus, back to Philippi, and finally back to Corinth, and thence to Macedonia. This thesis is supported by the possibility that Luke was the "brother" that Paul sent with Titus from Ephesus to Corinth in AD 52 (2

the numerous philosophers of Athens brought him to Ares Hill (the Areopagus) to hear what philosophy he espoused. Paul's sermon was elegant and persuaded some to believe, including Dionysus the Areopagite and a woman named Damaris and others with them, although most of the Athenians seemed only mildly interested. Paul left Athens without being persecuted or thrown out, for once, and proceeded to Corinth, farther south.

CORINTH

In Corinth, around January AD 50, Paul met Aquila and his wife Priscilla, Christian Jews from Rome. Possibly this couple had been converted to Christianity in Rome by Peter in AD 43, seven years before. In any case, they were forced to leave Rome by a decree that the emperor Claudius made in the ninth year of his reign, AD 49. Claudius was weary of the persecution of Christian Jews by non-Christian Jews, so he expelled all Jews, of whatever persuasion, from Rome. Paul had a family trade. He was a tentmaker. Since Aquila and Priscilla were of the same trade, Paul stayed and worked with them.

Paul preached in the Corinthian synagogue every Sabbath. Silas and Timothy reached Corinth from Macedonia, around February AD 50. Then the violent opposition of the Jews forced Paul to start preaching in a house next to the synagogue. Possibly this was when Aquila and Priscilla risked their necks to save Paul (Rom 16:4). This house was owned by a Jewish Christian named Titus Justus. No doubt to the horror of the non-Christian Jews, Crispus, the leader of their synagogue, and his whole household became Christians. Crispus was one of the few people Paul personally baptized in Corinth. Paul said Christ did not send him to baptize but to preach the gospel (1 Cor 1:14-17). They presumably went next door to join the church in Justus's home. Paul remained in Corinth one year and six months (Acts 18:11).

ILLYRICUM

At some point during this sojourn, Paul must have made a side trip to Illyricum, the Roman province west of Greece on the Adriatic Sea (modern Albania, Montenegro, Bosnia, Herzegovina, and coastal Croatia). The evidence for this is that Paul wrote in Romans 15:19, "from Jerusalem and all the way around to Illyricum I have fulfilled the ministry of the gospel of Christ." Obviously, the trip occurred before he wrote Romans in AD 54, and there is no other place in Paul's itinerary when he was so near to Illyricum and had the time to go. If Paul walked to Illyricum, it would have taken about thirty-three days each way. If he sailed from Corinth, it would have taken about eight

---

Cor 12:18). Or Luke may have been somewhere else during this entire interval of fifty-four months, from November AD 49 to April AD 54. Either thesis is possible, but, since Luke was Paul's Boswell, this author prefers the thesis that Luke accompanied Paul for this entire time.

days each way. Thus, if he sailed in good weather, the whole trip might have taken a month or less. If he went overland in the winter, it would have taken over two months. We know nothing about Paul's work there except for this passing remark.

JESUS SPOKE TO PAUL A THIRD TIME

In Corinth, around February 20, AD 50, Jesus spoke for the third recorded time to Paul, saying "Do not be afraid, but go on speaking and do not be silent, for I am with you, and no one will attack you to harm you, for I have many in this city who are my people" (Acts 18:9–10).

FIRST AND SECOND THESSALONIANS

In AD 50, Paul sent Timothy back to Thessalonica to check on the church's status and strengthen their faith (1 Thess 3:1–2). Timothy brought back a very encouraging report. Despite the riotous behavior of the Thessalonian Jews, the church in Thessalonica had remained faithful to the gospel, even though Paul had presented it "in the midst of much conflict" (1 Thess 2:2). Paul gladly wrote 1 Thessalonians to them. He sent greetings from himself, Silas, and Timothy, as Timothy was probably the return courier.

After reading 1 Thessalonians, and after receiving a fake, alarming letter from someone pretending to be Paul (2 Thess 2:2), the Thessalonians had further questions. Probably they wrote Paul a letter or sent a messenger asking them. The questions included whether Jesus had already come a second time, something about the resurrection from the dead, and something about a "man of lawlessness." Reading 2 Thessalonians is like hearing one half of a phone conversation. Paul reminded the Thessalonians of things he already had told them. We do not know what he had told them. He said they knew what was restraining the "man of lawlessness." We do not know what was restraining him, much less who the "man of lawlessness" was. Presumably, the Holy Spirit was restraining him, but certain passages of 2 Thessalonians are frankly a mystery without a solution. In this letter, Paul again sent greetings from himself, Silas, and Timothy, suggesting that the courier carrying the letter was someone else.

GALLIO

The Jews complained about Paul to Gallio, the Roman proconsul of Achaia (Greece). Junius Annaeus Gallio was the brother of Seneca, the Roman Stoic philosopher, playwright, and advisor to the emperor Nero. Gallio ignored the complaints of the Corinthian Jews, saying:

> If it were a matter of wrongdoing or vicious crime, O Jews, I would have reason to accept your complaint. But since it is a matter of questions about words

and names and your own law, see to it yourselves. I refuse to be a judge of these things. (Acts 18:14–15)

FOURTH RETURN TO JERUSALEM: AD 51.

Paul remained many days longer in Corinth after this hearing. He had his hair shaved in the nearby village of Cenchreae because he had made a vow of some kind. Then he, Aquila, Priscilla, Timothy, Silas, and Luke sailed for Ephesus. At this time, Apollos, a powerful preacher of the gospel, left Alexandria in Egypt and headed for Ephesus. In Ephesus, Paul reasoned with the Jews in the synagogue. He declined to stay there a long time but promised to return. He and Luke left Aquila and Priscilla in Ephesus and sailed to Caesarea at the end of summer, AD 51. After Paul left Ephesus, Apollos arrived there and met Aquila and Priscilla. For the fourth time, Paul returned to Jerusalem. He was in time to celebrate the Jewish fall holy days.

APOLLOS IN EPHESUS: AD 51

At about the same time, Apollos arrived in Ephesus and met Aquila and Priscilla there. He just missed Paul.

> [Apollos] was an eloquent man, competent in the Scriptures. He had been instructed in the way of the Lord. And being fervent in spirit, he spoke and taught accurately the things concerning Jesus, though he knew only the baptism of John. He began to speak boldly in the synagogue, but when Priscilla and Aquila heard him, they took him aside and explained to him the way of God more accurately. And when he wished to cross to Achaia (Greece), the brothers encouraged him and wrote to the disciples to welcome him. When he arrived, he greatly helped those who through grace had believed, for he powerfully refuted the Jews in public, showing by the Scriptures that the Christ was Jesus. (Acts 18:24–28)

THIRD MISSIONARY JOURNEY: AD 51–54

From Jerusalem, Paul returned to Antioch. After a brief rest there, he began his third missionary journey. He walked through Galatia and Phrygia. Again, he must have passed by his hometown of Tarsus. Whether he paused to greet his family or, knowing their aversion to his Christian faith, walked sadly by can only be imagined. He then returned to Ephesus, a trek of about 710 miles. It is probable that he walked, because the time of year was October and November of AD 51, a season when storms made it too dangerous to sail (Acts 27:9).

EPHESUS

Apollos had moved on to Corinth, but Aquila and Priscilla were awaiting Paul in Ephesus. He again joined them in earning a living by making tents so that he could pay his own way and not burden the faithful. He began in Ephesus by teaching twelve believers who, until then, had only known the baptism of John. Paul baptized them in the Holy Spirit (Acts 19:1–6). Then he taught in the synagogue for three months, where he spoke boldly. But some in the synagogue became stubborn and spoke evil of the gospel before the congregation, so Paul withdrew and took his disciples with him. He then taught daily in the hall of Tyrannus from eleven in the morning till four in the afternoon for two years, from about November AD 51 to about February AD 53. The identity of Tyrannus is uncertain. He was probably a teacher with a private school or lecture room.

While in Ephesus, God performed many miracles through Paul. Even handkerchiefs and aprons that he touched healed the sick when they touched them. Seven sons of the chief Jewish leader, Sceva, attempted to imitate Paul's exorcisms, but a demon-possessed person beat and wounded the would-be exorcists, saying, "I recognize Jesus, and I know about Paul, but who are you?" Then the man who had the evil spirit jumped on them and overpowered them all. He gave them such a beating that they ran out of the house naked and bleeding.

Paul's teaching so triumphed over his phony rivals that the Ephesians turned away from superstitions and sorcery. They burned books of magic worth 50,000 pieces of silver. In 2022, the metallic value of this was about $124,700. But money had greater purchasing power in the first century than it has today. Since a piece of silver was about a day's wages, this was a value equivalent to more than 136 years of work. Converting this sum to the average day's wages in the United States in 2022, the current equivalent purchasing power would be about $8.9 million.

BETWEEN EPHESUS AND CORINTH

This is a phase of Paul's third missionary journey that can be difficult to follow because the details of Paul's actions and travels are embedded throughout Acts and 1 and 2 Corinthians. Mixed in with Paul's actions and travels are the actions and travels of Apollos, Timothy, Titus, Luke, Erastus, Sosthenes, Chloe's people, Stephanas, Fortunatus, and Achaicus (who may be Chloe's people). The following summary of events will aid the reader in following Paul's story, as well as the turbulent story of the newly planted Corinthian church.

- Paul traveled from Antioch to Ephesus between September 25 and October 24, AD 51 (Acts 18:23, 19:1).
- Apollos was in Corinth at that time (Acts 19:1).

- Timothy, Titus, and probably Luke ("the brother who is praised by all the churches for his work in the gospel") either went with Paul from Antioch to Ephesus or they joined Paul in Ephesus (1 Cor 4:17; 2 Cor 8:18, 12:18).

- Someone from Corinth brought news of jealousy, quarreling, factionalism, litigation, adultery, incest, and other kinds of immorality in the Corinthian church. Probably the messenger was Apollos. This stands to reason because if Apollos was in Corinth when Paul arrived in Ephesus (Acts 19:1) and then in Ephesus refusing Paul's request for him to return to Corinth (1 Cor 16:12), Apollos must have traveled from Corinth to Ephesus between these two incidents.

- Paul wrote a lost warning letter to Corinth (1 Cor 5:9). Timothy took it to them (1 Cor 4:17). Since traveling alone might be dangerous, it is reasonable to suspect that Titus went with him.

- Paul's lost first letter did not fix the problems. The Corinthians wrote Paul a lost letter back with questions about proper sexual mores (1 Cor 7:1), entrusting it to Timothy, Chloe's people, Stephanas, Fortunatus, Achaicus, and Sosthenes, the synagogue leader in Corinth (Acts 18:17; 1 Cor 1:1, 11, 16:17).

- Paul wrote a second letter, 1 Corinthians, in part answering the Corinthians' lost letter to Paul and in part addressing the generally scandalous practices in the Corinthian church. Timothy took 1 Corinthians to Corinth (1 Cor 4:17, 16:10), accompanied by Chloe's people, Stephanas, Fortunatus, Achaicus, and perhaps Sosthenes.[18] Apollos refused to return to Corinth at this time (1 Cor 16:12). Apparently, he was fed up with the Corinthian mess.

- The Corinthian church did not respond well to 1 Corinthians. Timothy was probably the messenger who brought this news back to Paul in Ephesus.

- Paul wrote a lost, painful letter of tears and anguish to Corinth (2 Cor 2:4, 7:8, 12). Probably Timothy brought this back to Corinth.

- Concluding, after sending the lost letter of tears, that Corinth needed a more personal intervention, Paul made a second quick and painful trip Corinth (2 Cor 12:14, 13:1). This is evident because Paul could not have made a third trip to Corinth without making a second one.

- Paul returned from Corinth to Ephesus. This is evident, because Paul could not have left Ephesus after his second trip to Corinth (2 Cor 12:14, 13:1) and before

---

18. From Ephesus, Paul sent greetings to the Corinthians from himself and Sosthenes (1 Cor 1:1). Perhaps this implies that Sosthenes remained in Ephesus with Paul for some time, since Paul would not need to send Sosthenes's greetings if Sosthenes accompanied the epistle back to Corinth. On the other hand, perhaps Sosthenes did accompany 1 Corinthians back to Corinth but Paul included his greetings in the letter to add Sosthenes's authority, as leader of the Corinthian synagogue (Acts 18:17), to the epistle.

his third trip to Corinth (Acts 20:1–3) without first returning from Corinth to Ephesus.

- From Ephesus, Paul sent Titus and probably Luke to Corinth to help steady the church on the right course until Paul should return (2 Cor 8:18, 12:18).
- Paul sent Timothy and Erastus ahead of him to Macedonia (Acts 19:22).
- Paul sent Aquila and Priscilla back to Rome to see how the Roman church was faring.
- Paul traveled to Troas, hoping to meet Titus there, but Titus missed the rendezvous (2 Cor 2:12–13).
- Paul went on to Philippi and met Timothy (and Erastus) there (2 Cor 1:1).
- Titus arrived in Philippi, bringing Paul news of the apparently improved state of the church in Corinth (2 Cor 7:6–7, 14).
- Paul wrote 2 Corinthians from Philippi, adding greetings from Timothy (2 Cor 1:1, 9:2–5).
- Titus, probably Luke, and other brothers carried 2 Corinthians to Corinth (2 Cor 8:17–18, 9:3).
- Paul promised that he would come again to Corinth for a third time (2 Cor 12:14, 20–21, 13:1).
- In Corinth, Titus collected funds for the Jerusalem church, while Paul collected funds in Macedonia (2 Cor 8:6).
- Paul arrived in Corinth and remained there for three months (Acts 20:2–3).
- In Corinth, Paul added the funds Titus had collected for the Jerusalem church to those he had collected in Macedonia (Rom 15:25–26).
- In Corinth, Paul wrote Romans and sent greetings to Prisca (Priscilla) and Aquila and many others (Rom 16:3) from Timothy, Lucius,[19] Sosipater, Paul's kinsman, Tertius, Paul's scribe, and four others (Rom 16:21–23).

TROUBLE IN CORINTH

While in Ephesus, Paul received troubling news from Corinth, probably brought to him by Apollos. Members of the church there were indulging in jealousy, quarreling, factionalism, litigation, adultery, incest, and other kinds of immorality. He probably wanted to travel immediately to Corinth to correct them, but since this was around November AD 51, the sailing weather was too dangerous. Even if Paul had been

---

19. This Lucius may have been Lucius of Cyrene (Acts 13:1) or some otherwise unknown person with this common Roman name. He was probably not Luke the evangelist, because his name in Greek was Loukas, not Lucius.

willing to risk the winter storms, most sea captains would not do so. So, from Ephesus, Paul wrote a lost warning letter to the Corinthian church. It had to travel overland so it would reach Corinth only by the end of AD 51. Timothy was the messenger. Since traveling alone was risky, it is reasonable to suspect that Titus went with him.

Paul's lost first letter did not fix the problems. The Corinthians wrote Paul a lost letter back with questions about proper sexual mores, entrusting it to Timothy, Chloe's people, Stephanas, Fortunatus, Achaicus (who may have been Chloe's people), Sosthenes (the synagogue leader in Corinth), and probably Titus. Paul probably only received this delegation from Corinth by February AD 52. The news prompted him to write 1 Corinthians (which, despite its name, was actually Paul's second letter to Corinth). This grand epistle scolded the church in Corinth for its licentious behavior and acknowledged that he appreciated Apollos's ministry there. He referred to Apollos as his coworker who was watering the seed of faith that Paul had planted. Paul also defined moral sexual behavior (1 Cor 7) and expressed many lofty theological concepts.

JESUS SPOKE TO PAUL A FOURTH TIME

In 1 Corinthians, written in Ephesus around March AD 52, Paul wrote:

> I received from the Lord what I also delivered to you, that the Lord Jesus on the night when he was betrayed took bread, and when he had given thanks, he broke it, and said, "This is my body, which is for you. Do this in remembrance of me." In the same way also he took the cup, after supper, saying, "This cup is the new covenant in my blood. Do this, as often as you drink it, in remembrance of me." For as often as you eat this bread and drink the cup, you proclaim the Lord's death until he comes. (1 Cor 11:23)

This is a beautiful summation of the Eucharist. The account is also remarkable because Paul says that he did not learn of this from Peter or John, who were present at the Last Supper, but that Jesus told taught him this personally.

BACK TO CORINTH

Since the weather was now fair, Paul sent Timothy with 1 Corinthians to Corinth, accompanied by Chloe's people, Stephanas, Fortunatus, Achaicus, and probably Sosthenes (unless he remained for some time with Paul in Ephesus). Apollos refused to return to Corinth at this time. Apparently, he was fed up with the Corinthian mess.

Unfortunately, 1 Corinthians was still not well received. Timothy returned to Ephesus and reported this to Paul, probably around May AD 52. Paul responded with a lost severe, tearful letter to the Corinthians. Since the sailing weather was still fine, the letter probably reached Corinth before June AD 52. Probably Timothy was the courier again.

Paul realized that he needed to revisit all his churches in Greece, and he made plans for a sweeping journey through Macedonia, Greece, back to Jerusalem, and ending up in Rome (Acts 19:21). Unwilling, however, to wait that long to intervene in Corinth, and probably concluding, after sending three letters, that letters alone would not fix the problems there, Paul made a second quick round trip to Corinth around June AD 52.

The proof that Paul made this second, quick trip to Corinth is as follows. Since 2 Corinthians says that Paul was planning to come to Corinth a third time (2 Cor 10:2, 12:14, 20–21, 13:1), there had to have been a second time. From this comes the inescapable inference that Paul made a second quick trip to Corinth between his first visit there (Acts 18:1) and before his return there (Acts 20:2–3). In 2 Corinthians, however, written about eighteen months after this quick trip, Paul made apparently contradictory statements about traveling to Corinth.

"I wanted to come to you first, so that you might have a second experience of grace. I wanted to visit you on my way to Macedonia and to come back to you from Macedonia and have you send me on my way to Judea. Was I vacillating when I wanted to do this? Do I make my plans according to the flesh, ready to say yes, yes and no, no at the same time? . . . I call God to witness against me, it was to spare you that I refrained from coming again to Corinth . . . for I made up my mind not to make another painful visit to you . . . and I wrote to you as I did so that when I came I might not suffer pain from those who should have made me rejoice . . . for I wrote to you out of much affliction and anguish of heart with many tears" (2 Cor 1:15–23, 2:1–4).

Paul wrote that before writing 2 Corinthians he was planning to go to Corinth to give them a second blessing of grace (outreach). Since his first outreach to Corinth was his first trip there, it is obvious that if he went to Corinth again, that would be his second outreach. His original idea was to go to Macedonia and from Macedonia to go to Corinth again. In 1 Corinthians, he said he would come to Corinth again soon (1 Cor 4:19–21, 11:34, 16:2), but he specified that it would be only after he passed through Macedonia (1 Cor 16:5). He also said that he would not come quite yet, because he did not want to make just a quick, passing visit: "I do not now want to see you in passing. I hope indeed to remain a certain time with you if the Lord permits. I will remain, however, in Ephesus until Pentecost" (1 Cor 16:7–8).

But then Paul sent 1 Corinthians to Corinth and received an unsatisfactory response. He shot off an anguished letter of tears (2 Cor 2:4). He did this in lieu of making a second painful visit to Corinth (2 Cor 2:1). But then he changed his mind. He decided he must make a personal intervention in Corinth without delay. So, he went to Corinth a second time, returned to Ephesus, went to Macedonia, returned to Corinth a third time, and then returned, via Macedonia and Asia, to Jerusalem. Of this apparent vacillation in his plans he wrote, "Did I not use lightness in thus planning? Or do I plan according to the flesh so that with me there should be yes, yes and no, no?" (2 Cor 1:17). In this epistle, written after his promise in 1 Corinthians to follow a certain itinerary and after his changing that itinerary, Paul was excusing his seeming inconsistency. He followed a course of action different from what he originally planned (2 Cor 2:1). Yet the circumstances made his revised plan the right one. After the second trip to Corinth, Paul returned to Ephesus, completing his two-year mission there, and then resumed his original plan to travel back through Macedonia and Achaia to Corinth and thence back to Jerusalem (but via Macedonia again, as a Jewish plot changed his original plan once again).

SENDING OUT HIS TEAM

From Ephesus, Paul then sent Timothy and Erastus to Macedonia (Acts 19:22) to prepare the way for his next grand journey. He sent Titus to Corinth to help steady the church on the right course until Paul should return. He also gave Titus instructions to raise funds for the Jerusalem church and meet him in Troas afterwards. This rapid sequence of letters and trips to Corinth imply how concerned Paul was for this wayward church.

Around AD 53, Paul apparently sent Aquila and Priscilla back to Rome to see how the church there had survived Claudius's decree expelling all Jews and to lay the groundwork for his planned visit there (Acts 19:21; Rom 15:22–24). This is implied because when Paul wrote Romans from Corinth in AD 54 Aquila and Priscilla were already back in Rome (Rom 16:3). They probably felt it was safe to return despite the edict of AD 49. While Claudius's edict would expire with his death on October 13, AD 54, even before he died, government inefficiency being what it always is, the decree probably had relaxed. This happened with a similar decree by Tiberius in AD 19, which became a "dead letter" before Tiberius's death.[20]

ARTEMIS OF THE EPHESIANS

However, before Paul could leave Ephesus in November AD 53, a riot erupted. The temple in Ephesus contained a famous statue of Artemis, the Greek goddess of the hunt. Devout pilgrims bought silver facsimiles of her image until Paul's preaching undermined this cult. Demetrius, the head of the silversmiths' guild, roused the populace. He gathered the tradesmen and made the following speech:

> Men, you know that from this business we have our wealth. And you see and hear that not only in Ephesus but in almost all of Asia this Paul has persuaded and turned away a great many people, saying that gods made with hands are not gods. And there is danger not only that this trade of ours may come

---

20. Bruce, "Christianity under Claudius," 317.

into disrepute but also that the temple of the great goddess Artemis may be counted as nothing, and that she may even be deposed from her magnificence, she whom all Asia and the world worship. (Acts 19:25–27)

Demetrius's hearers were enraged, and they began to shout, "Great is Artemis of the Ephesians!" The city was filled with confusion. The mob dragged Paul's Macedonian traveling companions, Gaius and Aristarchus, into the theater. Paul wanted to address the crowd, but his disciples would not let him. Many of the agitators were swept away by the hysteria but did not even know why they had come together. The Jews in the crowd pushed a Jew named Alexander forward so that he could address the mob. Perhaps he was Alexander the coppersmith, who Paul says did him great harm (2 Tim 4:14). He may have had a trade connection with Demetrius. Given the great harm he may have done to Paul, he was either a non-Christian Jew or he was a Christian Jew who later betrayed Paul. In any case, when the mob heard that Alexander was a Jew, they drowned him out, crying out with one voice for about two hours, "Great is Artemis of the Ephesians!" At last the town clerk quieted the crowd, saying:

> Men of Ephesus, who is there who does not know that the city of the Ephesians is temple keeper of the great Artemis, and of the sacred stone that fell from the sky? Seeing then that these things cannot be denied, you ought to be quiet and do nothing rash. For you have brought these men here who are neither sacrilegious nor blasphemers of our goddess. If therefore Demetrius and the craftsmen with him have a complaint against anyone, the courts are open, and there are proconsuls. Let them bring charges against one another. But if you seek anything further, it shall be settled in the regular assembly. For we really are in danger of being charged with rioting today, since there is no cause that we can give to justify this commotion. (Acts 19:35–40)

With that, he dismissed the assembly.

TROAS

After this, Paul and Timothy traveled to Troas, where he expected to meet Titus, who was not, however, there. Possibly this was because the riot caused Paul to leave Ephesus earlier than expected, and so he arrived before the planned rendezvous. Possibly it was because Titus, in winter, had to make the slower land journey from Corinth back east and simply did not make the rendezvous in time. Paul preached in Troas for a little, but, concerned at missing Titus, he and Timothy pushed on to Macedonia.

JESUS SPOKE TO PAUL A FIFTH TIME

Sometime around AD 53, Paul prayed for the Lord to remove the "thorn in his flesh." He said that it was a messenger of Satan, sent to harass him, to keep him from becoming conceited. Three times he pleaded with the Lord to make it leave him, but Jesus replied, "My grace is sufficient for you, for my power is made perfect in weakness" (2 Cor 12:9).

WRITING 2 CORINTHIANS

In Philippi Titus finally caught up with him and brought him news about the apparently improved state of affairs in the Corinthian church (2 Cor 7:6-7, 14). Gratified, Paul wrote 2 Corinthians, a letter milder in tone and full of theological insights. (What we call 2 Corinthians was really his fourth letter to Corinth, for two letters have been lost.) In this letter, Paul warned the Corinthians not to be deceived by "super apostles," that is, false teachers who presented a gospel different from what they had accepted from Paul. He pointed out that he was in no way inferior to such teachers, since he had performed the signs of a true apostle among them, including signs, wonders, and mighty works. He also implied that the "super apostles" were hustlers, looking for financial support, because, in contrast to them, Paul did not burden the Corinthians financially (2 Cor 11:5-9, 12:11-13). Since it was around November AD 53, Paul must have sent this epistle overland. Titus, probably Luke, and other brothers carried 2 Corinthians to Corinth. Timothy was probably not the courier, because Paul sent Timothy's greetings to Corinth in the letter (2 Cor 1:1). In Corinth, Titus resumed collecting alms for the Jerusalem church, while in Macedonia Paul did the same (2 Cor 8:4-6).

PAUL'S THIRD VISIT TO CORINTH

Paul continued traveling further west, revisiting and strengthening the churches in Thessalonica and Berea. He then finally returned to Corinth. He remained there for about three months, between January and April AD 54 (Acts 20:2-3). There he met Titus and collected funds for the Jerusalem church (Rom 15:25-26). He probably received news from Aquila and Priscilla about the state of the church in Rome, prompting him to write the book of Romans. When the sailing weather was fair, at the end of March or in early April AD 54, Phoebe, a deacon of the church in Cenchreae, took the epistle to the Romans from Corinth (Rom 16:1), probably to Aquila and Priscilla, who were still in Rome.[21]

BACK TO MACEDONIA

Learning of a Jewish plot to kill him, rather than sailing for Syria, Paul sailed from Corinth back to Macedonia. He sent Sopater of Berea, Aristarchus and Secundus of

---

21. At some point prior to writing Romans, Paul's relatives, Andronicus and Julia, who had become Christians before Paul and who were well-known to the apostles, were imprisoned together with Paul (Rom 16:7). They are not listed as Paul's fellow prisoners in Philippi, Caesarea, or either time in Rome, but Paul did write that he had been imprisoned many times (2 Cor 6:5, 11:23).

Thessalonica, Gaius of Derbe, Timothy, and Tychicus and Trophimus of Asia went ahead of him to Troas (Acts 20:4).

Paul and Luke reached Philippi in April. There they collected more funds for the Jerusalem church. They then sailed away after Passover, on April 17, 22 Nisan, AD 54. They arrived in Troas after five days, on April 22, AD 54, where they remained for seven days (Acts 20:6).

RAISING EUTYCHUS

On their last day in Troas, April 29, AD 54, Paul and the Trojan church ate together, and afterwards Paul spoke until midnight. A young man named Eutychus, sitting on a third story windowsill, dozed during Paul's sermon, fell to the ground, and died. Paul resurrected Eutychus and then continued to talk to the gathering until daylight, leaving the congregation greatly comforted. There can have been few sermons in the history of the church quite as dramatic as that (Acts 20:7–12).

TO MILETUS

Luke, Sopater, Aristarchus, Secundus, Gaius, Timothy, Tychicus, and Trophimus then sailed to Assos, where they awaited Paul with a ship. Paul walked overland, arriving on May 1. The team then made a short sailing trip to Mytilene. The next day they sailed to Chios, arriving there on May 2. The following day, they sailed to Samos, arriving there on May 3. The next day, May 4, they reached Miletus. Since Paul was in a hurry to reach Jerusalem before Pentecost, and also because the Jews of Ephesus had plotted to kill him, he bypassed Ephesus and sent for the elders of the Ephesian church meet him at Miletus. The distance between Ephesus and Miletus is about thirty-nine miles, so it would have taken two days for Paul's messenger to reach Ephesus and two days for them to reach Miletus. This meeting therefore occurred after four days of travel, on May 6 (Acts 20:13–38).

JESUS SPOKE TO PAUL A SIXTH TIME

Paul told the Ephesian elders to be on guard against deceivers and quoted Jesus, saying, "It is more blessed to give than to receive" (Acts 20:35) This saying of Jesus is recorded nowhere else in the Bible, so probably Paul received it by special revelation. It is also possible that he learned it from one of the other apostles, although he had previously insisted that he received his learning from Jesus directly, not from them (Gal 1:1, 19, 2:6, 9; 1 Cor 9:1).

BACK TO JERUSALEM

After praying and bidding an emotional farewell, Paul sailed to Cos on May 7, to Rhodes on May 8, and then to the seaport of Patara on May 9. In Patara, they boarded a ship bound for Phoenicia, and, sailing south of Cyprus, they reached Tyre around May 11. Paul's team stayed in Tyre seven days, between May 12 and 18 (Acts 21:1–6). After that, they proceeded to Ptolemais (Acre) and stayed there one day, May 19 (Acts 21:7). He then walked to Caesarea, on Judea's Mediterranean coast, which was a journey of two days. He thus arrived on May 21 and stayed "for many days" at the house of Philip the Evangelist (not the apostle, but one of the seven deacons chosen to care for the poor and widows in the church). A prophet named Agabus, the same one who had correctly prophesied the famine in Judea fourteen years earlier, came from Judea to Caesarea and prophesied that the Jews would bind Paul if he went to Jerusalem. Skeptics claim that Agabus was a false prophet because he foretold that the Jews would bind Paul, whereas it was the Romans who did so. In fact, the Jews did bind Paul before the Romans took him into custody (Acts 24:6). Despite his companions' pleading not to go into harm's way, Paul determined to press on. Paul and his team (and probably Agabus) walked from Caesarea to Jerusalem, a sixty-eight mile, two-day journey, arriving there on May 28, 5 Sivan, the eve of Pentecost, as he had planned. He stayed at the home of Mnason (Acts 21:16).

PENTECOST

On Pentecost, May 29, 6 Sivan, AD 54, in Jerusalem, Paul delivered the alms he had collected in Greece and Macedonia for the Jerusalem church. The brothers and sisters received him gladly, and the day after arriving Paul and his team visited James, the half-brother of Jesus, and all the elders. He told the brothers all that God was doing among the gentiles, and they praised God (Acts 21:17–20).

The Jewish-Christian leaders told Paul that because thousands of Jews had put their faith in Jesus, many accused Paul of teaching the Jews in the diaspora to forsake Moses and not to circumcise their sons. To prevent trouble, they recommended that Paul join four other men who were under a vow and that he pay for all to shave their heads, purify themselves, and make offerings at the temple. Their recommendation was political, meant to keep the peace. It was not a compromise of the decision made by the Jerusalem Council five years ago. Paul agreed to this, and seven days later he completed his vow, on June 5, AD 54.

But Jews from Asia Minor recognized him in the temple and incited non-Christian Jews to riot. Having seen Trophimus the Ephesian with Paul in Jerusalem, they falsely accused Paul of bringing an uncircumcised gentile into the temple. Paul's team of non-Jewish disciples must have been conspicuous in Jerusalem, consisting, as they did, of

Luke, Sopater of Berea, Aristarchus and Secundus of Thessalonica, Gaius of Derbe, Timothy, Tychicus and Trophimus of Asia (modern Turkey), and probably Titus.

A JEWISH RIOT

A mob seized Paul and dragged him outside the temple to kill him, but the commander of the Roman cohort, Claudius Lysias, stopped them and brought the crowd to order. Paul appealed to Lysias and obtained permission to address the Jews in their own language. He told them the story of his conversion and of his mission to bring salvation to the gentiles.

The Jews erupted in anger and resumed their murderous threats. Probably persuaded by the mob's rage that Paul must have been guilty of something, Lysias seized Paul and planned to question him under torture. Paul, however, announced that he was a Roman citizen. And his citizenship was superior to that of Lysias, for Lysias had purchased his citizenship for a large sum, while Paul was born a Roman. Afraid of committing false arrest, Lysias unchained Paul and allowed him to stand trial before his accusers, the Jewish Council.

PAUL'S JERUSALEM TRIAL

During Paul's trial, Ananias (Annas), the high priest, gave the order to strike Paul on the mouth.[22] This was obviously out of order in a legal trial. Angrily, Paul said to him, "God is going to strike you, you whitewashed wall! Are you sitting to judge me according to the law, and yet contrary to the law you order me to be struck?" (Acts 23:3).[23] What then transpired was dramatic.

> Those who stood by said, "Would you revile God's high priest?" And Paul said, "I did not know, brothers, that he was the high priest, for it is written, 'You shall not speak evil of a ruler of your people.'" Now when Paul perceived that one part were Sadducees and the other Pharisees, he cried out in the council, "Brothers, I am a Pharisee, a son of Pharisees. It is with respect to the hope and the resurrection of the dead that I am on trial." And when he had said this, a dissension arose between the Pharisees and the Sadducees, and the assembly was divided. For the Sadducees say that there is no resurrection, nor angel, nor spirit, but the Pharisees acknowledge them all. Then a great clamor arose, and some of the scribes of the Pharisees' party stood up and contended sharply,

---

22. This was Ananias ben Nebedeus (Josephus, *Ant.*, 20:5:2), not the defrocked high priest Ananias (Annas) who was the father-in-law of Joseph Caiaphas and who joined in the trial of Jesus in AD 33. This Ananias served from AD 46 to 58. Although Paul had been in Jerusalem in AD 48 and in AD 51, probably, as a Jewish Christian, he did not meet the high priest either time. This is why Paul did not recognize that Ananias was the high priest.

23. Paul was echoing Jesus' rebuke of the Sadducees, when he called them whitewashed tombs, beautiful on the outside but filled on the inside with dead people's bones and filth (Matt 23:27).

"We find nothing wrong in this man. What if a spirit or an angel spoke to him?" And when the dissension became violent, the tribune, afraid that Paul would be torn to pieces by them, commanded the soldiers to go down and take him away from among them by force and bring him into the barracks. (Acts 23:4–10)

JESUS SPOKE TO PAUL A SEVENTH TIME

Lysias took Paul into custody to save his life. This was polite custody, not incarceration, for Lysias did not dare to keep a fellow Roman citizen in chains (Acts 22:29). That night Jesus spoke to Paul directly for the seventh time. He said, "Take courage, for as you have testified to the facts about me in Jerusalem, so you must testify also in Rome" (Acts 23:11). Jesus did not say that Paul would be the first to take the gospel to Rome, because he was not. When Paul finally reached Rome for the first time in AD 57, he found many Christians already there. Peter probably had founded the Roman church in AD 43, eleven years before. And Romans present at the birth of the church on Pentecost in Jerusalem probably brought the faith back to Rome as early as AD 33 (Acts 2:10).

ESCAPE TO CAESAREA

The next day, more than forty Jews pledged to kill Paul. The son of Paul's sister heard of the plot. He told his uncle Paul in the Roman barracks.[24] The would-be assassins swore they would neither eat nor drink until they killed Paul. Paul lived for another fourteen years, so either they broke their vow or they died of fasting.

Paul asked a centurion to inform Lysias of the plot. Lysias reacted immediately, ordering two of his centurions to assemble 470 cavalry, infantry, and spearmen to accompany Paul out of Jerusalem. This was a huge escort for a political prisoner. Pontius Pilate never deployed any comparable force to deal with Jesus or his followers. It suggests how intense the rage of the Jews must have become and how much the Romans feared civil unrest in troublesome Judea. The military detachment took Paul to Caesarea, the seat of Roman government on the Mediterranean Sea. They did not wait until the next day, but set out for the coast at 9 p.m., further emphasizing the urgency of the mission. They arrived in Antipatris, thirty-seven miles, the halfway point, at around 9 a.m. the following morning. Probably considering that the remainder of the journey would be safe, the Roman infantry and spearmen returned to their barracks in Jerusalem. The remaining seventy cavalry accompanied Paul the rest of the way to Caesarea. Cavalry trots at about eight miles per hour, so the squadron made the thirty-five-mile ride in a little over four hours, arriving in Caesarea after noon.

---

24. It is intriguing to speculate why Paul's sister lived in Jerusalem. This side of heaven, barring a great archaeological find, we may never know.

BIOGRAPHIES OF THE APOSTLES

IN THE CUSTODY OF FELIX

In Caesarea, Paul passed into the custody of Antonius Felix, procurator of Judea (AD 52–60), the top Roman official on station. The next day the high priest Ananias (Annas), a lawyer, and other representatives of the Jerusalem Council came to Caesarea to accuse Paul. Since this was a twenty-two hour walk, assuming no breaks, the Jewish accusers must have set out from Jerusalem no later than the same day that Paul left Antipatris. They must have been outraged that Paul had flown the coop, so they lost no time. After listening to the complaints of the Jewish elders, Felix decided to call for Claudius Lysias to hear his side of the story before making a decision. He then dismissed the frustrated Jewish elders.

Felix and his Jewish wife Drusilla (daughter of Herod Agrippa I) conversed with Paul privately. Paul's teachings of righteousness, self-control, and God's judgment discomfited Felix. Perhaps Felix was conscious that he was not a model of righteousness and self-control and therefore feared God's wrath. Felix did not hand Paul over to his Jewish accusers. He hoped Paul would bribe him to gain his freedom, but Paul offered no money. So Felix kept Paul in custody for two years, until the arrival of his successor as governor of Judea, Porcius Festus, during which time Paul's friends were free to visit and minister to him. Felix frequently sent for Paul and talked with him, perhaps fishing for that bribe or perhaps tentatively interested in the gospel.

1 TIMOTHY

During this two-year interval, Paul must have sent Timothy back to Ephesus to take charge of the church there. While in Caesarea, Paul wrote the epistle of 1 Timothy, offering Timothy pastoral advice (1 Tim 1:2–3). Many scholars suppose that Paul wrote 1 Timothy from Philippi to Timothy in Ephesus. The basis for assuming that Paul wrote 1 Timothy from Philippi is this verse: "As I urged you when I was going to Macedonia, remain at Ephesus so that you may charge certain persons not to teach any different doctrine" (1 Tim 1:3). However, as shown above, after the riot in Ephesus Paul traveled with Timothy to Troas and back to Philippi in Macedonia. He returned to Corinth, and Timothy was with him, since when he left Corinth, he sent Timothy and others ahead of him to Troas (Acts 20:4–5). Therefore, in Paul's swing from Ephesus to Philippi to Corinth, Timothy was with Paul and was not in Ephesus. When Paul pushed on from Troas to Jerusalem, Timothy was almost certainly still with him, since (1) on this trip Paul bypassed Ephesus (Acts 20:16), (2) Timothy and Trophimus were part of the same missionary team (Acts 20:4), and (3) Trophimus ended up in Jerusalem with Paul (Acts 21:29).

So, when Paul was leaving Ephesus for Macedonia, he took Timothy with him. The meaning of 1 Timothy 1:2–3 must be that as Paul and Timothy were departing Ephesus, Paul was ordaining him to return in future to take charge of the Ephesian church. Timothy had the opportunity to do this only during Paul's incarceration in Caesarea.

IN THE CUSTODY OF FESTUS

In AD 56, Porcius Festus replaced Felix as procurator. Three days after his arrival in Judea, Festus traveled from Caesarea to Jerusalem, where the Jewish leaders laid their complaints about Paul before him. They were still agitated about Paul after his being immobilized for two years. They wanted Festus to send Paul to Jerusalem, ostensibly to question him further, but really because they planned to ambush and kill him. Festus was too shrewd to fall into that trap. He told the Jewish elders that he was keeping Paul in custody at Caesarea and, if they wished, they could send some men of authority there to present their accusations against Paul. After eight or ten days, Festus returned to Caesarea. The Jews went with Festus. The day after they arrived, Festus held a meeting of Paul and his Jewish accusers. They brought many serious charges against him, none of which they could prove. Paul said, "neither against the law of the Jews, nor against the Temple, nor against Caesar have I committed any offense." Festus asked Paul if he would go to Jerusalem to stand trial. Paul insisted that he was in Caesar's tribunal and that he had appealed to Caesar. Festus said, "To Caesar you have appealed. To Caesar you shall go" (Acts 25:12), following the Roman habit of washing his hands of Jewish religious disputes (as did Pilate and Gallio).

After some days had passed, King Herod Agrippa II (the son of Herod Agrippa I and the great-grandson of Herod the Great) and his sister, Bernice, visited Festus. After staying in Caesarea for many days, Agrippa asked to hear Paul, and Festus arranged an audience. He thought it was a good idea because it might inform him of what to write about Paul when he sent him to Nero, since, so far, Festus had discerned no crime that Paul had committed. Paul told the story of his conversion and proclaimed the gospel. As he was speaking, Festus said with a loud voice, "Paul, you are out of your mind; your great learning is driving you out of your mind." Paul replied, "I am not out of my mind, most excellent Festus, but I am speaking true and rational words." Paul then appealed to King Agrippa to verify his testimony. "I am persuaded that none of these things has escaped [the king's] notice, for this has not been done in a corner. King Agrippa, do you believe the prophets? I know you believe," said Paul. Agrippa replied, "In a short time would you persuade me to be a Christian?" Paul answered, "Whether short or long, I would to God that not only you but all who hear me this day might become such as I am, except for these chains." Then the king, Bernice, Festus, and all who were with him rose and agreed that Paul had done nothing to deserve death or imprisonment. Agrippa said to Festus, "This man could have been set free if he had not appealed to Caesar" (Acts 26:32). Festus then made plans to send Paul to Rome where he could make his appeal to Nero.

VOYAGE TO MALTA

Paul and his companions (including Luke and Aristarchus, a fellow prisoner, and other unnamed prisoners) embarked on a ship for Italy under Julius, a kindly Roman commander of the Augustan Cohort, and several soldiers under his command, around August 24, AD 56. Julius, like Cornelius, was one of the most ancient and influential family names in Rome. Julius was either somebody or he was related to somebody. Aristarchus was a disciple from Thessalonica. He was apparently also arrested and sent to Rome with Paul, although under what charge Scripture does not say (Acts 27:2; Col 4:10).

They made port in Sidon, Lebanon, where they met friends, probably around Yom Kippur ("the Fast"), August 28, 1 Tishri, AD 56 (Acts 27:9). They put out to sea again from Sidon, but, because the wind was against them (coming out of the west), they sailed to Cyprus, reaching its lee shore around September 3, AD 56. Since they could not sail into the west wind, they tacked north across the open sea from Cyprus to Cilicia (modern Turkey and Paul's home province), reaching the coast around September 9, AD 56. They followed the coastline westward, tacking to and fro as they headed into the wind. They followed the shore from Cilicia to Pamphylia to Myra,[25] on the southwest coast of modern Turkey. They put into port there around September 28, AD 56.

In Myra, Julius found a grain ship from Alexandria, Egypt, and he transferred his charges to it. This would have been one of the largest vessels to ply the Mediterranean, carrying stores of grain from the fertile Nile Valley to the ever-hungry populace of Rome. As a centurion on official business, Julius would have been able to commandeer berths for himself, his soldiers, and his charges aboard. The sailing season in the Mediterranean normally ended by October, so the captain of this ship was flirting with luck. The profits he would gain in Rome were immense, and he probably thought he had a good chance of slipping through to Italy before the winter storms began.

The Alexandrian ship put to sea around October 2, AD 56. It sailed westward to Cnidus, a city at the tip of a fingerlike peninsula that juts out into the Aegean Sea on the southwest coast of Turkey, just north of the island of Rhodes, arriving around October 10, AD 56. The wind, however, continued to blow against the freighter, out of the west. The captain no doubt had hoped to sail from Cnidus northwest to Greece, island hopping all across the Aegean Sea. There, having made it halfway to Rome, he could winter snugly in any of the excellent safe harbors, such as Piraeus. But he could not sail west, so, probably in frustration, he chose another tack. He sailed southwest from Cnidus to Crete, setting out around October 18, AD 56.

The ship reached Salmone on the far eastern tip of Crete around October 21, AD 56. But the wind continued to blow out of the west. Sailing upwind, the ship tacked back and forth along the southern coast of Crete until it reached the port of

---

25. Myra is the city where Saint Nicholas (Santa Claus) was born in the third century AD.

Fair Havens, probably around October 23, AD 56. Since it was now fifty-seven days past Yom Kippur ("the Fast") and well into the dangerous winter sailing weather, Paul warned the ship's captain and crew not to press on but to spend the winter in Fair Havens (Acts 27:9–10). Julius and the ship's captain (who was also its owner) ignored Paul's warning and decided to sail for Phoenix farther west on the south coast of Crete and spend the winter there. They probably realized that Paul was right. It was time to give up trying to reach Greece. But they probably did not like the idea of wintering in Fair Havens because it was not a very secure port. It was wide open to the east wind, and just north of it was the rich agricultural Messara Valley. If, during the winter, the dreaded northeasterly storms came crashing down through the valley, they might batter the ship to pieces or rip it free of its moorings and drive it helplessly across the open sea into the Gulf of Sidra off Libya and into the dreaded shoals of Syrtis, the graveyard of many ships. It may be that "Fair Havens" was a humorously ironic name, given to the port by sea captains who knew it was anything but. The ship put out from Fair Havens about October 26, AD 56.

At first, the decision of Julius and the captain seemed a propitious one. The wind swung out of the west and now blew gently from the south, allowing the ship to follow the coast of Crete placidly toward Phoenix. They continued on this course until around October 28, AD 56. Then, around October 29, a terrible storm moved in from the northeast, blowing the ship off course. It scudded before the wind to the island of Cauda, about twenty-three miles south of Crete, alone on the open Mediterranean Sea. They managed to get under Cauda's lee shore. They had so far been pulling the ship's boat behind the freighter. In the lee of Cauda they managed, with some difficulty, to pull in the ship's boat and to haul it out of the water, securing it on deck. This would prevent the boat's line from getting tangled in the freighter's rudder. If that happened, they might be unable to steer. It would also keep the boat secure in case they needed to abandon ship

The storm continued to drive them along, and they lowered the sails and cast out a stern anchor to slow the ship down, because the fear of being driven all the way to the shoals of Syrtis continued to haunt them. Then they threw some of the ship's cargo overboard, suggesting that the ship was beginning to take on water and sink. The storm did not abate, and on November 1, AD 46, the crew jettisoned some of the ship's tackle. The word "tackle" in Greek is *skeué*, which means equipment.[26] This does not, therefore, mean that the crew began to throw over gear essential to navigate the ship, but that they began to jettison non-essential furniture. When neither the sun nor the stars appeared for many days and the storm raged on, they abandoned all hope of being saved.

The crew had eaten nothing for many days (and with the seasickness that even tough sailors experience in bad storms, no wonder). Paul told them that an angel of God had come to him in the night and told him that they would all be saved because

26. Strong, *Concordance*, 4631.

Paul must stand before Caesar. He urged them to take heart because he had faith that God would do exactly as promised. He added that they would soon run aground on some island.

After midnight on about November 14, the sailors suspected they were approaching land. They took soundings with a lead line and found twenty fathoms. They threw a lead line again and found fifteen fathoms. They were sure they were approaching land. Now fearing that they might run up on the rocks, they threw out four anchors off the ship's stern to slow their speed and lessen the possible impact.

Paul noticed that some of the crew, thinking they could escape the ship and reach the beach, were lowering the ship's boat into the sea, under the pretense of laying anchors down from the bow. He warned the centurion, Julius, and his soldiers that "unless these men stay in the ship, you cannot be saved." The centurion, his soldiers, and his prisoners were not qualified to manage the ship. They needed all hands on deck to ensure their best chance of survival. At Julius's command, the Roman soldiers cut away the ropes of the ship's boat and let it go, bobbing in the waves.

As day dawned, Paul urged everyone to take some food. They had eaten nothing in the fourteen days since they had secured the ship's boat on the lee shore of Cauda. They needed their strength, and he promised that all 276 men aboard would be saved. They were encouraged and ate. Then they lightened the ship further, to soften the impact of running aground, by throwing the cargo of Egyptian grain overboard.

SHIPWRECK

Paul and everyone aboard the Egyptian freighter were shipwrecked, and all hands survived. This was Paul's fourth shipwreck. In 2 Corinthians 11:25, he wrote, four years before, in AD 52, "Three times I was shipwrecked; a night and a day I was adrift at sea."

Just before the shipwreck, Paul's ship was "being driven about . . . in the Adria" (Acts 27:27).[27] The ESV translates this as "being driven across the Adriatic Sea." A glance at a modern map shows that the Adriatic Sea extends from Venice to Lecce on the heel of the Italian boot on its western shore and to Albania on its eastern shore. This is a long way from Malta, the traditional site of Paul's shipwreck. The Adria in ancient parlance, however, was not the same as the modern Adriatic Sea. Ptolemy speaks of the Adria as extending from Crete[28] in the east to Sicily in the west.[29] Given this understanding, Luke's reference to the body of water across which they had been driven would be accurate, although on a modern map we would say that the ship had been driven across the Ionian or the Mediterranean Sea.

---

27. This author's translation.
28. Ptolemy, *Geography* 3:15:1.
29. Ptolemy, *Geography* 3:4:1.

MALTA

The Maltese showed kindly hospitality to the shipwrecked mariners. They kindled a fire because it had begun to rain and was cold. As Paul gathered a bundle of sticks for the fire, a snake fastened onto his hand and hung there. Thinking that this species of snake was lethal, the Maltese natives expected him to swell up and fall down dead. They suspected that he was a murderer, because having survived a shipwreck, Justice had nevertheless condemned him to die. When he shook the snake off into the fire and survived with no ill effects, however, they decided Paul must be a god. This perhaps fulfilled Jesus' prophecy that his apostles would suffer no ill effects, even from the deadly bite of serpents (Mark 16:18).

Some doubt has been cast upon the identity of Paul's shipwreck site, because there are now no venomous snakes on Malta, and there is no archeological evidence that there ever were. This has given rise to the theory that Paul did not land on Malta but on the island of Meleda, now called Mjlet, off the coast of Croatia.[30] The Greek name for the island on which Paul beached is Melite (Acts 28:1). The horned viper (*Vipera ammodytes*) lives on Mjlet and throughout southern Europe and parts of the Middle East. It is the most dangerous of European vipers, because of its large size, long fangs, and highly toxic venom. The island of Mjlet was so overrun by poisonous snakes until 1911 that mongooses were introduced to eliminate them. But for Paul's ship, driven by a northeast gale, to make its way northwest from Crete halfway up the modern Adriatic Sea to Mjlet seems hardly credible.

There are better explanations. Possibly there was a venomous snake native to Malta in Paul's day that went extinct, and the evidence of its existence is as yet undiscovered. Possibly Paul encountered the European cat snake (*Telescopus fallax*), a venomous rear-fanged colubrid that does live on Malta. Its mouth is too small to bite humans easily, but it can do so if handled. Possibly Paul encountered a viper not native to Malta that had stowed away on the Alexandrian grain ship and had nestled among the sticks Paul gathered. The objection to this is that the Maltese seemed to recognize the snake and knew of its toxicity. That does not mean that the snake had to be native to Malta. Many ships put into the harbor at Malta and many animals had no doubt stowed away on some of them and landed on the island. The Maltese may simply have recognized what they had seen before. Or possibly the snake Paul encountered was not venomous at all. The Greek word for this snake is *echidna*, which may mean "viper" or simply "serpent."[31] The Bible does not say the snake bit Paul. It says it "fastened on his hand" and was "hanging from his hand" (Acts 28:3–4). So, it is possible that the people simply assumed, as people often do, that this snake was poisonous and deadly, and that naturally Paul would bloat and die. In conclusion, the problem of which

---

30. Meinardus, "St. Paul Shipwrecked in Dalmatia," 145.
31. Strong, *Concordance*, 2191.

snake Paul encountered after his shipwreck does not undermine the identification of his shipwreck site with Malta, which it almost certainly was.

Publius, the chief man on Malta, hosted Paul and his team. Paul healed Publius's father of fever and dysentery, and then Paul healed many others during his three-month stay on Malta (Acts 28:7–10).

VOYAGE TO ROME

Julius then transferred Paul and his other charges to another Alexandrian ship, the *Castor and Pollux*, which had wintered in Malta. He sailed to Syracuse in Sicily, then to Reghium in southern Italy, then to Puteoli, on the Bay of Naples. Finding fellow Christians there, Paul stayed with them for seven days. Julius the centurion must have been exceptionally lenient.

Paul and his entourage then walked north to Rome. Along the Appian Way, Christians came out from Rome to meet them at the village called Three Taverns. On seeing the welcoming party, Paul thanked God and took courage. He reached Rome around March 8, AD 57. He was allowed to stay there by himself under the light guard of one soldier. Three days after reaching Rome, Paul proclaimed the gospel to the Roman Jews on Saturday, the Sabbath, March 10, AD 57 (Acts 28:17–29). On the next Sabbath, March 17, Paul addressed the whole congregation of Roman Jews at Paul's place of lodging, and, after hearing him from morning to evening, they rejected the gospel. Thus, Paul turned to preaching to the gentiles in Rome (Acts 28:23–28).

ROME: AD 57–59

Paul remained in Rome under house arrest for two years. Even so, he preached the gospel boldly and without hindrance (Phil 1:12). He had a relative in Rome, Herodian (Rom 16:11). From Rome he wrote the books of Ephesians, Philippians, Colossians, Philemon, and a lost letter to the church of Laodicea. Paul's letter to the Philippians says that while in a Roman prison he converted members even of Caesar's household (Phil 1:13, 4:22). Mark arrived in Rome sometime during Paul's stay at this time. Also with him were Timothy, Luke, Onesimus, Aristarchus, and Demas (Phlm 1). Peter also arrived in Rome between AD 57 and 59 and resumed leadership of the Roman church, which he had founded. Silas joined him and perhaps acted as his scribe (1 Pet 5:12). All these details suggest that Paul was not in a dungeon with dripping walls, infested with rats. He was under reasonably comfortable house arrest, surrounded by colleagues.

PHILEMON AND ONESIMUS

While in Rome, Paul encountered Onesimus, a slave who had run away from his master, Philemon, the head of the church in Colossae (Phlm 1:1). While imprisoned, Paul led Onesimus to the Lord (Phlm 1:10) and wrote a letter to Philemon, pleading with him to emancipate Onesimus. Paul sent Epaphroditus to Philippi and Tychicus to Ephesus, armed with copies of Paul's letters to the churches in Greece and Asia, namely Ephesians, Philippians, Colossians, and a lost letter to the Laodiceans (Eph 6:21; Phil 2:25; Col 4:7, 16).[32] Since Paul asked the Colossians and the Laodiceans to read each other's letters, it seems that he wanted all the churches to read all four letters.

The letter to Philemon was different. It was personal. Philemon had a decision to make: punish Onesimus for running away or forgive him and set him free. Paul was sure Philemon would comply with Paul's plea on Onesimus's behalf since Paul had led Philemon to Christ (Phlm 19). Onesimus may have been less certain. He must have spent many an anxious hour as, at Paul's command, he traveled with Epaphras back to Colossae. Philemon did free Onesimus. If he had not done so, he surely would not have made Paul's letter public. Since the letter is published in our Bible, we can be sure that Philemon complied with Paul's request. Onesimus eventually succeeded Timothy as the bishop of the church at Ephesus.

Paul wrote in his letter to Philemon that he was "an old man and a prisoner for Jesus Christ." He was probably between fifty-two and fifty-four years old. He would survive another ten to twelve years.

NERO'S VERDICT

Paul's trial under Nero ended in acquittal. This was the early period of Nero's reign, before the emperor went mad and began persecuting Christians. At this time, after January AD 59, Luke, who was with Paul in Rome, completed his book of Acts. Since Luke states that Acts was his second book, Luke obviously had completed his first book, the Gospel of Luke, before this date. It is intriguing to consider that Mark and Luke were together in Rome during Paul's first imprisonment (Col 4:10–14; Phlm 1:24) and under the sacerdotal leadership of Peter at the same time. It is hard to imagine that they failed to read each other's books and shared their experiences of composing Scripture under the auspices of the Holy Spirit.

Nero acquitted Paul possibly because the young emperor wanted to distance himself from the anti-Jewish policy of his late uncle, Claudius. If so, that benevolent spirit would last for only five years.

---

32. Paul says the Colossians should read the letter "from Laodicea." He does not mean that the Laodiceans wrote a letter to the Colossians. He means that his letter to Laodicea would be delivered there first, after which the Laodiceans were meant to send the letter from Laodicea to Colossae.

Paul's movements after this are less certain. If Paul wrote the book of Hebrews, dictating it to Luke as his scribe, this is probably when he did so. He says he had released[33] Timothy on some mission away from Rome and hoped he would return in time to rejoin him on his travels and ultimately go with him back to Jerusalem (Heb 13:23).

ITALY, SPAIN, ILLYRICUM, ASIA MINOR, CRETE, AND GREECE

Since Paul's acquittal probably occurred in January AD 59, the sailing weather would be bad until spring, so he probably evangelized in the nearby regions. Hippolytus said he evangelized in Italy and Illyricum.[34] After that, he probably traveled to Spain, as he wrote that he hoped to do (Rom 15:24). From there he probably returned to the churches in Greece. He went to Crete and founded churches there, leaving them in the care of his fellow-worker, Titus (Titus 1:5). He then went to Ephesus. At some point, Aquila and Priscilla had returned to Ephesus from Rome (2 Tim 4:19). Paul probably visited the churches in Asia Minor, including Miletus (2 Tim 4:20), and then returned to Philippi, Thessalonica, and Corinth. From Corinth Paul wrote his letter to Titus in Crete probably between September 11, AD 60, and September 14, AD 64 (Titus 1:5).[35] While in Corinth Paul sent Artemas or Tychicus from Corinth to Titus, asking him to leave Crete and meet Paul in Nicopolis (Greece) if he could (Titus 3:12). All this probably happened in the good spring sailing weather, around March or April of AD 65. Paul did not simply trudge around the world conducting missions solo. He made disciples to whom he delegated the task of making disciples and sent them around the world. They included Silas, Timothy, Titus, Aquila, Priscilla, Tychicus, Epaphroditus, Phoebe, and doubtless many more.

THE NERONIAN PERSECUTION

The Great Fire of Rome broke out between July 18 and 26, AD 64. Taking advantage of the land that the fire cleared, the emperor Nero claimed a large plot on which he proposed to build a luxurious golden palace. The resentful mob of common Romans spread the rumor that Nero had set the fire himself with this result in mind. Their mutinous mood was lethal, and it terrified Nero. He tried every possible means to mollify them. When nothing worked, he hit upon the scheme of blaming the Christians in

---

33. The word "released" in Greek is sometimes translated "set free," as if Timothy were liberated from jail. There is no record, however, of Timothy in prison, so probably by "released" Paul means "sent away."

34. Hippolytus, "List of the Apostles and Disciples."

35. The clue is that Paul asked Titus to meet Paul in winter in Nicopolis, which is in western Greece between the Ambracian Gulf and the Ionian Sea. This suggests that Paul was positioning himself for a return to Illyricum, to the north, when the spring weather came.

Rome for setting the fire. Even the anti-Christian Roman historian Tacitus realized this was a lie. To impress the surly crowd, Nero began a merciless persecution of Christians. Tacitus described this as follows.

> Neither human help, nor imperial munificence, nor all the modes of placating Heaven, could stifle scandal or dispel the belief that the fire had taken place by order. Therefore, to scotch the rumor, Nero substituted as culprits, and punished with the utmost refinements of cruelty, a class of men, loathed for their vices, whom the crowd styled Christians. Christus, the founder of the name, had undergone the death penalty in the reign of Tiberius, by sentence of the procurator Pontius Pilatus, and the pernicious superstition was checked for a moment, only to break out once more, not merely in Judea, the home of the disease, but in the capital itself, where all things horrible or shameful in the world collect and find a vogue. First, then, the confessed members of the sect were arrested; next, on their disclosures, vast numbers were convicted, not so much on the count of arson as for hatred of the human race. And derision accompanied their end: they were covered with wild beasts' skins and torn to death by dogs; or they were fastened on crosses, and, when daylight failed were burned to serve as lamps by night. Nero had offered his Gardens for the spectacle, and gave an exhibition in his Circus, mixing with the crowd in the habit of a charioteer, or mounted on his car. Hence, in spite of a guilt which had earned the most exemplary punishment, there arose a sentiment of pity, due to the impression that they were being sacrificed not for the welfare of the state but to the ferocity of a single man.[36]

All this terror served to make the populace more sympathetic to the Christians and more inimical to Nero.

Meanwhile, Paul returned to Asia Minor, ending up in Ephesus and finally Troas.[37] In AD 66, the Jews launched their ill-fated war of independence against Rome. Caught up in the reverberations of this turmoil, Paul was arrested at Troas, probably unexpectedly, which would explain why he left his cloak and needed books with Carpus (2 Tim 4:13). His captors left him no time to pack. The fact that he was arrested so far from Rome implies that Nero's persecution of Christians spread far beyond the capital city. From Troas, Paul was taken to Ephesus, capital of the province of Asia. Titus, Crescens, Tychicus, Trophimus, Carpus, Demas, and Alexander the coppersmith were possibly all with Paul when he was arrested. Paul left Trophimus, who was ill, at Miletus (2 Tim 4:20). Alexander the coppersmith did Paul great harm, opposing Paul's message and that of Timothy, too. Titus went to Dalmatia, Crescens to Galatia, and Tychicus to Ephesus, no doubt to carry on the mission of proclaiming

---

36. Tacitus, *Annals* 15:44.

37. This largely unrecorded interval is a little over four years, so Paul had plenty of time to make a return circuit, or even multiple circuits, of all the churches in Asia, Macedonia, Achaia, Illyricum, and even a return trip to Rome and Spain if he chose.

the gospel and working with Timothy. Erastus remained in Corinth. Mark was probably also with this team somewhere in Asia Minor (modern Turkey), since Paul asked Timothy to bring Mark to Rome. When Paul made his defense in his second Roman incarceration, no one came to his support. They all deserted him, except Luke. Demas, who Paul called his fellow-worker in his letter to Philemon (Phlm 1:24) and who joined in sending greetings in Paul's letter to the Colossians (Col 4:14), had deserted him for love of the world and had gone to Thessalonica (2 Tim 4:10).

SECOND ROMAN INCARCERATION

This time in Rome Paul was imprisoned possibly in the Mamertine prison, where Nero had also incarcerated Peter.[38] This was very different from the relatively comfortable house arrest of his fist imprisonment. At this time Paul wrote his last epistle, 2 Timothy. In it, he begged Timothy to rejoin him and to bring Mark. The rift between him and Mark, arising at the start of Paul's second missionary journey seventeen years before, had mended. Of his non-Roman followers, only Luke remained with him, but Eubulus, Pudens, Linus, Claudia, and other brothers were with him in Rome, possibly also as prisoners of Nero (2 Tim 4:21).

PAUL'S DEATH

In 2 Timothy, Paul poured out his heart in this profound and moving epistle. He knew that this time the Romans would not set him free. He knew he was going to die.

> I am already being poured out as a drink offering, and the time of my departure has come. I have fought the good fight, I have finished the race, I have kept the faith. Henceforth there is laid up for me the crown of righteousness, which the Lord, the righteous judge, will award to me on that day, and not only to me but also to all who have loved his appearing. (2 Tim 4:6–8)

Jerome says that Paul suffered martyrdom on the same day as Peter.[39] As a Roman citizen, Paul died a dignified death, by the sword, while Peter, a non-citizen and a Jewish enemy of the state in wartime, died upside down on a cross.[40] Their deaths occurred near the end of Nero's reign, about AD 68.[41] Nero committed suicide on June 9, AD 68.[42] Had Nero delayed the execution but for a few months, Peter and Paul would have survived his evil reign.

---

38. De Montor, *The Lives and Times of the Roman Pontiffs*, 26.
39. Jerome, *On Illustrious Men*.
40. Roman law strictly forbade beating, imprisoning, or crucifying a Roman citizen without due process of law. Cicero, *Against Verres*, 2:5:161-163.
41. Finegan, *Handbook*, 380.
42. Finegan, *Handbook*, 379.

PAUL'S EPILOGUE

Back in AD 51, still five years before his famous shipwreck in Malta and seventeen years before his execution, Paul wrote a catalog of what he already had suffered for Jesus:

> Five times I received from the Jews the forty lashes minus one. Three times I was beaten with rods, once I was stoned, three times I was shipwrecked, I spent a night and a day in the open sea, I have been constantly on the move. I have been in danger from rivers, in danger from bandits, in danger from my own countrymen, in danger from Gentiles; in danger in the city, in danger in the country, in danger at sea; and in danger from false brothers. I have labored and toiled and have often gone without sleep; I have known hunger and thirst and have often gone without food; I have been cold and naked. (2 Cor 11:24–27)

"I am an ambassador in chains," wrote Paul in Ephesians 6:20. Paul preached the gospel for thirty-four years.[43] If he began studying under Gamaliel at the age of twenty-nine, he probably died at the age of sixty-four. As he wrote in 2 Timothy, penned shortly before his execution, Paul had fought the good fight, finished the course, and kept the faith.

---

43. Hippolytus says "Paul entered into the apostleship a year after the assumption of Christ; and beginning at Jerusalem, he advanced as far as Illyricum, and Italy, and Spain, preaching the Gospel for five-and-thirty years. And in the time of Nero, he was beheaded at Rome and was buried there" (Hippolytus, "List of the Apostles and Disciples"). The year of the assumption (ascension) of Christ was AD 33. So, if Paul began his ministry the year after that, AD 34, and his ministry ended with his death after thirty-five years, he would have died in AD 69, a year after Nero died (on June 10, AD 68). Clicking back thirty-five years from the date of Nero's death, assuming that Nero had Paul killed shortly before his demise, arrives at a starting date for Paul's ministry of June 8, AD 33 (June 10, Julian Calendar), which is certainly not "a year after the assumption of Christ." So Hippolytus is off by one year. Paul ministered for thirty-four years, from AD 33 to 68.

James the Just, the Half-Brother of Jesus

JAMES WAS THE HALF-BROTHER of Jesus, the second-eldest son of Joseph the carpenter and of Mary. Scripture identified the half-siblings of Jesus as James, Joses, Judas, Simon and more than three[1] unnamed sisters (Matt 13:55–56; Mark 6:3). The Gospels probably listed the brothers in order of seniority, so James was the oldest after Jesus. He was married (1 Cor 9:5).

DOUBTING JESUS

During Jesus' earthly ministry, James, Jude, and Jesus' other half-brothers did not believe in him (John 7:5). Twice, in AD 30, they and Mary tried to muzzle their egregious brother, thinking him "out of his mind" (Matt 12:46–50; Mark 3:21, 31–35; Luke 8:19–21). During the High Holy Days of AD 31, Jesus' brothers scornfully suggested that Jesus should go to Jerusalem and show off his miracles. Jesus told them to go up to the feast but that he would not go yet (John 7:2–6). After Jesus' resurrection, Jesus appeared personally to his half-brother James (1 Cor 15:7), who then believed and became the "bondservant of God and of the Lord Jesus Christ" (James 1:1). Because James and his brothers did yet not believe in Jesus' divinity at the cross, Jesus put their mother, Mary, into the care of John, the disciple Jesus loved, not in the care of his half-brother and her son, James. How bitter must have been the family divide until the risen Jesus appeared to his half-brother James.

THE NAZIRITE

James was called "just" because of his righteousness and piety. Like Samson, Samuel, and John the Baptist, his cousin, he was a Nazirite, one who took a vow to separate himself to the Lord, abstain from wine, spirits, and grapes or raisins, to let his hair grow long and not cut it, to avoid touching a dead body. A Nazirite vow might be lifelong or a temporary pledge to the Lord.

---

1. Matt 13:56 refers to "all," not "both of," Jesus' sisters; so, there were three or more.

CHURCH LEADER

Acts, Galatians, and 1 Corinthians depict James as a leader in the early church. Eusebius says the other apostles made him the first bishop of Jerusalem.[2] Paul referred to James as an apostle (Gal 1:6) and called James, along with Peter and John, one of the pillars of the church (Gal 2:9). When Peter escaped miraculously from prison and had to flee Jerusalem in AD 44 to escape Herod Agrippa I's persecution, he asked that James be informed (Acts 12:17). At the Council of Jerusalem in AD 49, James was the last to speak, after Peter, Paul, and Barnabas, before the Apostolic Council delivered its decree on Judaizing gentile Christians (Acts 15:19). When Paul went to Jerusalem with money he had raised in Greece and Macedonia for the faithful there, he met James, who advised Paul to ritually cleanse himself in the temple to disprove rumors that he was teaching against Mosaic law (Acts 21:18). James was the author of the inspired book of James. All these facts imply that James is rightly included among the apostles.

WORKS AND GRACE

Some see Paul teaching salvation by grace, not works, and James teaching salvation by works, not grace. This view arises from contrasting two statements by Paul and James. The first is, "For by grace you have been saved through faith. And this is not your own doing; it is the gift of God, not a result of works, so that no one may boast" (Eph 2:8-9). The second is:

> What good is it, my brothers, if someone says he has faith but does not have works? Can that faith save him? If a brother or sister is poorly clothed and lacking in daily food, and one of you says to them, "Go in peace, be warmed and filled," without giving them the things needed for the body, what good is that? So also, faith by itself if it does not have works, is dead. (James 2:14-17)

In fact, James and Paul taught the same gospel. Their statements are like two bookends on the same shelf. Salvation by faith produces the fruit of good works. Good works are a result of salvation, not the cause of it. Jesus said, "Every good tree bears good fruit, but a bad tree bears bad fruit" (Matt 7:17).

Grace, faith, and works are three indispensable ingredients of salvation. Grace is God reaching out to man, offering salvation. Faith is man believing in and accepting the free gift of God's grace. When this "handshake" happens, God produces salvation. And salvation transforms man, inspiring him to good works. Grace, faith, and good works: wherever salvation is, all three are there.

---

2. Eusebius, *Church History* 2:1:2.

THE BOOK OF JAMES

The book of James is somewhat like a New Testament version of Proverbs. It deals with six main topics, skipping from one to the other: (1) patience in trials, (2) wisdom, (3) faith, (4) the rich and the poor, (5) speech, and (6) obedience. James quotes the Sermon on the Mount more than any other New Testament author. As the wise leader of the Jerusalem church, he was to his half-brother, Jesus, somewhat as wise Solomon was to his prophetic father, David. David wrote many of the Psalms and strove as a man "after God's own heart" to create a godly kingdom (1 Sam 13:14). Solomon, his son, followed him and wrote inspired books of wisdom (Proverbs, Ecclesiastes, and Song of Songs). Jesus, God's Son, established the new covenant kingdom and spoke the wisest words ever uttered. James, his half-brother, assumed leadership of the church in Jerusalem and wrote an inspired book of wisdom, richly quoting his brother and Lord.

THE LIFE OF JAMES

The most complete account of James's life from antiquity is by Jerome:

> James, who is called the brother of the Lord, surnamed the Just . . . after our Lord's passion at once ordained by the apostles bishop of Jerusalem, wrote a single epistle, which is reckoned among the seven Catholic Epistles . . . Hegesippus who lived near the Apostolic Age, in the fifth book of his *Commentaries*, writing of James says: "After the apostles, James the brother of the Lord surnamed the Just was made head of the Church at Jerusalem. Many indeed are called James. This one was holy from his mother's womb. He drank neither wine nor strong drink, ate no flesh, never shaved or anointed himself with ointment or bathed. He alone had the privilege of entering the Holy of Holies, since indeed he did not use woolen vestments but linen and went alone into the Temple and prayed on behalf of the people, insomuch that his knees were reputed to have acquired the hardness of camels' knees." Ananias the high priest, the youthful son of Ananias of the priestly class . . . assembled a council and publicly tried to force James to deny that Christ is the son of God. When he refused, Ananias ordered him to be stoned. Cast down from a pinnacle of the Temple, his legs broken, but still half alive, raising his hands to heaven he said, "Lord, forgive them for they know not what they do." Then, struck on the head by the club of a fuller, such as fullers are accustomed to wring out garments with, he died. James was of so great sanctity and reputation among the people that the downfall of Jerusalem was believed to be on account of his death. And so he ruled the church of Jerusalem thirty years, that is, until the seventh year of Nero,[3] and was buried near the Temple from which he had been cast down. His tombstone with its inscription was well known until the siege of Titus and the end of Hadrian's reign.[4]

---

3. Nero reigned form October 13, AD 54, to June 9, AD 68, so James died in AD 62.
4. Jerome, *On Illustrious Men*.

Joseph Barnabas, the Encourager

LUKE'S INSPIRED BOOK, ACTS, calls Barnabas an apostle, together with Paul (Acts 14:14), and so on the authority of Scripture, Barnabas was an apostle. Barnabas (which means "Son of Encouragement") was born of Jewish parents on the island of Cyprus about the beginning of the first century (Acts 4:36). A Levite, Barnabas spent time in Jerusalem. He may have settled there. His relatives, the family of John Mark the Evangelist and Mark's mother, Mary, also had a home there, and Barnabas may have owned land nearby. A rather late tradition recorded by Clement of Alexandria and Eusebius says that Barnabas was one of the seventy-two disciples that Jesus commissioned. The church always seemed to hold him in high regard.

IN THE EARLY CHURCH

Barnabas was very much an encourager. At Pentecost, he encouraged the young church with a rich gift of land. A certain couple, Ananias and Sapphira, imitated him, but lied to the apostles and died through the conviction of the Holy Spirit. And Barnabas encouraged Paul to enter the mission field by going to Tarsus and coaxing him out of retirement. Generations of Christians are in Barnabas's debt.

SPONSORING PAUL

When Saul the persecutor, later Paul the apostle, made his first visit to Jerusalem after his conversion, the church there was slow to accept that he was a sincere believer (Acts 9:26). Barnabas sponsored him and had him received by the apostles, though Paul then met only Peter and James, the half-brother of Jesus (Acts 9:27; Gal 1:18–19).

Paul went to his family home at Tarsus where he lived in obscurity for six years. In the dispersion that followed Stephen's death, approved of by Paul, some disciples from Cyprus and Cyrene began preaching to the gentiles. They met with great success among the Greeks at Antioch in Syria, where Peter founded the church in AD 34. When the apostles in Jerusalem heard of this, they sent Barnabas to investigate what his fellow Cypriots were doing (Acts 11:22). Though a Jew, Barnabas saw these gentile converts as part of God's plan. He at once saw the possibility of an immense mission field. Paul evidently had impressed Barnabas at their earlier meeting because he thought of him for this work. In AD 43, Barnabas set out for Tarsus and persuaded Paul to join the Antioch church and begin preaching (Acts 11:25). Together they labored at Antioch for a year and "taught a great multitude."

FAMINE RELIEF

In AD 43, a prophet named Agabus predicted that a famine would strike Jerusalem. In AD 44, Barnabas, Paul, and Titus carried offerings from the Antioch brethren to the mother church (Acts 11:30; Gal 2:1). Some discussion occurred about whether Titus should submit to circumcision, but Peter, John, James, Paul, and Barnabas agreed that this was unnecessary for his salvation (Gal 2:3). The apostles gave Paul and Barnabas the right hand of fellowship (Gal 2:9). They acknowledged that Jesus had commissioned Paul directly, and they authorized him to go preach to the gentiles. When Paul and Barnabas returned to Antioch, they brought with them the cousin of Barnabas, John Mark, the future author of the first Gospel (Acts 12:25).

FIRST MISSIONARY JOURNEY

In the same year, AD 44, the church of Antioch felt inspired by the Holy Spirit to send out missionaries to the gentile world. They named Barnabas and Paul to do the work. The church laid hands upon them, and they embarked for Cyprus, with John Mark as helper. First, they evangelized Barnabas's native land, Cyprus, and then they crossed over to Paul's home, Asia Minor.

Here, at Perga in Pamphylia, the first stop, John Mark left them. Paul considered this desertion. One may conclude that Mark was an inexperienced boy, not quite up to the rigors of evangelism. But this may not be the case. If Mark had traveled to Rome with Peter in AD 43,[1] Mark's Gospel would have been complete at this time; perhaps Mark felt called to disseminate his Gospel rather than pursue this missionary trip with Paul and Barnabas. Perhaps he felt that by leaving Paul and Barnabas a copy of his Gospel he was equipping them, not deserting them. Furthermore, Acts records that Mark was neither called by the Holy Spirit nor chosen by the Antioch elders for this trip. The Holy Spirit did, however, call Mark to write—and presumably to circulate—his Gospel. Perhaps at this time, Mark returned to Jerusalem and then went to Alexandria, where he founded the Egyptian church.

Barnabas and Paul alone ventured into the interior of a wild country, preached at Antioch of Pisidia, Iconium, Lystra, Derbe, and other cities. At every step they met with opposition and even violent persecution from the Jews, who incited mobs against

---

1. Eusebius, *Church History* 2:14–15.

them. The most striking incident of the journey was at Lystra, where the superstitious populace took Paul, who had just cured a lame man, for Hermes "because he was the chief speaker," and Barnabas for Zeus. The people were about to sacrifice a bull to these "gods" when the apostles prevented them. The Jews from Iconium, who had followed them to Lystra in outrage, persuaded the mob to turn and attack the apostles. They wounded Paul almost fatally. Still, Paul and Barnabas made many converts on this journey and retraced their steps to Perga, organizing churches and ordaining elders. They testified, on returning to Antioch in Syria, that God had "opened a door of faith to the Gentiles" (Acts 14:27).

THE JUDAIZERS

Barnabas and Paul had been "for no small time" at Antioch, when Jewish believers came from Jerusalem and threatened to undo their work of church planting among the gentiles. The Judaizers preached that circumcision was necessary for salvation, even for gentiles. Paul and Barnabas realized that their infant churches would wither in the face of this teaching.

Peter came to Antioch and associated with gentiles, eating with them. This displeased some disciples of James; in their opinion, Peter's act contradicted Mosaic law. Peter yielded to their criticism, apparently through fear of displeasing them, and stopped eating with the gentiles. Barnabas followed Peter's example. Paul considered that they "were not straightforward with the truth of the Gospel" and challenged them before the whole church. Peter apparently agreed with Paul's critique and accepted his public rebuke (Gal 2:14). Presumably, Barnabas followed suit.

THE JERUSALEM COUNCIL

The Antioch church wanted to settle the Judaizing question, so it sent Paul and Barnabas to Jerusalem in AD 49 to confer with the other apostles. The Jerusalem apostles received them and, at what is called the Council of Jerusalem, listened in silence to the signs and wonders God had done through Paul and Barnabas among the gentiles. The council decided in their favor, commissioning Paul, Barnabas, Judas Barsabbas, and Silas (Silvanus) to take the council's decree to Antioch. Paul and Barnabas then decided to revisit their young churches in Asia Minor. Barnabas wanted to take John Mark once more, but Paul objected because of Mark's earlier defection. A sharp dispute ensued, and Paul and Barnabas agreed to separate. Barnabas sailed with John Mark to his homeland, Cyprus, while Paul took Silas and revisited the churches of Asia Minor (Acts 15:39–41).

LATER YEARS

Little is known of the later career of Barnabas. He was still laboring as an apostle when Paul wrote 1 Corinthians, from which we learn that he, like Paul, earned his own living on an equal basis with other apostles (1 Cor 9:5–6). The reference suggests the friendship between the two was still strong. When Paul was a prisoner in Rome for the first time, from AD 57 to 59, John Mark was attached to him as a disciple (Phlm 24), which may indicate that Barnabas was no longer living, since Mark and Barnabas might otherwise have still been working as a team. It also demonstrates that whatever differences Paul and Mark may have felt at the time of Paul's second missionary journey, they must have patched up.

Various traditions represent Barnabas as the first bishop of Milan. He is supposed to have been martyred. Certain Jews coming to Syria and Salamis, where Barnabas was then preaching the gospel, were exasperated at his success. They ambushed him as he was teaching in a synagogue, dragged him out, tortured him, and then stoned him to death. His cousin, John Mark, witnessed his death and privately buried his body.

LEGACY

Barnabas appears to have been one of the most esteemed men of the first Christian generation. Luke wrote of him with affection, "He was a good man, full of the Holy Spirit and of Faith" (Acts 11:24). Tertullian credits Barnabas with the writing the book of Hebrews, although authorship of this book is also attributed to Paul and Apollos.

Others of the Apostolic Age

John the Baptist

JOHN THE BAPTIST IS not, perhaps, a person we associate with the apostles of Jesus, and yet, as the forerunner of the Messiah, obviously he was a uniquely appointed messenger of Christ. His story is entwined inextricably with the lives of Jesus and his apostles.

JOHN'S CONCEPTION

In the days of King Herod the Great, there was a priest (a Levite) named Zechariah. He had a wife who was also a Levite named Elizabeth. They were both righteous, obeying all the commandments of the law, but they had no child because Elizabeth was barren, and both were advanced in years. On Saturday, the Sabbath, March 1, 3 BC, while Zechariah was serving his turn as a priest before God in Jerusalem, he was chosen by lot to enter the temple and burn incense. It was the time of the afternoon prayer, 3 p.m., and a multitude of people were outside the temple, praying in anticipation of the Sabbath ending at sundown on that Saturday.

Inside the temple was the altar of incense which stood in front of the veil that divided the outer sanctuary from the inner sanctuary, the holy of holies. There, standing at the right side of the altar, an angel of the Lord appeared to Zechariah. Fear fell upon him, and he was troubled. But the angel said to him:

> Do not be afraid, Zechariah, for your prayer has been heard. Your wife Elizabeth will bear you a son, and you shall call him John. You will have joy and gladness, and many will rejoice at his birth. He will be great before the Lord. And he must not drink wine or strong drink. He will be filled with the Holy Spirit, even from his mother's womb. And he will turn many of the children of Israel to the Lord their God. He will go before him in the spirit and power of Elijah, to turn the hearts of the fathers to the children, and the disobedient to the wisdom of the just, to make ready for the Lord a people prepared. (Luke 1:13–17)

This message must have crowded Zechariah's brain. The first stunning prophecy was that he and Elizabeth would at last have a child. As a trained priest, however, Zechariah must have understood more. He no doubt realized from what the angel said that his son would be a Nazirite, like Samuel and Samson. As such, he would take vows to drink no alcohol, not to touch a corpse, and not to cut his hair or beard (Num 6:2–21). Nazirite vows could be for a time or for life, but since the angel was calling the boy a Nazirite from before his birth, it sounded like a lifelong vow. Samuel had kept his vows for life. Samson had violated his. Which prophet would Zechariah's son be like?

Even more impressions must have come flooding into Zechariah's thoughts. The angel said things about the boy that may have reminded the priest of the prophecy by Malachi made 428 years ago:

> Behold, I am going to send you Elijah the prophet before the great and awesome day of the Lord comes. And he will turn the hearts of fathers to their children and the hearts of children to their fathers, lest I come and strike the land with a decree of utter destruction. (Mal 4:5–6)

God had promised to send an Anointed One, a Messiah, a Christ, from as far back as Eden (Gen 3:16) and from the time of Moses (Deut 18:15). The sacred Scriptures were laced through with hints about this mysterious Savior (for example, Isaiah 53). The priests speculated about him endlessly, and, of course, wherever there are two priests, there are three opinions. But one thing all agreed upon was that Elijah would return to pave the way for the Messiah. The angel had just told Zechariah that his miracle son would come in the spirit and power of Elijah and that this was happening now and through him.

Like everyone else in the priesthood, and many among the common folk, Zechariah must have known Daniel's prophecy about the coming of Messiah the Prince (Dan 9:24–27). Daniel foretold that 490 years from the issuance of a decree to rebuild Jerusalem the Messiah would come, be cut off, and have nothing. Four hundred fifty-four years before, the Persian King Artaxerxes I had issued a decree permitting Ezra the priest to lead a second wave of survivors out of Babylonian exile back to Jerusalem. The earlier wave of returning survivors, under Zerubbabel the governor and Jeshua the priest, had already laid the foundation of the Second Temple, the start of restoring Solomon's First Temple that Nebuchadnezzar had destroyed in 586 BC. A second wave of Jewish survivors, under Ezra the priest and then under Nehemiah the governor, would rebuild the city of Jerusalem. It was thus this Persian decree that caused Daniel's prophetic clock to start ticking.

Daniel said that the Messiah would do many things: he would finish transgression, make an end of sin, make atonement for iniquity, bring in everlasting righteousness, seal up vision and prophecy, anoint a most holy place, make a firm covenant with many, put a stop to sacrifice and grain offering, but then be cut off and have nothing. After that would come a flood of war and desolations, ending with the destruction of Jerusalem and the temple.

Zechariah and everyone else could count. Daniel's prophetic clock had started ticking 454 years ago. The alarm would go off in the 490th year, a mere thirty-six years from the year Zechariah was speaking with the angel. For the Messiah to come and do all those prophesied things in the next thirty-six years did not leave much time. Many people believed that the Messiah would be born soon or was perhaps even alive already and walking anonymously among them. Now here was an angel, telling Zechariah that his unborn son would be the Elijah forerunner who would pave the Messiah's way.

It probably took mere seconds for all these long-embedded teachings to arise and swirl around Zechariah's brain, but, in the presence of this strange and frightening being, the angel, all he could reply was, "How shall I know this? For I am old, and my wife is advanced in years." The angel replied, "I am Gabriel." That name must have sent a shock through Zechariah's learned mind. Gabriel was the very angel who had appeared to Daniel and had told him all those things about the Messiah. This angel had appeared to no one else in history but to Daniel and now to Zechariah. Gabriel continued:

> I stand in the presence of God. I was sent to speak to you and to bring you this good news. Now, behold, you will be silent and unable to speak until the day that these things take place, because you did not believe my words, which will be fulfilled in their time. (Luke 1:19–20)

With that, Gabriel vanished. Zechariah tried to speak. Nothing. Probably he sank down and pondered, waiting for his racing heart and heavy breathing to calm down. Then he arose and came out of the temple into the slanting afternoon sunlight. Outside, the people assembled for the afternoon prayer were wondering at Zechariah's delay inside. When they perceived that he was unable to speak to them, he made signs and conveyed that he had seen a vision. There must have been a great deal of speculation among the families of Jerusalem as they sat down to their Sabbath meal after sundown on that astonishing day.

Zechariah was no doubt eager to return to his home in the Judean countryside to tell his wife, Elizabeth, what Gabriel had said. He had to wait, however, because his term of service continued for another week. Even then, when his turn ended on Friday, March 7, he could not travel home immediately, because that would entail violating the Sabbath ban on travel. So he remained in Jerusalem from sundown on Friday till sundown on Saturday, probably observing the Sabbath with relatives or friends, who noted that he continued to be mute. This was more than laryngitis. The angel had truly taken speech from him.

ZECHARIAH RETURNS TO ELIZABETH

Church tradition holds that Zechariah and Elizabeth lived in the town of Ein Karem, just an hour and a half walk from Jerusalem. On Sunday, March 9, Zechariah no doubt rose with the sun and set out eagerly for home. There was likely a youthful spring in his step that he had not felt for many years. When he met Elizabeth, it must have been a joyful reunion that reminded them both of when they had first met. Zechariah had to tell her the story, but he had no speech. So, like a good priest, he doubtless had written down every word that the angel had said to him, and he must have shown his journal to Elizabeth. Unlike Greek women of her day, Hebrew women were taught to read and do math, and so she could read all that had transpired, even though her husband remained mute. His speechlessness was a little frightening, perhaps, but Gabriel had said it would be temporary. Probably they joked about it. Elizabeth no doubt planned to enjoy this time when her husband would have to listen to whatever she said without being able to talk back.

Zechariah and Elizabeth were perhaps happier than they had ever been. The Holy Spirit was in their midst. As they embraced each other, Elizabeth conceived, counting the days of gestation backward from John's birth, sometime between that very evening, Sunday, March 9, and the next Sabbath, Saturday, March 15, 3 BC. Elizabeth could feel the life within her, even though there was no physical sign of it yet. "John," she probably kept murmuring to herself. She said happily to her husband, "Thus the Lord has done for me in the days when he looked on me, to take away my reproach among people" (Luke 1:25).

ELIZABETH IN HIDING

Elizabeth had long felt inadequate and lonely for being unable to bear children. Now her dream was coming true. But she hid herself for five months (Luke 1:24). Why? Probably in part she wanted time alone, to savor this miracle. Probably in part because her husband remained mute and could not explain the miracle to all the friends, neighbors, and relatives who would have pummeled them with questions. And probably in part because there may still have been a bit of doubt in her. What if the baby did not survive? What if he were stillborn? She was an elderly woman, and such pregnancies were often hard. Perhaps she would rather that nobody ever knew than to make her pregnancy public and then have it fail.

As the baby grew in Elizabeth's womb, Passover rolled around. As a priest obedient to the law of Moses (Exod 23:14–17; Deut 16:5–6), Zechariah doubtless made the pilgrimage to Jerusalem. The law did not require Elizabeth to go, although normally she might have gone, because it was a good chance to meet all her relatives who also made the pilgrimage. This special year, however, in her delicate and hidden state, she stayed at home.

ZECHARIAH RETURNS TO JERUSALEM FOR PASSOVER

Passover in 3 BC ran from Wednesday, April 9 until Thursday, April 17. Zechariah set out for Jerusalem, no doubt in the company of many friends and neighbors, no later than Tuesday, the day before the feast. When he arrived in Jerusalem, Zechariah probably found that he had become a minor celebrity. The story of his meeting Gabriel in the temple had surely circulated throughout the Jewish community, and everyone was no doubt eager to learn if he was still mute. He was.

In Jerusalem, Zechariah surely met Elizabeth's relatives from Galilee, who likely included Mary, the fiancée of Joseph, the son of Jacob. Mary, her parents, Joseph, and his parents probably all read Zechariah's written account of the angel Gabriel and of Elizabeth's miracle pregnancy. Zechariah's continuing muteness was testimony to the facts. The family probably experienced an awestruck Passover, as they reflected on the possible near-term fulfillment of the prophecies of Isaiah, Daniel, and Malachi. The Messiah was coming, indeed, and his advent was closely associated with the birth of their new little cousin, John.

ZECHARIAH RETURNS TO JERUSALEM FOR PENTECOST

After Passover, Elizabeth's pregnancy continued in health, and the months rolled around to the next great pilgrimage feast, Pentecost, which fell on Friday, May 30. Zechariah of course again traveled to Jerusalem, and Mary, Joseph, and their parents and relatives no doubt once more had the chance to meet him and observe that his muteness continued. They would also have learned that Elizabeth's pregnancy was proceeding well. Around Friday, August 15, Elizabeth's sixth month of pregnancy began. She came out of hiding. Her womb was swollen with life. The miracle foretold by Gabriel was now evident for all to see.

THE ANNUNCIATION

In the sixth month of Elizabeth's pregnancy, and in Elul, the sixth month of the Hebrew year (Luke 1:26), God sent the angel Gabriel to Nazareth, in Galilee, to Mary, a virgin betrothed to a man named Joseph of the house of David. He told her that the Holy Spirit would overshadow her and conceive Jesus, Son of the Most High, in her womb. Gabriel also informed her that Elizabeth had conceived a son in her old age and that this was the sixth month of her pregnancy, adding that nothing is impossible with God. And the angel Gabriel departed from her. Around that time, on Saturday, the Sabbath, September 13 (23 Elul), over midnight to Sunday, September 14 (24 Elul), 3 BC, the Holy Spirit immaculately conceived Jesus in the virgin womb of Mary.

On that Sunday, the teenage Mary believed she was pregnant. She knew the pregnancy was of the Holy Spirit. She trusted in God. But she probably did not have quite as much faith in her family, in Joseph, and in Joseph's family. If they did not believe her, if they thought she had become pregnant by another man, the penalty under Mosaic law would be either death by stoning or ignominious return to her father's house. Where was Mary to turn for help and support? Who would believe her?

Helpfully, the angel who spoke to Mary identified himself as Gabriel, the same angel who had spoken to her relative, Zechariah. Zechariah had experienced two miracles: (1) the angel had struck him dumb, and (2) Elizabeth had conceived a child and was six months pregnant. If anyone would accept Mary's story, Zechariah and Elizabeth might. So she wanted to go to them in haste. Perhaps they would help her break the news to the rest of the family. But the young Mary could hardly travel from Galilee to Judea alone. Who would escort her? And how would she explain her need to go quickly?

ARISING IN HASTE

Erev (the eve of) Rosh Hashanah, the Feast of Trumpets, was on a Friday in that year. As Jews from outside Jerusalem, tradition required that Galileans begin their observation of pilgrimage feasts a day early (so as not to miscalculate and miss the day). In this case, that meant celebrating in Jerusalem on Thursday. Jews in Galilee had to depart no later than Sunday to arrive on Wednesday, September 17, to be ready for their devotions on the following day.

The mandatory pilgrimage provided Mary with a chance to go to Judea with her family. Once there, she knew she would meet Zechariah, who also would make the pilgrimage faithfully to Jerusalem for the High Holy Days that fall. Of course, he would then return home. What could be more natural than for Mary to suggest that she go with him to attend to her relative, Elizabeth, who might have a difficult childbirth, given that she was expecting her first child at an advanced age? This was how Mary could get to Judea without attracting undue notice. But she had to move fast to get her family to agree to it and to be ready in time to join the caravan going south. Mary and her family, and probably Joseph and his family, departed from Galilee on the required journey to Jerusalem for Rosh Hashanah on Sunday, September 14 (the very day when Mary conceived Jesus). They probably reached Jerusalem on Wednesday, September 17. Mary was a quick-thinking young woman, and she arose in haste, indeed.

MARY VISITS ELIZABETH

At the end of the High Holy Days, on the last day of the Feast of Tabernacles (Sukkot), on Monday, October 13, in Jerusalem, Mary probably bade farewell to Joseph and her parents, who returned north to Galilee, while she traveled south with her mute relative Zechariah to stay with Elizabeth. Mary was in her second month of pregnancy.

She probably had morning sickness, but she did not show yet. She was getting away to the Judean hills just in time.

It took only an hour and a half to travel from Jerusalem to Ein Karem, the village where Zechariah lived. The pregnant Mary entered Zechariah's house and met the pregnant Elizabeth, and when Elizabeth heard the greeting of Mary, the baby John leaped in her womb. Elizabeth was filled with the Holy Spirit, and she exclaimed with a loud cry:

> Blessed are you among women and blessed is the fruit of your womb! Why is this granted to me that the mother of my Lord should come to me? For behold, when the sound of your greeting came to my ears, the baby in my womb leaped for joy. Blessed is she who believed that there would be a fulfillment of what was spoken to her from the Lord. (Luke 1:42–45)

God graciously spared Mary an awkward explanation. Before she said a word, God revealed to Elizabeth the sanctity of Mary's pregnancy and even went further. He gave Elizabeth the knowledge that Mary's child would be the Messiah. And Elizabeth supported Mary's belief in what she heard by saying Mary was blessed for believing what Gabriel had told her, a pointed contrast to her mute husband, Zechariah, who had not believed Gabriel and who was without doubt listening to these words of his wife, Elizabeth.

THE MAGNIFICAT

Mary was relieved and overjoyed by Elizabeth's understanding of what her pregnancy meant. Clearly inspired by the Holy Spirit, she uttered a beautiful psalm, known as the Magnificat, because the first sentence of Mary's psalm in Latin is *Magnificat anima mea Dominum:* "My soul magnifies the Lord." Zechariah surely heard all these things and must have marveled that over the course of human history the angel Gabriel had only appeared to three people: Daniel, himself, and his teenage relative, Mary. Although mute, Zechariah had ears, and his Levitical priestly training may well have moved him to write down every word that Mary spoke through the inspiration of the Holy Spirit, so that others might profit from this psalm in days and years to come.

THE BIRTH OF JOHN THE BAPTIST

Mary remained with Elizabeth and Zechariah for the rest of Elizabeth's pregnancy, about three months (Luke 1:56). When John the Baptist was born, around December 1, 3 BC, Mary was at her relative Elizabeth's side. On Tuesday, December 9, eight days after John's birth, the religious doctors in Zechariah's village came to circumcise the child (Luke 1:59). When Zechariah's family asked what the son's name should be, Elizabeth, remembering Gabriel's command to her husband, said it must be John.

The neighbors made signs to Zechariah, protesting that none of his family had the name John, and so his son should not either. It is amusing that the people made signs to Zechariah instead of speaking, because he was dumb, not deaf. This is what people often do with mutes: assume that just because they cannot speak, they cannot hear. This humorous detail adds a touch of verisimilitude to Luke's Gospel that tends to validate its authenticity. Then Zechariah wrote on a tablet:

"His name is John."

All the people marveled at that, but they wondered even more when Zechariah suddenly recovered his speech. Fear came upon them because they realized this was indeed a miracle child. Gabriel had not said that Zechariah would be mute until the birth of John, but that he would be mute "until all these things take place." So, John's circumcision was the great day, the day when the forerunner of the Messiah, the new Elijah, came into the covenant community of God.

Mary and Elizabeth witnessed the miraculous recovery of Zechariah's speech. The fulfillment of this promise by Gabriel must have reassured Mary that God would support her against possible human recriminations for her miraculous pregnancy. The hand of God was visibly at work.

ZECHARIAH'S PROPHECY

Inspired by the Holy Spirit, Zechariah pronounced a beautifully phrased prophecy, reminiscent of the psalm Mary had composed fifty-six days before. He said:

> Blessed be the Lord God of Israel, for He has visited and redeemed His people and has raised up a horn of salvation for us in the house of His servant David, as He spoke by the mouth of His holy prophets from of old, that we should be saved from our enemies and from the hand of all who hate us; to show the mercy promised to our fathers and to remember His holy covenant, the oath that He swore to our father Abraham, to grant us that we, being delivered from the hand of our enemies, might serve Him without fear, in holiness and righteousness before Him all our days. And you, child, will be called the prophet of the Most High; for you will go before the Lord to prepare His ways, to give knowledge of salvation to His people in the forgiveness of their sins, because of the tender mercy of our God, whereby the sunrise shall visit us from on high to give light to those who sit in darkness and in the shadow of death, to guide our feet into the way of peace. (Luke 1:68–79)

Zechariah was a priest, knew the Scriptures very well, and was in the grip of high emotions at the recovery of his speech and the circumcision of his miracle child. This was more than personal to him; since the child would be the forerunner to the Messiah, this was an event of national, historic, and religious significance. In a moment of inspiration, Zechariah spoke these exact words and, to preserve them for himself and for posterity, he undoubtedly wrote them down. Mary must have wondered at these words, for they were spoken about the child in her womb.

John would grow and become strong in spirit, and, as an adult, he would live in the wilderness eating wild locusts and honey until his public ministry began in AD 29, about thirty-two years later. Since Elizabeth and Zechariah were advanced in age at the time of John's birth, they probably did not live to witness the public ministry, and untimely execution, of their beloved son.

RENDEZVOUS IN JERUSALEM

On Thursday, December 11, Mary and Zechariah would have arrived on schedule in Jerusalem for the feast of Chanukah. Mary no doubt met her family and Joseph and his family at the feast, which began on Friday, December 12. They could have left for Jerusalem a day earlier, on Wednesday, but Zechariah would have wanted to wait a day to see how John recovered from the circumcision. He did fine, but there was probably another reason for a day's delay. After nine months of being mute, he probably had much he wanted to say to his wife, Elizabeth.

The pilgrimage to Jerusalem for Chanukah was to commemorate the Maccabees' recapture of Jerusalem from the Greek king Antiochus IV Epiphanes and the purification of the temple and restoration of worship there 161 years before, on Monday, November 21 (25 Kislev), 164 BC. This was not a pilgrimage commanded in Mosaic law, but Jews commonly observed it, as Jesus did in AD 32 (John 10:22). This rendezvous was probably part of Mary's plan for Mary to go to Elizabeth's aid. She had traveled south with the family on the Rosh Hashanah pilgrimage in September, traveled with Zechariah from Jerusalem to his house in Judea, stayed with Elizabeth until Elizabeth gave birth, and returned to Jerusalem in December (Chanukah) so that Mary's family could escort her back to her home in Galilee. Since the Jewish calendar and human gestation were predictable, Mary needed no prophetic powers to lay down this plan.

Mary was now about three months pregnant. She probably still did not yet "show," but probably at this time she confided to Joseph and to her family that she had conceived by the Holy Spirit. The accumulation of miracles in the life of Zechariah (his meeting with Gabriel, his loss of speech, the miracle birth of John the Baptist, and the recovery of his speech) no doubt helped Joseph's and Mary's families to accept Mary's account. Also, Mary probably repeated her Magnificat and Zechariah probably repeated his prophecy for the families to hear. After all, if these psalms have been preserved for us, surely Mary and Zechariah shared them with their families then. These must have been among the "things Joseph considered" (Matt 1:20) when resolving to divorce Mary quietly.

JOSEPH ACCEPTS MARY

Joseph probably believed Mary's story as soon as he heard it. He probably did not need the dream of an angel to accept what she said as truth. Living in a small town like Nazareth, as a young teenager, Mary had little, if any, opportunity for an illicit sexual encounter. When she traveled to visit her relative Elizabeth, she was chaperoned by her priestly relative, Zechariah. Moreover, Joseph probably trusted Mary personally. Mary was a special person. God chose her of all the billions of women ever born to be the mother of the Messiah. God saw much good in Mary, and if God did, Joseph would, as well. Mary was undoubtedly a person whose candor and purity made believing her easy.

As a just man, Joseph was a Jew who revered Mosaic law (Matt 1:19). If he mistrusted Mary, the law would require him to denounce her to the community and face death by stoning for adultery (Lev 20:10; Deut 22:22). Instead, he took the decision to divorce her quietly (Matt 1:19), probably not because he doubted her but because he believed her. Joseph may have felt unworthy to be the stepfather of Mary's miracle child, the Messiah. The pronouncements about the infant Jesus overawed him (Luke 2:33). He may have feared to accept so great a role. After all, God had sent an angel to Mary, but no angel to him yet.

But then an angel of the Lord did appear to him in a dream, saying, "Joseph, son of David, do not fear to take Mary as your wife, for that which is conceived in her is from the Holy Spirit. She will bear a son, and you shall call his name Jesus, for he will save his people from their sins" (Matt 1:20–21).

THE COMING OF JOHN THE BAPTIST

> In the fifteenth year of the reign of Tiberius Caesar, Pontius Pilate being governor of Judea, and Herod being tetrarch of Galilee, and his brother Philip tetrarch of the region of Ituraea and Trachonitis, and Lysanias tetrarch of Abilene, during the high priesthood of Annas and Caiaphas, the word of God came to John the son of Zechariah in the wilderness. (Luke 3:1–2)

The fifteenth regnal year of Tiberius Caesar began on Saturday, August 19, AD 28, and ended on Saturday, August 18, AD 29. Using all the time markers in the Gospels, it is possible to pinpoint that John baptized Jesus on Sunday, September 2, AD 29.[1] So, John began his ministry some days before that date, before mid-August AD 29. He went into all the region around the Jordan, proclaiming a baptism if repentance for the forgiveness of sins, saying, "Repent, for the kingdom of heaven is at hand" (Matt 3:2).

John's base of operations was the village of Bethany on the Jordan (not Bethany on the Mount of Olives).

---

1. See "Pinpointing the Start of Jesus' Ministry" in the Appendices. No other date works.

THE MISSION OF JOHN THE BAPTIST

Luke says the word of God came to John. John says God sent John to witness the light. Matthew, Mark, and Luke say that John came preaching repentance. John was he of whom Isaiah the prophet spoke when he said:

> Behold, I send my messenger before your face, who will prepare your way, the voice of one crying in the wilderness, "Prepare the way of the Lord; make His paths straight. Every valley shall be filled, and every mountain and hill shall be made low, and the crooked shall become straight, and the rough places shall become level ways, and all flesh shall see the salvation of God." (Matt 11:10; Mark 1:2–3; Luke 3:4–5)

CONFLATED PROPHECIES

Matthew, Mark, and Luke purposely conflated the words of two prophets, Malachi and Isaiah.

> "Behold, I am going to send my messenger, and he will clear the way before me. And the Lord, whom you seek, will suddenly come to His Temple; and the messenger of the covenant, in whom you delight, behold, He is coming," says the Lord of hosts. (Mal 3:1)

> Behold, I will send you Elijah the prophet before the great and awesome day of the LORD comes. And he will turn the hearts of fathers to their children and the hearts of children to their fathers, lest I come and strike the land with a decree of utter destruction. (Mal 4:5–6)

> A voice is calling, "Clear the way for the Lord in the wilderness; Make smooth in the desert a highway for our God." (Isa 40:3)

As a kind of shorthand, the evangelists cited only Isaiah, because he was the more famous of the two prophets. John wrote in his Gospel that the Baptist came from God not as the light but as a witness to the light of Jesus, crying out that Jesus, who was coming after him, ranked before him. John wore a garment of camel's hair and a leather belt and ate locusts and wild honey. Elijah "wore a garment of hair, with a belt of leather about his waist" (2 Kgs 1:8). John the Baptist came in the spirit and form of Elijah and had a similar appearance.

THE MULTITUDES WHO CAME TO JOHN THE BAPTIST

People from Jerusalem, from all over Judea, and from the region all around the Jordan were going out to see John the Baptist. He proclaimed a baptism of repentance for the forgiveness of sins. Everyone who came confessed their sins and were baptized by him in the River Jordan.

This was the season of Israel's High Holy Days. Judea was filled with pilgrims (perhaps as many as 2.7 million Jews from around the world).[2] John was preaching and baptizing downhill from Jerusalem, past Jericho, on the Jordan River, a distance of about twenty miles or five hours' walk.

The Jews of Galilee made their pilgrimages to Jerusalem by avoiding Samaria. They followed the Jordan River southward from the Sea of Galilee, turned west toward Jericho, and climbed the ascent to Jerusalem. Galilean pilgrims would all pass John's place of ministry at Bethany beyond the Jordan along their way to Jerusalem. John may have been in the wilderness, but he was at a strategic crossroads.

THE RITUAL OF BAPTISM

Baptism of repentance for confessed sins was John's innovation. Probably he got the idea from Leviticus 15, in which God's law required that anyone who had become unclean should bathe his body and clothes to become clean again by evening. Without this immersion, an unclean person would be an outcast from the covenant community. John applied the practice to symbolize repentance (confessing the uncleanness of sin and turning away from it) and desiring to become clean in God's eyes. The idea was that the pollution of sin made a man an outcast from the kingdom of heaven. John never said that baptism produced the forgiveness of sins. Baptism was a symbol of the desire to repent and to receive God's gracious cleansing, which alone produces salvation.

THE BROOD OF VIPERS

The High Holy Days, Monday, August 20, through Thursday, September 20, were ample time for the Jewish religious leaders to hear of John's unusual ministry and send representatives to investigate. When John saw many of the Pharisees and Sadducees coming to his baptism, he said to them:

> You brood of vipers! Who warned you to flee from the wrath to come? Bear fruit in keeping with repentance. And do not presume to say to yourselves, "We have Abraham as our father," for I tell you, God is able from these stones to raise up children for Abraham. Even now the axe is laid to the root of the trees. Every tree therefore that does not bear good fruit is cut down and thrown into the fire. (Matt 3:7–10)

Hearing this stunning rebuke of their leaders, the crowds asked John what they should do. He told them that whoever had two tunics should share with him who had

2. Josephus, *War* 6:9:3.

none, and whoever had food should do likewise. Tax collectors, the despised collaborators with Rome, also came to be baptized and asked what they should do. John told them to collect no more in taxes than they were authorized to do, a radical departure from their customary rapacious practice. Soldiers came to John and asked what they should do. He told them not to extort money from anyone by threats or false accusations and to be content with their wages. This was another radical departure from the profession of soldiering in those days. The religious leaders questioned John, but they felt no need to repent. The common people confessed their sins and asked John what to do about them.

The people were full of expectation. They all were questioning in their hearts whether John might be the Christ. John said that the one coming after him was mightier than he and that John was not worthy to carry his sandals or to stoop down and untie them. He said that he had baptized the people with water, but the Messiah would baptize them with the Holy Spirit and with fire. The Messiah's winnowing fork was in his hand. He would clear his threshing floor and gather his wheat into the barn, but he would burn the chaff with unquenchable fire. So, with these and many other exhortations, John preached to the people.

The common people suspected that John was the Messiah. The religious leaders feared he might be the Messiah. But John told them that the Messiah was coming after him and was infinitely more worthy and mighty than he was. John also explained that his baptism was of simple water and was symbolic. But the baptism of the Messiah would be of the Holy Spirit and would be real.

Gathering the wheat was a metaphor that the Jews understood to mean reuniting faithful Israel. Burning the chaff they thought meant throwing off the hated yokes of Rome, the Herods, and the Hellenizing Jews. John made no attempt to ingratiate himself with the Jewish leaders. He said they needed to repent as much, if not more, than anyone.

JESUS' BAPTISM: GOD SPEAKS AUDIBLY

Jesus left Galilee no later than Tuesday, August 28. He arrived at John's place on the Jordan no later than Thursday evening or Friday morning. He would have observed the Sabbath both from piety and because there would be few Jews to witness his baptism until the Sabbath was over. On Sunday, September 2, AD 29, Jesus came to John to be baptized by him. John would have prevented him, saying:

"I need to be baptized by you, and do you come to me?"

John said he was unworthy to baptize his cousin, Jesus. Jesus, being sinless, had nothing of which to repent. But Jesus answered him, "Let it be so now, for thus it is fitting for us to fulfill all righteousness."

Then John consented. And when Jesus was baptized, immediately he went up from the water, and the heavens were torn open to him, and he saw the Spirit of God descending in bodily form, like a dove, and coming to rest on him; and a voice from heaven said, "You are my beloved Son; with You I am well pleased."

God's voice spoke audibly from heaven, endorsing Jesus' divinity. God would speak audibly two other times during Jesus' earthly ministry, at the transfiguration in AD 32 and at the Jerusalem temple during the passion week of AD 33.

JESUS IN THE WILDERNESS

Jesus, full of the Holy Spirit, returned from the Jordan, and the Spirit immediately drove him into the wilderness for forty days and forty nights to be tempted by the devil. This occurred from Monday, September 3, to Saturday, October 13, AD 29.

THE JEWISH LEADERS QUESTION JOHN AGAIN

On Monday, October 15, the Jews sent priests and Levites from Jerusalem to ask John the Baptist who he really was. He confessed he was not the Christ. They asked if he was Elijah. He said he was not. They asked if he was the Prophet (foretold by Moses in Deut 18:15). He said no. They asked him to say who he was so that they could give an answer to their Pharisee masters in Jerusalem. John replied that he was the voice of one crying in the wilderness, "Make straight the way of the Lord." They asked him why, then, was he baptizing if he was neither the Christ, nor Elijah, nor the Prophet. He replied that he baptized with water but that already standing among them was one they did not know, one who would come after John, the strap of whose sandal he was unworthy to untie.

THE UNACCEPTABLE SACRIFICE

Something unusual was motivating the Sadducees and Pharisees to go out in the wilderness and question John the Baptist about his mysterious identity and his ominous message. Around August of AD 29, John the Baptist began his ministry. On Sunday, September 2, AD 29, John baptized Jesus, publicly recognizing him as the Messiah. On Thursday, October 4, AD 29, Yom Kippur, the Day of Atonement, the first of forty unacceptable sacrifices was presented in the temple. This was the thirty-second day of Jesus' forty-day fast in the wilderness. So the Yom Kippur of AD 29 was the first of forty unacceptable sacrifices presented in the temple before its destruction in August AD 70. Here is how that worked.

On the Day of Atonement, the high priest of Israel sacrificed a bull for his own sins. He then presented two goats in the temple to cover the sins of all Israel. Chosen by lot, one goat became the Lord's goat, offered as a blood sacrifice, whose blood the high priest took into the holy of holies and sprinkled on the mercy seat on the lid of the ark of the covenant. The other goat became the "Azazel"[3] goat, or scapegoat, to be sent away into the wilderness. The high priest confessed the sins of the nation and asked Yahweh to place them on the head of the scapegoat, who took them away into the wilderness, atoning for them. According to the Babylonian Talmud, *Yoma* 39b, the priests determined whether God accepted the national sacrifice by tying a crimson thread to one horn of the scapegoat. If God turned the thread white, he had pardoned Israel. But from AD 29 until AD 69, the year before Rome destroyed Jerusalem and the temple, for forty consecutive years, according to the Talmud, the thread remained red.[4] God did not pardon Israel for all those years.

This is not a biblical test. Paul warned believers against putting faith in man-made traditions (Col 2:20–23), and this certainly was one. Nevertheless, according to the Talmud, the Jews did believe it, and their concerns were justified, because Jesus' better, new covenant had come to replace the old covenant (Heb 7:22, 8:6). So, while the unacceptable scapegoat of Israel wandered in the wilderness, ten days after Yom Kippur, Satan tempted Jesus, the Lamb of God, unsuccessfully, in the wilderness. On Yom Kippur of AD 29, Jesus acted as Israel's scapegoat, and when he returned from the wilderness John the Baptist hailed him as the "Lamb that takes away the sins of the world." (Jesus' message in cleansing the temple during the next year's Passover in AD 30 was that the old covenant was no longer effective for salvation from sin. God's new covenant had come.)

Monday, October 15, AD 29, was the first day (when travel was not forbidden) when the Jewish leaders could walk to the Jordan and challenge John again to give them better answers. They came with very specific questions. John said he was not a reincarnation of Elijah. Jesus later would explain that the Jewish leaders misunderstood the prophecy of Elijah's return. John's function was to act like Elijah, not be Elijah. Elijah in fact would come again, with Moses, on the Mount of Transfiguration, three years later and after the death of John (Matt 17:3).

They also asked if John was the Prophet that Moses had foretold in Deuteronomy 18:15, the Messiah. John repeated what he had said before, that the Messiah was coming after him and was more worthy than he was. But John added this spine-tingling news: The Messiah was standing among them. John had already baptized his cousin Jesus, whose ministry clock had begun to tick.

THE LAMB OF GOD

The next day, Tuesday, October 16, John saw Jesus coming toward him, and said, "Behold the Lamb of God, who takes away the sins of the world! This is he of whom I said, 'after me comes a man who ranks before me, because he was before me'" (John

---

3. The meaning of Azazel is uncertain. There is no biblical warrant for the legend that it is the name of a fallen angel.

4. *Yoma* 39b.

1:29–30). John went on to say that he did not know Jesus, but he came for the purpose of baptizing with water to make Jesus known to Israel. He declared that he had witnessed the Spirit descend on Jesus like a dove, remaining on him, and that God had told John that Jesus would baptize with the Holy Spirit. John testified that Jesus was the Son of God.

John was Jesus' cousin. He grew up with stories of the miracles and prophecies of his and Jesus' births, and he undoubtedly met his cousin Jesus year after year in Jerusalem on the annual pilgrimages. By saying he did not know Jesus, John was saying that he did not fully comprehend Jesus' Messianic identity until God revealed it to him. Later, when in prison, John would send to ask Jesus if he really were the promised Messiah or if they should wait for another (Matt 11:3; Luke 7:19).

JOHN THE BAPTIST EXALTS JESUS

In AD 30, after the Passover, on Sunday, April 7 (15 Nisan), Jesus and his disciples went south into the Judean countryside, and he remained there with them, as the disciples baptized (John 3:22). At this time, John the Baptist went north to Aenon, where he was baptizing because water was plentiful there. Many people came to be baptized.

A discussion arose between some of John's disciples and a Jew over purification. They brought the dispute to John, and the conversation turned to Jesus. They said, "Rabbi, he who was with you across the Jordan, to whom you bore witness: look, he is baptizing and all are going to him" (John 3:26). John replied by saying that a person can receive nothing unless it comes from heaven. He reminded them that he had borne witness that he was not the Christ but that he had been sent before him. He said that the bridegroom has the bride, and the bridegroom's friend stands aside and rejoices for him. John said his joy was now complete and that Jesus must increase while John decreased. He added:

> He who comes from above is above all . . . he whom God has sent utters the words of God, for He gives the Spirit without measure. The Father loves the Son and has given all things into His hand. Whoever believes in the Son has eternal life; whoever does not obey the Son shall not see life, but the wrath of God remains on him. (John 3:31–36)

This is the fourth time in recorded history that anyone received the title "rabbi." The first two rabbis in history were Jesus and his relative, John the Baptist. John spoke of Jesus in clearly Messianic terms. Far from being jealous, he was joyful that he must decrease as Jesus increased.

THE ARREST OF JOHN THE BAPTIST IN AD 30

John the Baptist criticized the immoral marriage of Herod Antipas I to Herodias, the granddaughter of Herod the Great and wife of Herod Antipas's brother, Herod Philip. This provoked Herod Antipas to arrest John the Baptist. The backstory is as follows.

Herod Antipas was originally married to the daughter of King Aretas, ruler of Arabia Petraea, a kingdom to the east of the tetrarchy of Galilee, that is, modern Jordan. Antipas's brother, Herod Philip, was married to Herodias, the granddaughter of Herod the Great. When Philip was on a journey to Rome, Antipas visited his brother Philip's home, fell in love with Herodias, and married her. He then put away his first wife, the daughter of King Aretas. John the Baptist rebuked Herod Antipas for the crimes of adultery (having sexual relations with the wife of another man) and incest, since Herodias was his brother's wife (Lev 18:16). Aretas declared war on Herod Antipas over the offense to his daughter and defeated him.[5]

No doubt smoldering with resentment at the loss of the war and at John's rebuke, Herod Antipas wanted to kill John but feared to do so because so many people considered John a prophet. Herodias, the adulterous wife, also wanted to put John to death, but she could not, for Herod feared John, knowing that he was a righteous and holy man. When he heard John, Herod was greatly perplexed, and yet he heard him gladly. However, after all the evil things that Herod had done, he added this to them all, that he locked up John in prison. He sent and seized John and bound him for the sake of Herodias, his brother Philip's wife. He held John in jail for about one year, and Herodias conspired to have him murdered (Matt 14:3–5; Mark 6:17–19).

John's arrest occurred at Aenon, in Samaria, the province once ruled by Herod Antipas's brother, Archelaus, but now ruled for the Roman emperor by Pontius Pilate, the procurator. Herod Antipas ruled Galilee and Peraea, so arresting John the Baptist in a city under Pilate's rule was an act that exceeded Herod's authority. Probably John the Baptist, a wandering holy man, concerned Pilate very little, and Pilate was residing in Caesarea, all the way across the province on the Mediterranean coast. He probably did not hear of the surprise arrest until it was a *fait accompli*. Still, this would have added to the enmity between Pilate and Herod. Herod thought he should have inherited his brother Archelaus's territory when Archelaus proved insane and Augustus deposed him. Herod perceived Pilate as the agent of a usurper. Considering all that his father, Herod the Great, had done to help secure Judea for the empire against Rome's archenemy, Parthia, this was ingratitude. There was nothing, however, Herod could do against the reigning and dangerous emperor, Tiberius.

---

5. Josephus, *Ant.* 18:5.

JESUS' WITHDRAWAL TO SAMARIA

When Jesus heard that John had been arrested and learned that the Pharisees had heard that Jesus was making and baptizing more disciples than John (although Jesus himself did not baptize, but only his disciples), he left Judea and departed again for Galilee. And he had to pass through Samaria. So, he came to a town of Samaria called Sychar (Shechem in the Old Testament, Sebastia in Israel today), near the field that Jacob had given to his son Joseph. Jacob's well was there; so, Jesus, wearied as he was from his journey, was sitting beside the well. It was about the sixth hour.

The Pharisees considered both John and Jesus a threat to their authority. They were probably pleasantly intrigued that their old enemy, Herod Antipas, had arrested John. Perhaps they could persuade Herod to arrest Jesus as well, solving two problems at once. Probably Jesus recognized this threat and so left for Galilee without delay.

It took about fifteen and a half hours to walk from Jerusalem to Sychar. If Jesus left Jerusalem at 3 p.m. and walked through the evening and night, Jesus would arrive at dawn. He met the Samaritan woman at the well at the "sixth hour," referring to the Roman method of timekeeping (the method John always used), which counts the zero hour, as we do, from midnight. Since sunrise in Judea was 5:59 a.m. on April 19, AD 30, Jesus met the woman at about 6 a.m. Jesus paused at the well because he was weary from his hasty journey. The evidence of haste is supported also by the fact that Jesus took the shorter route from Judea to Galilee, through Samaria. Jews normally avoided Samaria when traveling between Galilee and Judea because the Jews and Samaritans were hostile to each other. This was an emergency retreat.

A QUESTION ABOUT FASTING

The year rolled around to Tisha B'Av, the ninth day of the Jewish month of Av, or Thursday, July 25, in AD 30. The Pharisees were fasting because this day commemorated the destruction of Solomon's Temple by Nebuchadnezzar in 586 BC. Tisha B'Av is a religious day established "from the bottom up," that is, God did not ordain it. The Jews made it up. The prophet Zechariah stated that God would convert these man-made fasts from times of mourning into times of joy (Zech 8:19). Why? Because even though the Romans would destroy the Second Temple in a manner eerily like how the Babylonians had destroyed the First Temple, Jesus claimed that, in his resurrection, he would replace the temple with a new and better covenant. Thus would Tisha B'Av, a day of mourning, become a day of joy.

We know Jesus and his disciples went to Jerusalem around Tisha B'Av in this year, because after this event, the Gospels describe him "returning" and "crossing again in the boat to the other side." They could not have "returned" if they did not go in the first place, and they could not have "crossed again" if they had not crossed a first time.

They did not fast, because Jesus was conscious of his fulfillment of Zechariah's prophecy. As far as Jesus was concerned, the new covenant had already come. The temple was already a thing of the past. There was nothing left to mourn, only joy in the acceptable day of the Lord (Isa 58:5, 61:1–3; Luke 4:18).

So, Jesus and his five disciples (at least) sailed from Capernaum to the southern shore of the Sea of Galilee and walked along the Jordan Valley to Jerusalem. This would be a likely place for John's disciples to meet him because John was in prison in Machaerus, west of the Dead Sea, and John's disciples seem to have continued to meet along the Jordan River. John's disciples went to Jesus and asked why they and the Pharisees were fasting, while Jesus' disciples were not fasting. Jesus replied, "Can you make wedding guests fast while the bridegroom is with them? The days will come when the bridegroom is taken away from them, and then they will fast in those days" (Luke 5:34–35).

Jesus, using the analogy of himself as the bridegroom at a wedding feast, made the point that being with Jesus was better than having the temple. By cleansing the temple at the Passover earlier that same year, Jesus had declared the end of the old covenant and the beginning of the new covenant. In AD 70, the Roman general (later emperor) Titus would destroy the Second Temple, ironically again on 9 Av, thirty-seven years after Jesus had ascended into heaven. The Jews would certainly fast in that day; more than fast, many died of starvation in the Roman siege. They would watch the last traces of the old covenant go up in flames and watch their nation condemned to millennia of exile. But those who understood Jesus' new and better covenant (Heb 7:22, 8:6), would rejoice that in Jesus something better than the temple had come (Matt 12:6).

MESSENGERS FROM JOHN THE BAPTIST

Herod Antipas was holding John in prison in Machaerus in the hills west of the Dead Sea (Madaba in today's Jordan). John had been incarcerated for about 152 days, yet he still had disciples who were free to visit him; they probably had to feed him, as Herod probably did not provide for his prisoners' sustenance.

John learned of Jesus' many deeds and sayings, and he sent two messengers to ask Jesus if he really was the Messiah, or if they should still look for another. Those messengers would not have violated the Sabbath or Rosh Hashanah by traveling on those days, and so they probably caught up with Jesus in Jerusalem on Monday, September 16, AD 30.

Although John had testified that Jesus was the Lamb of God and had baptized him and had heard God's voice from heaven, after nearly a year in jail, John still craved affirmation from Jesus. God does not rebuke those who have sincere doubts and ask for his reassurance.

John's messengers arrived just when Jesus was healing many people of diseases, casting out demons, and restoring sight to many who were blind. Jesus replied to John's query by saying they had seen and heard of the following miracles he had done:

1. The blind received sight.
2. The lame walked.
3. Lepers were cleansed.
4. The deaf heard.
5. The dead were raised (Jairus's daughter and the son of the widow of Nain, at least).
6. Good news was preached to the poor (the Jubilee).

And then Jesus said that blessed was he who was not offended by Jesus. Why would someone be offended at all his good deeds? Jesus himself would marvel, shortly thereafter, at the leaders of his generation who were offended by his doing good.

When John's messengers had gone, Jesus began to speak to the crowds concerning John, "What did you go out into the wilderness to see? A reed shaken by the wind? What then did you go out to see? A man dressed in soft clothing? Behold, those who wear soft clothing are in kings' houses. What then did you go out to see? A prophet? Yes, I tell you, and more than a prophet" (Matt 11:7–9).

About 594 days before this date, more than one and a half years before, John the Baptist had launched his ministry. Jesus asked the crowds (the Jews of Judea or Jews from around the world who had come to Jerusalem for the Passover and had not yet started their homeward trek) what had drawn them in the first place to John the Baptist during the High Holy Days of AD 29. He was not a reed shaken in the wind, a mere voice. He was not a rich man, a mere purse. He was a prophet, but more than a prophet, because he was the prophesied forerunner of the Messiah.

> This is he of whom it is written, "Behold, I send my messenger before your face, who will prepare your way before you." Truly, I say to you, among those born of women there has arisen no one greater than John the Baptist. Yet the one who is least in the kingdom of heaven is greater than he. From the days of John the Baptist until now the kingdom of heaven has suffered violence, and the violent take it by force. For all the Prophets and the Law prophesied until John, and if you are willing to accept it, he is Elijah who is to come. He who has ears to hear, let him hear. (Matt 11:10–15)

"When all the people heard this, and the tax collectors too, they declared God just, having been baptized with the baptism of John, but the Pharisees and the lawyers rejected the purpose of God for themselves, not having been baptized by him" (Luke 7:29–30).

Jesus said that no one born of a woman, meaning all mankind, was greater than John, but then he said that, nevertheless, the least person in the kingdom of God was

JOHN THE BAPTIST

greater than John. This is just a rhetorical way of saying that John was the forerunner, which makes him the fulfiller of Elijah's prophesied return and therefore great. Because John was great, his testimony about Jesus as Messiah was trustworthy. From the time John baptized Jesus until that date, the kingdom of heaven suffered violence because the religious leaders were failing to embrace the Messiah as they should have done. But all the prophecies about the forerunner focused on John, so no one should expect Elijah to come after John or expect a Messiah after Jesus.

> To what then shall I compare the people of this generation, and what are they like? They are like children sitting in the marketplace and calling to their playmates, "We played the flute for you, and you did not dance; we sang a dirge, and you did not mourn." For John came neither eating nor drinking, and they say, "He has a demon." The Son of Man came eating and drinking, and they say, "Look at him! A glutton and a drunkard, a friend of tax collectors and sinners!" Yet wisdom is justified by her deeds. (Matt 11:16–19)

Jesus compared the rituals and religious learning of the leaders to children's games, a shocking trivialization of the traditions they held sacred. John the Baptist was a Nazirite. He did not touch alcoholic drink and his diet was ascetic. Jesus said the response of the religious leaders was to call him demon possessed. By contrast, Jesus was not an ascetic. He ate and drank normally, even turning water into an abundance of wine at the wedding in Cana and feasting with Matthew's sinful tax collector cronies. The response of the religious leaders was to reject Jesus.

Jesus was criticizing the Jewish leaders for being illogical and inconsistent and rejecting the teaching of God hypocritically. They were not really offended by John's asceticism or Jesus' indulgence; they just did not want God to disturb their comfortable lives as professional Jews. Jesus concluded that what justifies wisdom is what comes of it, its "deeds" or "children." He meant the scribes and Pharisees had no evidence to prove themselves good. But the least in the kingdom of God was as good as ever one could be.

THE DEATH OF JOHN THE BAPTIST

The date of Herod Antipas's birthday is unknown, but since he killed John the Baptist between April 2 and May 24 of AD 31, it must have been between these dates. Herodias, the wife of Herod Antipas, hated John the Baptist for denouncing her incestuous marriage. She had first been the wife of Herod's brother, called Herod II or Herod Philip. She broke the laws of Israel and divorced her first husband while he was yet alive and married Herod Antipas, Herod Philip's brother. Herodias seized the occasion of Herod Antipas's birthday to hatch a plot to kill John, her despised critic. Salome was the daughter of Herodias and Herod Philip, her first husband.[6] At Herod

---

6. Salome is not named in the New Testament. Josephus identifies her name in *Antiquities of the*

Others of the Apostolic Age

Antipas's birthday feast, Salome danced before Herod and his guests. The girl's dancing so pleased him that Herod told her to ask for whatever she wished, and he would grant it, up to half his kingdom.

Rather than answer directly, Salome went out to her mother and asked Herodias, "For what should I ask?" Herodias replied, "The head of John the Baptist." Salome immediately came with haste to the king and said, "I want you to give me at once the head of John the Baptist on a platter." Salome added to Herodias's demand that she wanted John's head "at once" and "on a platter." She was not an innocent pawn, but equally as vicious and bloodthirsty as her evil parents.

The king was exceedingly sorry, but because of his oaths and his guests he did not want to break his word to Salome. So he sent an executioner immediately with orders to bring John's head. Herod's executioner had to travel from Herod's court (in Galilee) to Machaerus, where John was imprisoned. This was a thirty-two-hour walk, which means about three days outbound and three days to return (unless Herod gave his executioner a horse). Since March 7 and 8 were a Friday and Saturday, it is likely that the executioner would depart early on Wednesday, March 5 to arrive before the Sabbath sunset on Friday. Probably Herod and his executioner were not religiously observant, but the Jewish authorities were, and Herod was always anxious to avoid displeasing them. It would have been needlessly impolitic to mix up this deadly mission with Sabbath breaking.

The executioner must have killed John in Machaerus, because leading him back to Galilee to be beheaded would incur the risk of John's escape, and in these strange times of Jesus' miracles it might have seemed quite possible to Herod that John would pull some stunt like Elijah (of whom he was meant to be the reincarnation) and fly to heaven in a chariot of fire (2 Kgs 2:11).

Matthew specifically says that John's disciples acquired and buried John's body. These disciples of John were probably already in Machaerus, continuing to hear John's teaching and attending to his needs. Since it is unlikely that Herod's executioner would have bothered to lug John's body back to Herod's court in Tiberias with his head, John's disciples probably had to carry the Baptist's headless corpse home. This inference is supported by the extrabiblical tradition that John the Baptist was buried in Sebastia, or Sychar (modern Sebastia), although why they would choose to bury him in Samaria, of all places, rather than in Bethany on the Jordan, in the place where he baptized Jesus, or in his parents' home town of Ein Karem, is unclear. Nevertheless, the body had to get from Machaerus back home somehow, and since John's disciples surely buried it, they probably transported it, too.

Neither the Bible nor any ancient source say what became of John the Baptist's head. Four sites contend for the honor of harboring the relic: (1) Damascus, (2) Rome, (3) Amiens, France, and (4) Munich, Germany. It seems more likely that John's disciples asked Herod for the Baptist's head, joined John's head and body together, and

---

Jews 18:5:4.

buried his remains respectfully. Accounting for the time to make the homeward journey from Machaerus, John's disciples would have buried John and told Jesus about it on Wednesday, 2 Nisan, March 12, AD 30.

To escape Herod's desire to see him and possibly in grief over John, Jesus withdrew to a desolate place, which probably occurred no later than 3 Nisan, Thursday, March 13. In this desolate place, Jesus fed the five thousand. The reason this is time-bound is that Jesus had to choose his Passover lamb in Jerusalem on 10 Nisan (Exod 12:3), Thursday, March 20. Working backward, it is evident that Jesus had only just the right amount of time to feed the five thousand on 3 Nisan, Thursday, March 13, walk on water and reach Gennesaret the next day, Friday, 4 Nisan, March 14, walk to Capernaum, teach in the Capernaum synagogue on Saturday, 5 Nisan, March 15, leave for Jerusalem on 6 Nisan, Sunday, March 15, or 7 Nisan, Monday, March 17, and reach Jerusalem by 10 Nisan, Thursday, March 20. It thus follows logically that the Pharisees would at that time object to his disciples not washing their hands during the Passover in Jerusalem, since handwashing is such an important part of the Passover ritual and since the Pharisees had a better chance of observing the disciples' meal habits when they were in Jerusalem than when they were in Galilee.

HEROD SEEKING JESUS

Herod Antipas heard about the fame of Jesus and the remarkable things that Jesus was doing. Feeling perplexed, he concluded that Jesus' miracles only made sense if Jesus was John the Baptist resurrected. Others thought Jesus was Elijah come back to life (Matt 14:2; Mark 6:14; Luke 9:7). Obviously, Herod Antipas was haunted by his murder of John, and his information about Jesus was garbled.

Jesus had explained that John the Baptist had come to fulfill the Elijah-like role of forerunner to the Messiah (Matt 17:11; Mark 9:12). John explicitly said that he was the fulfiller of Elijah's mission, not his reincarnation (John 1:21). Elijah would literally come back at the transfiguration very soon, in April of AD 31 (Matt 17:3; Luke 9:30).

Furthermore, John the Baptist was Jesus' cousin and was six months older than Jesus. Jesus and John were contemporaries. It would be impossible for John, already in his thirties, to die and come back to life as Jesus, who was also already in his thirties. Still, Herod Antipas concluded, "John, whom I beheaded, has been raised." And he sought to see Jesus.

When Jesus heard that Herod Antipas was seeking him, he and the Twelve took a boat, probably one of the fleet of the four fishermen, and sailed across the Sea of Galilee to Bethsaida, a fishing village on the north shore. He eluded both the crowds following him and Herod Antipas.

Others of the Apostolic Age

After landing at Bethsaida, they took the boat along the north shore to the east, where there was no village, only desolate countryside. There they moored the boat and went inland to a grassy knoll. It was there that Jesus fed the five thousand.[7]

THE MISSION OF ELIJAH

From Bethsaida, Jesus led his disciples to the villages of Caesarea Philippi[8] in the far north of Israel, about thirty-five miles away. To walk straight there would take about eleven and a half hours. Jesus probably arrived there over a journey of two easy days' walking. He went from village to village, pausing sometimes to pray. Jesus asked his disciples who the crowds said the Son of Man was. They said that some believed he was John the Baptist, others Elijah, and others Jeremiah or one of the prophets risen from the dead. Jesus asked them who they thought he was. Peter replied, "You are the Christ, son of the living God" (Matt 16:16). Jesus answered him:

> Blessed are you, Simon Bar-Jonah! For flesh and blood as not revealed this to you, but my Father who is in Heaven. And I tell you, you are Peter, and on this rock, I will build my Church, and the gates of Hell shall not prevail against it. I will give you the keys of the Kingdom of heaven, and whatever you bind on earth shall be bound in Heaven, and whatever you loose on earth shall be loosed in Heaven. (Matt 16:17–19)

Jesus' statement about the gates of hell demonstrates that he expected the kingdom of heaven to be a conquering force. Gates are a defensive structure, not an offensive weapon. By saying that the gates of hell would not prevail against the kingdom of heaven, Jesus did not envision hell invading the kingdom of heaven but the reverse. The kingdom of heaven would invade and conquer hell. "For the law of the Spirit of life has set you free in Christ Jesus from the law of sin and death" (Rom 8:2). "In all these things we are more than conquerors through him who loved us" (Rom 8:37).

Jesus then strictly charged the disciples to tell no one that he was the Christ. Probably the reason why Jesus did not want this discussion to go public yet was the expectation of the Jews that the Messiah would be a conqueror, not a martyr. He

---

7. Tour guides in Israel today will tell you that Jesus fed the five thousand near the village of Tabgha, on the shoreline south of Capernaum, but that does not square with the geographical points of reference in the Gospels, especially Luke 9:10.

8. There were two cities in the region named Caesarea, in honor of the Roman emperor, whose title was uniformly "Caesar," the cognomen (or third name) of Gaius Julius Caesar. Caesarea Maritima was on the Mediterranean Coast. It was originally a Phoenician port known as Strato's Tower. Rome awarded the city to Herod the Great in 30 BC, who renamed it in honor of Augustus Caesar. Herod rebuilt the city and harbor between 22 and 9 BC When Judea became a Roman province in AD 6, Caesarea Maritima replaced Jerusalem as the civilian and military capital of the Roman governor. Caesarea Philippi was an inland city at the southwestern base of Mount Hermon. It was originally called Paneas, after the Greek god Pan. Herod's son, Herod Philip, improved the city and made it the capital of his tetrarchy. He, too, renamed the city Caesarea in honor of Caesar Augustus.

probably did not want the people agitating to make him king, as they had done after he fed the five thousand.

Nathanael had stated that he thought Jesus was the Messiah the first day he began following Jesus, back in the fall of AD 29. The idea was not really new to any of them. But none of them would grasp the full significance of Jesus' identity or the form of his Messianic mission until after the resurrection. This moment of recognition was one further step in the direction of comprehending the whole truth.

The words Jesus spoke to Peter in Matthew 16:18 are better translated in this way: "You, Peter, are a pebble, but on this boulder," indicating himself, "I will build my Church." Jesus was not saying that the church would be built on Peter, the rock, but on the rock of Jesus. Peter was, so to speak, a chip off the old block. His real name was Simon Bar-Jonah (son of Jonah), but because of this saying of Jesus he acquired the nickname "Peter" or "Cephas," the words for stone in Greek and Aramaic, respectively. Roughly translated, Simon's nickname was "Rocky."

From that time, Jesus began to teach them that the Son of Man must go to Jerusalem and suffer many things and be rejected by the elders and the chief priests and the scribes and be killed and after three days rise again. And he taught this plainly.

While in Caesarea Philippi, Jesus took Peter, James, and John up the slope of Mount Hermon, where he was transfigured and where Moses and Elijah with him. This event was not what Jesus foretold that Nathanael would see, because Nathanael was not present at the transfiguration. As they were coming down Mount Hermon on the next day, Jesus told Peter, James, and John to tell no one of the transfiguration until after he would rise from the dead. The disciples did not yet really grasp that Jesus would die a premature death and be resurrected, despite Jesus' plainly telling them of it. Still, they must have understood enough to keep this story quiet for the present, although it must have been hard to do so.

Grappling with the implications of Jesus rising from the dead, they asked why the scribes said Elijah must come first before all things would be restored, meaning before the advent of the Messiah. They had, in fact, just seen Elijah a moment ago. He had come first! Jesus explained that although they had just seen Elijah, the prophecy about Elijah coming in fact referred figuratively to the mission of John the Baptist. Moreover, the Messiah's restoration of all things would be preceded by men treating him with contempt and killing him, as they had done to John.

THE LORD'S PRAYER, A SECOND TIME

Jesus was praying in a certain place, possibly Gethsemane on the Mount of Olives, a place he seemed to favor. He had just observed the Sabbath with Mary, Martha, and Lazarus in Bethany, and the Mount of Olives was nearby. When he finished praying, one of his disciples asked him to teach them how to pray, as John the Baptist had, evidently, taught his disciples. Jesus once again taught them the Lord's Prayer (Luke

11:2–4) as he had taught his four disciples, Peter, Andrew, James, and John, during the Sermon on the Mount (Matt 6:9–13) one hundred days earlier.

JOHN THE BAPTIST: THE LAST OF THE PROPHETS

The Pharisees, who were lovers of money, and whose wealth came in large part from the taxes and tithes the common people paid them, heard all these things, and they ridiculed him.

> And He said to them, "You are those who justify yourselves before men, but God knows your hearts. For what is exalted among men is an abomination in the sight of God. The Law and the Prophets were until John; since then the good news of the Kingdom of God is preached, and everyone forces his way into it. But it is easier for Heaven and Earth to pass away than for one dot of the Law to become void." (Luke 16:15–17)

Jesus was plainly telling them that a new covenant had replaced the old. The law and the prophets, he said, were valid until the coming of John the Baptist, whose ministry began in AD 29. Since then, Jesus had preached the good news of the kingdom of God, which did not abolish the law and the prophets, but fulfilled them. The coming of the Messiah did, however, abolish the priestly class.

THE BAPTISM OF JOHN

On Tuesday morning of the passion week in AD 33, as soon as Jesus entered the temple, he began preaching the gospel. The chief priests (Annas and Caiaphas), flanked by the scribes and elders, went up to him and asked who gave him the authority to perform miracles and teach. Rather than reply directly to a question whose answer was obvious, Jesus asked them a question: Was the baptism of John from heaven or from man?

The religious leaders feared that the pro-Jesus crowds would stone them to death if they said, "from man," because they believed John was a real prophet. They also feared to say, "from heaven," because Jesus would then ask them why they had not believed him, since John had taught that Jesus was the Messiah. So they replied that they did not know. Having trapped them in hypocritical deceit, Jesus refused to answer them, either.

Jesus then offered a parable illustrating that he understood exactly where the religious leaders stood. The parable was of two sons. One refused to obey his father but eventually did. The other promised to obey but never did. Jesus asked the religious leaders a simple question: Which son was obedient?

They answered, of course, "The first."

Jesus said to them, "Truly, I say to you, the tax collectors and the prostitutes go into the Kingdom of God before you. For John the Baptist came to you in the way of righteousness, and you did not believe him, but the tax collectors and the prostitutes believed him. And even when you saw it, you did not afterward change your minds and believe him." (Matt 21:31–32)

This is the last biblical reference to John the Baptist. He was an ambassador for Christ before and during Jesus' ministry. Unlike others of the Apostolic Age, he died before Jesus' crucifixion and resurrection, but, like them, his influence endured far beyond his earthly mission and death.

Nicodemus and Joseph of Arimathea, Christian Pharisees

NICODEMUS AND JOSEPH OF Arimathea may have been among the Christian Pharisees who were present at the Jerusalem Council (Acts 15:5). Nicodemus was a prominent Pharisee in the Sanhedrin and a follower of Jesus, proving that not all Pharisees were Jesus' enemies (John 3:1; Mark 15:43). Indeed, a large number of Jewish priests became Christians (Acts 6:7), and Luke may have written both his Gospel and the book of Acts to one of the high priests, Theophilus.[1] Nicodemus was the fourth person to call Jesus "rabbi" (John 3:2), after Andrew, John (John 1:38), and Nathanael (John 1:49). Judas Iscariot was the last (Matt 26:49; Mark 14:45). Joseph of Arimathea (a village in Judea) was a rich, good, and upright man who came to believe in Jesus before the crucifixion (Matt 27:57). He was also, apparently, a member of the Sanhedrin (Luke 23:50–51).

SECRET MEETING WITH JESUS

During the first Passover of Jesus' ministry in AD 30, Nicodemus came to see Jesus at night, in private.

> Now there was a man of the Pharisees named Nicodemus, a ruler of the Jews. This man came to Jesus by night and said to him, "Rabbi, we know that you are a teacher come from God, for no one can do these signs that you do unless God is with him. (John 3:1–2)

Since Jesus had no home (Matt 8:20; Luke 9:58), and since the meeting was private, the venue was probably the Jerusalem house of the apostle John, since he must have been present to record the interview (John 3:1–20). Since John was personally known to the high priest of Israel, Joseph Caiaphas, and to his father, the ex-high priest Ananias or Annas (John 18:13), possibly Nicodemus approached Jesus through John. The meeting was after sunset, Thursday, April 4 (15 Nisan). That Nicodemus

---

1. Theophilus ben Ananus reigned as high priest from AD 37 to 41. Josephus, *Ant.* 14:6:2.

was open to Jesus' teaching at the start of his ministry shows how expectant knowledgeable Jews were in Jesus' day for the coming of the Messiah.

> Jesus answered him, "Truly, truly, I say to you, unless one is born again, he cannot see the Kingdom of God." Nicodemus said to Him, "How can a man be born when he is old? Can he enter a second time into his mother's womb and be born?" Jesus answered, "Truly, truly, I say to you, unless one is born of water and the Spirit, he cannot enter the Kingdom of God. That which is born of the flesh is flesh, and that which is born of the Spirit is spirit. Do not marvel that I said to you, 'You must be born again.' The wind blows where it wishes, and you hear its sound, but you do not know where it comes from or where it goes. So it is with everyone who is born of the Spirit." (John 3:5–8)

Unlike so many other Pharisees, Nicodemus did not take offense at Jesus' pointing out that he needed higher instruction. The phrase "born again" is in Greek, "born from above." Being born of blood means being born of a mother's womb. Being born of water means to be baptized. Being born of the Spirit, or from above, means spiritual regeneration.

Jesus gave a brilliant answer to the atheist or agnostic who complains that he cannot believe in a God he cannot see. We cannot see the wind, but we see its effects, and no sane person would deny the existence of the wind. We cannot see God, but we can see his effects, which are far greater than the effects of any wind. God makes himself obvious.

> Nicodemus said to Him, "How can these things be?" Jesus answered him, "Are you the teacher of Israel and yet you do not understand these things? Truly, truly, I say to you, we speak of what we know, and bear witness to what we have seen, but you do not receive our testimony. If I have told you earthly things and you do not believe, how can you believe if I tell you heavenly things? No one has ascended into Heaven except He who descended from Heaven, the Son of Man. And as Moses lifted up the serpent in the wilderness, so must the Son of Man be lifted up, that whoever believes in Him may have eternal life." (John 3:9–15)

Jesus said, "We speak of what we know." Who were "we"? The Father, Son, and Holy Spirit. Jesus, as God, was using the same language of plural unity that God used in Genesis: "Let us make man in our image."

What was the reference to Moses lifting up a serpent in the wilderness? During the last part of the Exodus, in 1407 BC, the second generation of Israelites in the wilderness complained about being led out of Egypt after the first generation had all died off in the wilderness for just such complaining. God sent fiery serpents among them, and they bit the people so that many died. The people appealed to Moses, who prayed. God told Moses to make a bronze serpent and set it on a pole. "Everyone who is bitten, when he sees it, shall live," said God (Num 21:8). This was not idolatry since God would not violate his own laws by exalting an idol. As proof of this, 683 years later, King Hezekiah broke Moses' bronze snake in pieces (2 Kgs 18:4) because the Jews had formed the habit of burning incense to it, turning it into an idol. The snake by then had acquired the name "Nehushtan," whose meaning is unclear. So how were the Israelites saved? God saved them. God provided a focal point. Looking up at the snake reminded the people of the Lord's power and right to punish their disobedience and of God's desire to show mercy. When the people considered the justice of their punishment and sought the mercy of God, God withheld punishment and granted salvation. This was the exact mission of the Messiah: to convict and pardon the repentant and to be lifted up on the cross, pointing the way to God. Jesus continued:

> For God so loved the world, that He gave His only Son, that whoever believes in Him should not perish but have eternal life. For God did not send His Son into the world to condemn the world, but in order that the world might be saved through Him. Whoever believes in Him is not condemned, but whoever does not believe is condemned already, because he has not believed in the name of the only Son of God. And this is the judgment: the light has come into the world, and people loved the darkness rather than the light because their works were evil. For everyone who does wicked things hates the light and does not come to the light, lest his works should be exposed. But whoever does what is true comes to the light, so that it may be clearly seen that his works have been carried out in God. (John 3:16–20)

Jesus made clear that God loved the world, not just a chosen few, so much so that "whoever" believes might have eternal life. Eternal life is designed for everyone. This must have come as a bit of a shock to Nicodemus, a Pharisee ("one set apart") of the chosen people. Notably, Jesus says, "Whoever does what is true comes to the light." This phrase suggests that good works may lead a person to the light. Good works do not produce salvation, but if they lead a person to the light, and if, seeing the light, the person believes, he may then be saved and not condemned. The relationship between faith and works in the Bible is synergistic. It is impossible to be saved without faith (Luke 7:50; Rom 10:9; Eph 2:8–9), but it is also impossible to have faith and be saved without producing good works (Matt 7:17; James 2:14, 24). An absence of good works, according to Jesus, would be like bad fruit on a tree, indicating a bad tree, meaning lack of faith and thus a lack of salvation.

OPPOSING THE SANHEDRIN

In the following year, AD 31, on the last day of the Feast of Tabernacles, Nicodemus objected to his fellow Pharisees' desire to arrest Jesus without a fair trial (John 7:50–51). Joseph of Arimathea also did not consent to the actions of the Sanhedrin against Jesus (Luke 23:50–51).

LAYING JESUS IN THE TOMB

On Good Friday, AD 33, Joseph of Arimathea asked Pilate if he could take the body of Jesus from the cross. Pilate granted the request, and Joseph and Nicodemus reverently laid it in Joseph's tomb (John 19:39–42), from which Jesus rose on Resurrection Sunday. Joseph and Nicodemus were boldly risking a strong taboo, for touching Jesus' dead body would render them unclean until sundown (Lev 11:40). Since Jesus died between 1:12 p.m. and 2:10 p.m. on Friday, April 1, AD 33, and since the sun set in Israel at 5:07 p.m. on that day, Joseph and Nicodemus had only between four to five hours to accomplish this task, reach their homes, wash, and be purified before sunset so that they could observe the Passover.

They would not have made this request of Pilate before they saw Jesus die, and so they probably did not start out for the Roman fortress before 2:10 p.m. When they gained an audience with Pilate, they probably found him in a distressed state of mind. Jerusalem had been bathed in darkness from 10:14 a.m. to 2:10 p.m. (Matt 27:45; Luke 23:44). An earthquake had rocked the city at the moment Jesus died, the temple curtain was torn in two, from top to bottom, and there were reports of the dead being raised and appearing to many throughout the city (Matt 27:51–53). Pilate probably granted the request of Nicodemus and Joseph with a trembling hand. A gesture, however, would not be good enough. The centurion at Golgotha would need to see a written order. Exasperated, Pilate probably called for writing instruments and jotted down the release. This probably occurred no sooner than 2:45 p.m.

Assuming the two Pharisees could make it to Golgotha by 3:00 p.m., probably running with a nervous eye on the declining sun, they still had to get Jesus off the cross. Since the centurion in charge, after seeing the awesome events of the last few hours, acknowledged that Jesus was the Son of God (Matt 27:54), he probably was willing to order his soldiers to help, after inspecting Pilate's order. This cannot have been accomplished sooner than 3:30 p.m. Now Joseph and Nicodemus had to carry Jesus' body from Golgotha to Joseph's tomb. Perhaps they reached the tomb as soon as 3:45 p.m., although with their burden it might have been as late as 4:00 p.m. Mary Magdalene and the other Mary (Jesus' mother) were sitting opposite the tomb, watching (Matt 27:61; Mark 15:47). To be there, they must have followed Joseph and Nicodemus as they struggled along with the body of Jesus. The men laid Jesus' body in the tomb hastily and without much ceremony because they were pressed for time. They rolled the stone over the tomb, probably no earlier than 4:15 p.m. They and the women now had only fifty-two minutes to reach their homes by sunset, in time for Passover. The reason the women came to the tomb with spices on Resurrection Sunday is that they wanted to make up for the unceremonious haste with which Jesus had been laid to rest. Their intentions were good, but they had no idea how they were going to remove the tombstone. By God's grace, they did not have to do so.

CHRONOLOGY OF THE DAY OF THE CROSS

Roman timekeeping is like ours. From midnight to sixty minutes thereafter is zero hour. From sixty minutes after midnight to 119 minutes after midnight is the first hour of the day, and so on. In our timekeeping, an hour is always sixty minutes long, no matter what the season of the year may be.

By contrast, traditional Jewish timekeeping took the hours between sunrise and sunset and divided them into twelve equal units and called them "hours." As the days grew longer and shorter over the course of the year, there were always twelve hours of daylight, by Jewish reckoning, but the length of the hours increased or decreased proportional to the season. This is known as *halachic* time-keeping: timekeeping according to *halacha* or Jewish rabbinical tradition. So, summer "hours" were longer than winter "hours" because they were subsets of a longer day.

On the day of the cross, April 1, AD 33 in Jerusalem, the sun rose at 5:20 a.m. and set at 6:02 p.m. The hours of daylight therefore consisted of 760 minutes, so every "hour," by Jewish reckoning, was actually 58.71 minutes long on that day. The table "Hours on the Day of the Cross" in the Appendices shows the relationship of the Jewish hours to the Roman hours on the day of the cross (with a slight rounding error). Understanding the references to time in the Gospels on this day requires understanding which method of timekeeping each Gospel author was using. John used the Roman method. The others used the Jewish method.

We should avoid "reading history backwards." Ancient peoples, including the Jews and the Romans, were remarkably efficient at keeping time, but obviously they did not have our modern computers and atomic clocks. So, when this study notes that the sun rose at 5:20 a.m. on April 1, AD 33 in Jerusalem, a contemporary Roman or Jew would likely have noted the time as "half past the fifth hour" or "half past the last hour," respectively. When John says that Pontius Pilate presented Jesus to the Jewish mob and said, "Behold your king," (John 19:14) at "about the sixth hour," John meant about 6 a.m. We can feel sure John was using the Roman method of timekeeping, because if John were using the Jewish method, the sixth hour would mean around 11 a.m., which fails to fit with the rest of the narrative of the day of the cross. When Mark says the Romans crucified Jesus in the third hour (using the Jewish method of timekeeping), we can calculate today that the third hour was from 7:18 a.m. to 8:16 a.m. And when Matthew and Luke say that the sky grew dark from the sixth to the ninth (Jewish) hours, we can calculate today that this could be anytime between 10:15 a.m. (the beginning of the sixth hour) until 2:10 p.m. (the end of the ninth hour). The Gospel writers probably thought of this as simply meaning from mid-morning until mid-afternoon.

HOURS ON THE DAY OF THE CROSS (24-HOUR FORMAT)

April 1, AD 33	From Time	To Time	Roman Cardinal Hour	Roman Ordinal Hour	Jewish Ordinal Hour	Notes
Midnight	23:26	0:24	0:00	0		
Jesus tried before dawn	0:25	1:23	1:00	1st		
	1:24	2:22	2:00	2nd		
	2:23	3:21	3:00	3rd		
	3:22	4:20	4:00	4th		
	4:21	5:19	5:00	5th		
Sunrise: Pilate tells the Jews, "Behold your king."	5:20	6:18	6:00	6th	1st	John 19:14: about the sixth (Roman) hour
	6:19	7:17	7:00	7th	2nd	
Jesus hangs on the Cross	7:18	8:16	8:00	8th	3rd	Mark 15:25: in the third (Jewish) hour
	8:17	9:15	9:00	9th	4th	
	9:16	10:14	10:00	10th	5th	
Jesus hangs on the Cross in darkness	10:15	11:13	11:00	11th	6th	Matt 27:45, Luke 23:44: from the sixth–ninth (Jewish) hour.
	11:14	12:12	12:00	12th	7th	
	12:13	13:11	13:00	13th	8th	
Jesus dies in darkness	13:12	14:10	14:00	14th	9th	
Jesus hangs on the cross, dead	14:11	15:09	15:00	15th	10th	
	15:10	16:08	16:00	16th	11th	
Jesus is buried before sundown	16:09	17:07	17:00	17th	12th	Matt 27:57–60, Mark 15:42, Luke 23:54, John 19:38–42
Night—Jesus' body is in the tomb	17:08	18:06	18:00	18th		
	18:07	19:05	19:00	19th		
	19:06	20:04	20:00	20th		
	20:05	21:03	21:00	21st		
	21:04	22:02	22:00	22nd		
	22:03	23:01	23:00	23rd		
	23:02	0:00	0:00	24th		

Stephen, the Martyr

THE SERVANT

In the Jerusalem church, between June and December AD 33, when the disciples were increasing in number, the Hellenist Christians complained that the widows of the Jewish Christians were unfairly taking precedence in the daily distribution of alms. The Hellenist Christians were Jewish converts to Christianity from Greek communities. The twelve apostles convened the full number of disciples and said:

> It is not right that we should give up preaching the word of God to serve tables. Therefore, brothers, pick out from among you seven men of good repute, full of the Spirit and of wisdom, whom we will appoint to this duty. But we will devote ourselves to prayer and to the ministry of the word. (Acts 6:2–4)

This pleased the whole gathering, and they chose Stephen, "a man full of faith and the Holy Spirit" (Acts 6:5) and Philip (not the apostle, obviously), Prochorus, Nicanor, Timon, Parmenas, and Nicolaus, a proselyte of Antioch. The seven men all had Greek names, suggesting that they all came from the Hellenist portion of the congregation. Either there were more Hellenists than Jewish Christians voting, or the Jewish Christians generously voted with the Hellenists.

They set these men before the apostles who ordained them by praying over them and laying hands upon them. "And the word of God continued to increase, and the number of the disciples multiplied greatly in Jerusalem, and a great many of the priests became obedient to the faith" (Acts 6:7). The fact that a great many priests, Levites who served in the temple, were becoming Christians explains the wrath and alarm of the Sanhedrin and Saul (Paul). Christian Judaism was threatening to eclipse non-Christian Judaism.

MIRACLE WORKER

Stephen, full of grace and power, was working miracles, "great wonders and signs," among the people. A group of non-Christian Jews rose up and disputed with Stephen.

They included Jews from Cyrene (Libya), Alexandria in Egypt, Cilicia, Asia (modern Turkey), and some who belonged to the synagogue of freedmen. The freedmen or *libertini* were the descendants of Jews whom Pompey had led captive back to Rome after his conquest of Jerusalem in 63 BC. They settled in the trans-Tiberine district of Rome in large numbers, where they had synagogues. When Tacitus described Claudius's expulsion of Jews from Rome, he mentions "four thousand of the Freedmen" as banished to Sardinia.[1]

ACCUSED

These accused Stephen of speaking blasphemously about Moses and God. But the wisdom and Spirit with which Stephen spoke overpowered them. Unable to defeat Stephen in debate, they secretly instigated men against him, who stirred up a Jewish mob. They seized Stephen and brought him before the Sanhedrin. There false witnesses testified against him, saying, "This man never ceases to speak words against this holy place and the law. We have heard him say that Jesus of Nazareth will destroy this place and will change the customs that Moses delivered to us" (Acts 6:13–14). Yet as they gazed at Stephen, everyone who sat in the council saw that his face was like the face of an angel, which probably means it was radiant like the face of Moses when he descended from Mount Sinai (Exod 34:29–35).

ON TRIAL

The high priest, Joseph Caiaphas, asked Stephen, "Are these thing so?" Stephen replied with a long discourse, reciting the history of Israel from Abraham to the patriarchs to Moses. In accurately recounting these well-known facts, Stephen proved that he knew the orthodoxy of Judaism well. At the end of his discourse, however, he pulled the rug out from under his listeners by pointing out that the Jews (of which he was one) had throughout their history fallen short of the glory of God. He said:

> You stiff-necked people, uncircumcised in heart and ears, you always resist the Holy Spirit. As your fathers did, so do you. Which of the prophets did your fathers not persecute? And they killed those who announced beforehand the coming of the Righteous One [the Messiah], whom you have now betrayed and murdered, you who received the law as delivered by angels and did not keep it. (Acts 7:51–53)

Enraged, his audience ground their teeth at him. But Stephen, full of the Holy Spirit, gazed into heaven and saw the glory of God. He said, "Behold, I see the heavens opened and the Son of Man standing at the right hand of God." This was perilously close to Daniel's Messianic oracle: "I saw in the night visions, and behold, with the

---

1. Tacitus, *Annals* 2:85.

clouds of heaven there came one like a son of man, and he came to the Ancient of Days and was presented before him" (Dan 7:13).

MARTYRDOM

Stephen's audience shouted, stopped their ears, and rushed him. They dragged him outside the city and stoned him. As they did so, they stripped off their outer garments and laid them at the feet of a young man named Saul, who approved of the execution. As Stephen was suffering from the blows of the stones, he cried out, "Lord Jesus, receive my spirit." Then he fell to his knees and said in a loud voice, "Lord, do not hold this sin against them." Having said this, he "fell asleep," that is, he died. Devout men buried Stephen and made a great lamentation over him. The Catholic Feast of Saint Stephen commemorates his martyrdom on December 26, and while that date, like many feast days, may not be exact, it fits well with the overall chronology of the Apostolic Age. Stephen was the first Christian martyr to die for his faith. Martyr in Greek means "witness."

AFTERMATH

On that day, a great persecution of the church arose, and all the Christians in Jerusalem, except for the resolute apostles, scattered throughout Judea and Samaria (Acts 8:1). Thus, the stoning of Stephen, far from squelching the infant church, catalyzed the spread of Christianity, because "those who scattered went about preaching the word" (Acts 8:4). Reacting to this unintended consequence, Saul began ravaging the church, entering house after house, and dragging off men and women to prison. Pursuing the scattered believers to Damascus, he would encounter Jesus on the Damascus Road and become no longer a persecutor of the church but a tireless apostle of Christ and church planter, under a new name, Paul.

John Mark, the Gospel Author

JOHN MARK (GREEK: *MARKOS*, from Latin *Marcus*, meaning "consecrated to the god of war, Mars") is the individual referred to in Acts as John Mark, John, and Mark, and is identical with the Mark mentioned by Paul (Col 4:10; Phlm 1:24; 2 Tim 4:11) and by Peter (1 Pet 5:13). Paul wrote that Mark was the cousin of Barnabas (Col 4:10) and thus *The Golden Legend* identifies him, like Barnabas, as a Levite; at least one of his parents was of that tribe.[1] Peter called Mark his son (1 Pet 5:13). Since Mark was the biological son of a woman named Mary (Acts 12:12), not Peter's wife, in calling Mark his "son," Peter probably meant that he baptized him.

Mark's names are curious. His first name, John, is "dove" in Hebrew, associated with peace and God's Holy Spirit. His second name, Mark, is Roman and means consecrated to the Roman god of war, Mars. Oddly, his name conjoins peace and war. Also odd is his having a Latin name. The god of war in the Greek pantheon was Ares; Mars was the corresponding Roman god. This possibly suggests that Mark may have been the son of a Roman proselyte. It also might explain how he might have known Latin and thus have been able to act as Peter's interpreter in Rome. (The eastern Roman empire used Greek as its official and culturally dominant language. Latin was the language of Italy and the western empire.)

MARK'S UPPER ROOM

Mark's account of Jesus' arrest in Gethsemane makes an unusual reference to a young man. "And a young man followed him, with nothing but a linen cloth about his body. And they seized him, but he left the linen cloth and ran away naked"[2] (Mark 14:51–52).

---

1. De Voragine, *The Golden Legend*, 59: "Saint Mark, Evangelist."
2. The word naked in Greek is *gymnos*, which may mean stark naked or may mean wearing only an under-garment (Strong, *Concordance*, s.v. 1131). The meaning in this case is probably that the young man was wearing only a linen garment, not a coat, and that when he lost his coat, he was clothed only in a loincloth. It seems unlikely that a young Jewish man on the eve of Passover would be wandering about in public stark naked under only a linen cloth. In Jewish culture, public nakedness was shameful. Adam and Eve were remarkable for being naked and not being ashamed (Gen 2:25). God commanded that priests should not approach God's altar by going up steps because that would expose their nakedness as they ascended (Exod 20:26). God condemned apostate Judah by saying,

If this "young man" were Mark, Mark may have been present at the Last Supper. He must at least have been nearby, because immediately after singing the hymns of praise that ended the Passover meal, Jesus led the disciples to the Mount of Olives. This was late at night. For Mark to have been with the disciples late on Passover night and to have followed them to the Mount of Olives, Mark would have had either (1) to have left his home to make a late-night rendezvous with Jesus, (2) to have been in the house where Jesus and the disciples were having the meal and have joined them when they left the house, or (3) to have participated in the Last Supper with Jesus and disciples. Any of the three options is possible, but the first is unlikely.

As a Jerusalem resident, Mark would not have been celebrating the Passover that night unless it were with Jesus. Mark would normally have celebrated the Passover on Friday, after the crucifixion, not on Thursday. Jesus and his disciples, as non-residents of Jerusalem, celebrated two Passovers, one on Thursday and one on Friday, as was the custom for Jews from other parts of the world to ensure that they did not miss the sacred night by miscalculating the phase of the full moon. Passover always occurs by the full moon, and the determination of the phase of the moon was official only according to the observation of the priests in Jerusalem. Outlying communities did their best to keep track of the lunar calendar, but when making pilgrimages to Jerusalem, they held double ceremonies to err on the side of safety and thus not miss any of God's mandatory feasts. Jerusalem residents had no need to do this because they could consult the priests daily.

Mark might have been wandering around late at night, seeking Jesus, and might have stumbled upon him and the disciples heading for Gethsemane, but that is rather random. If Mark was in the house where Jesus was having the Last Supper, it is reasonable to deduce that the house was that of Mark. Mark's mother, Mary, had a house in Jerusalem (Acts 12:12). Jesus had sent Peter and John to meet a man carrying a jar, the owner of a house with an upper room, and to ask him for the use of it for Jesus' Passover meal (Luke 22:8–13). He told them simply to say that "the Teacher" wanted to use the guest room to eat the Passover with his disciples (Mark 14:14; Luke 22:11). Since it was only necessary to identify Jesus as "the Teacher" or "the rabbi" to this man, the owner of the house must have known Jesus. It is therefore logical to surmise that the man may have been the husband of Mary, the mother of Mark, who, like her son, was a believer in Christ.

Mark's mother was a prominent member of the infant church at Jerusalem and was probably fairly wealthy. Peter went to her house after his third arrest in AD 44. Mary's house had a porch, there was a servant girl named Rhoda to open the door, and the house was a meeting-place for the brethren, "many" of whom were praying there the night Peter arrived from prison. It was no small house. It makes sense that Mark's large house may have contained the upper room where Jesus held the Last Supper,

---

"Your nakedness will be uncovered. Your shame will be exposed" (Isa 47:3). And God showed his compassion for Judah by saying, "I spread my skirt over you and covered your nakedness" (Ezek 16:8).

where the apostles gathered on Resurrection Sunday when Jesus appeared to them with Thomas absent, where the apostles gathered the following Monday when Jesus appeared to them with Thomas present, and where they gathered after the ascension.

TRAVELS WITH PETER

Peter, after having established the church in Antioch in AD 34, preached to Jews in Pontus, Galatia, Cappadocia, Asia, and Bithynia. Reading Acts, one may get the impression that Paul was the first to bring the gospel to these parts of the world. In fact, Peter and Mark preceded him. From Bithynia, Peter and Mark pushed on to Rome in the second year of Claudius, AD 43.[3] John Mark accompanied Peter as his disciple and interpreter.[4] Probably Mark could speak Latin, whereas Peter probably could speak only Greek, Aramaic, and Hebrew. In Rome Peter confronted and brought down the renegade Simon Magus, who was posing as a sorcerer.

THE GOSPEL OF MARK

The Christians in Rome were so inspired by Peter's teaching that they were not satisfied with hearing it once only. They entreated Mark to leave them a written monument of the doctrine Peter had orally communicated to them. Nor did they cease until they had prevailed on him, and this was the occasion of his composing the Gospel of Mark. Mark wrote down accurately, although not in order, whatever he remembered Peter teaching about the words and deeds of Christ. He was careful not to omit any detail and not to record anything falsely. Peter approved Mark's Gospel and published it to the churches to be read by his authority.[5]

Mark's Gospel was thus in circulation by AD 43.[6] It would have been available very early not only to the church at large but to Matthew, Luke, and John, who would soon write their own Gospels. Matthew and Luke would incorporate a great deal of Mark's material into their books.

THE FIRST MISSIONARY JOURNEY

Peter and Mark returned to Jerusalem, and in AD 43 Agabus, a prophet, journeyed from Jerusalem to Antioch and predicted that a great famine would devastate Judea. The Antioch church sent Barnabas and Saul to Jerusalem with famine relief one year in advance of the disaster (Acts 11:29–30). After Herod Antipas's death in AD 44,

---

3. Jerome, *On Illustrious Men*.
4. Eusebius, *Church History* 3:39:15.
5. Jerome, *On Illustrious Men*; Eusebius, *Church History* 2:15:1–2, 3:39:15.
6. Finegan, *Handbook*, 382.

Paul, Barnabas, and Mark returned to Antioch and then embarked on Paul's first missionary journey. Mark may have brought his Gospel with him, and Paul and Barnabas may have made use of it as they preached to the new churches they planted along the way.

When Paul and Barnabas resolved to push on from Perga into central Asia Minor, Mark left them and returned to Jerusalem. What his reasons were for turning back Luke does not record; the account seems to suggest that he feared the toil (Acts 15:38). But this may not be the case. If Mark had traveled to Rome with Peter in AD 43, as Eusebius asserts, Mark's Gospel would have been complete at this time. Perhaps Mark felt called to circulate his Gospel rather than to pursue this missionary trip with Paul and Barnabas. Acts records that Mark was neither called by the Holy Spirit nor chosen by the Antioch elders for this trip. The Holy Spirit did, however, call Mark to write his Gospel. Moreover, Paul and Barnabas were taking the gospel into this region for the first time, but he and Peter had covered the territory before they went to Rome.

TO EGYPT

Jerome wrote that Mark took his Gospel to Alexandra, where he founded the Egyptian church "so admirable in doctrine and continence of living that he constrained all followers of Christ to his example."[7] It is therefore probable that Mark founded the church in Egypt at this time, between AD 44 and 49. Probably this is what called him away from the missionary journey of Barnabas and Paul.

SECOND MISSIONARY JOURNEY

Paul did not forget the incident in Perga. He refused to take Mark with him on his second missionary journey. This refusal led to a sharp disagreement between Paul and Barnabas, who, taking Mark with him, sailed back to his native Cyprus (Acts 15:39). At this point Mark disappears from the pages of Acts.

BACK IN ROME

When Peter wrote his first epistle from Rome, sometime between AD 49 and 59, Mark and Silas (Silvanus) were with him, and Silas probably acted as Peter's scribe (1 Pet 5:12–13). The fact that Peter sent Mark's greeting to a number of churches in the region recalled the evangelistic journey he and Peter had made between AD 41 and 43.

Mark was with Paul in Rome during Paul's first imprisonment there because Paul sent Mark's greetings to the church at Colossae and to Philemon (Col 4:10; Phlm 24). Obviously, Paul and Mark had patched up their previous estrangement.

---

7. Jerome, *On Illustrious Men*.

FURTHER JOURNEYS

After Paul was released from prison, Mark may have accompanied him to Spain and then may have gone back to the east. In any case, by AD 68, Mark had returned to Asia Minor because Paul, writing in Rome shortly before his death to Timothy at Ephesus, asked Timothy to bring Mark to him, saying that "he is very useful to me for ministry" (2 Tim 4:11). If, as Paul asked, Mark did return to Rome at this time, he may have witnessed Paul and Peter being martyred.

MARK'S DEATH

Jerome wrote that Mark died in the eighth year of Nero's reign, which was AD 62.[8] Jerome is wrong, because Mark was alive when Paul wrote 2 Timothy in AD 68. The more likely year of Paul's death is AD 68, but even the often earlier-proposed year of AD 64 contradicts Jerome. Jerome wrote more than three centuries after Mark lived, and Jerome is not always error-free. So, Mark probably died in or after AD 68.

As to the manner of his death, early tradition makes Mark a martyr and says that he died being dragged through the streets of Alexandria, Egypt by enraged pagan priests.[9] Perhaps after daring to join Paul in Rome during the Neronian persecution and witnessing the martyrdom of Peter and Paul there, Mark returned to his church in Egypt. Mark's body was removed from Alexandria to Venice where he became the patron saint. In Christian literature and art Mark's symbol is the lion.

APOSTLESHIP

Was Mark an apostle? Let us apply the five tests of apostleship to Mark. Did he know the Incarnate Lord? Yes. Did Jesus call him directly? Possibly. Did the Holy Spirit work through him? Yes, since he wrote an inspired book of Scripture. Did he teach God's word, not his own philosophy? Yes. Did God work miracles through him? We do not know. The uncertain answers to questions two and five make it impossible to assert that he was officially an apostle.

---

8. Jerome, *On Illustrious Men*.
9. De Voragine, *The Golden Legend*, 59: "Saint Mark, Evangelist."

Luke, the Beloved Physician

LUCAS OR LUKE WAS a doctor and a helper of Paul. According to Eusebius, Luke was born at Antioch, Syria, and was a physician by profession (Col 4:14).[1] Luke was a gentile (Col 4:11). We know nothing of Luke's conversion, but since Peter founded the church in Antioch in AD 34, perhaps Luke first heard the gospel then.

THEOPHILUS

Luke wrote two New Testament books, the Gospel of Luke and the Acts of the Apostles. He addressed each of his books to someone named Theophilus, as follows:

> Inasmuch as many have undertaken to compile a narrative of the things that have been accomplished among us, just as those who from the beginning were eyewitnesses and ministers of the word have delivered them to us, it seemed good to me also, having followed all things closely for some time past, to write an orderly account for you, most excellent Theophilus, that you may have certainty concerning the things you have been taught. (Luke 1:1–4)

> In the first book, O Theophilus, I have dealt with all that Jesus began to do and teach, until the day when he was taken up, after he had given commands through the Holy Spirit to the apostles whom he had chosen. He presented himself alive to them after his suffering by many proofs, appearing to them for forty days and speaking about the kingdom of God. (Acts 1:1–3)

The name Theophilus is Greek for "friend of God." Possibly Luke was using this as a generic term, addressing any reader who was a believer. There is, however, another intriguing possibility. The high priest of Israel from AD 37 to 41 was Theophilus ben Ananus, the son of Ananus (Ananias, Annas), the high priest from AD 6 to 15. Ananus was the first high priest appointed by Rome, so his posting was political, not consecrated. The Roman procurator of Judea, Gratus, deposed Ananus in AD 15 for executing capital punishment, an authority reserved to the Romans alone. Although defrocked, Ananus continued to exercise the power behind the high priestly throne.

---

1. Eusebius, *Church History* 3:4:7.

From AD 16 to 17, his son Eleazar reigned as high priest. From AD 18 to 36, his son-in-law, Joseph Caiaphas, reigned. Ananus looked over Caiaphas's shoulder and encouraged the plot to murder Lazarus of Bethany (John 12:10). He also drove the conspiracy to have the Romans kill Jesus. From AD 36 to 37, Ananus's son Jonathan reigned, followed by his son Theophilus from AD 37 to 41. In AD 43, another son of Ananus officiated, and Ananus's son Jonathan was restored in AD 44. The arrogant and evil Ananus, as much despised by Jews as by Christians, perished in the final conflagration Jesus foretold in Matthew 24, when the Romans destroyed Jerusalem and the temple in AD 70.

So Luke may have addressed his two books to the high priest Theophilus, son of the evil Ananus, who persecuted Jesus. Theophilus, like many Jewish priests of his day, may have come to see Jesus as the Messiah (Acts 6:7). He must have liked Luke's first book, the Gospel, or Luke probably would not have dedicated his second book to him.

LUKE'S GOSPEL

Luke completed Acts no later than the end of Paul's first imprisonment in Rome, which ended in AD 59 (Acts 28:30). This was eighteen years after Theophilus's last year in office. Most scholars think Luke wrote his Gospel after the publication of the Gospels by Mark and Matthew. Mark composed his Gospel in AD 43. Matthew composed his Gospel in AD 49. Therefore Luke must have composed his Gospel after AD 49 and before AD 59, the end of Paul's first imprisonment in Rome. But there is a hint that Luke probably finished his Gospel as early as AD 49.

In Acts 16:10, Luke's narrative switches from the pronouns "he" or "they" to the pronoun "we," suggesting that Luke caught up with Paul at Troy and joined him on the rest of his missionary journeys. Perhaps Luke had been in Jerusalem working on his Gospel. Having finished it, he may have brought a copy and caught up with Paul, after which he began work on the book of Acts. Eusebius corroborated this: "They say that Paul meant to refer to Luke's gospel wherever, as if speaking of some gospel of his own, he used the words 'according to my gospel'" (Rom 2:16, 16:25, 2 Tim 2:8).[2] It is possible that when Paul wrote in AD 53 of "the brother whose praise [is] in the Gospel through all of the churches" (2 Cor 8:18)[3] that he was referring to Luke and Luke's Gospel, which Luke may have then completed as early as AD 49.

It may seem a bit rushed for Luke to have completed his Gospel in the same year that Matthew completed his, especially if Luke used Matthew's Gospel as a source. However, this is not necessarily problematic. Luke said he decided to compose his Gospel because many others had undertaken to compile a narrative of Jesus' ministry, but he wanted to write an orderly account so that Theophilus could have certainty about the things being taught. It is unlikely that Luke was denigrating the Gospels of

2. Eusebius, *Church History* 3:4:8.
3. This author's literal translation from Greek.

Mark and Matthew. Rather, he was probably referring to the abundance of disorganized notes in the hands of the other apostles.

Jesus called his disciples "scribes who [had] been trained for the kingdom of heaven . . . like a master of a house, who brings out of his treasure what is new and what is old" (Matt 13:52). It would be surprising if the disciples had ignored this and had failed to make notes during Jesus' ministry. Consider, for example, that Matthew was not present at the Sermon on the Mount. Yet only Matthew recorded it. Either Jesus or Peter, James, and John, the only disciples present (Matt 4:18–21, 5:1), gave Matthew the text. These apostolic scribes would bring out of their treasure what is new, the new covenant teaching of Jesus, and what is old, the old covenant promises that Jesus fulfilled. Since the Gospels record several long intervals in which Jesus and his disciples disappeared from the pages of history,[4] it is plausible that Jesus used these times to rehearse his disciples in all his teaching and that they, as scribes, wrote their notes and checked them with Jesus for accuracy. In this way, when Jesus ascended and the disciples became apostles, they would have been well equipped with sermon notes that would empower them to take the gospel to all nations, as the Great Commission required.

Luke may have begun work on his Gospel in Jerusalem as early as AD 33. He may have taken many notes from the other apostles, and he doubtless conducted many first-person interviews with such key persons as Mary, the mother of Jesus. He probably also kept his own eyewitness notes of events in the early church which he would later use in composing Acts. As he asked to peruse the notes of the other apostles, he may have had the opportunity in Jerusalem to review Matthew's emerging composition. It is not unreasonable to imagine that Matthew may have published his Gospel in the summer of AD 49 and Luke may have finished his Gospel in the fall of the same year. There is no need to build dogma on this, but the conjecture is a comfortable fit. And the thesis has ancient support: "Luke not only was taught the gospel history by the apostle Paul who was not with the Lord in the flesh, but also by the other apostles."[5]

Luke's Gospel gives special attention to gentiles, which makes sense because he was a gentile. Only his Gospel records: (1) the parable of the good Samaritan (Luke 10:30), (2) Jesus praising the gentile widow of Zarephath and Naaman the Syrian (Luke 4:26–27), and (3) the story of the one grateful leper who was a Samaritan (Luke 17:16–18).

Luke's Gospel records six miracles and eighteen parables not found in the other Gospels, including: (1) the story of the Annunciation (Luke 1:28), (2) Mary's visit to Elizabeth (Luke 1:39–40), (3) Mary's Magnificat (Luke 1:46–55), (4) the presentation

---

4. Jesus' ministry lasted 1,350 days, spanning five calendar years (AD 29–33), fifty calendar months, and 44.36 months (calculated as being of 30.5 days' average duration). The Gospels have gaps in their narratives in which Jesus disappears from the pages of history. The gaps total 770 days, which is about two years, representing fifty-seven percent of Jesus' total ministry time.

5. Jerome, *On Illustrious Men*.

of Jesus to Simeon and Anna (Luke 2:25–38), (5) the story of the boy Jesus' disappearance in Jerusalem (Luke 2:41–50), (6) the story of the forgiven woman disrupting the feast by washing Jesus' feet with her tears (Luke 7:36–50), (7) the story of the prodigal son (Luke 15:11–32), and (8) the story of Lazarus and the rich man after death (Luke 16:19–31). Why is this?

Remember Luke's stated reason for writing his Gospel. What Luke literally wrote in Greek was, "It seemed good also to me, having followed closely from the first with all things carefully in consecutive order to you to write, most excellent Theophilus."[6] The implication is that Luke, being a Greek, felt the need to produce a history of Jesus in the Greek style. Greeks tended to write in a linear, chronologically consecutive style (like Herodotus and Thucydides), while Jews tended to write in a more topically organized and less chronological way (like Isaiah, Daniel, and Ezra). To accomplish this, Luke would very likely have interviewed everyone who was a trustworthy eyewitness and, in so doing, would seek to capture events in Jesus' ministry that the other evangelists might have omitted. John's Gospel supports this possibility, for he wrote: "Now Jesus did many other signs in the presence of the disciples, which are not written in this book" (John 20:30), and "There are many more things that Jesus did. If all of them were written down, I suppose that not even the world itself would have space for the books that would be written" (John 21:25).

Luke's Greek style, along with that of the author of Hebrews, is the most elegant in the New Testament. It is intriguing to think that the book of Hebrews might have come from the depths of Paul's mind by the grace of Luke's pen. Perhaps, in AD 59, the year of Paul's acquittal, he dictated Hebrews to Luke. That might explain the Pauline thinking and the Lukan style.

Luke's Gospel is longer than Matthew's, and his book of Acts is about as long as all of Paul's surviving epistles together. Of all the historians of ancient times, Luke is perhaps the finest. The historical and geographical details of Luke's writing are astonishingly accurate. Every turn of the archeologist's spade has validated Luke's testimony. Since Luke wrote with such uncommon precision about historical facts, he is credible with respect to supernatural accounts. The integrity of Luke's work is a great testimony to the gospel and a frustrating stumbling block to skeptics.

TRAVELING WITH PAUL

Luke first joined Paul's company at Troas in AD 49 (Acts 16:20) and accompanied him to the island of Samothrace, then to Neapolis, and finally to Philippi in Macedonia. Because Luke continued to employ the first-person plural pronoun "us" in Acts 20:5, it seems that Luke was Paul's loyal comrade, accompanying him on most of his journeys. Perhaps this is the reason that the book of Acts focuses so much on the ministry of

---

6. This author's literal translation.

Paul. Luke also stayed with Paul when, between AD 57 and 59, he was first imprisoned in Rome. Paul wrote: "Epaphras, my fellow prisoner in Jesus, sends greetings to you, and so do Mark, Aristarchus, Demas, and Luke, my fellow workers" (Phlm 24).

Some assume that because Luke stopped using the pronoun "we" and reverted to the pronoun "they" at this time (Acts 16:16) that Luke did not accompany Paul to Thessalonica. Luke resumed using the pronoun "we" in Acts 20:5, when Paul sailed back to Macedonia after his third visit to Corinth. This begs the question of who recorded Paul's eloquent speech in Athens. Paul may have recited the details from memory to Luke later as he composed the book of Acts, but Luke's vivid account of the Athenian episode in Acts 17:20–34 seems like an eyewitness account. If Luke was in Athens, he may have made an insignificant pronoun shift between Act 17:1 and 20:5 purely as a literary decision. In that case, he may have accompanied Paul all the way from Philippi to Thessalonica to Berea to Athens to Corinth to Ephesus to Jerusalem, back to Ephesus, back to Philippi, and finally back to Corinth, and thence to Macedonia. This thesis is supported by the possibility that Luke was the "brother" that Paul sent with Titus from Ephesus to Corinth in AD 52 (2 Cor 12:18). Or Luke may have been somewhere else during this entire interval of fifty-four months, from November AD 49 to April AD 54. Either thesis is possible, but, since Luke was Paul's Boswell, this author prefers the thesis that Luke accompanied Paul for this entire time.

Luke and Mark were together in Rome between AD 57 and 59 in the company of Paul. Peter may also have arrived in Rome around this time to undertake his final ministry there. And so Luke, Mark, Peter, and Paul probably had ample opportunity to discuss the Gospel of Mark, the Gospel of Luke, and the book of Acts (which Luke was probably working on at that time). Although there is no direct evidence that they did confer in this way, it is hard to imagine that, given their obvious opportunities, they would have failed to do so. These two great apostles and two great evangelists, as sojourners together in a strange land, would hardly have missed the chance to share insights on the subject matter and details of these inspired New Testament books.

During Paul's second imprisonment, in AD 68, after everyone else had deserted him, Luke alone remained to the end. Paul wrote, "Only Luke is with me" (2 Tim 4:11).

LATER YEARS AND DEATH

The details of Luke's life after Paul's death are scanty. Julius Africanus states that Luke was unmarried and that he died at the age of seventy-four in Bithynia, filled with the Holy Spirit. Epiphanius says he preached in Dalmatia, Gallia (either Galatia or Gaul, France), Italy, and Macedonia.[7] Jerome says he was buried in Constantinople.[8]

---

7. New Advent, "Gospel of Saint Luke."
8. Jerome, *On Illustrious Men*.

APOSTLESHIP

Let us apply the five tests of apostleship to Luke. Did he know the Incarnate Lord? Perhaps. Did Jesus call him directly? We do not know. Did the Holy Spirit work through him? Yes, since he wrote two inspired books of Scripture. Did he teach God's word, not his own philosophy? Yes. Did God work miracles through him? We do not know. The uncertain answers to questions one, two, and four make it impossible to assert that he was officially an apostle.

Jude, the Half-Brother of Jesus

JUDE WAS THE HALF-BROTHER of Jesus and the fourth eldest son of Joseph the carpenter. Scripture identified the half-siblings of Jesus as James, Joses, Judas, Simon, and more than three unnamed sisters (Matt 13:55–56; Mark 6:3). Mark probably named them in order of seniority, so Jude was the youngest brother but one. Jude identified himself as a bondservant of Jesus Christ and brother of James (Jude 1). He was too humble to claim any rank related to the Lord. Jude's reference to himself and to James, his brother, simply by their first names argues for this identity. What other "James" and "Jude" could have been so famous among first-century Christians as to require no further identification, especially since James and Jude were such common names at that time? He was married (1 Cor 9:5).

DOUBTING JESUS

During Jesus' earthly ministry, Jude and Jesus' other half-brothers did not believe in him (John 7:5). Twice, in AD 30, they tried to muzzle their wayward brother, thinking him insane (Matt 12:46–50; Mark 3:21, 31–35; Luke 8:19–21). During the High Holy Days of AD 31, Jesus' brothers scornfully suggested that he should go to Jerusalem and show off his miracles. Jesus told them to go up to the feast but that he would not go yet (John 7:2–10).

LEADERSHIP

Jude became a bishop of the Jerusalem church. Since his brother James died in AD 62, and since the Romans destroyed Jerusalem in AD 70, he must have succeeded his brother as bishop between AD 62 and 70.

APOSTLESHIP

Since Jude wrote a book in the inspired canon of Scripture, Jude may possibly be included in the list of first-century apostles. However, since Jude refers to the apostles as "they" (Jude 18), he seems not to have claimed apostolic authority for himself. Let us apply the five tests of apostleship to Jude: Did he know the incarnate Lord? Yes. Did

Jesus call him directly? Probably. Did the Holy Spirit work through him? Yes, since he wrote an inspired book of Scripture. Did he teach God's word, not his own philosophy? Yes, that is the main message of the epistle of Jude. Did God work miracles through him? We do not know. The uncertain answers to questions two and five make it impossible to assert that he was officially an apostle.

THE BOOK OF JUDE

The book of Jude contains passages very similar to 2 Peter. It is hard to know which author may have imitated the other, if either of them did. Jude vigorously denounced heretics who had crept in among the church. He quoted apocryphal works, including The *Assumption of Moses* and *The Book of Enoch* (neither of which was written by Moses or Enoch). This does not demean the authority of Jude any more than Paul's quoting the pagan poet Epimenides (Titus 1:12) undermines the canonicity of Titus.

JUDE'S GRANDCHILDREN

Hegesippus, a second-century Christian writer, mentioned the descendants of Jude living in the reign of the emperor Domitian (AD 81–96). The emperor commanded that the descendants of David should be slain. Capitalizing on this, enemies of the church brought accusation against the two grandchildren of Jude on the grounds that they were descendants of David.

A certain Evocatus brought them before Domitian, for he feared the second coming of Christ just as Herod had feared his first coming. The emperor asked them if they were descendants of David. They confessed that they were. He asked them how much property and money they owned. Both answered they had only a thirty-nine acre plot of land between them. It was worth only nine thousand *denarii*. They showed their calloused hands and explained that they worked the land for their subsistence and to pay their taxes. Domitian asked them about Christ's kingdom. They replied that it was not a temporal or earthly kingdom, but a heavenly and angelic one, which would appear at the end of the world, when Christ should return in glory to judge the quick and the dead and give to everyone reward or punishment according to his works. Hearing this, Domitian "did not pass judgment against them but, despising them of no account, he let them go, and by a decree put a stop to the persecution of the church." When they were released, they led the churches as witnesses and relatives of the Lord. They lived in peace until the time of the emperor Trajan (AD 98–117).[1] Eusebius wrote that Symeon, Jesus' uncle, also a Jewish bishop of Jerusalem, suffered martyrdom after many days of torture under Trajan.[2]

---

1. Eusebius, *Church History* 3:19–20.
2. Eusebius, *Church History* 3:32.

Timothy, the Bishop of Ephesus

TIMOTHY'S NAME IN GREEK means "honoring God" or "honored by God." He was the first bishop of Ephesus, who, according to tradition, died around the year AD 97. Timothy was from the Lycaonian city of Lystra in Asia Minor. He was the son of Eunice and the grandson of Lois, both of whom were godly women (2 Tim 1:5). From an early age, Timothy had shown signs of being prophetically gifted (1 Tim 1:18, 4:14). He was frequently in poor health (1 Tim 5:23).

When Paul and Barnabas first visited Lystra in AD 44, Paul healed a man crippled from birth. This miracle astonished the Lystrans, who thought Paul and Barnabas must be gods come to earth. The apostles managed to dissuade the priest of Zeus from sacrificing a bull to them, but angry Jews from Antioch (in Asia Minor) and Iconium (modern Konya) arrived and incited the mob to stone Paul. They dragged him out of the city, leaving him for dead (Acts 14:19). Despite all this, some of the Lystrans believed, and Paul and Barnabas planted a church there.

CALLED BY PAUL

Five years later, in AD 49, Paul wrote his letter to the Galatians, which was probably distributed to all the churches that he and Barnabas had planted on their first missionary journey, including the church in Lystra. Paul returned to Lystra later that year, this time with Silas (Silvanus) as his companion. There Paul met Timothy, a young man whose father was Greek and whose grandmother, Lois, and his mother, Eunice, were Jewish. Lois and Eunice had a sincere faith that Paul especially noted (2 Tim 1:5).

Timothy was well spoken of in the church of Lystra, and Paul wanted to take him along with him and Silas to help in their mission. Since Timothy's father was Greek, Timothy had not been circumcised. Paul had this done (Acts 16:3) to ensure Timothy's acceptability to the Jews to whom they would proclaim the gospel. This was a practical, not a theological, act. It did not compromise the decision made at the Council of Jerusalem, that gentile believers did not need to be circumcised to be Christians. In fact, as they moved on, they promulgated the decisions of the council in all the churches along their way (Acts 16:4).

ON TO EUROPE

Paul, Silas, and Timothy walked to Mysia (in the northwest of modern Turkey) and wanted to enter Bithynia (along the shore of the Black Sea in modern Turkey), but the Holy Spirit prevented them (Acts 16:7). Instead, they walked to Troas, near ancient Troy on the Aegean coast. At this point Luke joined them. In Troas, Paul saw a vision in the night of a man in Macedonia (northern Greece), saying, "Come over and help us." At this, the team immediately went to Philippi, the capital of Macedonia. Timothy witnessed Paul and Silas being thrown in jail in Philippi, the earthquake that set them free, and Paul's conversion of the jailer and his entire family.

Timothy was with Paul when he founded the church in Thessalonica. He was there when the Thessalonian Jews rioted against Paul. Timothy retreated with him to Berea, where the reception was more noble. The outraged Thessalonian Jews followed Paul to Berea, however, so the believers sent Paul, probably Luke, and possibly some others to Athens. Paul left Timothy and Silas in Berea. He gave Timothy instructions to visit the church in Thessalonica to see how they had survived the tumultuous circumstances of the church planting (1 Thess 3:1–2) and then to bring Silas and join him in Corinth later.

THESSALONIAN LETTERS

Timothy and Silas reached Corinth around February AD 50 (2 Cor 1:19). Timothy brought a very encouraging report form Thessalonica, and Paul happily wrote 1 Thessalonians back, sending greetings from himself, Silas, and Timothy. After reading the first letter and receiving a fake letter from someone posing as Paul (2 Thess 2:2), the Thessalonians seemingly had some questions, and probably they wrote Paul a letter posing them. Paul replied from Corinth with 2 Thessalonians, in which he answered their questions and again included greetings from himself, Silas, and Timothy.

TO EPHESUS

Timothy stayed with Paul as he traveled to Ephesus for the first time and then went to Jerusalem and then went to Antioch in Syria. When Paul embarked on his third missionary journey from Antioch, Timothy was with him. As they trekked through Asia Minor, they must have passed by Paul's hometown of Tarsus and must surely have visited Eunice and Lois as they passed through Lystra. At length they reached the seaport of Ephesus on the Aegean Sea and settled in.

CORINTHIAN TROUBLES

Paul preached in Ephesus in the hall of Tyrannus for two years. But troubling news of rampant immorality arrived from the church in Corinth, probably brought by Apollos. Paul wrote a lost warning letter to Corinth probably around November AD 51. Since it was winter, when it was dangerous to sail, the letter must have travelled overland. Timothy was the messenger (1 Cor 4:17). The letter reached Corinth only by the end of AD 51.

More distressing reports from Corinth reached Paul in Ephesus around the end of February AD 52, brought by Timothy and Chloe's people, Stephanas, Fortunatus, Achaicus, and Sosthenes, the synagogue leader in Corinth.

In response, Paul wrote 1 Corinthians, probably around the beginning of March. Since the sailing weather was becoming fairer, Paul sent Timothy to Corinth, bearing 1 Corinthians with him. He tried to persuade Apollos to go with Timothy but, probably annoyed at the mess in Corinth, Apollos was unwilling to go (1 Cor 16:12). The letter was not well received, so Timothy returned quickly to Ephesus, probably around May AD 52, and reported the bad news to Paul.

Paul's blood was up. He wrote a lost, severe letter of tears to the Corinthians around May AD 52. Since the sailing weather was still fine, the letter probably reached Corinth before June of AD 52, probably carried by Timothy. Paul apparently felt that the letter might not be enough. He proposed to return to Macedonia and Achaia (Greece), after which he would return to Jerusalem and then go to Rome. But this was long-term planning. The situation at Corinth was urgent, and so Paul sailed from Ephesus on a lightening, second trip to Corinth around June of AD 52. After chastising the Corinthian church, Paul returned to Ephesus around July AD 52. Timothy came back with him, because he had to return to Ephesus first before Paul could send him from Ephesus to Macedonia (Acts 19:22).

BACK TO MACEDONIA

From Ephesus, Paul launched Timothy and Erastus ahead of him to Macedonia, where he would meet them later (Acts 19:22). Paul knew he would be returning to Corinth soon, but he wanted a trusted lieutenant on site to keep the church in line. So, he sent Titus and probably Luke (the brother), who sailed while navigation was still safe, before Yom Kippur of AD 52 (2 Cor 8:6, 23, 12:18). In the summer of AD 53, Paul apparently sent Aquila and Priscilla from Ephesus to Rome to see how the church had survived Claudius's expulsion edict. He left Ephesus in November AD 53, and met Timothy and Erastus in Philippi. There he met Titus, who was probably arriving overland from Greece. Titus brought him news of his successful mission in Corinth (2 Cor 7:6–7). Overjoyed, Paul wrote 2 Corinthians around November AD 53. Titus then returned to

Corinth, carrying the epistle with him (2 Cor 8:17). The letter asked the Corinthians to let Titus organize the collections of alms for the Christians at Jerusalem.

BACK TO CORINTH

Paul then made a return tour of the churches in Greece, ending at Corinth (Acts 20:2). Timothy accompanied him. They stayed in Corinth for three months, between January and April AD 54 (Acts 20:3). At this time, Paul composed his epistle to the Romans, in which he sent Timothy's greetings to the Roman church (Rom 16:21).

BACK TO PHILIPPI

Learning of a Jewish plot to kill him, Paul did not sail for Ephesus from Corinth but diverted instead to Macedonia (Acts 20:3). Paul sent the missionary team of Sopater of Berea, Aristarchus and Secundus of Thessalonica, Gaius of Derbe, Timothy, and Tychicus and Trophimus of Asia ahead of him to Troas (Acts 20:4), while he and Luke went to Philippi. They left Philippi after Passover, April 17, 22 Nisan, AD 54 (Acts 20:6).

TO JERUSALEM

On his way back to Jerusalem in AD 54, Paul and his team did not take the time to stop in Ephesus. They were carrying the funds they had collected in Greece and Macedonia for the poor of Jerusalem, which must have exposed them to some risk of banditry on the way. Also, there was a Jewish plot to kill him afoot in Ephesus (Acts 20:3). Moreover, Paul wanted to reach Jerusalem before Pentecost, probably because that would be a celebratory occasion on which to give the funds to the Jerusalem church. So, Paul had the Ephesian elders come meet him in nearby Miletus (Acts 20:17).

BACK TO EPHESUS

After returning to Jerusalem, Paul was arrested by the angry Jewish elite, whisked away by the Romans to Caesarea, and imprisoned there by the Roman proconsul, Festus, for two years. At this time Paul sent Timothy to Ephesus, where he assumed the leadership of the church there. Paul wrote 1 Timothy in Caesarea to Timothy in Ephesus. The letter was full of pastoral advice. Paul even wrote, "No longer drink only water, but use a little wine for the sake of your stomach and your frequent ailments" (1 Tim 5:23).

Many scholars suppose that Paul wrote 1 Timothy from Philippi to Timothy in Ephesus, but this is not possible. As shown above, after the riot in Ephesus Paul traveled with Timothy to Troas and back to Philippi in Macedonia. He returned to

Corinth, and Timothy was with him, since when he left Corinth, he sent Timothy and others ahead of him to Troas. Therefore, in Paul's swing from Ephesus to Philippi to Corinth, Timothy was with Paul and was not in Ephesus. When Paul pushed on from Troas to Jerusalem, Timothy was almost certainly still with him, since (1) on this trip Paul bypassed Ephesus (Acts 20:16), (2) Timothy and Trophimus were part of the same missionary team, and (3) Trophimus ended up in Jerusalem with Paul (Acts 21:29).

The basis for assuming that Paul wrote 1 Timothy from Philippi is this verse: "As I urged you when I was going to Macedonia, remain at Ephesus so that you may charge certain persons not to teach any different doctrine" (1 Tim 1:3). As shown, when Paul was leaving Ephesus for Macedonia, he took Timothy with him. So the meaning of this verse must be that as Paul and Timothy were departing Ephesus, Paul was ordaining him to return in the future to take charge of the Ephesian church. Timothy had the opportunity to do this only after Paul's arrest in Jerusalem.

TO ROME

When, in AD 56, Festus sent Paul to stand trial before Nero Caesar in Rome, Timothy, Luke, John Mark, Tychicus, and Erastus either accompanied him or met him in Rome (Acts 27:1; Eph 6:21; Col 1:1; Phil 2:19; Phlm 23). Paul was acquitted by Nero and set free in AD 59. The author of Hebrews mentions Timothy as being released (Heb 13:23). If Paul wrote Hebrews, this clue suggests that Paul may have sent Timothy on some mission away from Rome,[1] just as he sent Tychicus from Rome to Colossae and Ephesus (Col 4:7; Eph 6:21) and Epaphroditus to Philippi (Phil 2:25) bearing the Epistles to the Colossians, the Ephesians, the Philippians, and Philemon. If this is correct, Nero evidently acquitted Paul while Timothy was still away, and Paul looked forward to his return so that they could resume their missionary journeys together. There is no record of how much time Timothy spent with Paul after Paul's first imprisonment in Rome.

BACK TO EPHESUS

In Paul's final and fatal imprisonment in Rome, in AD 68, Paul wrote his last and most heartbroken letter, 2 Timothy. Timothy was not in Rome with Paul during the first part of this second incarceration. Probably what happened is that Nero's officials seized Paul suddenly in Troas. This arrest was not as polite as the previous one. Nero was now killing Christians just for being Christians, and Paul was a famous preacher and therefore a prime target. The suddenness of the capture is suggested by Paul's words to Timothy: "Luke alone is with me. Get Mark and bring him with you, for he is very useful to me for ministry. When you come, bring the cloak that I left with Carpus

---

1. This is a strong argument for Pauline authorship of Hebrews, because in the New Testament Timothy appears consistently as serving under the leadership of Paul.

at Troas, also the books, and above all the parchments" (2 Tim 4:11–13). Paul would scarcely have left his cloak, books, and parchments behind if those who arrested him had given him time to pack. This also implies that at the time of his arrest Timothy was in nearby Ephesus and was in a position to gather Paul's belongings in Troas and bring them to Rome.

The Romans probably did not allow Paul to travel with an entourage, as he had done on his first trip to Rome, so Timothy, Mark, and Luke had to make their own way there. Although Paul says that he had sent Crescens to Galatia, Titus to Dalmatia, Tychicus to Ephesus (2 Tim 4:10–12) and had left Erastus in Corinth and Trophimus in Miletus (2 Tim 4:20), this does not mean that he dispatched all these disciples from Rome. He probably sent them out before his arrest.

In 2 Timothy, Paul poured out his heart. He knew that this time the Romans would not set him free. He knew he was going to die.

> I am already being poured out as a drink offering, and the time of my departure has come. I have fought the good fight, I have finished the race, I have kept the faith. Henceforth there is laid up for me the crown of righteousness, which the Lord, the righteous judge, will award to me on that day, and not only to me but also to all who have loved his appearing. (2 Tim 4:6–8)

TIMOTHY'S DEATH

The apocryphal *Acts of Timothy* states that in the year AD 97, the then-eighty-year-old bishop tried to halt a pagan festival in Ephesus. The angry revelers beat him to death with clubs and stones. They buried him outside the city at a place called Pion. In AD 356, the relics of Timothy were transferred to Constantinople and placed in the Church of the Holy Apostles.[2]

---

2. "The Acts of Timothy."

Silas or Silvanus, the Colleague of Paul

SILAS (SILVANUS) WAS A Christian colleague of Paul (Acts 15:40). He was a Jew (Acts 17:4). Like Paul, he was a Roman citizen whose Latin name was Silvanus (Acts 16:37). He was also a prophet (Acts 15:32). Silas was at the Jerusalem Council in AD 49 and was, with Paul, Barnabas, and Judas Justus Barsabbas, one of the four men the council entrusted to bring their decree to the gentile converts in Antioch.

FIRST MISSIONARY JOURNEY

After fulfilling this mission, Paul and Barnabas decided to bring that edict to the churches they had founded in Cyprus and Asia Minor. When Paul and Barnabas fell out over whether to take John Mark on this second missionary journey, Paul chose Silas instead and set out to visit the churches he and Barnabas had founded in Asia Minor, while Barnabas returned to his native Cyprus with John Mark (Acts 15:39–40).

Paul and Silas walked from Antioch in Syria to Lystra, where they met Timothy, who, after being circumcised, joined their mission. The three journeyed on to Mysia (in northwestern Turkey) and tried to enter Bithynia (along Turkey's Black Sea coast), but the Holy Spirit stopped them, so they walked to Troas (near ancient Troy) on the Aegean Sea. There Luke joined them (Acts 16:10).

TO EUROPE

Paul had a dream one night about a man asking them to go over to Macedonia and help them (Acts 16:9). Immediately the three sailed to Samothrace and Neapolis (Acts 16:11). Probably the reason for the stop on the island of Samothrace was that it was October, dangerous sailing weather, and so the ship's captain was only making short island-hopping journeys. The fact that they took the risk of traveling by sea at all rather than trekking overland shows how urgent Paul considered the Macedonian call to be. From Neapolis they walked to Philippi, an important city in Macedonia.

PHILIPPI

In Philippi, they converted Lydia, a woman of Thyatira who became the first Christian in Greece (but not in Europe, because there already were Christians in Rome). In Philippi, a slave girl began following Paul and his team around, crying out, "These men are servants of the Most High God, who proclaim to you the way of salvation" (Acts 16:17). This was a perfectly true statement, but the girl annoyed Paul by shouting this repeatedly over many days, so he suddenly turned and said to the spirit, "I command you in the name of Jesus Christ to come out of her" (Acts 16:18). The spirit came out of her that very hour. The girl's masters, however, were outraged because they had been using this slave to charge for fortune-telling. They had Paul and Silas brought up before the magistrates, severely beaten, and thrown in jail. Luke and Timothy were spared.

That night in jail, though badly bruised, Paul and Silas were singing hymns to God, and the other prisoners were listening to them. Suddenly, an earthquake struck the jailhouse. Its doors flung open and the bonds restraining the prisoners were broken. (Probably the bonds were stocks, not chains, for an earthquake would probably not have split chains). The jailer, thinking his prisoners had escaped, prepared to commit suicide. He knew that the Roman penalty for losing a prisoner was death, and if the jailer ran away to escape capital punishment, the Roman officials would kill his whole family instead. To spare them, he planned to take his own life. Paul, however, restrained him, and that night the jailer and his whole family believed.

The next day the magistrates gave orders to release Paul, but he indignantly demanded that they come to him and apologize, for Paul and Silas were Roman citizens. It was a dire offense to punish or imprison a Roman citizen without a trial. Terrified, the magistrates apologized, released Paul and his team, and begged them to leave Philippi. Paul did not hasten away. He and his team first went to Lydia's house and then left the city when they were quite ready.

TO THESSALONICA AND CORINTH

Silas accompanied Paul, Luke, and Timothy to Thessalonica, where they founded a church. When the Thessalonian Jews rioted against Paul, the team moved on to Berea, where they founded another church. When the Thessalonian Jews pursued Paul to Berea, Paul, Luke, and some others went to Athens while Silas and Timothy remained in Berea (Acts 17:14). Paul left instructions for Timothy to return to Thessalonica to see how well the newly planted church had survived the tumult that accompanied its founding. After that, Timothy and Silas were to rejoin Paul in Corinth. There they preached together with Paul (2 Cor 1:19). In his first letter to the Thessalonians, Paul sent greetings to them from himself, Timothy, and Silas (1 Thess 1:1). Silas remained in Corinth with Paul while Timothy made a return trip to Thessalonica. When

Timothy returned to Corinth with encouraging news, Paul sent a second letter to the Thessalonian Christians with greetings from himself, Timothy, and Silas (2 Thess 1:1).

Probably sometime during Paul's first imprisonment in Rome from AD 57 to 59, Silas, Peter, and Mark also arrived in Rome. Silas probably acted as Peter's scribe in the composition of 1 Peter (Col 4:10; 1 Pet 5:12–13). The Bible makes no mention of Silas thereafter.

Titus, the Bishop of Crete

TITUS WAS A DISCIPLE of Paul the apostle, who wrote a biblical epistle to him. He was a Greek from Antioch, which is where Paul led him to Christ (Gal 2:1; Titus 1:4).

IN JERUSALEM

Paul and Barnabas brought famine relief from Antioch to Jerusalem in AD 44 (Acts 11:29–30; Gal 2:1). After the famine was over, Paul, Barnabas, and Titus returned to Jerusalem in AD 48. There the Judaizers in the Jerusalem church spied on Titus, saw that he was not circumcised, and tried to force his circumcision. Paul refused. Peter, John, and James (the half-brother of Jesus) agreed that Titus's circumcision was unnecessary. Paul, Barnabas, and Titus then returned to Antioch (Gal 2:1–11).

IN EPHESUS AND CORINTH

Titus was with Paul during his two-year sojourn in Ephesus. From Ephesus, Paul sent Titus and probably Luke to Corinth in AD 52 to help steady the church on the right course until Paul should return. He also gave Titus instructions to raise funds for the Jerusalem church and meet him in Troas afterwards, as Paul would pass through Troas when leaving Ephesus.

IN MACEDONIA

After a riot in Ephesus, Paul and Timothy traveled to Troas, where he expected to meet Titus, who was not, however, there. Possibly this was because the riot caused Paul to leave Ephesus earlier than expected, and so he arrived before the planned rendezvous. Possibly it was because Titus, in winter, had to make the slower land journey from Corinth back east and simply did not make the rendezvous in time. Paul preached in Troas for a little, but concerned at missing Titus, he and Timothy pushed on to Macedonia.

In Philippi Titus finally caught up with Paul and brought him news about the apparently improved state of affairs in the Corinthian church (2 Cor 7:6–7, 14). Gratified, Paul wrote 2 Corinthians, a letter milder in tone and full of theological insights. (What we call 2 Corinthians was really his fourth letter to Corinth, for two letters have been lost.) Since it was around November AD 53 and the winter sailing weather was risky, Paul must have sent this epistle overland. Titus, probably Luke, and other brothers carried 2 Corinthians to Corinth (2 Cor 8:16–23, 9:1–5, 12:18).

BACK TO CORINTH AND JERUSALEM

Second Corinthians asked the Corinthians to let Titus organize the collections of alms for the Christians at Jerusalem. Paul continued traveling further west, revisiting and strengthening the churches in Thessalonica and Berea. He then finally returned to Corinth. He remained there for about three months, between January to April AD 54 (Acts 20:2–3). There he met Titus and gathered in the funds for the Jerusalem church (Rom 15:25–26). Titus probably accompanied Paul from Corinth back to Jerusalem when Paul delivered those funds in AD 54.

CRETE

For a long interval, Scripture makes no mention of Titus. Perhaps he went to Rome on Paul's first voyage there, or perhaps he went to visit Paul in Rome during his two-year Roman incarceration. In any case, Paul and Titus teamed up again after Paul's acquittal (Titus 1:5). Paul founded churches in Crete with Titus and left Titus there to lead them, probably in AD 63 (Titus 1:5).

Around AD 65, Paul was back in Corinth. From there he sent Apollos and Zenas, a lawyer, to Crete, bearing his letter to Titus (Titus 3:3). He asked Titus to speed them on their way, seeing that they lacked nothing. This suggests that Apollos and Zenas were being sent to assume leadership of some of the churches in Crete, which, by then, had probably spread all over the large island. Paul also said he would soon be sending Artemas and Tychicus to Crete, and he urged Titus to join him in Greece after Paul spent the winter in Nicopolis (Titus 3:12). This suggests that he was relieving Titus of his mission in Crete and sending other leaders to take up the charge.

DALMATIA

Later, during Paul's second imprisonment in Rome, Titus traveled to Dalmatia (2 Tim 4:10). This is the last reference to Titus in Scripture.

HIS RELICS

Titus's relics, now consisting only of his skull, are venerated in the Church of Saint Titus in Heraklion, Crete, to which it was returned in 1966 after being removed to Venice during the Turkish occupation.

Aquila and Priscilla, Tentmakers from Rome

AQUILA AND PRISCILLA (ALSO called Prisca) were a married couple. Paul called them his fellow workers in Christ Jesus (Rom 16:3). At some point, in some unrecorded way, they risked their lives for Paul (Rom 16:4). Perhaps they saved Paul when the Jews attacked him in Corinth (Acts 18:12).

They were originally from Pontus, an ancient kingdom located in what is now Turkey on the southern shore of the Black Sea. They moved to Italy, where they became Christians, probably through the ministry of Peter, who founded the church there in AD 43. Thus, they probably knew Peter before they met Paul. But they then were forced to leave, because, as Suetonius wrote, "since the Jews constantly made disturbances at the instigation of Chrestus [Christ], [Claudius] expelled them from Rome"[1] (Acts 18:2). This occurred in the ninth year of Claudius's reign or AD 49.[2] This was not without precedent. In AD 19, the emperor Tiberius also expelled the Jews from Italy.[3] Claudius probably did not distinguish between Christian and non-Christian Jews, seeing them as squabbling sects of the same religion.

When Paul and Luke first arrived in Corinth around January 26, AD 50, Paul met Aquila and Priscilla. Because they were tentmakers as Paul was, he stayed and worked with them (Acts 18:3). It might seem odd that Paul, who evidently came from a family wealthy enough to send him to study with Gamaliel in Jerusalem, was a tentmaker, but it is consistent with his culture. A Jewish proverb says, "He who does not teach his son a trade teaches him to be a thief."

EPHESUS AND APOLLOS

Paul, Luke, Priscilla, and Aquila left Corinth for Ephesus around August 24, AD 51 (Acts 18:18). Around August AD 51, Apollos, a Christian Jew in Alexandria, left Egypt for Ephesus. Paul stayed only a short time in Ephesus, but Aquila and Priscilla

---

1. Suetonius, *Lives of the Twelve Caesars*, "Claudius."

2. Orosius, *Histories Against the Pagans* 7:6:15. Claudius's first regnal year began on January 24, AD 41, so his ninth year began on January 24, AD 49.

3. Merrill, "The Expulsion of Jews from Rome under Tiberius," 365.

remained there, while Paul went on to Jerusalem, leaving Priscilla and Aquila behind (Acts 18:19). Apollos then arrived in Ephesus, just missing Paul.

> [Apollos] was an eloquent man, competent in the Scriptures. He had been instructed in the way of the Lord. And being fervent in spirit, he spoke and taught accurately the things concerning Jesus, though he knew only the baptism of John. He began to speak boldly in the synagogue, but when Priscilla and Aquila heard him, they took him aside and explained to him the way of God more accurately. (Acts 18:24–26)

Apollos then went to Corinth, and Paul returned to Ephesus and stayed there for two years, from November 8, AD 51, to February 7, AD 53 (Acts 19:1, 8–10). Apollos and Paul had just missed meeting again. But Aquila and Priscilla were with Paul. The Ephesian church, or at least a small group, met in their house (1 Cor 16:19).

BACK TO ROME

In the summer of AD 53, Paul apparently sent Aquila and Priscilla from Ephesus to Rome to see how the church had survived Claudius's expulsion edict. This is suggested because when Paul wrote Romans, the couple was already back in Rome, where the church, or at least a small group, met in their house (Rom 16:3–5). Aquila and Priscilla probably felt it was reasonably safe to return to Rome despite Claudius's edict because even before Claudius died on October 13, AD 54, the decree had probably relaxed. The similar edict of Tiberius in AD 19 likewise "became a dead letter" before Tiberius's death.[4]

Paul left Ephesus and eventually returned to Corinth, where he remained for three months, between January and early April AD 54 (Acts 20:3). There he probably received news from Aquila and Priscilla about the state of the church in Rome, which likely prompted him to write his letter to the Romans. When the sailing weather was fair again, in spring, Paul entrusted the manuscript of Romans to Phoebe, a deacon of the church in Cenchreae near Corinth, and she took the letter to the Roman church (Rom 16:1). She probably handed it to Aquila and Priscilla, who were still there.

BACK TO EPHESUS

At some point, possibly AD 60 but definitely before AD 68, the year of Paul's death, Aquila and Priscilla returned from Rome to Ephesus. We know this because Paul greets them there during his second, fatal imprisonment in Rome (2 Tim 4:19). After this, Aquila and Priscilla disappear from the pages of Scripture.

---

4. Bruce, "Christianity under Claudius," 317.

LEGACY

Paul called Priscilla and Aquila his "coworkers in the ministry of Christ Jesus" (Rom 16:3). In this verse, Paul puts Priscilla before her husband Aquila, conferring upon her an intriguing rank. The fact that he calls both Priscilla and Aquila his "coworkers" is a strong argument that Paul was not opposed to all female leadership in the church, although he did oppose the leadership of untutored and unruly women, like those of Corinth and Ephesus (1 Cor 14:34; 1 Tim 2:12).

Apollos, the Eloquent Preacher

APOLLOS WAS A JEWISH Christian from Alexandria. Perhaps he was a member of a church that arose after Egyptian Jews became Christians on Pentecost in AD 33 (Acts 2:10). Or perhaps he was member of the church Mark planted in Egypt between AD 44 and 49. Jerome wrote that the church Mark founded there was "so admirable in doctrine and continence of living that he constrained all followers of Christ to his example."[1] Perhaps it was under the tutelage of the learned Mark that Apollos gained his theological insight. Some scholars speculate that Apollos may have composed the epistle to the Hebrews.

TO EPHESUS

Apollos left Egypt and arrived in Ephesus around September 4, AD 51, barely missing a meeting with Paul, who had just left Ephesus for Jerusalem. Aquila and Priscilla were still in Ephesus when Apollos arrived.

> [Apollos] was an eloquent man, competent in the Scriptures. He had been instructed in the way of the Lord. And being fervent in spirit, he spoke and taught accurately the things concerning Jesus, though he knew only the baptism of John. He began to speak boldly in the synagogue, but when Priscilla and Aquila heard him, they took him aside and explained to him the way of God more accurately. When Apollos wanted to go to Achaia [Corinth], the brothers and sisters encouraged him and wrote to the disciples there to welcome him. When he arrived, he was a great help to those who by grace had believed. For he vigorously refuted his Jewish opponents in public debate, proving from the Scriptures that Jesus was the Messiah. (Acts 18:24–28)

CORINTHIAN TROUBLES

While Apollos was in Corinth, Paul returned to Ephesus, where he remained for two years (Acts 19:1, 8–10). Fed up with the jealousy, quarreling, litigation, factionalism,

---

1. Jerome, *On Illustrious Men*.

adultery, incest, and other kinds of immorality in the Corinthian church, apparently Apollos traveled to Ephesus around November AD 51. There he brought the bad news from Corinth to Paul, which prompted Paul to write a lost warning letter to the Corinthians (1 Cor 5:9). Timothy was the messenger who took it back, overland, since the winter sailing weather was too dangerous. He probably arrived in Corinth at the end of AD 51.

Apparently, the Corinthians rejected Paul's admonishments. Timothy, Chloe's people, Stephanas, Fortunatus, Achaicus, and Sosthenes, the synagogue leader in Corinth, brought Paul news back from Corinth (1 Cor 1:11). Paul's first letter had not fixed the problems. They probably arrived around the end of February AD 52. In response, Paul wrote 1 Corinthians around March AD 52. Paul chastised the Corinthians for dividing into rival camps. He appealed to them to be united in the same mind, saying that Chloe's people had reported quarreling among them, with some saying, "I follow Paul," or "I follow Apollos," or "I follow Cephas," or "I follow Christ." He wrote:

> Is Christ divided? Was Paul crucified for you? Or were you baptized in the name of Paul? I thank God that I baptized none of you except Crispus and Gaius, so that no one may say that you were baptized in my name. (I did baptize also the household of Stephanas. Beyond that, I do not know whether I baptized anyone else.) For Christ did not send me to baptize but to preach the Gospel, and not with words of eloquent wisdom, lest the Cross of Christ be emptied of its power. (1 Cor 1:13–17)

Paul went on to say that he could not address the Corinthians as spiritually mature, but as infants in Christ. He said he had fed them milk, for they were not ready for solid food. He chastised them for their jealousy and strife, writing:

> Are you not of the flesh and behaving only in a human way? For when one says, "I follow Paul," and another, "I follow Apollos," are you not being merely human? What then is Apollos? What is Paul? Servants through whom you believed, as the Lord assigned to each. I planted, Apollos watered, but God gave the growth. So neither he who plants nor he who waters is anything, but only God who gives the growth. He who plants and he who waters are one, and each will receive his wages according to his labor. For we are God's fellow workers. You are God's field, God's building . . . So let no one boast in men. For all things are yours, whether Paul or Apollos or Cephas or the world or life or death or the present or the future—all are yours, and you are Christ's, and Christ is God's. (1 Cor 3:3–9, 21–23)

In this epistle, Paul used himself and Apollos as examples of teachers who in their preaching did not go beyond what was written in Scripture (1 Cor 4:6), which was what spared believers from becoming puffed-up partisans.

Since the sailing weather was now safe, Paul dispatched Timothy (1 Cor 4:17, 16:10), along with Chloe's people, Stephanas, Fortunatus, Achaicus, and Sosthenes (unless Sosthenes remained with Paul in Ephesus) to take 1 Corinthians to Corinth. Apollos refused to return to Corinth at this time (1 Cor 16:12). Apparently, he was fed up with the Corinthian mess. Scripture says nothing more of Apollos until Paul mentions his mission to Crete.

TO CRETE

Seven years later, after Nero acquitted Paul in AD 59, Paul made various missionary journeys and ended up in Corinth again around AD 65. From there he sent Apollos and Zenas, a lawyer, to Crete, bearing his letter to Titus (Titus 3:13). He asked Titus to speed them on their way, ensuring that the new arrivals would lack nothing. This suggests that Apollos and Zenas were being sent to assume leadership of some of the churches in Crete, which by then had probably spread all over the large island (Titus 3:13). Paul also said he would soon be sending Artemas and Tychicus to Crete, and he urged Titus to join him in Greece after Paul spent the winter in Nicopolis (Titus 3:12). This suggests that Apollos, Zenas, Tychicus, and Artemas were now in charge of the Cretan church. After this, Apollos vanishes from the pages of Scripture.

Minor Characters in the New Testament

ACTS AND THE EPISTLES mention a number of minor characters who may have had pivotal roles but of whom Scripture says little, sometimes no more than their names. They are listed below.

ACHAICUS

He was a believer in Corinth. He was an emissary from Corinth to Paul in Ephesus (1 Cor 16:17).

ALEXANDER

He was the brother of Rufus and the son of Simon of Cyrene (Mark 15:21).

ALEXANDER THE COPPERSMITH

He was probably the same person as Alexander the Jew of Ephesus, who was put forward to quell (unsuccessfully) the tumult at the temple of Artemis (Acts 19:33–34). He was probably also the same person that Paul "delivered to Satan" to teach him not to blaspheme. This was before or during the time Paul was languishing in Roman captivity in Caesarea (1 Tim 1:20). During Paul's second incarceration in Rome, Paul wrote that Alexander strongly opposed the gospel, that he had done Paul much harm, and that the Lord would repay Alexander for his deeds (2 Tim 4:14–15).

AMPLIATUS

He was in Rome when Paul wrote Romans in Corinth, and Paul called him his beloved in the Lord (Rom 16:8).

ANDRONICUS AND JUNIA

They were Jews and Paul's kinsmen, living in Rome at the time Paul wrote Romans. They were well known to the apostles, and they became followers of Christ before Paul did. At some point in Paul's adventures, they had been imprisoned with him (Rom 16:7). Since Paul wrote Romans before his imprisonment in Caesarea and before his first imprisonment in Rome, they were not his fellow-prisoners there. He was imprisoned previously in Philippi, but no mention of his kinsmen is made in that narrative, so they were not likely his fellow prisoners there. However, Paul stated that he had been imprisoned many times (2 Cor 6:5, 11:23), so it was probably on one of these unspecified occasions that Andronicus and Junia were arrested with Paul.

APELLES

He was in Rome and was approved in Christ (Rom 16:10).

APPHIA

She was a believer in Colossae who was of the church that met in Philemon's house (Phlm 1:2).

ARCHIPPUS THE COLOSSIAN

He was a believer in Colossae, a fellow soldier in Christ, who was of the church that met in Philemon's house (Phlm 1:2).

ARCHIPPUS THE LAODICEAN

He was in Laodicea and had a ministry that the Lord had given him to fulfill (Col 4:17).

ARISTARCHUS

He was originally from Thessalonica. He, with Gaius, was seized by the mob in Ephesus during the riot concerning Artemis (Acts 19:29). He apparently traveled with Paul from Ephesus, to Macedonia, to Corinth, and back to Ephesus (Acts 20:4). He was a Jewish Christian who accompanied Paul on his first voyage to Rome (Acts 27:2). He was also under arrest like Paul, although under what charge Scripture does not reveal (Col 4:10). When, during his first incarceration in Rome, Paul wrote to Colossae and Philemon, he added greetings from Aristarchus (Col 4:10; Phlm 1:24).

ARISTOBULUS

His family was of the church in Rome (Rom 16:10).

ARTEMAS

He was a Christian that Paul sent to Titus in Crete (Titus 3:12).

ASYNCRITUS

He was a believer in Rome along with other unnamed brothers (Rom 16:14).

CARPUS

He was an associate of Paul in Troas. When Paul was arrested there, apparently suddenly, Paul left his cloak, books, and precious parchments with him (2 Tim 4:13).

CHLOE

She was someone in Corinth whose people reported the quarrels and immorality in the Corinthian church to Paul (1 Cor 1:11).

CLAUDIA

She was a Christian in Rome during Paul's second incarceration there. Paul sent her greetings to Timothy (2 Tim 4:21).

CLAUDIUS LYSIAS

He was the Roman tribune who saved Paul from the Jewish mob and had him sent under military escort from Jerusalem to the procurator Felix in Caesarea. He respected Paul for being a citizen by birth, for Lysias had bought his citizenship for a large sum (Acts 22:24–28, 23:17–33).

CLEMENT

He was a fellow worker with Paul in Philippi (4:3).

CRESCENS

He was with Paul during his second Roman incarceration, but he left Paul and went to Galatia (2 Tim 4:10).

CRISPUS

He was the synagogue leader in Corinth. During Paul's first sojourn there. He and all his household became Christians. Paul baptized him (Acts 18:8, 1 Cor 1:14).

DAMARIS

She was an Athenian woman, one of the few who heard Paul's speech in Athens and believed (Acts 17:34).

DEMAS

He was with Paul during his first Roman incarceration, and Paul sent greetings from him to the Colossians and to Philemon (Col 4:14; Phlm 1:24). During Paul's second Roman incarceration, Demas deserted Paul and went to Thessalonica "because he loved the world" (2 Tim 4:10).

DIONYSIUS THE AREOPAGITE

He was one of the few who heard Paul's speech in Athens and believed (Acts 17:34).

THE ELECT LADY

She was the person to whom John wrote his second epistle (2 John 1:1). There is no certain way to identify this lady.

EPAENETUS

He was the first convert to Christ in the Roman province of Asia (Rom 16:5).

EPAPHRAS

He was a native of Colossae and was the believer who brought the gospel to that city (Col 1:7, 4:12). He was with Paul during his first Roman incarceration. Paul sent his greetings to Colossae and Philemon from Epaphras in two of his epistles (Col 4:12;

Phlm 1:23). Paul called Epaphras "my fellow prisoner in Christ Jesus." Perhaps Epaphras was also incarcerated in Rome during Paul's first imprisonment there. Perhaps he became a Christian through the ministry of his fellow prisoner Paul. Or perhaps Epaphras was a believer who traveled with Paul to Rome and Paul was using the phrase "fellow prisoner" metaphorically, meaning that Epaphras was sticking with Paul during Paul's incarceration.

EPAPHRODITUS

He was from Philippi and was Paul's coworker. He was one of the couriers who took Paul's epistle to the Philippians to them (Phil 2:25–29). He brought gifts and news from Philippi to Paul in Rome during Paul's first incarceration there (Phil 4:18).

ERASTUS

He was the city treasurer of Corinth (Rom 16:23). He evidently accompanied Paul from Corinth to Ephesus, because when Paul wrote 1 Corinthians, he sent Erastus and Timothy to deliver the epistle to the Corinthian church (Acts 19:22). No doubt Erastus, as an important public official in Corinth, added weight to Paul's letter. During Paul's second Roman incarceration, Erastus remained at Corinth (2 Tim 4:20).

EUBULUS

He was a Christian in Rome during Paul's second incarceration there. Paul sent his greetings to Timothy (2 Tim 4:21).

EUODIA

She was a fellow laborer with Paul in Philippi with whom Paul pleaded to make up her disagreement with another female believer, Syntyche (Phil 4:2).

FORTUNATUS

He was a believer in Corinth. He was an emissary from Corinth to Paul in Ephesus (1 Cor 16:17).

GAIUS OF CORINTH

He was a believer whom Paul baptized during his first sojourn in Corinth (1 Cor 1:14). Either he or Gaius of Derbe offered hospitality to Paul and the whole Corinthian church. While Paul was in Corinth for the third time, Paul sent greetings from Gaius to the church in Rome (Rom 16:23). These greetings might have been from Gaius of Corinth or Gaius of Derbe.

GAIUS OF DERBE

Either he or Gaius of Corinth offered hospitality to Paul and the whole Corinthian church. While Paul was in Corinth for the third time, Paul sent greetings from Gaius to the church in Rome (Rom 16:23). These greetings might have been from Gaius of Corinth or Gaius of Derbe. Gaius of Derbe traveled with Paul from Corinth back to Ephesus (Acts 20:4).

GAIUS OF MACEDONIA

He, along with Aristarchus, was a Macedonian traveling companion of Paul. He, with Aristarchus, was seized by the mob in Ephesus during the riot concerning Artemis (Acts 19:29).

GAIUS THE ELDER

John wrote his third epistle to this person, who might have been any of the other three men named Gaius in the New Testament or might have been a fourth Gaius. Gaius was a common Roman name (3 John 1:1).

HERMAS

He was a believer in Rome along with other unnamed brothers (Rom 16:14).

HERMES

He was a believer in Rome along with other unnamed brothers (Rom 16:14).

HERMOGENES

He was a former disciple who, like Phygelus, turned away from Paul in Asia (2 Tim 1:15).

HERODIAN

He was in Rome and was Paul's kinsman (Rom 16:11).

Others of the Apostolic Age

HYMENAEUS

He was an apostate who, like Alexander the Coppersmith, Paul "handed over to Satan to learn not to blaspheme" (1 Tim 1:20).

JASON

He was a denizen of Thessalonica who accepted the gospel from Paul. The enraged Jews of the Thessalonian synagogue attacked Jason's house, thinking to find Paul there. When they did not find him, they dragged Jason before the city authorities and declared (falsely) that the Christians were acting against the decrees of Caesar and saying there was another king, Jesus. The authorities, who were disturbed, took money as a security from Jason and the other Christians (a bribe) and let them go (Acts 17:5–9).

JESUS CALLED JUSTUS

He was a Jewish Christian who was with Paul during his first imprisonment in Rome. When Paul wrote to Colossae, he sent Justus's greetings (Col 4:11).

JOSEPH BARSABBAS

He was one of the two men nominated to replace Judas Iscariot (Acts 1:23). Matthias won that honor (Acts 1:26).

JUDAS JUSTUS BARSABBAS

He was a leader among the believers and a prophet (Acts 15:32). The Jerusalem Council chose him and Silas (Silvanus) to go with Paul and Barnabas to Antioch to bring the council's decree (Acts 15:22).

JULIA

She was a believer in Rome along with other unnamed saints (Rom 16:15).

JULIUS

He was the centurion who escorted Paul to Rome for his first trial there. He was kind and lenient with Paul (Acts 27:1, 3, 6, 11, 31, 43). His name suggests that he was from an influential Roman family.

LINUS

He was a Christian in Rome during Paul's second incarceration there. Paul sent his greetings to Timothy (2 Tim 4:21).

LUCIUS OF CYRENE

He was a prophet and teacher in Antioch and a colleague of Barnabas and Paul. One day as he, Paul, Barnabas, Simeon Niger, and Manaen were praying and fasting, the Holy Spirit called for the appointment of Barnabas and Paul for a special assignment. Lucius, Simeon, and Manaen laid hands on Barnabas and Paul and sent them on Paul's first missionary journey (Acts 13:1–3). He was possibly the same Lucius who was with Paul during his third visit to Corinth (Rom 16:21).

LYDIA

She was a denizen of Philippi, originally from the city of Thyatira in what is now Turkey. She was a dealer in purple cloth, a luxurious item. She was a worshipper of God. She and her whole household accepted the gospel from Paul. She took Paul and Silas (Silvanus) into her house (Acts 16:14–15, 40). She seems to have been the first leader of the Philippian church.

MANAEN

He was a lifelong friend (or foster brother) of Herod Antipas I, the tetrarch. He was a prophet and teacher in Antioch and a colleague of Barnabas and Paul. One day as he, Paul, Barnabas, Simeon Niger, and Lucius of Cyrene were praying and fasting, the Holy Spirit called for the appointment of Barnabas and Paul for a special assignment. Lucius, Simeon, and Manaen laid hands on Barnabas and Paul and sent them on Paul's first missionary journey (Acts 13:1–3).

MARY

She was a believer in Rome who had worked hard for the church (Rom 16:6).

MNASON

He was one of the early believers from Cyprus. Possibly he came to Christ when Paul and Barnabas and Mark preached in Cyprus during Paul's first missionary journey. Mnason hosted Paul and his team in his home on Paul's last return to Jerusalem (Acts 21:16).

NARCISSUS

His family was of the church in Rome (Rom 16:11).

NEREUS AND HIS SISTER, OLYMPAS

They were believers in Rome, along with other unnamed saints (Rom 16:15).

NICANOR

He was one of the seven men, full of the Spirit and wisdom, whom the church chose to distribute food to the widows in the congregation. Unlike Nicolas, one of the seven, he was born a Jew (Acts 6:5).

NICOLAS OF ANTIOCH

He was one of the seven men, full of the Spirit and wisdom, whom the church chose to distribute food to the widows in the congregation. He was a convert to Judaism (Acts 6:5).

NYMPHA

She was a believer in Laodicea. The church there, or at least a small group, met in her house (Col 4:15).

ONESIMUS

Onesimus was a slave owned by Philemon, the leader of the church in Colossae, near Ephesus. Paul had led Philemon to the Lord. Onesimus ran away to Rome. The penalty of a runaway slave was death, but in Rome he encountered Paul, who led him to Christ. Paul sent Onesimus back to Colossae with a private letter to Philemon, entreating him to set Onesimus free. No doubt Philemon did so; otherwise, he probably would have destroyed the epistle. Since it became public and part of the New Testament, he surely did set Onesimus free. Onesimus eventually became the bishop of the church in Ephesus.

ONESIPHORUS

In Ephesus, he rendered great service to Paul. He followed Paul to Rome and searched for him diligently. This was during Paul's incarceration (probably the first one). Onesiphorus refreshed Paul and was not ashamed of his chains (2 Tim 1:16–18).

PARMENAS

He was one of the seven men, full of the Spirit and wisdom, whom the church chose to distribute food to the widows in the congregation. Unlike Nicolas, one of the seven, he was born a Jew (Acts 6:5).

PATROBAS

He was a believer in Rome along with other unnamed brothers (Rom 16:14).

PERSIS

He was in Rome, he was beloved, and he worked hard in the Lord (Rom 16:12).

PHILIP THE EVANGELIST

He was one of the seven men, full of the Spirit and wisdom, whom the Jerusalem church chose to distribute food to the widows in the congregation. Unlike Nicolas, one of the seven, he was born a Jew (Acts 6:5). He subsequently lived in Caesarea, where he hosted Paul and his team. He had four unmarried daughters who prophesied (Acts 21:8–9). He is not Philip the apostle.

PHILOLOGUS

He was a believer in Rome along with other unnamed saints (Rom 16:15).

PHLEGON

He was a believer in Rome along with other unnamed brothers (Rom 16:14).

PHOEBE

She was a deacon of the church in Cenchreae, near Corinth. She was at least one of the couriers who took Paul's epistle to the Romans to Rome (Rom 16:1).

PHYGELUS

He was a former disciple who, along with Hermogenes, turned away from Paul in Asia (2 Tim 1:15).

PROCORUS

He was one of the seven men, full of the Spirit and wisdom, whom the church chose to distribute food to the widows in the congregation. Unlike Nicolas, one of the seven, he was born a Jew (Acts 6:5).

PUBLIUS

He the chief man on Malta who hosted Paul and his team after the shipwreck and whose father Paul healed of fever and dysentery (Acts 28:7–8).

PUDENS

He was a Christian in Rome during Paul's second incarceration there. Paul sent his greetings to Timothy (2 Tim 4:21).

QUARTUS

He was a believer in Corinth. While Paul was there on his third visit to the city, he sent Quartus's greetings to the church in Rome (Rom 16:23).

RUFUS

He was in Rome. He was chosen in the Lord, and his mother was like a mother to Paul (Rom 16:13). Perhaps he was the brother of Alexander and the son of Simon of Cyrene (Mark 15:21).

SECUNDUS

He was from Thessalonica. He accompanied Paul from Corinth after his third sojourn there back to Ephesus (Acts 20:4).

SIMEON NIGER

He was a prophet and teacher in Antioch and a colleague of Barnabas and Paul. One day as he, Paul, Barnabas, Lucius of Cyrene, and Manaen were praying and fasting, the Holy Spirit called for the appointment of Barnabas and Paul for a special assignment. Lucius, Simeon, and Manaen laid hands on Barnabas and Paul and sent them on Paul's first missionary journey (Acts 13:1–3).

SIMON OF CYRENE (MODERN LIBYA)

He was father of Alexander and Rufus (Mark 15:21). As the Roman soldiers led Jesus away to Golgotha, Jesus carried his own cross (John 19:17), but the soldiers also seized Simon and forced him to carry one end of the cross, following behind Jesus, probably because Jesus, after his torment, was too weak to carry it alone (Matt 27:32, Luke 23:26).

SOPATER

He was the son of Pyrrhus from Berea. He accompanied Paul from Corinth after his third sojourn there back to Ephesus (Acts 20:4).

SOSTHENES

He was the synagogue leader in Corinth who succeeded Crispus. A crowd of Jews beat him in front of the Roman proconsul, Gallio, because he failed to suppress Paul's preaching of the gospel (Acts 18:17). He apparently followed Paul back to Ephesus (and no wonder) because Paul sent Sosthenes's greetings back to Corinth (1 Cor 1:1).

STACHYS

He was in Rome. Paul called him beloved (Rom 16:9).

STEPHANAS

He and his household were the first converts in Corinth. They devoted themselves to the service of the saints. Paul baptized him and his household. He was an emissary from Corinth to Paul in Ephesus (1 Cor 16:15–17).

SYNTYCHE

She was a fellow laborer with Paul in Philippi with whom Paul pleaded to make up her disagreement with another female believer, Euodia (Phil 4:2).

TERTIUS

He was Paul's scribe in Corinth when Paul composed Romans (Rom 16:22).

TIMON

He was one of the seven men, full of the Spirit and wisdom, whom the church chose to distribute food to the widows in the congregation. Unlike Nicolas, one of the seven, he was born a Jew (Acts 6:5).

TITIUS JUSTUS

He was a worshiper of God whose house was next door to the synagogue in Corinth. When the synagogue expelled Paul, he went to Justus's house and carried on teaching (Acts 18:7).

TROPHIMUS

He was from Ephesus (Acts 21:29). He was, with Timothy, part of Paul's missionary team. He followed Paul to Corinth and then to Jerusalem (Acts 20:4), where some Jews from Ephesus recognized him and believed Paul had brought him, an uncircumcised gentile, into the temple (Acts 21:29). The whole city was aroused, and the mob seized Paul, leading to his arrest by the Romans, his escape to Caesarea, and his first trip to Rome. Before Paul's second Roman incarceration, he left Trophimus in Miletus because Trophimus was ill (2 Tim 4:20).

TRYPHAENA

A woman in Rome who was a worker in the Lord (Rom 16:12).

TRYPHOSA

A woman in Rome who was a worker in the Lord (Rom 16:12).

TYCHICUS

He was from the Roman province of Asia, probably Ephesus. He was a helper of Paul. He traveled with Paul and his ministry team from his third visit to Corinth back to Macedonia (Acts 20:4). He was at least one of the couriers who, during Paul's first Roman incarceration, delivered the letter to the Ephesians to the church in Ephesus (Eph 6:21) and Colossians to the church in Colossae (Col 4:7–9). Paul sent him to Titus when Titus was leading the churches in Crete (Titus 3:12). Before or during Paul's second Roman incarceration, Paul sent Tychicus to Ephesus, no doubt to curate the church there in Paul's absence.

URBANUS

He was in Rome. Paul called him his fellow worker in Christ (Rom 16:9).

ZENAS

He was lawyer Paul sent with Apollos to Titus in Crete (Titus 1:1).

Appendices

Proposed Timeline of Jesus' Life and the Apostolic Age

THIS TIMELINE WAS CAREFULLY constructed on an Excel spreadsheet of 1,427 pages with one column representing every day from 2 BC to AD 70 (in both Hebrew and Gregorian dates). The method used was to anchor every certain date in the timeline (such as Jewish holy days or the Great Fire of Rome) and then to arrange all approximate dates around the anchors. When biblical characters walked or sailed from one place to another, ancient sailing records[1] or Google Maps with walking times were employed to estimate the probable length of such journeys. The result is a meticulous chronology which is to some extent conjectural but which fits Scripture perfectly and has a high probability of being accurate overall.

3 BC

- Zechariah, the father of John the Baptist, began his service rotation in the Jerusalem Temple on the Sabbath, Saturday, March 1, 3 BC (Luke 1:5–10).
- Zechariah heard from an angel that his wife, Elizabeth would conceive, was struck dumb, and completed his temple service on Friday, March 7, 3 BC (Luke 1:11–22).
- John the Baptist was conceived between Tuesday, March 11, and Sunday, March 16, 3 BC (Luke 1:24).
- Elizabeth went into hiding for five months, Monday, March 17, 3 BC (Luke 1:24).
- Elizabeth came out of hiding, around Thursday, August 14, 3 BC.
- Mary received the annunciation from the Angel Gabriel and conceived Jesus by the Holy Spirit probably between Saturday, the Sabbath, September 13 (23 Elul), over midnight to Sunday, September 14 (24 Elul), 3 BC[2] (Luke 1:26–38).

---

1. Casson, *Speed under Sail of Ancient Ships*.
2. This a preferred date for the conception of Jesus because it occurs within the sixth month of Elizabeth's pregnancy, and the sixth month of the Hebrew year, Elul; this fits well with the rest of the

- Mary and her family departed on the fall pilgrimage to Jerusalem, Monday, September 15, 26 Elul, 3 BC.
- Rosh Hashanah fell on the Sabbath, Saturday, September 20, 1 Tishri, 3 BC.
- After Sukkot, the Feast of Tabernacles, Mary accompanied her relative, Zechariah, to his home to meet Elizabeth, Sunday, October 12, 23 Tishri, 3 BC (Luke 1:39–45).
- Mary delivered the Magnificat, Sunday, October 12, 3 BC (Luke 1:46–55).
- Mary remained with Elizabeth until the birth of John the Baptist on Monday, December 1, 3 BC (Luke 1:56–58).
- Zechariah circumcised John and regained his speech on December 8, 21 Kislev, 3 BC (Luke 1:59–75).
- Zechariah and Mary made the one-day pilgrimage to Jerusalem for Chanukah around Tuesday, December 9, 3 BC.
- Mary probably rejoined her family and her betrothed, Joseph, in Jerusalem over Chanukah, which lasted from Thursday, December 11, 24 Kislev, to Saturday, the Sabbath, December 20, 4 Tevet, 3 BC. It was probably at this time, with her pregnancy showing, that she explained to Joseph and her family the truth of her miraculous conception three months before. She no doubt received moral support from Zechariah, who could attest that the Angel Gabriel and appeared to him also and that many miracles had surrounded the birth of John.
- Joseph heard from an angel and accepted Mary (Matt 1:18–25).

2 BC

- John the Baptist was dedicated at the temple on Friday, January 9, 2 BC.
- Joseph and the pregnant Mary made their pilgrimage to Jerusalem for Pentecost, starting out on Tuesday, May 12, 29 Iyar, 2 BC.
- Joseph and Mary probably left Jerusalem for Bethlehem around Sunday, June 14, 2 BC (Luke 2:1–6).
- Jesus was born, probably on Wednesday, June 17, 6 Tammuz, 2 BC (Luke 2:6–20).[3]
- Jesus was circumcised, probably on Wednesday, June 24, 13 Tammuz, 2 BC (Luke 2:21).
- Jesus was presented at the temple, probably on Sunday, 16 Av, 2 BC (Luke 2:22–38).
- The magi set out for Judea, probably around Sunday, August 2, 2 BC (Matt 2:1–2).

Biblical timeline; and it coincides with the important astronomical phenomena described in Matthew.

3. See "Pinpointing the Date of Jesus' Birth" in the Appendices.

Proposed Timeline of Jesus' Life and the Apostolic Age

- The magi reached Jerusalem probably just before Chanukah, around November 29, 24 Kislev, 2 BC (Matt 2:1–2).
- Chanukah fell between November 30, 25 Kislev and December 8, 3 Tevet, 2 BC.
- The magi met Herod probably after Chanukah on Wednesday, December 9, 2 BC (Matt 2:3–8).
- The magi visited Jesus in Bethlehem, Wednesday, December 23 (25 December by the Julian Calendar), 18 Tevet, 2 BC (Matt 2:9–11).
- The magi departed for Babylon around Thursday, December 24 (Matt 2:12).
- An angel warned Joseph to take Jesus and Mary to Egypt, Thursday, December 26, 2 BC. He left at once (Matt 2:13–15).
- Herod slaughtered the male infants of Bethlehem, probably around Monday, December 28, 2 BC (Matt 2:16–18).

1 BC

- Herod burned two rabbis alive, probably around January 6, 1 BC.
- There was a total lunar eclipse in Jerusalem, Saturday, January 9, 6 Shevat, 1 BC.
- Herod the Great died between around March 1, 1 BC (not in 4 BC, as many texts erroneously assert).[4]
- Passover fell on Wednesday, March 17, 14 Nisan, 1 BC.
- An angel told Joseph to return from Egypt, Friday, March 26, 23 Nisan, 1 BC (Matt 2:19–20).
- Joseph and his family began their homeward journey after about three months in Egypt, probably around Sunday, March 28, 1 BC (Matt 2:21).
- Skirting Judea, which was in political turmoil under Herod Archelaus, Joseph, Mary, and Jesus went to Nazareth, probably arriving around Sunday, April 4, 2 Iyar, 1 BC (Matt 2:22–23; Luke 2:39–40).

AD 11

- The twelve-year-old Jesus conversed with the teachers in the temple, Friday, April 11, 25 Nisan, AD 11 (Luke 2:41–52).

---

4. See "Pinpointing the Date of Jesus' Birth" in the Appendices.

APPENDICES

AD 5

- Paul was born in Gischala in upper Galilee,[5] perhaps around AD 5. If so, he was about seven years younger than Jesus.

AD 7

- When the Roman hegemon Quirinius absorbed Galilee into the Roman province of Judea in AD 7,[6] Paul's family moved from Galilee to Tarsus in Asia Minor (modern Turkey).[7]

AD 14–37

- Tiberius reigned as Roman emperor from AD 14 to 37.

AD 29

- Jesus' thirty-first birthday fell on June 17, AD 29.
- John the Baptist started baptizing, before Saturday, August 18, 22 Av, AD 29, because that was the last day of Tiberius's fifteenth regnal year (Matt 3:1–2; Mark 1:4; Luke 3:1–3; John 1:6–8).
- John rebuked the Pharisees and Sadducees, calling them a generation of vipers, Monday, August 20, 24 Av, AD 29 (Matt 3:7–10; Luke 3:7–9).
- John baptized Jesus, Sunday, September 2, 7 Elul, AD 29 (Matt 3:13–17; Mark 1:9–11; Luke 3:21–22).
- Jesus began his forty days in the wilderness, Monday, September 3, 8 Elul, AD 29 (Matt 4:1–2; Mark 1:12; Luke 4:1–2).
- The fifteenth year of Tiberius ended Saturday, August 18, 22 Av, AD 29 (Luke 3:1).
- Rosh Hashanah fell on Tuesday, September 25, 1 Tishri, AD 29.
- Yom Kippur fell on Thursday, October 4, 10 Tishri, AD 29.
- Sukkot, the Feast of Tabernacles, began, Tuesday, October 9, 15 Tishri, AD 29.

---

5. Jerome, *On Illustrious Men*.
6. Josephus, *Ant.* 18:1:1.
7. Jerome, *On Illustrious Men*.

- Satan tempted Jesus, Saturday, the Sabbath, October 13, 29 Tishri, AD 29 (Matt 4:1–11; Mark 1:13; Luke 4:1–13).

- Priests and Levites questioned John the Baptist again, Monday, October 15, 21 Tishri, AD 29 (John 1:19–28).

- John declared that Jesus is the Lamb of God, Tuesday, October 16, 22 Tishri, AD 29 (John 1:29–34).

- Sukkot, the Feast of Tabernacles, ended, and John again declared that Jesus is the Lamb of God, Wednesday, October 17, 23 Tishri, AD 29. Andrew, John, and probably Peter stayed with Jesus in a tabernacle (John 1:35–42).

- Jesus called Philip and Nathanael. Jesus and Andrew, John, Peter, Philip, and Nathanael set out for Galilee, Thursday, October 18, 24 Tishri, AD 29 (John 1:43–51).

- Jesus and the five disciples arrived in Cana for a wedding, where Jesus turned water in to wine, Sunday, October 21, 27 Tishri, AD 29 (John 2:1–11).

- Jesus, his family, and the five disciples took a holiday in Capernaum by the Sea of Galilee, Tuesday, October 22, 28 Tishri, AD 29 (John 2:12).

- Jesus vanished from the pages of Scripture for 157 days or over five months.

AD 30

- Jesus reappeared on the pages of Scripture with a bang, cleansing the Jerusalem Temple for the first time on Friday, March 29, 9 Nisan, AD 30 (John 2:13–22).

- Jesus performed unrecorded miracles in Jerusalem around the Passover, Wednesday, April 3, 14 Nisan, AD 30 (John 2:23–24, 3:2).

- Jesus taught Nicodemus, Thursday, April 4, 15 Nisan, AD 30 (John 3:1–21).

- Jesus' disciples baptized in the Judean countryside, Sunday, April 6, AD 30 (John 3:22).

- John the Baptist exalted Jesus, Monday, April 9, AD 30 (John 3:23–36).

- John the Baptist was arrested, Thursday, April 18, AD 30 (Matt 4:12, 14:3–5; Mark 1:14–15, 6:17–20; Luke 3:19–20).

- Jesus retreated overnight to Samaria (John 4:1–6).

- Jesus met the Samaritan woman at the well around 6 a.m., Friday, April 19, AD 30 (John 4:7–27).

- Jesus spent the Sabbath with the Samaritans, Friday, April 19–Sunday April 21, AD 30 (John 4:28–42).

- Jesus arrived in Galilee, taught throughout the Galilean synagogues, and performed unrecorded miracles (Matt 4:12; Mark 1:14-15; Luke 4:14-15; John 4:43-45), starting Monday, April 22, AD 30.
- Jesus read Isaiah 61 in the Nazareth synagogue where he was rejected there for the first time, Saturday, the Sabbath, April 27, AD 30 (Luke 4:16-30).
- In Cana, Jesus healed the official's son in Capernaum, Sunday, April 28, AD 30 (John 4:46-54).
- Jesus settled in Capernaum, Tuesday, April 30, AD 30 (Matt 4:13-17).
- Jesus called Peter, Andrew, James, and John into full-time ministry, Wednesday, May 1, AD 30 (Matt 4:18-22; Mark 1:16-20; Luke 5:1-11).
- Jesus preached in Galilee, from the Sabbath, Saturday, May 4 through the Sabbath, Saturday, May 11, AD 30 (Matt 4:23-25).
- Jesus delivered the Sermon on the Mount[8] (Matt 5-7), healed the first leper (Matt 8:2-4), healed the first centurion's servant (Matt 8:5-13), taught in the Capernaum synagogue (Mark 1:21-22; Luke 4:31-32), healed a demoniac (Mark 1:23-28; Luke 4:33-37), healed Peter's mother-in-law (Matt 8:14-15; Mark 1:29-31; Luke 4:38-39), and healed many (Matt 8:16-17; Mark 1:32-34; Luke 4:40-41) all on Saturday, the Sabbath, May 18, AD 30.
- Jesus departed for a desolate place, Sunday, May 19, AD 30 (Mark 1:35-38; Luke 4:42-43).
- Jesus made the Jerusalem pilgrimage for Pentecost, Tuesday, May 21, 3 Sivan, AD 30.
- Pentecost fell on Friday, May 24, 6 Sivan, AD 30.
- Jesus conducted a brief Judean ministry from Saturday, the Sabbath, May 25 to Saturday, the Sabbath, June 8, AD 30 (Luke 4:44).
- Jesus returned to Galilee, Sunday, June 9, AD 30 (Mark 1:39).
- Jesus cleansed a second leper (Mark 1:40-45; Luke 5:12-16), calmed a storm (Matt 8:23; Mark 4:35-36; Luke 8:22), cast demons into the Gadarene swine (Matt 8:28-34; Mark 5:1-20; Luke 8:26-39), healed a paralytic (Matt 9:1-8; Mark 2:1-12; Luke 5:17-26), called Matthew Levi (Matt 9:9-13; Mark 2:13-14; Luke 5:27-28), and attended Matthew's feast (Matt 9:10-13; Mark 2:15-17; Luke 5:29-32), all between June 15 and July 25, AD 30.
- The next section of the Gospels presents complex chronological challenges. There are two options: (1) move Matthew to fit the sequencing of Mark and Luke, or (2) move Mark and Luke to fit Matthew's sequencing. Option 2 producers a better

---

8. On Mount EremoDelete this bullet and join this paragraph with the paragraph pertaining to the previous bullet..

Proposed Timeline of Jesus' Life and the Apostolic Age

harmony of the synoptics and therefore seems preferable. Considering Matthew to be the chronological authority seems the better choice. This assumes that Matthew's accounts are in a more chronological order while the other two Synoptic Gospels are in a more topical order. Any other attempt to organize the sequence of events fails, but this convention works well.

- Jesus' thirty-second birthday fell on June 17, AD 30.
- Jesus raised Jairus's daughter, healed a woman with a hemorrhage, and healed two blind men on Tuesday, July 30, AD 30 (Matt 9:18–31; Mark 5:21–43; Luke 8:40–56).
- Jesus healed a mute man, Wednesday, July 31, AD 30 (Matt 9:32–34).
- Nazareth rejected Jesus a second time, Saturday, the Sabbath, August 17, AD 30 (Mark 6:1–6).
- Jesus called the twelve disciples into full-time ministry 111 days after calling the four fishermen and 352 days after his baptism. He also delivered the Sermon on the Plain and healed the second centurion's servant. All this occurred on Monday, August 19, AD 30 (Matt 10:1–4; Mark 3:13–19; Luke 6:13–19, 7:1–10).
- Jesus' family tried to seize him, thinking he was out of his mind, Tuesday, August 20, AD 30 (Mark 3:20–21).
- Jesus raised the widow's son in Nain, Wednesday, August 21, AD 30 (Luke 7:11–17).
- Jesus sent out the Twelve for twenty-three days while he went to preach in cities on his own, after which they all met again in Jerusalem from Thursday, August 22 to Thursday, September 12, AD 30 (Matt 10:5–42, 11:1; Mark 6:7–9, 30; Luke 9:1–10; John 5:1).
- Jesus healed a man at Bethesda Pool on Rosh Hashanah, the Sabbath, Saturday, September 14, 1 Tishri, AD 30 (John 5:2–9).
- John the Baptist sent messengers to Jesus, Monday, September 16, AD 30 (Matt 11:2–3; Luke 7:18–20).
- A sinful woman anointed Jesus, Saturday, the Sabbath, September 21, 8 Tishri, AD 30 (Luke 7:36–49).
- Yom Kippur fell on Monday, September 23, 10 Tishri, AD 30.
- Sukkot, the Feast of Tabernacles, fell on Friday, September 27, 14 Tishri, AD 30.
- Jesus' disciples plucked grain on the Sabbath, Saturday, September 28, 15 Tishri, AD 30 (Matt 12:1–2; Mark 2:23–24; Luke 6:1–2).
- Jesus healed a man with a withered hand on the Sabbath, Saturday, October 5, 22 Tishri, AD 30 (Matt 12:9–10; Mark 3:1–4; Luke 6:2–9).

APPENDICES

- Jesus withdrew to avoid a Pharisaical plot, Sunday, October 6, 23 Tishri, AD 30 (Matt 12:15–21). Jesus healed a blind-mute demoniac on Sunday, October 6, AD 30 (Matt 12:22–30; Mark 3:22–27).
- Sukkot, the Feast of Tabernacles, ended on Monday, October 7, 24 Tishri, AD 30.
- Jesus' mother and brothers again tried to stop his ministry (Matt 12:46–50; Mark 3:31–35; Luke 8:19–21), and Jesus called his disciples new scribes in the kingdom of heaven (Matt 13:51–52), Wednesday, October 9, AD 30.
- Nazareth rejected Jesus for the third time on the Sabbath, Saturday, October 12, AD 30 (Matt 13:53–58).

AD 30–31

- Jesus vanished from the pages of Scripture for 151 days, almost five months, from Sunday, October 14 AD 30 to Wednesday, March 12, AD 31.

AD 31

- Herod Antipas celebrated his birthday, and Herodias's daughter demanded John the Baptist's head on a platter, possibly on Tuesday, March 4, AD 31 (Matt 14:6–7; Mark 6:21–22).
- John the Baptist was executed in Machaerus, probably on Sunday, March 9, AD 31.
- The head of John the Baptist was presented to Herodias's daughter, Tuesday, March 11, AD 31 (Matt 14:8–11; Mark 6:23–28).
- News of John's death reached Jesus, Wednesday, March 12, AD 31 (Matt 14:12).
- Jesus withdrew to Bethsaida, a desolate place, fed the five thousand, and the disciples were caught in a storm, Thursday, March 13, AD 31 (Matt 14:13–24; Mark 6:31–47; Luke 9:10–17; John 6:1–21).
- Jesus walks on water, returns to Gennesaret, and crowds follow him to Capernaum, Friday, March 5, AD 31 (Matt 14:25–36; Mark 6:48–56; John 6:19–27).
- Jesus taught in the Capernaum synagogue, Saturday, the Sabbath, March 6, AD 31 (John 6:22–71).
- Jesus and his disciples departed for Jerusalem to observe the Passover, Monday, March 17, 7 Nisan, AD 31.
- The Passover fell on Monday, March 24, 14 Nisan, AD 31.

Proposed Timeline of Jesus' Life and the Apostolic Age

- The Pharisees confronted Jesus about washing hands, Tuesday, March 25, 15 Nisan, AD 31 (Matt 15:1–2; Mark 7:1–5).

- Jesus departed for Galilee, Sunday, March 30, 20 Nisan, AD 31.

- Jesus arrived in Galilee, Tuesday, April 1, 22 Nisan, AD 31.

- Jesus left for Sidon and Tyre, Sunday, April 6, AD 31 (Matt 15:21; Mark 7:24).

- Jesus arrived in the region of Sidon and Tyre and healed the demon-possessed daughter of a Syrian woman, Tuesday, April 8, AD 31 (Matt 15:22–28; Mark 7:25–30).

- Jesus left for the Decapolis, Sunday, April 13, AD 31.

- Jesus healed a deaf man in the Decapolis, Wednesday, April 16, AD 31 (Mark 7:31–37).

- Jesus healed many, Thursday, April 17, AD 31 (Matt 15:29–31).

- Jesus fed the four thousand and sailed to Dalmanutha, Friday, April 18, AD 31 (Matt 15:32–39; Mark 8:1–10).

- Jesus sailed to Bethsaida and healed a blind man, Sunday, April 20, AD 31 (Matt 16:4; Mark 8:13–26).

- Jesus set out for Caesarea Philippi, Monday, April 21, AD 31 (Mark 8:27).

- Jesus was transfigured on Mount Hermon, Tuesday, April 29, AD 31 (Matt 17:2–3; Mark 9:2–4; Luke 9:29–32).

- Jesus healed a demon-possessed boy that his disciples could not heal, Wednesday, April 30, AD 31 (Matt 17:17–18; Mark 9:19–27; Luke 9:41–43).

- Jesus told Peter to pay the temple tax from coins found in a fish, Wednesday, May 21, AD 31 (Matt 17:24–27).

- Jesus' thirty-third birthday fell on June 17, AD 31.

- Jesus' brothers and disciples departed for Jerusalem while Jesus remained behind, Sunday, August 31, AD 31 (John 7:2–12).

- Rosh Hashanah fell on Thursday, September 4, 1 Tishri, AD 31.

- Yom Kippur fell on Saturday, the Sabbath, September 13, AD 31.

- Jesus departed for Jerusalem, Sunday, September 14, 11 Tishri, AD 31 (John 7:10–13).

- Jesus arrived in Jerusalem, Tuesday, September 16, 13 Tishri, AD 31.

- Sukkot, the Feast of Tabernacles, fell on Wednesday, September 17, 14 Tishri, AD 31.

- Temple officers failed to arrest Jesus on Saturday, the Sabbath, September 20, 17 Tishri, AD 31 (John 7:32–36).

APPENDICES

- On the last day of Sukkot, the Feast of Tabernacles, Jesus declared that he was the source of living water, Saturday, the Sabbath, September 27, 24 Tishri, AD 31 (John 7:37–39).
- Jesus pardoned a woman caught in adultery and declared that he was the light of the world, Sunday, March 28, AD 31 (John 7:53—8:11).
- Jesus healed a man born blind on Saturday, the Sabbath, October 4, 1 Cheshvan, AD 31 (John 9:1–12).
- Jesus departed for Galilee on Sunday, October 5, AD 31.

AD 31–32

- Jesus vanished from the pages of Scripture for 174 days, nearly six months, from Monday, October 6, AD 31 to Saturday, March 27, AD 32.

AD 32

- Jesus traveled toward Judea, Sunday, March 28, AD 32 (Matt 19:1–2; Mark 10:1; Luke 9:51).
- A Samaritan village rejected Jesus, Monday, March 29, AD 32 (Luke 9:52–56).
- Jesus sent out the seventy-two for a ministry outreach of ten days, from Tuesday, March 30, 1 Nisan to Thursday, April 8, 10 Nisan, AD 32 (Luke 10:1–12).
- Jesus and the seventy-two met again in Jerusalem, Thursday, April 8, 10 Nisan, AD 32 (Luke 10:17–20) just in time to choose their lamb for the Passover.
- The Passover fell on Monday, April 12, 14 Nisan, AD 32.
- Jesus visited Martha, Mary, and Lazarus in Bethany on the Mount of Olives, Friday, April 23, AD 32 (Luke 10:25–37).
- Jesus vanished from the pages of Scripture for thirty-five days, from April 24 to May 29, AD 32.
- Jesus told the parable of the narrow gate, Sunday, May 30, AD 32 (Luke 13:22–30).
- Pentecost fell on Wednesday, June 2, 6 Sivan, AD 32.
- Jesus healed a man with dropsy on Saturday, the Sabbath, June 5, AD 32 (Luke 14:1–6).
- Jesus vanished from the pages of Scripture for 106 days, from June 6 to September 19, AD 32.
- Jesus' thirty-fourth birthday fell on June 17, AD 32.

- Jesus healed ten lepers on Monday, September 20, AD 32 (Luke 17:11–19).
- The children came to Jesus on Rosh Hashanah, Thursday, September 23, 1 Tishri, AD 32 (Matt 19:13–15; Mark 10:13–16; Luke 18:15–17).
- Yom Kippur fell on Saturday, the Sabbath, October 2, 10 Tishri, AD 32.
- Jesus called the rich, young ruler on Sunday, October 3, AD 32 (Matt 19:16–18; Mark 10:17–18; Luke 18:18–19).
- Jesus vanished from the pages of Scripture for seventy-one days, from October 4 to December 14, AD 32.
- Jesus taught in Jerusalem during Chanukah, from Tuesday, December 14, 24 Kislev to Wednesday, December 22, 2 Tevet, AD 32 (John 10:22–30).
- Jesus went to Bethany on the Jordan, Thursday, December 23, AD 32 (John 10:40–42).
- Lazarus fell ill and died, Thursday, December 30, AD 32 (John 11:1–5).

AD 33

- Jesus raised Lazarus, Sunday, January 2, AD 33 (John 11:38–44).
- Jesus vanished from the pages of Scripture for seventy-six days, over 2.5 months, staying with his disciples in Ephraim, from Monday, January 3 to Saturday, March 19, 1 Nisan, AD 33.
- Jesus set out for Jericho, Sunday, March 20, 2 Nisan, AD 33.
- Jesus foretold his death, and James and John requested special treatment in the kingdom of heaven, Tuesday, March 22, 4 Nisan, AD 33 (Matt 20:17–21; Mark 10:32–37; Luke 18:31–34).
- Jesus healed blind Bartimaeus and met Zacchaeus, Wednesday, March 23, 5 Nisan, AD 33 (Mark 10:46–52; Luke 18:35–43; 19:1–10).
- Jesus healed two blind men, Thursday, March 24, 6 Nisan, AD 33 (Matt 20:29–34).
- Mary of Bethany anointed Jesus, Friday, March 25, 7 Nisan, AD 33 (John 12:1–8).
- On Palm Sunday, Jesus entered Jerusalem, met some Greeks, and cleansed the temple for the second time, Sunday, March 27, 9 Nisan, AD 33 (Matt 21:1–16; Mark 11:1–11; Luke 19:29–48; John 12:12–36).
- Jesus cursed the fig tree and cleansed the temple for the third time, Monday, March 28, 10 Nisan, AD 33 (Matt 21:18–19; Mark 11:12–19).

- The fig tree withered, Jesus delivered the Olivet Discourse, and he predicted that he would die on Friday, Tuesday, March 29, 11 Nisan, AD 33 (Matt 21:20–22, 24:1–46; Mark 11:20–26, 13:1–31; Luke 21:5–24).

- A woman anointed Jesus at the house of Simon the Leper, and Judas made his deal to betray Jesus, Wednesday, March 30, 13 Nisan, AD 33 (Matt 26:6–13; Mark 14:3–9; Luke 22:3–6).

- Jesus celebrated the Last Supper, Thursday, March 31, 13 Nisan, AD 33 (Matt 26:17–35; Mark 14:12–31; Luke 22:7–38; John 13–17:15).

- Judas died (Matt 27:5–10; Acts 1:18–20), and Jesus died on the Passover, Friday, April 1, 14 Nisan, AD 33 (Matt 27:48–50; Mark 15:36–37; Luke 23:45; John 19:28–30).

- Jesus was resurrected on Firstfruits, appeared to Peter, appeared on the Emmaus Road, and appeared to ten of his disciples in the upper room, Sunday, April 3, 16 Nisan, AD 33 (Matt 28:1–15; Mark 16:1–13; Luke 24:1–49; John 20:1–23; 1 Cor 15:3–8).

- Jesus appeared to eleven of his disciples, including Thomas, and Monday, April 11, 24 Nisan, AD 33 (John 20:24–29).

- Jesus met his disciples by the Sea of Galilee, on Mount Eremos where he gave the Great Commission, at a Sabbath meal in Galilee, and appeared to over five hundred people over forty days between April 3 and May 12, AD 33 (Matt 28:16–20; Mark 16:14–18; John 21:1–25; 1 Cor 15:3–8).

- Jesus' ascension occurred on Friday, May 13, AD 33 (Mark 16:19–20; Luke 24:50–53; Acts 1:9–11).[9] His ministry, from his baptism to his ascension, spanned five calendar years, from AD 29 to 33, fifty calendar months, and 1,350 days or a little over forty months' time (calculated at 30.5 days per month).

- Probably around AD 33, when he was twenty-nine, Paul went to Jerusalem to study under Gamaliel (Acts 22:3).[10]

- The apostles chose Matthias to replace Judas on Sunday, May 13, AD 33 (Acts 1:26).

---

9. This was Friday, 26 Iyar. The Sabbath would begin at sundown on that day, which is why Acts says that the disciples "returned to Jerusalem from the mount called Olivet, a Sabbath day's journey away."

10. Paul said in Acts 22:3 that he was "brought up" in Jerusalem, where he studied at the feet of the famous rabbi, Gamaliel. The word "brought up" in Greek, *anatrepho*, means "nurtured or nourished" (Strong *Concordance*, s.v. 397). Paul was in Jerusalem at the stoning of Stephen, which occurred in December AD 33. Paul was probably not in Jerusalem much earlier than that. If Paul had been in Jerusalem for the Passover of AD 33, he would have been aware in the first person of the Crucifixion and the resurrection. If so, given Paul's intellect and curiosity, his initial hostility to the church (Acts 7:58, 8:1–3) might not have been as harsh as it was. He might have shared the more sympathetic view that his fellow Pharisees, Nicodemus (John 3:1–2, 7:50–51, 19:39) and Joseph of Arimathea, (Matt 27:57; Mark 15:43; Luke 23:50–51; John 19:38) and many of the Jewish priests (Acts 6:7) had.

Proposed Timeline of Jesus' Life and the Apostolic Age

- The Holy Spirit descended after Peter's sermon on Pentecost, Sunday, May 22, 6 Sivan, AD 33 (Acts 2:1–4).[11]
- Peter and John went to the temple, where Peter healed a lame beggar and then preached in Solomon's portico. The Sanhedrin arrested Peter and John, who defended themselves boldly. The council threatened them but released them on May 27, AD 33 (Acts 3:1—4:23).[12]
- The believers had everything in common from May 27, AD 33 and ongoing (Acts 4:32–35).
- Joseph Barnabas donated a field to the apostles on May 30, AD 33 (Acts 4:36).
- Ananias and Sapphira donated a field to the church but lied about its value and died on June 1, AD 33 (Acts 5:1–11).
- The apostles worked many signs and wonders. Multitudes of believers were added to the Lord on June 5, AD 33 (Acts 5:12–16).
- The Sanhedrin arrested Peter and John again on June 6, AD 33. An angel freed them, and they continued to preach (Acts 5:17–21).[13]
- Peter and John returned to the Temple and resumed preaching. The Sanhedrin arrested them again. They refused to obey the Sanhedrin, saying they must obey God rather than men. The council wanted to kill them, but Gamaliel urged patience. Peter and John were released, June 7, AD 33 (Acts 5:22–41).
- The apostles continued to preach Jesus every day from June 7, AD 33 and ongoing (Acts 5:42).
- The apostles chose seven to serve the church between June 7 and December 25, AD 33 (Acts 6:1–6).[14]
- The number of disciples in Jerusalem, including many priests, multiplied in Jerusalem (Acts 6:7).
- Thaddaeus, at Thomas's instigation, went to Edessa in Greater Armenia, healed King Abgarus, and converted the whole city, AD 33.[15]
- Chanukah: 24 Kislev to 3 Tevet, starting Saturday, the Sabbath, December 3, AD 33.

---

11. Added to the church that day were "about three thousand souls." At this assembly were Jews from Rome (Acts 2:10). These converts probably were the first to take the gospel there.

12. The release was probably no later than 3 p.m., because this was the Sabbath Eve, Friday, 11 Sivan.

13. The high priest scolded them for preaching in the name of Jesus. Peter and the apostles said they must obey God rather than men. The council wanted to kill them, but Gamaliel counseled otherwise, so the council beat the apostles, warned them to stop preaching about Jesus, and let them go.

14. The seven were Stephen, Philip, Prochorus, Nicanor, Timon, Parmenas, and Nicolaus (a proselyte of Antioch).

15. Eusebius, *Church History* 1:13.

APPENDICES

- Members of the synagogue of freedmen (*libertini*) and Jews from Cyrene, Alexandria, Cilicia, and Asia disputed with Stephen, who was doing great signs and wonders, and stirred up opposition to him, between December 18 and 25, AD 33 (Acts 6:8–11).[16]

- The anti-Christian Jews seized Stephen and dragged him before the council. Stephen testified to them, and they stoned him to death, with Paul approving, on December 26, AD 33 (Acts 6:12–8:1, 22:20).[17]

AD 33–34

- Paul ravaged the church in Jerusalem between December 29, AD 33, and March 28, AD 34 (Acts 8:1–3).[18]

AD 34

- All believers except the apostles scattered throughout Judea and Samaria and went about preaching the word, reaching as far as Antioch (Acts 8:1, 4, 11:19).

- Philip proclaimed Christ in Samaria, between January 1 and 15, AD 34 (Acts 8:5–8).[19]

- Peter and John visited Samaria, preached, and converted both men and women in many villages there, and rebuked Simon Magus, who sought to buy the gift of the Holy Spirit, between January 15 and 22, AD 34 (Acts 8:9–25).

- Jewish Christians from Jerusalem preached to the Jews in Antioch between January 23 and February 6, AD 34 (Acts 11:19).[20] Probably Peter was one of them, because he is thought to have founded the church in Antioch.[21]

- On the road from Jerusalem to Gaza, Philip converted the Ethiopian eunuch on January 23, AD 34 (Acts 8:26–38).[22]

16. The synagogue of freedmen (*libertini*) probably consisted of Jews from Rome who had been taken there as slaves after Pompey's conquest of Judea in 63 BC and who subsequently had been freed.

17. This is Saint Stephen's Day in the Catholic Church, commemorating his martyrdom. The church does not always get dates right, but there is nothing wrong with this date, and it fits the rest of the timeline of Acts.

18. The assumption is that Paul devoted at least ninety days to this campaign, presumably studying under a possibly hesitant Gamaliel as he did so.

19. This was a journey of about forty-five miles from Jerusalem.

20. They traveled 354 miles overland to plant a Jewish Christian church in Syria, demonstrating that Paul's concern with the spread of Christianity to Syria was merited.

21. Perhaps Peter led Luke, a native of Antioch, to Christ at this time. Or, given Luke's closeness to Paul, maybe Paul led Luke to the Lord after AD 43.

22. This was a journey of about eighty-four miles.

Proposed Timeline of Jesus' Life and the Apostolic Age

- The Holy Spirit led Philip to Azotus (Ashdod) on January 24, AD 34 (Acts 8:39–40).[23]
- Philip preached in villages from Azotus all the way to Caesarea (Acts 8:40).[24]
- Jewish Christians from Cyprus and Cyrene preached in Antioch, converting many gentiles, between February 13 and 20, AD 34 (Acts 11:20–21).
- The Jerusalem church sent Barnabas to Antioch between March 29 and April 2, AD 34 (Acts 11:22–24).[25] Barnabas encouraged the believers in Antioch, where believers were first called Christians. Even more came to the Lord.
- Paul encountered the risen Jesus for the first time on the Damascus Road around Sunday, April 2, AD 34. This was when Jesus spoke to Paul for the first time (Acts 9:3–9, 22:4–11, 26:12–18).[26]
- Ananias healed and baptized Paul, April 8, AD 34 (Acts 9:10–19, 22:12–16).[27]
- Paul proclaimed Christ in the Damascus synagogues, between April 15 and May 6, AD 34 (Acts 9:20–22).[28]
- In the summer of AD 34, James the son of Zebedee may have sailed on a missionary journey to Spain.
- Paul traveled to Arabia between May 7 and 22, AD 34 (Gal 1:17, 4:25).[29]

AD 34–37

- Paul remained in Arabia from AD 34 to 37 (Gal 1:18).[30]

AD 37

- Tiberius died. Caligula became emperor, AD 37.

23. This was a journey of about sixteen miles.
24. This was a journey of about sixty miles.
25. This was a journey of about 354 miles.
26. Although the certain date is unknown, this timing fits. Luke gives three accounts of this event in Acts, which complement but do not contradict each other. This was a journey of about 195 miles.
27. Luke gives two accounts of this in Acts which complement but do not contradict each other.
28. This assumes he did so on three Sabbaths.
29. It would have taken Paul about fifteen days to travel the 435 miles to Mount Horeb (Sinai) in Arabia, the present Jabal al–Laws in Saudi Arabia. This is a conjectural but logical destination, and, as Paul says, the Mountain of Moses is not in the Sinai Peninsula, but in Arabia (Gal 4:25).
30. Paul's trip to Arabia and back to Damascus took about 2.9 years (about 1,059 days). Paul said that after three years he returned to Jerusalem. "After three years" means three years after his conversion.

APPENDICES

- Paul returned to Damascus and preached in the synagogues there again between March 30 and April 21, AD 37 (Gal 1:17).[31]

- When the ethnarch under the Syrian King Aretas demanded that Paul be arrested and killed, Paul escaped Damascus in a basket around April 22, AD 37 (Acts 9:23–25; 2 Cor 11:32–33).[32]

- Paul returned to Jerusalem, between April 22 and 26, AD 37, and stayed fifteen days with Peter (Acts 9:26; Gal 1:18).[33]

- The apostles, other than Peter and James, Jesus' half-brother, were absent from Jerusalem and therefore probably abroad in mission fields (Gal 1:19).

- Paul preached in Jerusalem. He attempted to join the disciples, but they feared him. Barnabas reconciled them, and Paul disputed with the Hellenist Jews, who sought to kill him, between April 28 and May 12, AD 37 (Acts 9:26–29, 26:20).[34]

- Jesus spoke to Paul for the second time in the temple, May 9, AD 37 (Acts 22:17–21).[35]

- Since the Hellenic Jews wanted to kill him, the brothers took Paul to Caesarea, between May 13 and 16, AD 37 (Acts 9:28–30).[36]

- Paul returned to Tarsus, between May 20 and 24, AD 37 (Acts 9:30).[37]

- Paul remained in Tarsus for six years, between May 24, AD 37, and May 19, AD 43 (Acts 11:25–26).[38]

31. Paul traveled 435 miles back to Damascus. This assumes he preached there over three Sabbaths.

32. Luke used the phrase "when many days had passed" (Acts 9:23) to cover the three years since Paul's conversion (Gal 1:18). This is not the only time Luke makes such a breathtaking abridgement. He does so in his Gospel (Luke 9:51). In this verse, Luke says "as the days drew near for Him to be taken up, [Jesus] set His face to go to Jerusalem." Reading the four Gospels "horizontally," it is clear that this verse is set in the beginning of AD 32, more than a year before the crucifixion. Jesus did not make a beeline for the cross from Luke 9:51; rather Luke, a selective historian, trained his telescope on the cross from that vantage point. John, in his Gospel, also abridges AD 32 dramatically. John 10:21 skips from October AD 31 to John 10:22 in December (Chanukah) AD 32, a gap of thirteen months.

33. It would have taken him about four days to get back to Jerusalem. On the way, he would have had to pass the spot on the Damascus Road where he met Christ.

34. This assumes he preached over three Sabbaths. The Hellenist Jews were probably the Sadducees (the family of Annas and Caiaphas).

35. This was Saturday, a Sabbath, 7 Sivan, the second day of Pentecost. Jesus said to Paul, "Make haste and get out of Jerusalem quickly, because they will not accept your testimony about me . . . Go, for I will send you far away to the Gentiles."

36. This was a journey of about sixty-nine miles. Peter probably went to Lydda at the same time. Possibly Paul and Peter walked together from Jerusalem to the coast.

37. This was a journey of about 112 miles. He could sail this time, as the season was safe for navigation.

38. Paul's trip to and from Arabia took three years. He served in Antioch one more year. Paul and Barnabas took famine relief to Jerusalem in the year Herod Agrippa I killed James the son of Zebedee, which was AD 44. The interval between the Paul's conversion and the death of James (AD 34–44)

- In June AD 37, Peter went to Lydda and healed Aeneas (Acts 9:31–34).[39]
- Peter went to Joppa and raised Tabitha (Dorcas) from the dead (Acts 9:36–42).
- Peter went to Caesarea around June 10, AD 37 (Acts 10:1–24).[40]
- Peter entered Cornelius's household and led the whole family to the Lord, probably on June 11, AD 37 (Acts 10:25–48).[41]
- Peter justified the conversion of Cornelius's gentile household to the Jewish Christians in Jerusalem between June 16 and 19, AD 37 (Acts 11:1–18).[42]

AD 39

- Paul (or someone) was taken up into the third heaven, AD 39 (2 Cor 12:2–3).[43]

AD 41

- Caligula died. Claudius became emperor on January 24, AD 41.

AD 41–43

- Peter and Mark preached to Jews in Pontus, Galatia, Cappadocia, Asia, and Bithynia, sometime between AD 41 and 43.

AD 43

- Peter and Mark pushed on from Bithynia to Rome around April AD 43.[44]

---

equals ten years. Subtracting three years in Arabia and one year in Antioch leaves six years; hence Paul remained in obscurity in Tarsus for six years.

39. This was a journey of about thirty miles.
40. This was a journey of about forty-two miles.
41. This was a journey of about forty-two miles.
42. This was a journey of about sixty-nine miles.
43. This is fourteen years prior to when Paul wrote 2 Corinthians.
44. Eusebius says that Simon Magus, after being rebuked by Peter, went to Rome, where he developed a cult that revered Simon as a god. In the reign of Claudius (January 24, AD 41–October 13, AD 54), Peter pursued him to Rome and defeated the cult, establishing the gospel in the Eternal City. Eusebius, *Church History* 2:14–15. This was a journey of about 1,968 miles.

Appendices

- Nathanael Bartholomew and Judas Thaddaeus Lebbaeus brought the gospel to Armenia in AD 43.[45]

- Peter preached in Rome, formally founded the church there, and John Mark, his companion, recorded his sermon notes as the Gospel of Mark. This was between May 6 and August 13, AD 43.[46]

- Barnabas brought Paul from Tarsus to Antioch, between May 20 and 24, AD 43 (Acts 11:25–26; Gal 1:21).[47]

- Peter and John Mark arrived back in Jerusalem from Rome, around September 1, AD 43, before the sailing weather became dangerous at the time of Yom Kippur (Acts 27:9).[48]

- James, the son of Zebedee, may have arrived back in Jerusalem from Spain before Yom Kippur of AD 43.

AD 44

- Paul served in the Antioch church for one year. Paul led Titus to Christ there, between May 24, AD 43, and May 23, AD 44 (Acts 11:26; Titus 1:4).

- Agabus traveled from Jerusalem to Antioch between December 30, AD 43, and January 5, AD 44.[49] He predicted a famine in Judea.[50] The Antioch church decided to send a relief fund to Jerusalem by the hands of Barnabas and Paul (Acts 11:27–30).

- Paul and Barnabas took famine relief from the rich Antioch church to the poor church in Jerusalem between March 16 and 21, AD 44 (Acts 11:29–30).[51]

- Herod Agrippa I killed James, the brother of John, March 31, 15 Nisan, AD 44 (Acts 12:1–2).

- Herod arrested Peter on April 1, 16 Nisan, AD 44 (Acts 12:3–5).

---

45. "Saints Thaddaeus and Bartholomew," *The Armenian Prelacy*.
46. Finegan, *Handbook*, 382.
47. This was a journey of about 124 miles.
48. This was a journey of about 1,992 miles.
49. This was a journey of about 195 miles.
50. Josephus, *Ant.* 20:2. As foretold by the prophet Agabus and recorded by Josephus, famine raged in Judea under the procurator Cassius Fadus (AD 44–47). Orosius, in his *Histories against Pagans*, 7:6:9, 12, placed it in the fourth year of Claudius's reign. Claudius began to reign on January 24, AD 41, so his fourth year began on January 24, AD 45. The famine therefore endured from the Passover of AD 45 to the Passover of AD 47, 739 days or slightly over two years.
51. This was a journey of about 195 miles.

Proposed Timeline of Jesus' Life and the Apostolic Age

- An angel rescued Peter on April 2, 17 Nisan, AD 44 (Acts 12:6–18). After his escape, Peter went to the house of Mary, the mother of John Mark. It was a large house and probably contained the upper room where Jesus held the Last Supper.

- Peter left for Caesarea on April 3, 18 Nisan, AD 44 (Acts 12:19).[52] He spent some time there.

- Herod addressed the people of Tyre and Sidon after Passover and was struck down around April 8, AD 44 (Acts 12:20–23).

- Herod died around April 13, AD 44 (Acts 12:23). Herod probably did not die at the same moment he was struck down. Luke says in Greek that he was immediately struck down and that, having been eaten by worms, he breathed his last. The idea is probably that he collapsed, lingered a few days, died, and when the royal physicians examined his corpse, they found he had been infested by parasites.

- The word of God multiplied, and Paul, Barnabas, and Titus returned to Antioch with John Mark, April 14–19, AD 44 (Acts 12:24–25).[53]

- Barnabas, Paul, and John Mark set out on the first missionary journey between May 25 and September 6, AD 44 (Acts 13:1–3, 5).

- Paul and his team landed in Cyprus, May 26, AD 44 (Acts 13:4–5).[54]

- Paul preached in Cypriot synagogues from May 28 to June 18, AD 44 (Acts 13:5–6).[55]

- The Roman proconsul Sergius Paulus believed the gospel when Paul blinded Elymas bar Jesus, around June 19, AD 44 (Acts 13:6–12).

- Paul, Barnabas, and John Mark sailed to Perga between June 20 and 26, AD 44 (Acts 13:13).[56]

- John Mark left Paul and Barnabas and returned to Jerusalem, June 26 to July 4, AD 44 (Acts 13:13).[57]

- Paul and Barnabas walked to Pisidian Antioch between June 27 and July 1, AD 44 (Acts 13:14).[58]

- Paul preached in Antioch, around July 2, AD 44 (Acts 13:14–43).

- Paul preached in Antioch again, around July 9, AD 44 (Acts 13:44–52).

---

52. This was a journey of about 69 miles.
53. This was a journey of about 451 miles.
54. The distance traveled from Antioch was 124 miles.
55. This occurred probably over at least three Sabbaths, traveling across the island from Salamis to Paphos, about 149 miles.
56. The distance traveled was about 214 miles.
57. The distance traveled was about 656 miles.
58. The distance traveled was about 118 miles.

Appendices

- The Jews of Antioch stirred up persecution against them, so Paul and Barnabas walked to Iconium, around July 10 and 14, AD 44 (Acts 13:51).[59]

- Paul preached in Iconium for a long time, from July 16 to 31, AD 44 (Acts 14:1–5).

- Controversy arose in Iconium, and gentiles and Jews, together with their rulers, threatened to mistreat them, so Paul and Barnabas fled to Lystra, around August 1, AD 44 (Acts 14:4–7).[60]

- John Mark may have founded the church in Egypt, between AD 44 and 49.[61]

- Paul healed a cripple and rejected worship by the Lystrans as the god Hermes around August 2, AD 44 (Acts 14:8–18).

- Jews from Antioch and Iconium arrived and stoned Paul, leaving him for dead, around August 2, AD 44 (Acts 14:19).[62]

- Paul and Barnabas went to Derbe, between August 3 and 5, AD 44 (Acts 14:20).[63]

- Paul and Barnabas preached in Derbe and made many disciples, between August 6 and 13, AD 44 (Acts 14:21).[64]

- Paul and Barnabas returned to Lystra,[65] returned to Iconium,[66] and returned to Pisidian Antioch,[67] between August 14 and 24, AD 44 (Acts 14:21–23).

- Paul and Barnabas returned to Perga and Attalia, between August 25 and 31, AD 44 (Acts 14:24–25).[68]

- Paul and Barnabas sailed to Syrian Antioch, between September 1 and 6, AD 44 (Acts 14:26–27).[69] They arrived thirteen days before Yom Kippur. They reported to the church that God had opened the door of faith to the gentiles. Paul's first missionary journey took 103 days or about 3.5 months. The distance traveled was about 1,319 miles.

- Yom Kippur fell on September 19 in AD 44.

---

59. The distance traveled was about ninety-three miles.
60. The distance traveled was about twenty-four miles.
61. The distance traveled was about four hundred miles.
62. The Jews traveled ninety-three miles to do this.
63. The distance traveled was about fifty-three miles.
64. This probably occurred over two Sabbaths.
65. The distance traveled was about fifty-three miles.
66. The distance traveled was about twenty-four miles.
67. They appointed elders in every church and committed them to the Lord. The distance traveled was 152 miles.
68. The distance traveled was about 118 miles.
69. It was not safe to navigate the Mediterranean after Yom Kippur (Acts 27:9). The distance traveled was about 443 miles.

AD 45–46

- Famine struck Judea from AD 45 to 47 (Acts 11:28).[70]

AD 48

- Paul, Barnabas, and Titus sailed to Caesarea and walked to Jerusalem to see how the survivors of the famine had fared. This was a logical time for the trip, because it was the third springtime since the famine began, when, if the famine were really over, the signs of fresh growth would be evident. Judaizers spied on Titus and tried to compel him to be circumcised sometime in AD 48 fourteen years after Paul's conversion (Gal 2:1–5).[71] Paul and Barnabas refused to submit to the Judaizers.
- James the half-brother of Jesus, Peter, and John gave Paul and Barnabas "the right hand of fellowship" and confirmed the mission Jesus had given them, of bringing the gospel to the uncircumcised sometime in AD 48 (Gal 2:9).
- Paul and his companions returned to Antioch sometime in AD 48.[72]

AD 49

- Paul and Barnabas remained in Syrian Antioch for no little time with the disciples from the end of the first missionary journey in September AD 44 until around May AD 49 (Acts 14:28).[73]
- The Roman emperor Claudius expelled the Jews from Rome in AD 49, the ninth year of his reign (Acts 18:2).[74]

---

70. Josephus, *Ant.* 20:2. As foretold by the prophet Agabus and recorded by Josephus, famine raged in Judea under the procurator Cassius Fadus (AD 44–46). Orosius, in his *Histories against Pagans*, 7:6:9, 12, placed it in the fourth year of Claudius's reign. Claudius began to reign on January 24, AD 41, so his fourth year began on January 24, AD 45. The famine therefore endured from the Passover of AD 45 to the Passover of AD 47, 739 days or slightly over two years.

71. Paul said this was fourteen years after his conversion; since his conversion occurred around April 2, AD 34, this trip to Jerusalem occurred just before Passover, 14 Nisan, Monday, April 13, AD 48. This was a logical time for the trip, because it was the third springtime since the famine began, when, if the famine were really over, the signs of fresh growth would be evident.

72. This whole round trip covered about 926 miles.

73. Luke was given to sweeping condensations in his historical narratives, so "no little time" is about two years. New Testament writers masterfully combined literary economy with historical precision.

74. Orosius, *Histories against the Pagans* 7:6:15. Claudius's first regnal year began on January 24, AD 41, so his ninth year began on January 24, AD 49.

- Judaizers from Jerusalem taught the church in Antioch that they must become Jewish to be Christians, between March 24 and 27, AD 49 (Acts 15:1; Gal 2:12).

- Paul and Barnabas debated the Judaizers in Antioch, around March 25–28, AD 49 (Acts 15:2).

- Peter visited Antioch, between March 30 and April 15, AD 49 (Gal 2:11).

- Fearing criticism by the Judaizers, Peter refused to eat with gentiles, and Barnabas joined him in this, between March 3 and April 10, AD 49 (Gal 2:12–13).[75]

- Paul rebuked Peter publicly, around April 10, AD 49 (Gal 2:14).[76]

- Peter sailed to Caesarea and returned to Jerusalem, between April 15 and 20, AD 49 (Acts 15:7).[77]

- The Antioch church appointed Paul and Barnabas to go to Jerusalem and consult all the apostles on the question of Judaizing, between May 2 and 10, AD 49 (Acts 15:2).

- In Antioch, Paul wrote the book of Galatians telling the gentiles they did not need be become Jews to become Christians (3:23–25, 5:12). He sent off copies to the churches in Perga, Pisidian Antioch, Iconium, Lystra, and Derbe (Greater Galatia) between May 13 and 19, AD 49 (Gal 1:2).[78]

- Paul and Barnabas walked from Antioch to Jerusalem, preaching in Phoenicia (modern Lebanon) and Samaria as they went, May 27 to June 17, AD 49 (Acts 15:3–4).[79]

- The Jerusalem Council met, between June 21 and 23, AD 49 (Acts 15:5–29). All the apostles were present except James, son of Zebedee, who had died in AD 44.

- Matthew probably composed his Gospel in AD 49 and then began missionary journeys to Macedonia, and Parthia.[80]

- After AD 49, Peter preached in Pontus, Galatia, Cappadocia, Betania, Asia Minor (Bithynia), and Italy. His missionary journeys culminated in Rome, probably before AD 57–59.[81]

---

75. This was over the Passover, Saturday, April 3 to Sunday, April 11, AD 49.
76. This might have been in the synagogue on the last Sabbath of Passover week.
77. Peter had to return from Antioch to Jerusalem to be present at the Jerusalem Council.
78. Paul did not mention the Jerusalem Council in Galatians, meaning that he must have written and sent the epistle prior to the council. Otherwise, he would not have needed to write Galatians; he could simply have sent the churches in Galatia the council's decree, which is what he did in his second missionary journey (Acts 15:25, 16:4).
79. The distance covered was about 451 miles.
80. Davies and Allen, *Matthew 1–7*.
81. Hippolytus, "List of the Apostles and Disciples." Peter's travels took him at least 3,000 miles.

Proposed Timeline of Jesus' Life and the Apostolic Age

- Paul and Barnabas walked to Caesarea, between June 17 to July 1, AD 49 (Acts 15:33–35).[82]

- Paul and Barnabas sailed from Caesarea to Antioch, between July 1 and 6, AD 49 (Acts 15:35).[83]

- Paul and Barnabas remained in Antioch for "some days," between July 7 and 28, AD 49 (Acts 15:36).[84] They decided to return to the churches they had planted on the first missionary journey to see how they were faring. The churches had been on their own for five years.

- Paul and Barnabas separated over taking John Mark on a second missionary journey. Instead, Paul and Silas (Silvanus) set out for Syria around July 29, AD 49. Barnabas and Mark returned to Cyprus (Acts 15:37–40; Gal 1:21).

- Paul and Silas walked from Antioch back to the churches in Syria and Cilicia. Paul had to bypass his hometown of Tarsus again, August 4–28, AD 49 (Acts 15:41).

- Paul disseminated the letter of the Jerusalem Council, and the churches grew, between August 4 and October 12, AD 49 (Acts 16:4–5).

- Paul met Timothy in Lystra in the house of his mother Eunice and grandmother Lois, around August 29 to September 7, AD 49 (Acts 16:1–3). Paul circumcised Timothy.

- Paul, Silas, and Timothy walked to the border of Mysia and attempted to enter Bithynia, but the Holy Spirit prevented them, between September 8 and October 12, AD 49 (Acts 16:6–7).[85]

- Paul walked to Troas, between October 13 and 16, AD 49 (Acts 16:8).[86]

- Luke probably finished his Gospel in the fall of AD 49.

- Changing from the pronoun "they" to "we," Luke joined Paul, Silas, and Timothy in Troas between October 13 and 20, AD 49 (Acts 16:10).

- Paul saw a vision calling him to Macedonia, around October 19, AD 49 (Acts 16:9–10).

- Paul, Silas, Timothy, and Luke sailed to Samothrace and Neapolis and walked to Philippi, between October 20 and 22, AD 49 (Acts 16:11–12).[87]

---

82. The distance traveled was about 68 miles.
83. The distance traveled was about 390 miles.
84. Perhaps Paul converted Luke in Antioch at this time.
85. The distance traveled was more than 600 miles.
86. The distance traveled was about 200 miles.
87. This was a dangerous time of year to sail (Acts 27:9). The fact that Paul chose to travel by sea via Samothrace suggests that he felt the Macedonian call was too urgent to permit the longer route overland. On the other hand, this was not a long ocean voyage, so the risk was not as great as sailing

- Paul converted Lydia in Philippi on a Sabbath, October 23, AD 49 (Acts 16:13–15).
- Paul exorcised a slave girl, around November 15, AD 49 (Acts 16:16–18).[88]
- The slave girl's owners had Paul and Silas beaten and thrown into a Philippian prison, while Luke and Timothy were spared, around November 17, AD 49 (Acts 16:19–40). An earthquake broke them out of jail. The jailer and his whole household came to the Lord.
- After their release, Paul and his team walked to Thessalonica, between November 21 and 24, AD 49 (Acts 17:1).[89]
- Paul preached in Thessalonica over three Sabbath days, between November 27 and December 11, AD 49 (Acts 17:2–4).
- Jews in Thessalonica rioted against Paul, around December 12, AD 49 (Acts 17:5–9).
- The believers in Thessalonica sent Paul to Berea, between December 13 and 14, AD 49 (Acts 17:10).[90]

AD 49–50

- Paul preached in the Berean synagogue, where many believed, between December 18, AD 49, and January 1, AD 50 (Acts 17:11–12).

AD 50

- Jews from Thessalonica followed Paul to Berea, between January 2 and 3, AD 50 (Acts 17:13).
- The Berean believers sent Paul with the other followers for Athens (probably including Luke), around January 4, AD 50 (Acts 17:14–15).[91]
- Paul and probably Luke arrived in Athens, around January 6, AD 50 (Acts 17:16).[92] He sent some of his followers back to Berea, instructing Silas and Timothy to rejoin him in Corinth.

---

to Rome, Alexandria, or Antioch. The ship could island-hop and did so, stopping at Samothrace. The distance traveled was about 620 miles.

88. This assumes that Paul preached in Philippi over four Sabbaths.
89. The distance traveled was about 94 miles.
90. The distance traveled was 47 miles.
91. The distance traveled was about 250 miles.
92. This was still a dangerous time of year to sail (Acts 27:9), but the need to get Paul out of Berea was pressing, and ships traveling from Macedonia to Athens could hug the coast and shelter in the Pagasetic, Malian, North Euboean, and Petalioi Gulfs, if needed.

- Paul preached in the Athenian synagogue, between January 8 and 15, AD 50 (Acts 17:17).

- Paul conversed with Epicurean and Stoic philosophers, between January 16 and 22, AD 50 (Acts 17:18–21).

- Paul addressed the Areopagus, around January 23, AD 50 (Acts 17:22–34). Dionysius the Areopagite and a woman named Demaris were among the few Athenians who believed.

- Paul left, probably with Luke, for Corinth, around January 25, AD 50 (Acts 18:1).

- Paul and Luke arrived in Corinth and met Aquila and Priscilla, Christian Jews evicted from Rome by Claudius, around January 26, AD 50 (Acts 18:2–3). They were tentmakers, like Paul, and Paul took up residence with them.[93]

- Paul first preached in the Corinthian synagogue around February 5, AD 50 (Acts 18:4).

- Paul preached in the synagogue every Sabbath, between February 5 and 19, AD 50 (Acts 18:4).[94]

- Silas and Timothy reached Corinth from Macedonia, around February 13, AD 50 (Acts 18:5).[95]

- Timothy brought encouraging news about the faith of the church in Thessalonica, and Paul wrote 1 Thessalonians to the believers there probably around February, AD 50 (1 Thess 1:1, 3:6).

- The Jews rejected the gospel, and Paul turned to the gentiles, around February 19, AD 50 (Acts 18:5–8).

- After this Paul remained in Corinth one year and six months. Timothy and Silas (and probably Luke) were with him (Acts 18:5, 11; 2 Cor 1:19).

- During this sojourn, Paul must have made a side trip to evangelize Illyricum,[96] since this occurred before he wrote the book of Romans in AD 54 (Rom 15:19).[97]

- Jesus spoke directly to Paul for the third time in Corinth, around February 20, AD 50 (Acts 18:9–10).[98]

93. The distance traveled was about 56 miles.
94. The conjecture here is that "every" Sabbath means at least three Sabbaths.
95. Possibly Silas and Timothy remained in Berea to settle the church there. Possibly they walked from Berea to Thebes and then to Corinth, as ships' passage at this time of year was dangerous (Acts 27:9) and perhaps hard to secure. Either way, they had a delayed arrival in Corinth.
96. Eusebius, *Church History* 4:1
97. If Paul walked to Illyricum, it would have taken about thirty-three days each way. If he sailed from Corinth, it would have taken about eight days each way; thus, if he sailed in good weather, the whole trip might have taken a month or less.
98. Jesus said, "Do not be afraid, but go on speaking and do not be silent, for I am with you, and no one will attack you to harm you, for I have many in this city who are my people." The distance traveled

APPENDICES

- In Corinth, Paul wrote 2 Thessalonians, probably around April AD 50. The Thessalonians must have had some questions about Paul's description of the coming of the Lord in 1 Thessalonians, which they must have put to Paul by letter or messenger, for in 2 Thessalonians Paul clarified that the Lord had not yet come and referred to a man of lawlessness and to a discussion about this man between Paul and the Thessalonians whose details he assumed they knew but which he did not disclose to third-party readers of this letter (2 Thess 2:1–12).

AD 51

- Junius Gallio became proconsul of Achaia (Greece), around July AD 51 (Acts 18:12).[99]
- Gallio dismissed the Jews' charges against Paul, around July 28, AD 51 (Acts 18:13–16).[100]
- Paul remained "many days" longer in Corinth before sailing to Syria, between July 29 and August 22, AD 51 (Acts 18:18).[101]
- Paul had his hair shaved at Cenchreae in the Jewish custom, marking the end of a vow, around August 23, AD 51 (Acts 18:18).
- Paul, Priscilla, Aquila, Timothy, Silas, and Luke sailed for Ephesus, August 24, AD 51 (Acts 18:18–19).
- Paul arrived in Ephesus and reasoned with the Jews in the synagogue, around August 28, AD 51 (Acts 18:19).[102]
- Paul stayed only a short while in Ephesus this time but promised to return, between August 28 and 30, AD 51 (Acts 18:20–21).[103]
- Paul sailed from Ephesus to Caesarea, between August 30 and September 3, AD 51 (Acts 18:22–23).[104]

---

round trip was about 800 miles.

99. Gallio was the elder brother of the famous Roman philosopher and mentor of Nero, Seneca.

100. Frustrated, the Jews beat Sosthenes, the synagogue leader, in front of Gallio, who was indifferent.

101. The "many days" is probably a subset of Paul's total sojourn in Corinth of one year and six months. The significance of the "many days" is that Gallio's refusal to appease the non-Christian Jews meant that Paul could safely leave Corinth at his leisure.

102. The distance traveled was about 310 miles by sea.

103. Aquila and Priscilla remained in Ephesus.

104. The distance traveled was about 900 miles.

Proposed Timeline of Jesus' Life and the Apostolic Age

- Paul traveled from Caesarea to Jerusalem, between September 3 and 6, AD 51 (Acts 18:22–23).[105]

- Apollos, a Christian Jew from Egypt, left Alexandria for Ephesus, around the end of August AD 51. He arrived in Ephesus around September 4. He barely missed meeting Paul. Apollos spoke boldly in Ephesus (Acts 18:24–26).[106]

- Paul arrived in Antioch[107] and spent "some time" there, between September 12 and 25, AD 51 (Acts 18:22–23).[108]

- Apollos went to Corinth, between September 17 and 21, AD 51 (Acts 18:27–28).[109]

- Paul's second missionary journey took 776 days or a little over two years and covered about 4,345 miles.

- Paul embarked on his third missionary journey, walking through Galatia and Phrygia, between September 25 and October 24, AD 51 (Acts 18:23). Either Timothy and Titus were with him or they joined him from elsewhere when he reached Ephesus (1 Cor 4:17; 2 Cor 12:18).[110]

- Paul walked to Ephesus, between October 24 and November 7, AD 51. Apollos was in Corinth at this time (Acts 19:1).[111]

- Paul taught twelve believers who until then had only known John's baptism (Acts 19:1–7), and he preached in the Ephesian synagogue for three months (Acts 19:8). The main congregation in the synagogue opposed him, and so he continued to teach in the hall of Tyrannus in Ephesus for two years, from November 8, AD 51 to February 7, AD 53 (Acts 19:8–10).[112]

- Paul received news of jealousy, quarreling, litigation, factionalism, adultery, incest, and other kinds of immorality in the Corinthian church, probably from Apollos, around November AD 51 (Acts 19:1, 1 Cor 16:12).

- Paul might have been itching to travel to Corinth to sort out the church's problems, but the sailing weather in winter was too dangerous. Even if Paul would have braved it, most sea captains would not. So, from Ephesus, Paul wrote a lost

---

105. The distance traveled was about 68 miles.

106. Having just missed meeting Paul, Apollos would receive instruction from Aquila and Priscilla.

107. The distance traveled was about 451 miles.

108. "Some" time in Greek does not necessarily mean a long time. Paul's second missionary journey took 788 days or about 25.8 months or about 2.16 years. The total distance traveled was about 5,014 miles.

109. He powerfully refuted the Jews in public, showing that Jesus was the Messiah. This was the last window of the year for a safe, long trip by sea.

110. The distance traveled was about 410 miles.

111. From Antioch to Ephesus was a trip of about 710 miles.

112. The three months mentioned in Acts 19:8 is a subset of the two years mentioned in Acts 19:10. No doubt in this interval Paul established many satellite churches in the region, probably including Colossae and the seven churches in Revelation.

APPENDICES

warning letter to the Corinthians, around November 10, AD 51 (1 Cor 5:9).[113] It had to travel overland so it would reach Corinth around the end of AD 51. Timothy was the messenger (1 Cor 4:17).

AD 52

- The Ephesian Jews rejected the gospel, around February 8, AD 52, and Paul left their synagogue and taught in the lecture hall of Tyrannus daily for two years (Acts 19:9–10).[114]
- Paul worked miracles in Ephesus and the sons of Sceva received a demonic rebuke, around February 8, AD 52, and ongoing (Acts 19:11–20).[115]
- Timothy, Chloe's people, Stephanas, Fortunatus, Achaicus, and Sosthenes, the synagogue leader in Corinth, brought Paul news and a letter back from Corinth enquiring about proper sexual mores (1 Cor 1:11). Paul's first letter had not fixed the problems. This news probably reached Paul around the end of February AD 52.
- In Ephesus, Paul wrote 1 Corinthians, probably around the beginning of March AD 52 (1 Cor 1:2). In this letter, Paul revealed that he appreciated Apollos's ministry in Corinth. He acknowledged that he had planted the seed of Christianity in Corinth, and Apollos, his coworker, watered it (1 Cor 3:6–9). He also expounded on many lofty theological themes.
- Probably around this time in Ephesus, Jesus spoke to Paul for the fourth time (1 Cor 11:23).
- Now that the sailing weather was fairer, Timothy took 1 Corinthians to Corinth (1 Cor 4:17, 16:10), along with Chloe's people, Stephanas, Fortunatus, Achaicus, and probably Sosthenes (unless he remained in Ephesus with Paul). Apollos refused to return to Corinth at this time (1 Cor 4:17, 16:12). Apparently, he was fed up with the Corinthian mess.
- First Corinthians was not well received, and Timothy and Titus probably returned quickly to report this to Paul. They probably arrived back in Ephesus around May AD 52.
- In Ephesus, Paul wrote a lost severe letter of tears and anguish to the Corinthians, around May AD 52 (2 Cor 2:4–9, 7:8–12).[116] Since the sailing weather was now

---

113. The warning was not to associate with sexually immoral people.
114. This was the last Sabbath in this three-month interval.
115. The word of the Lord increased and prevailed mightily.
116. He said that he wrote the letter with many tears and to test their obedience, even if it grieved them.

fine, the letter probably reached Corinth before June AD 52. Timothy was the messenger again, along with the Corinthian delegation.

- Probably realizing that the Greek churches needed his personal support, Paul conceived a plan to return to Macedonia, Achaia (Greece), and Jerusalem and then go to Rome (Acts 19:21; 1 Cor 4:18–21; 2 Cor 2:1, 13:1–2; Rom 15:22–24).[117]

- Concluding, after sending the lost letter of tears, that Corinth needed a more personal and urgent intervention, Paul was unwilling to leave Corinth adrift until his planned longer trip. So, he made a second quick round trip to Corinth, around June AD 52 (2 Cor 2:1, 12:14, 13:1).[118]

- Paul and Timothy returned from Corinth to Ephesus, around July AD 52.[119] This is evident because Paul could not have left Ephesus after his second trip to Corinth (2 Cor 2:1, 12:14) and before his third trip to Corinth (Acts 20:1–3) without first returning from Corinth to Ephesus.

- From Ephesus, Paul sent Titus and probably Luke (the brother) to Corinth to help steady the church on the right course until Paul should return (2 Cor 12:18). He sent them off while the sailing weather was still good, before Yom Kippur of AD 52.[120]

AD 53

- In the summer of AD 53, Paul apparently sent Aquila and Priscilla from Ephesus to Rome to check how the church had survived Claudius's expulsion edict. This is suggested because when Paul wrote Romans they were back in Rome, where the church, or at least a small group, met in their house (Rom 16:3–5).[121]

- Paul sent Timothy and Erastus ahead of him from Ephesus into Macedonia (Acts 19:22).

---

117. Paul appears to be musing here, but not making specific dates. He probably made a quick trip to Corinth during his Ephesian sojourn, but his full tour of Macedonia, Greece, Jerusalem, and Rome would not happen until AD 54–57.

118. The distance traveled round trip was about 621 miles by sea.

119. Paul remained in Ephesus for a total interval of two years. The quick, roundtrip intervention in Corinth must have been a subset of this time frame.

120. He instructed Titus to meet him in Troas, but Titus would not actually rendezvous with Paul until Paul reached Macedonia.

121. Aquila and Priscilla probably felt it was safe to return to Rome despite Claudius's edict of AD 49 expelling all Jews. While Claudius's edict surely expired with his death on October 13, AD 54, even before he died the decree had probably relaxed, as a similar edict of Tiberius in AD 19 also "became a dead letter" before Tiberius's death. Bruce, "Christianity under Claudius," 317. The distance traveled was about 1,035 miles.

APPENDICES

- A riot broke out in Ephesus, around November 4, AD 53 (Acts 19:23–41).[122]
- Paul gathered the disciples in Ephesus, encouraged them, and set out for Macedonia (Acts 20:1).
- Paul traveled to Troas, around November 7–20, AD 53 (2 Cor 2:12–13).[123] He was sorry to miss Titus there, so he pushed on to Macedonia.[124]
- At or before this time, Jesus spoke to Paul a fifth time (2 Cor 12:9).
- In Macedonia, Paul met Timothy, Erastus, and Titus, who had probably arrived overland from Greece after the last fair sailing season, which ended in September. This is probably why Titus was delayed and failed to make the rendezvous with Paul in Troas.[125]
- Titus brought Paul good news from Corinth, between November 21, AD 53, and January 7, AD 54 (Acts 20:2, 2 Cor 7:6–14).
- In Philippi, Jesus spoke to Paul directly for the sixth time around AD 53 (2 Cor 12:9).
- In Philippi, in response to the good news from Corinth, Paul wrote 2 Corinthians, a letter of commendation, around November 30, AD 53 (2 Cor 7:6, 13–16).[126]
- Titus and probably Luke (the praised brother) carried 2 Corinthians to Corinth (2 Cor 8:16–23, 9:3–5).
- In Corinth, Titus collected funds for the Jerusalem church, while Paul collected funds in Macedonia (2 Cor 8:6–7).

AD 53–54

- Paul arrived in Corinth and remained there three months, between January 8 and April 7, AD 54 (Acts 20:3).[127] There he met Titus, collected funds for the Jerusalem church (Rom 15:25), and probably received news from Aquila and

---

122. There is no certainty about this date, but the events occurred just before the end of Paul's sojourn in Ephesus.
123. He preached Christ there to good effect.
124. The distance traveled was about 209 miles.
125. The distance traveled was about 300 miles overland
126. Paul remarked that he had experienced affliction in Asia (2 Cor 1:8), which probably refers to the riot at Ephesus.
127. This was deep winter, dangerous sailing weather (Acts 27:9), so Paul no doubt took the overland route. Since he went through "those regions," he probably revisited the churches in Philippi, Thessalonica, Berea, Athens, and Corinth. All the while, he was raising funds for the poor of Jerusalem. The three months refers to his total time in Greece, not in Corinth only. He probably also visited Athens on his way from Macedonia. He collected more funds for the poor of Jerusalem.

Priscilla about the state of the church in Rome, prompting him to write the book of Romans (Rom 16:3).

AD 54

- When the sailing weather was fair, at the end of March AD 54, Phoebe, a deacon of the church in Cenchreae, took the epistle to the Romans from Corinth to Rome (Rom 16:1), probably to Aquila and Priscilla, who were still there.

- Learning of a Jewish plot to kill him, rather than sailing for Syria, Paul sailed from Corinth back to Macedonia and reached Philippi around April 7, 13 Nisan, AD 54 (Acts 20:3–6). With him were Sopater, son of Pyrrhus, Aristarchus and Secundus of Thessalonica, Gaius from Derbe, Timothy, Tychicus and Trophimus of Ephesus, and probably Luke and Titus (Acts 20:6; 2 Cor 8:18).[128]

- Paul sent Sopater, Aristarchus, Secundus, Gaius, Timothy, Tychicus, and Trophimus ahead of him to Troas (Acts 20:4).

- In Macedonia, Paul collected more funds for the Jerusalem church (Rom 15:25–27).[129]

- Paul and Luke sailed away from Philippi after Passover, April 17, 22 Nisan, AD 54 (Acts 20:6).

- Paul and Luke arrived in Troas after five days, on April 22, AD 54 (Acts 20:6).[130]

- Paul and his team (Sopater, Aristarchus, Secundus, Thessalonica, Gaius, Timothy, Tychicus, Trophimus, Titus, and Luke) stayed in Troas seven days, until April 29, AD 54. On that last day, Paul raised Eutychus from the dead (Acts 20:7–12).

- Paul walked to Assos, a forty-four mile, two-day journey. He arrived on May 1. His team met him there with a ship and made the short sailing trip to the island of Mytilene (Acts 20:13–14).

- The next day the team sailed to Chios, arriving there on May 2 (Acts 20:15).[131]

- The following day, they sailed to Samos, arriving there on May 3 (Acts 20:15).[132]

- The next day, they reached Miletus, arriving there on May 4 (Acts 20:15).[133]

---

128. The distance traveled was about 330 miles.
129. Paul said in Romans that he was on his way to Jerusalem to deliver the funds he had collected in Macedonia and Achaia. His plan was to reach Jerusalem before Pentecost.
130. The distance traveled was about 280 miles.
131. The distance traveled was about 157 miles.
132. The distance traveled was about 75 miles.
133. The distance traveled was about 40 miles.

- Paul did not stop in Ephesus because he wanted to reach Jerusalem by Pentecost, and because there was a Jewish plot to kill him in that city (Acts 20:3, 16).
- Paul sent for the Ephesian church leaders to meet him in Miletus. The distance between Ephesus and Miletus is about thirty-nine miles, so it would have taken two days for Paul's messenger to reach Ephesus and two days for them to return to Miletus. This meeting therefore occurred after four days of travel (Acts 20:17).
- Paul spoke to the Ephesian leaders in Miletus on May 6, AD 54 (Acts 20:18–38).
- At or before this time, Jesus possibly spoke to Paul a sixth time, as Paul revealed an otherwise unrecorded saying of Jesus, that "it is more blessed to give than to receive" (Acts 20:35). It is also possible that Paul learned of this saying by Jesus from one of the other apostles.
- On May 7, Paul and his team sailed to the island of Cos (Acts 21:1).[134]
- On May 8, the team sailed to the island of Rhodes (Acts 21:1).[135]
- On May 9, the team sailed to the seaport of Patara (Acts 21:1).[136]
- In Patara, they boarded a ship bound for Phoenicia, and, sailing south of Cyprus, they reached Tyre, probably around May 11 (Acts 21:2–3).[137]
- Paul's team stayed in Tyre seven days, between May 12 and 18, AD 54 (Acts 21:4). The disciples there pleaded with Paul not to go to Jerusalem.
- Paul's team proceeded to Ptolemais (Acre) and then stayed there one day, May 19, AD 54 (Acts 21:7).[138]
- Paul went to Caesarea, a forty-mile, two-day walk, arriving there May 21, AD 54 (Acts 21:8).[139]
- Paul stayed in Caesarea with Philip (the deacon and evangelist, not the apostle) "many days," from May 21 to 26, AD 54. Philip had four unmarried daughters who prophesied (Acts 21:8–9).
- Agabus came from Jerusalem and foretold Paul's imprisonment (Acts 21:10–14).
- Paul walked from Caesarea to Jerusalem, a sixty-eight-mile, two-day journey, arriving on May 28, 5 Sivan, AD 54, the eve of Pentecost. He and his team stayed at the house of Mnason, the Cypriot, an early disciple (Acts 21:15–16).[140]

---

134. The distance traveled was about 60 miles.
135. The distance traveled was about 85 miles.
136. The distance traveled was about 90 miles.
137. The distance traveled was about 635 miles.
138. The distance traveled was about 50 miles.
139. The distance traveled was about 40 miles.
140. The distance traveled was about 68 miles.

Proposed Timeline of Jesus' Life and the Apostolic Age

- On May 29, 6 Sivan, Pentecost, AD 54, Paul met James and the elders, delivered his alms to the church, and took a purification vow that lasted for nearly seven days, up until June 4, AD 54. (Acts 21:17–26).[141]

- Paul's missionary team of Greek Christians (Sopater, Aristarchus, Secundus, Thessalonica, Gaius, Timothy, Tychicus, Trophimus, Titus, and Luke) was conspicuous in Jerusalem. Jews falsely accused Paul of bringing Trophimus, an uncircumcised Greek, into the temple. They rioted, and Paul defended himself in Hebrew, around June 4, AD 54 (Acts 21:27—22:21).

- After hearing Paul's defense, the crowd threatened to kill him. To calm the mob, the Roman centurion on duty intended to flog Paul publicly, but Claudius Lysias, the Roman tribune, stopped him when he learned that Paul was a Roman citizen. Lysias took Paul into custody to protect him (Acts 22:22–29).

- Wanting to know the reason for accusations of the Jews, Lysias ordered the Jewish Council to assemble and arraign Paul, around June 5, AD 54 (Acts 22:30—23:9).

- To save him from a riot in the council, the Roman tribune took Paul into the Roman barracks, around June 5, AD 54 (Acts 23:10).

- Jesus spoke to Paul for the seventh time in the Roman barracks, on the night of June 5, AD 54 (Acts 23:11).[142]

- Forty Jews vowed to kill Paul, and Paul's nephew (his sister's son) alerted Paul, who passed the message to Lysias through one of the centurions in the barracks, around June 6, AD 54 (Acts 23:12–22). The would-be assassins swore they would neither eat nor drink until they killed Paul. Paul lived for another fourteen years, so either they broke their vow or they died of fasting.

- Lysias ordered two of his centurions to assemble two hundred Roman infantry, two hundred Roman spearmen, and seventy Roman cavalry, 470 soldiers in all, to escort Paul to Antipatris by night, around 9 p.m., June 6, AD 54 (Acts 23:23–31).[143]

- After traveling all night, the Roman infantry and spearmen returned to Jerusalem. The cavalry escorted Paul the rest of the way to Caesarea, arriving around noon, around June 7, AD 54 (Acts 23:32–35).[144]

- Five days later, meaning five days after Lysias had assembled the Council in Jerusalem on June 5, AD 54, the high priest Ananias (Annas)[145] came from Jerusalem

---

141. Paul's third missionary journey took about 976 days or about 32 months or about 2.67 years. The distance traveled was about 3,155 miles.

142. Jesus said, "Take courage, for as you have testified to the facts about me in Jerusalem, so you must testify also in Rome."

143. The distance traveled was about 40 miles.

144. The distance traveled was about 32 miles.

145. Not the same Annas who, with his son-in-law, Joseph Caiaphas, conducted the mock trial

to Caesarea and accused Paul before Felix, who also heard Paul's defense. Paul made his defense on June 10, AD 54, twelve days after he went up to Jerusalem to worship (Acts 24:11). Felix postponed the verdict for several days, until Lysias the tribune could come to Caesarea. Paul was under guard, but he was free to see his friends. This was from June 14 to 20, AD 54 (Acts 24:1–21).

- Felix and his Jewish wife Drusilla heard Paul's defense, around June 20, AD 54. Felix did not issue a verdict, but kept Paul in Caesarea, sending frequently to speak with him and hoping for a bribe (Acts 24:24–26).
- Paul sent Timothy back to Ephesus to take charge of the church (1 Tim 1:3).
- From Caesarea, Paul wrote 1 Timothy to Timothy in Ephesus, giving him pastoral advice, around April 12, AD 54 (1 Tim 1:3).
- Claudius died. Nero became emperor on October 13, AD 54.

AD 54–56

- Felix kept Paul in prison in Caesarea for two years, probably between June 21, AD 54 and June 19, AD 56, about when Porcius Festus succeeded Felix as governor (Acts 24:27).

AD 56

- After two years' custody under Felix, the new Roman governor Porcius Festus arrived on station in AD 56.[146]
- Three days after his arrival in Caesarea, Festus went to Jerusalem to hear the accusations of the Jews against Paul. This was about June 23, AD 56 (Acts 25:1).
- Festus returned to Caesarea after eight to ten days, around July 2, AD 56 (Acts 25:6).
- The next day, Festus interrogated Paul, around July 3, AD 56. He told Paul, "To Caesar you have appealed. To Caesar you will go" (Acts 25:7–12).
- After some days had passed, Paul testified to Festus, King Herod Agrippa II, and the king's sister, Bernice, around August 1, AD 56 (Acts 25:13—26:30).
- Finding Paul innocent, Festus nevertheless arranged to send him to Rome to grant his appeal to Nero Caesar (Acts 26:31–32).

---

of Jesus. This was Annas or Ananias son of Nebedeus, who officiated from AD 47 to 52. Josephus, *Antiquities*, 20:5:2.

146. Finegan, *Handbook*, 398.

Proposed Timeline of Jesus' Life and the Apostolic Age

- Paul sailed with Luke and Aristarchus, a fellow prisoner, plus some other unnamed prisoners (Acts 27:1, Col 4:10), on his fourth missionary journey in the custody of a kindly Roman centurion of the Augustan Cohort, Julius. This was around August 24, AD 56.[147]

- Paul arrived in Sidon and met friends there, around August 25, AD 56 (Acts 27:1–3).[148]

- He remained with friends in Sidon until about August 28, AD 56 (Acts 27:3). This was the date of Yom Kippur, 1 Tishri ("the Fast"), in that year (Acts 27:9).

- They put out to sea again around August 29, AD 56 (Acts 27:4).

- Because the wind was against them (coming out of the west), they sailed under the lee of Cyprus around September 3, AD 56 (Acts 27:4).[149]

- With the wind coming out of the west, they tacked north across the open sea to the coast of Cilicia, reaching the coast around September 9, AD 56 (Acts 27:5).

- They tacked west against the wind along the coastline of Cilicia and Pamphylia until they reached Myra in Lycia,[150] on the southwest coast of modern Turkey, around September 28, AD 56 (Acts 27:4–5).[151]

- They transferred to a grain ship from Alexandria and put out to sea around October 2, AD 56 (Acts 27:6).

- They reached Cnidus, a city at the tip of a promontory pointing west into the Aegean Sea north of Rhodes, about October 10, AD 56 (Acts 27:7).[152]

- Since the wind was against them and they could not sail further west, they tacked south to Crete, setting out around October 18, AD 56 (Acts 27:7).[153]

- They reached Salmone on the far eastern tip of Crete around October 21, AD 56 (Acts 27:7).

---

147. The distance traveled was about 116 miles.

148. Jerome, in his book *On Illustrious Men*, says that Paul was taken to Rome in "the twenty-fifth year after our Lord's passion, that is, the second [year] of Nero." Jerome was right about the second year of Nero, but wrong about the date of Jesus' passion. He was assuming Jesus' passion was in AD 30, which is a common mistake. Adding twenty-five years to AD 30 yields AD 55. Nero became emperor on October 13, AD 54, so his second regnal year was indeed AD 55, but he had only reigned for 365 days by October 12 of that year. He had reigned for two full years (730 days) by October 12, AD 56. So, AD 56 is the true year of Paul's journey to Rome, and that year was twenty-three, not twenty-five, years after the crucifixion. Jerome wrote more than three hundred years after the crucifixion and had none of our modern tools, like calendar software or spreadsheets, and so his error is understandable.

149. The distance traveled was about 186 miles.

150. Myra is the city where Saint Nicholas (Santa Claus) was born in the third century AD.

151. The distance traveled was about 310 miles.

152. The distance traveled was about 225 miles.

153. The distance traveled was about 186 miles.

APPENDICES

- Sailing against the west wind, they reached Fair Havens in Crete, around October 23, AD 56 (Acts 27:8). Since it was fifty-seven days past Yom Kippur ("the Fast") and well into the dangerous winter sailing weather, Paul warned the ship's captain and crew to winter in Fair Havens (Acts 27:9–10).[154]
- Julius the centurion, the pilot, and the ship's owner ignored Paul's warning and decided to sail for Phoenix in Crete and winter there, putting out to sea around October 26, AD 56 (Acts 27:11–12).
- They sailed with a gentle south wind along the coast of Crete toward Phoenix until around October 28, AD 56 (Acts 27:13).
- A terrible storm whipped in from the northeast and blew their ship to the island of Cauda, south of Crete, where they managed to get under the island's lee shore, around October 29, AD 56.[155]
- They secured the ship's boat on the deck of the large Alexandrian freighter around October 20, AD 56.
- The storm continued to drive them along, and they lowered the sails and dropped a sea anchor for fear that the storm would drive them into the Libyan gulf and the dreaded shoals of Syrtis.
- They threw some of the ship's cargo overboard to lighten the ship. This was around October 31, AD 56 (Acts 27:14–18).
- The storm did not abate, and around October 31, AD 56, the crew jettisoned some of the ship's tackle around November 1, AD 56 (Acts 27:19).
- The storm tossed their ship for many days. Neither sun nor stars appeared for many days. The crew lost all hope (Acts 27:13–20).
- Paul urged the crew to eat and take heart. He predicted that they would run aground on some island (Acts 27:21–26).
- On the fourteenth night, at midnight (which means the early morning of the next day), the sailors suspected that they were approaching land. The date was about November 12, AD 56 (Acts 27:29–32).
- Paul warned Julius that some of the crew were abandoning ship, so the soldiers cut away the ship's boat to prevent this.
- On the fourteenth morning (dawn after the events after the previous midnight), Paul urged the crew to take food and promised that all 276 men aboard would be saved. Then the crew threw their stores into the sea, about November 12, AD 56 (Acts 27:33–38).

---

154. The distance traveled was about 112 miles.
155. The distance traveled was about 40 miles.

Proposed Timeline of Jesus' Life and the Apostolic Age

- Paul was shipwrecked on Malta, around November 12, AD 56 (Acts 27:39–44).[156]
- Paul survived a lethal snakebite and healed many Maltese (Acts 28:3–10; Mark 16:18).
- Paul stayed on Malta for three months (probably about ninety-three days), from about November 12, AD 56, to about February 13, AD 57 (Acts 28:11).
- Paul sailed from Malta to Syracuse in Sicily on an Alexandrian ship, the *Castor and Pollux*, which had wintered in Malta, around February 13, AD 56 (Acts 28:11–12). Although the sailing season in the ancient Mediterranean normally began in March and ended in October,[157] Malta is the southernmost point in Europe and therefore the spring sailing season probably came earlier than in the northern Mediterranean.

AD 57

- Paul reached Syracuse in Sicily around February 19, AD 57 (Acts 28:12). He stayed there for three days.[158]
- Paul sailed from Sicily to Rhegium in southern Italy, around February 22, AD 57 (Acts 28:13).[159]
- One day after reaching Rhegium on February 22, AD 57, Paul reached Puteoli, on the Bay of Naples, on February 24, AD 57. He stayed there with local Christians for seven days, until March 2, AD 57 (Acts 28:13–14).[160]
- Paul and his entourage walked north to Rome, reaching the outskirts of the city, around March 8, AD 57. Roman Christians came out to meet him at the Forum of Appius and Three Taverns. In Rome, Paul was allowed to stay by himself, with only one solider guarding him (Acts 28:14–16).[161]
- After three days, Paul addressed the local Jewish leaders, on Saturday, the Sabbath, March 10, AD 57 (Acts 28:17–29).
- On the following Sabbath, Saturday, March 17, AD 57, Paul addressed the whole congregation of Roman Jews at his place of lodging.

---

156. This was Paul's fourth time being shipwrecked (2 Cor 11:25). The distance traveled was about 740 miles.

157. Bereford, *The Ancient Sailing Season*, 9.

158. The distance traveled was about 128 miles.

159. The distance traveled was about 108 miles.

160. The distance traveled was about 240 miles.

161. The distance traveled was about 133 miles. Paul's trip from Jerusalem to Rome took 1,006 days or nearly 33 months or about 2.76 years and covered about 2,596 miles.

APPENDICES

AD 57–59

- Paul was under house arrest in Rome for two years and wrote the books of Ephesians, Philippians, Colossians, Philemon, and a lost letter to the church of Laodicea (Eph 6:10; Phil 1:13; Col 4:10, 16; Phlm 1:10), between March 18, AD 57, and March 17, AD 59 (Acts 28:30–31).

- While in Rome, Paul encountered Onesimus, a slave who had run away from his master, Philemon, who was the head of the church in Colossae. Paul led Onesimus to the Lord in Rome (Phlm 1–10) and wrote the epistle to Philemon, entreating him to set Onesimus free (Phlm 15–16).

- Mark and Silas arrived in Rome sometime during Paul's first imprisonment (Col 4:10; 1 Pet 5:12–13). Peter also had arrived in Rome sometime between AD 57–59 and resumed his leadership of the Roman church, which he had founded. Peter remained in Rome until his death in AD 68.

AD 59

- Paul possibly wrote the book of Hebrews at this time.[162]
- Nero acquitted Paul around March 17, AD 59.[163]
- In Rome, Luke completed the book of Acts, no later than March AD 59.[164]
- Paul apparently had released[165] Timothy on some mission away from Rome and hoped he would return in time to rejoin him on his travels and ultimately go with him back to Jerusalem (Heb 13:23).

---

162. Paul may also have written Hebrews just after being acquitted by Nero at the end of his two-year imprisonment. The thesis that Luke wrote Hebrews is strong. The case against Paul's authorship is primarily linguistic; the style is more like Luke's than like Paul's (Allen, *Lukan Authorship of Hebrews*, 318–19). This author's thesis is that while in Rome, Paul dictated Hebrews and Luke wrote it, but, unlike an ordinary scribe, Luke added his elegant polish under the guidance of the Holy Spirit. Since Paul was reaching out via letters from Rome to the churches in Macedonia and Asia, it would make sense for him to reach out to the church in Jerusalem as well, especially since the author of Hebrews said he looked forward to visiting his readers in Jerusalem with Timothy soon (Heb 13:23). Since Luke was with Paul in Rome, he was available to coauthor the letter.

163. There is no certain date for this, but it could not have happened earlier.

164. Jerome, in his book *On Illustrious Men*, asserts that Luke completed Acts in AD 59. This means his Gospel must have been completed before then.

165. The word "released" in Greek is sometimes translated "set free," as if Timothy were liberated from prison. There is no record, however, of his being incarcerated, so probably by "released" Paul means "sent away."

Proposed Timeline of Jesus' Life and the Apostolic Age

- Paul probably evangelized in the Italian countryside before leaving for Spain in the spring of AD 59.[166]
- Paul probably sailed to Spain in the early summer of AD 59 (Rom 15:24).

AD 60–63

- Paul probably evangelized in Spain, possibly from AD 59 until AD 62 (Rom 15:24).
- The Sadducees threw James the Just, the half-brother of Jesus, down from the pinnacle of the temple to his death in AD 62.
- Paul probably sailed to Illyricum, perhaps stopping again in Rome, before October AD 62.
- Paul probably strengthened the churches in Illyricum and made his way to Thessalonica and visited all his churches in Macedonia and Greece, between AD 62 and 63.
- Paul probably sailed to Crete in AD 63.[167]
- Paul founded churches in Crete with Titus, probably for all of AD 63 (Titus 1:5).

AD 64–68

- Paul probably sailed to Ephesus in AD 64.
- The Great Fire torched Rome between July 18 and 26, AD 64.[168]
- Possibly in AD 64 Andrew died under the proconsul Aegeates in Achaia (Greece).
- Nero began his persecution of Christians, from around November 26, AD 64 until his death on June 9, AD 68.[169]

166. Paul was acquitted in AD 59, and he died in AD 68. What he did in this interval of 3,136 days or about 8.6 years is not recorded, but it is reasonable to believe that he realized his ambition to evangelize Spain (Rom 15:24), founded churches in Crete (Titus 1:5), and did what he had always done before, traveling to the churches he had planted, strengthening them, and founding new churches.

167. Some scholars think Paul sailed from Italy to Crete and then to Spain. This would not have made sense. If he went to Spain, it would be more economical for him to depart from Italy to Spain and then visit Crete on his return to the east.

168. Tacitus, *Annals* 15:38–44; Plutarch, "Life of Crassus," *Lives*. The fire gutted much of the city. Nero acquired the cleared land and built a magnificent golden palace for himself on it. The rumor circulated that he set the fire himself to acquire the land cheaply (a practice famously established by the avaricious Marcus Licinius Crassus 146 years before).

169. Unable to win back the mob when they suspected Nero of torching Rome, Nero hit upon the scheme of blaming the Christians for the fire and persecuting them publicly with extreme and sadistic cruelty. Tacitus said that rather than win sympathy Nero instead excited pity for the Christians and increased the public hatred of himself.

APPENDICES

- John probably wrote Revelation during the Neronian persecution, between AD 64 and 68.
- Judas Thaddaeus Lebbaeus died a martyr in Lebanon probably around AD 65.[170]
- At some point, definitely before AD 68, Aquila and Priscilla returned from Rome to Ephesus (2 Tim 4:19).
- Paul probably visited the churches in Asia Minor, including Miletus (2 Tim 4:20), and then returned to Philippi, Thessalonica, Corinth, Illyricum, and Nicopolis in western Greece, where he probably spent the winter. He then probably returned to Asia Minor, ending up in Ephesus and finally Troas, probably between AD 64 and AD 65 (Titus 3:12).[171] He probably then returned to Corinth in AD 65.
- From Corinth, Paul wrote his epistle to Titus in Crete, probably in AD 66. The clue is that Paul asked Titus to meet him in winter in Nicopolis, which is in western Greece between the Ambracian Gulf and the Ionian Sea. This suggests that Paul was positioning himself for a return to Illyricum, to the north.
- Zenas and Apollos were the messengers and probably had the assignment of assuming leadership of some the Cretan churches (Titus 3:13).
- Paul sent Artemas and Tychicus to Crete, probably to relieve Titus, and Titus probably sailed from Crete to Achaia (Greece) and joined Paul after his winter in Nicopolis in AD 66 (Titus 1:5, 3:12–13).
- Paul went to Nicopolis in western Greece and stayed for the winter, probably from September AD 65 to March AD 66.[172]
- The first Roman-Jewish War erupted in AD 66.
- Matthias returned to Jerusalem where he was stoned to death by anti-Christian Jews, possibly in AD 66.
- Nathanael Bartholomew brought the gospel to Armenia and died there as a martyr in AD 66.[173]

---

170. "Saints Thaddaeus and Bartholomew," *The Armenian Prelacy*.

171. This largely unrecorded interval is about eight years, so Paul had plenty of time to make a return circuit, or even multiple circuits, of all the churches in Asia, Macedonia, Achaia, Illyricum, and even a return trip to Rome and Spain if he chose. These many journeys took 3,136 days or 8.6 years and could easily have encompassed over 7,000 miles.

172. This was a journey of about 273 miles.

173. "Saints Thaddaeus and Bartholomew," *The Armenian Prelacy*.

Proposed Timeline of Jesus' Life and the Apostolic Age

AD 67

- Nero arrested Peter in Rome, possibly around July AD 67, holding him in the Mamertine prison for nine months before executing him on the same day that he executed Paul.[174]

AD 68

- Paul returned to Troas, where Nero's officials suddenly arrested Paul, possibly around March AD 68. The arrest was so sudden that Paul had no time to pack. He left his books and cloak with Carpus (2 Tim 4:13).[175]

- Titus, Crescens, Tychicus, Carpus, Demas, and Alexander the coppersmith were possibly all with Paul when he was arrested. Titus went to Dalmatia, Crescens to Galatia, and Tychicus to Ephesus, no doubt to carry on the mission of proclaiming the gospel and leading the churches there. Mark was probably also with this team somewhere in Asia Minor (modern Turkey) at this time. Demas, who stood by Paul faithfully during his first Roman imprisonment (Col 4:14), deserted Paul now. Alexander the coppersmith did Paul great harm, opposing his message. Erastus remained at Corinth, and Trophimus, who was ill, remained in Miletus (2 Tim 4:10–21).

- Paul was taken to the provincial capital of Ephesus, from whence he was escorted by sea to Rome, possibly between March and April AD 68. He was probably also jailed in the Mamertine prison, where Peter was incarcerated.[176] Only Luke was with him (2 Tim 4:11).[177]

- Paul wrote 2 Timothy from a Roman prison, around April AD 68 (2 Tim 1:8).[178] He greeted Priscilla, Aquila, and the household of Onesiphorus in Ephesus. Eubulus, Pudens, Linus, Claudia, and all the brothers of the Roman church (possibly also prisoners at this time) greeted Timothy as well (2 Tim 4:19–21).

---

174. De Montor, *The Lives and Times of the Roman Pontiffs*, 26.

175. When he reached Rome, Paul asked Timothy to bring the cloak he left with Carpus in Troas, along with his books and parchments (no doubt Scriptures and his own sermon notes). It is unlikely that he would have left these things voluntarily in Troas on a journey so far away as to Rome unless he were taken in Troas suddenly and by force.

176. De Montor, *The Lives and Times of the Roman Pontiffs*, 26.

177. The voyage to Rome took about one month by sea.

178. Paul said he was a prisoner and near death (2 Tim 4:6). This cannot be Paul's first imprisonment, because he said only Luke was with him and that Demas had deserted him. In his first imprisonment, the people with him were: Tychicus, Timothy, Epaphroditus, Onesimus, Aristarchus, John Mark, Jesus (Justus), Luke, and Demas. Paul urged Timothy to come to him in Rome, which distinguishes this letter absolutely from 1 Timothy.

- Nero executed Peter's wife, probably very near the day of Peter's execution.[179]
- Nero executed Paul and Peter on the same day, possibly around May 5, AD 68. Paul was probably around age sixty-four.[180]
- Mark died a martyr in Egypt, probably in AD 68.
- Nero committed suicide at age thirty-two, June 9, AD 68.[181]

AD 69

- AD 69 was the "Year of the Four Emperors" when, in the chaotic civil war following Nero's suicide, four Roman generals ruled as emperor in succession: Galba, Otho, Vitellius, and Vespasian. When Vespasian succeeded them all, he left his son Titus in Judea to finish the Roman-Jewish War.

AD 70

- The Romans under Titus sacked Jerusalem and burned the temple in August AD 70.

AD 73

- The Roman-Jewish war ended with the capture of Masada in AD 73.
- The emperor Domitian banished John to the island of Patmos around AD 94.[182]

---

179. Eusebius, *Church History* 3:30:2.

180. Jerome, in his book *On Illustrious Men*, writes that Paul and Peter died on the same day in the fourteenth year of Nero's reign, which was AD 68. Jerome also adds that this was twenty-seven years after the Lord's passion. This is either a scribal or a math error by Jerome. If one assumes that Christ died in AD 30 (which is not correct), twenty-seven years later would be AD 57. If one assumes that Christ died in AD 33 (which is correct), twenty-seven years later would be AD 60. Neither year, obviously, is close to the fourteenth year of Nero's reign.

181. Suetonius, *Lives of the Twelve Caesars*, "Nero." Jesus died at thirty-three, saved the world, and inspired billions of followers from then until this day. Nero, master of an empire of 59–76 million souls, killed himself at thirty-two, hunted down by his Praetorian Guard, terrified, hated, and disgraced.

182. Jerome, *On Illustrious Men*.

Proposed Timeline of Jesus' Life and the Apostolic Age

AD 81–96

- In Domitian's reign (AD 81–96), Philip, like Peter, was crucified upside down, in Hierapolis. At the same time, Bartholomew was crucified, but was released from his cross alive.[183]

AD 97

- Timothy died around AD 97.

AD 98

- The apostle John died of old age in Ephesus, probably in his nineties, around AD 98.

AD 115–17

- The second Roman-Jewish war erupted in the reign of the emperor Trajan. Jews in Cyrene, Cyprus, Mesopotamia, and Egypt revolted, slaughtering over 440,000 Roman citizens and others by cooking their flesh, making belts of their entrails, clothing of their skins, sawing them in half, anointing themselves with gentile blood, and making them fight as gladiators or feeding them to wild beasts. The Roman Berber general Lusius Quietus eventually crushed the rebellion.[184]

AD 123

- The apostle Simon the Zealot may have died at 120 years old around AD 123.[185]

AD 129–30

- Trajan's successor, the emperor Hadrian, changed the name of Jerusalem to Aelia Capitolina, commemorating his family name, Aelius, and the Roman god Jupiter

---

183. Hippolytus, "List of the Apostles and Disciples."
184. Cassius Dio, *Roman History* 75:32.
185. Hippolytus, *List of the Apostles and Disciples*.

Capitolinus. He established a temple to Jupiter on the site of the Jewish temple that Titus had destroyed in AD 70. He posted the Tenth Legion there with orders to prevent any Jews from returning to the city.

AD 132-36

- In the final Roman-Jewish war, Simon bar Kokhba, a Jewish rebel leader, whom many Jews thought was the Messiah, tried to expel the Romans from Judea by force. After three years, the emperor Hadrian sent six legions under general Sextus Julius Severus, who defeated the Jews. About 580,000 Jews perished in the war, and the Romans sold many more into slavery. In an attempt to erase the legacy of Israel, Hadrian wiped the name of Judea off the map, re-naming the province Syria Palaestina. The province retained the name of Palestine under the Byzantine and Islamic empires, until it became the Kingdom of Jerusalem under the Christian Crusaders from 1099 to 1187. In 1187, it again came under Islamic rule until World War I. Great Britain administered Palestine 1920–48. Then, after 1,812 years under the name Palestine, in 1948, David Ben-Gurion and the Jewish People's Council declared the establishment of the state of Israel.

Great Messianic Expectations

JESUS APPEARED IN HISTORY not as a total surprise, but at a time when everyone was expecting—or dreading—the Messiah. The Jews, as well as the pagan Greeks, Romans, and the magi of Persia, all knew prophecies about a new kind of king who would arise in the east at that time. Two important examples are Genesis 49 and Daniel 9.

SHILOH

In Genesis 49:10, Jacob (Israel) blessed his sons and specifically said of Judah: "The scepter shall not depart from Judah, nor the ruler's staff from between his feet, until Shiloh comes, and to him shall be the obedience of the peoples." Shiloh means, approximately, "him to whom it belongs." Jews taught that the prophecy meant that the kings of Israel would rule the tribe of Judah until the rightful king would come. They understood this to mean the Messiah.

In 43 BC, Herod the Great tried to take the throne of Judea away from Hyrcanus, scion of the Hasmonean (Maccabean) dynasty that had ruled an independent Jewish state for a century. Herod was an Idumean (Edomite), a descendant of Esau, and thus not a Jew. The Jews therefore regarded Herod as an enemy alien and fought to keep him from the throne. In 37 BC, the Romans helped Herod secure power in Judea and confirmed him as their puppet king of the Jews. The Jews lamented that the scepter had passed from Judah[1] while Shiloh (the Messiah) had not yet come. Yet he would come during the last years of Herod the Great, who had no trouble finding scholars who could identify where the prophesied infant would be born: Bethlehem (Mic 5:2; Matt 2:6).

---

1. In fact, the Hasmonaean dynasty, the Maccabees, was of the tribe of Levi, not Judah. But it was customary to refer to Israelites who had returned from Babylonian exile in 539 BC and who made up the restored nation of Judea as Jews (of the tribe of Judah), even though they consisted of people from the tribes of Judah, Benjamin, and Levi. There were even stragglers from the lost Ten Tribes, proven by the fact that the Prophetess Anna, who blessed the infant Jesus, was of the tribe of Asher (Luke 2:36).

DANIEL'S SEVENTY SEVENS

The second great biblical time marker for the advent of Messiah was the prophecy of Daniel's 490 years. In 539 BC, God said to Daniel that

> Seventy weeks are decreed about your people and your holy city, to finish the transgression, to put an end to sin, and to atone for iniquity, to bring in everlasting righteousness, to seal both vision and prophet, and to anoint a most holy place. Know therefore and understand that from the going out of the word to restore and build Jerusalem to the coming of an anointed one, a prince, there shall be seven weeks. Then for sixty-two weeks it shall be built again with squares and moat, but in a troubled time. And after the sixty-two weeks, an anointed one shall be cut off and shall have nothing. And the people of the prince who is to come shall destroy the city and the sanctuary. Its end shall come with a flood, and to the end there shall be war. Desolations are decreed. And he shall make a strong covenant with many for one week, and for half of the week he shall put an end to sacrifice and offering. And on the wing of abominations shall come one who makes desolate, until the decreed end is poured out on the desolator. (Dan 9:24–27)

The idea that Daniel 9 proposes 360-day "prophetic years" lacks support in Scripture. If Daniel's seventy weeks are equal to 490 periods of 360 days, then the total period would be 176,400 days or only 438.29 Gregorian years or only 478 Hebrew years. Neither of these metrics get us to "the coming of Messiah, the prince," no matter which Persian decree we start from. It seems that the concept of "prophetic years" is basically a human invention which arises from not correctly understanding the Hebrew calendar and halachic time-keeping. Some scholars assume that a year equals 360 days because the Hebrew calendar is lunar, but that is a misunderstanding. The Hebrew month is lunar, but the Hebrew year is solar. The average length of a Hebrew year is thus 369 days, and no Hebrew year ever equals 360 days.

The weeks refer to seven-year intervals or heptads, just as decades refer to intervals of ten years and centuries refer to intervals of one hundred years. Seventy heptads equal 490 years.

FIFTEEN EVENTS

The prophecy says that within 490 years, fifteen things would happen, all of which did happen by the end of Jesus' ministry:

1. Finish the transgression (Rom 5:15, 18).

2. Put an end to sin (John 1:29; Rom 6:7; 1 Pet 2:24).

3. Atone for iniquity (John 1:29; Heb 2:17, 10:12).

4. Bring in everlasting righteousness (Matt 3:15; Luke 1:33; Rom 5:18; 2 Cor 9:9).

Great Messianic Expectations

5. Seal both vision and prophet (Heb 1:1–2; Jude 1:3; Rev 22:18–19).

6. Anoint a most holy place (Luke 4:18; Acts 10:33; Heb 1:8–9).

7. Jerusalem shall be built with squares and a moat, but in a troubled time (Neh 6:15).

8. Coming of an anointed one, a prince, or Messiah the Prince (Matt 1:17, 2:4, 18:15–16; Mark 12:35; Luke 2:11, 3:15; John 1:41, 4:25–29, 7:26, 41, 20:31; Acts 3:20, 5:42, 17:3, 18:5, 28, 26:22–23).

9. An anointed one (Christ, the Messiah) shall be cut off and shall have nothing (Matt 27:45–50; Mark 15:33–39; Luke 23:44–48; John 19:23–24, 28–30).

10. A people of a prince shall come and destroy the city and the sanctuary. In the Roman-Jewish War of AD 67–73, the Romans (a people) led by Titus (a prince, the son of the emperor Vespasian), came to Jerusalem and destroyed the city and the temple.

11. The end shall come with a flood, with war till the end. Probably over one million Jews died in the Roman-Jewish War. With the destruction of the temple "the end" came, the end of the old covenant, for the Levitical priesthood could never again perform the sacrifices and feasts that the law of Moses required be done in the temple.

12. There will be decreed desolations. Malachi 4 clearly decreed the final desolation of Jerusalem if the Jews persisted in apostasy. Deuteronomy 28 made a long list of similar decrees. The fall of Jerusalem to the Romans in AD 70 was marked by famine, insanity, cannibalism, mass bloodshed, and the total destruction of the city and the Jerusalem Temple. The abomination that the Levitical priests had inflicted on the house of God, that is, continuing to offer sacrifices under the old covenant while rejecting the Messiah and the new covenant, had caused desolation, that is, God's abandonment of the temple to its destruction.

13. Someone shall make a strong covenant with many for one week (one seven-year period). This someone is the Messiah, not Titus, for Jesus said, "this is the blood of the covenant, which is poured out for many for the forgiveness of sins" (Matt 26:28; Mark 14:24; Luke 22:20)

14. In the midst of the last seven, that person shall put an end to sacrifice and offering. Jesus did this when he first cleansed the temple during the Passover of AD 30 (John 2:15), which was the fourth year of the final seven, exactly in the middle of that last seven. Jesus reaffirmed this when he cleansed the temple two more times in AD 33 (Matt 21:12; Mark 11:15; Luke 19:45)[2] and by his sacrifice on the cross in AD 33, the final year of the final seven. Jesus is the fulfillment of types

---

2. Jesus would cleanse the temple two more times, once on Palm Sunday, March 27, AD 33 (Matt 21:12), and again on the following Monday, March 28, AD 33 (Mark 11:15).

and shadows in the Old Testament. His new covenant made temple sacrifices not only unnecessary, but blasphemous. The torn veil of the holy of holies at Jesus' death signified that Jesus' atonement on the cross fulfilled and replaced the old covenant, as did his words at the point of death, "It is finished" (John 19:30; see also Heb 7:27, 8:6, 9:13–15, 24–26, 10:10–12).

15. On the wing of abominations (the rejection of the Messiah) shall come one who makes desolate, until the decreed end is poured out on the desolator (the Jewish elite). Jesus said that because the scribes and Pharisees had shut off the kingdom of heaven, because they were outwardly righteous but inwardly lawless, and because they had rejected Jesus and his apostles as they had killed the prophets, seven woes would come upon their generation. Jerusalem's house was being left to her desolate, and, according to Matthew, not one stone of the temple would be left standing upon another; all would be torn down (Matt 23—24).

THE PRINCE

Daniel 9:24-27 mentions "an anointed one, a prince" (Dan 9:25), "an anointed one" (Dan 9:26), and "the people of a prince who is to come" (Dan 9:26). The word prince is נָגִיד, *nagid*, in both verses 25 and 26, but in 25 the prince is "anointed" מָשִׁיחַ, *mashiach*, that is, clearly, the Messiah, whereas in 26 the prince is distinguished as being the leader of some people עַם, *am*, who is to come. Moreover, that same verse mentions the מָשִׁיחַ, *mashiach*, Messiah, and only eight words later (in Hebrew) mentions the prince, marking him as being the leader of a people to come. It seems that Daniel is being careful to distinguish between the anointed prince, the Messiah, and the prince who will destroy the city and the sanctuary. Considering the second prince, Titus, this fits history nicely. During AD 69, the Year of the Four Emperors, Vespasian suspended his war against the Jews to see which contender for the imperial throne would come out on top. When the Roman mob murdered the third contender, Vitellius, and Vespasian won, he rushed to Rome to claim the crown, leaving his son Titus in charge of the legions in Judea and giving him the order to finish off the war with the Jews. Titus resumed the siege of Jerusalem and ultimately destroyed the city and the temple between 8 and 10 Av (August 1–3), AD 70. At this stage in his career, Titus exactly fit the description of a prince of a people who was to come. The Romans were not already in Judea. They came from elsewhere. (The legions assembled for the war were the Fifth, from Macedon, the Fifteenth, from Egypt, and the Tenth, from Syria). Titus was not yet the emperor. He was the son of the emperor, hence a prince, not a king. (Although, when Vespasian celebrated a triumph commemorating the victory over the Jews, he elevated Titus so that the honor was for both father and son, literally as joint *imperatori*. The arch in the Roman Forum, which still stands, memorializing the sack of Jerusalem was named the Arch of Titus.)

THE DECREE

Daniel says that the Messiah will be come and be cut off "but not for Himself" after 483 years and that in the final week the Messiah will make a covenant with many, and in the middle of that week he will bring an end to sacrifice and offering. The starting point of the weeks must be a decree (רָבָד, *dabar*, word) "to restore and rebuild Jerusalem" (Dan 9:25). Added to that is the statement that until [the coming of] Messiah the Prince [there shall be] 7 + 62 weeks = 69 weeks = 483 years. Added to that statement is that the street and the wall [of Jerusalem] shall be built even in troublesome times. It is reasonable to think that two separate activities are in view. In 539 BC, Cyrus decreed that Jeshua and Zerubbabel could lead a return to Judah. They restored (בוּשׁ, *shub*) and built (הָנָב, *banah*, which also may mean "restore") Jerusalem. They first rebuilt the altar by Tishri (September 20–October 19) of 538 BC (Ezra 3:1, 10–11, 4:24). Then the Jews slacked off and stopped building the temple until encouraged by Haggai (Hag 1:1, 15; Ezra 4:24, 5:1).

In 520 BC, Tattenai, the Persian governor, tried to stop the reconstruction of the temple, but Darius issued a decree commanding that the work continue. The Jews completed the Second Temple on 3 Adar, Friday, February 13, 515 BC (Ezra 6:16) and celebrated the first Passover in the Second Temple on 14 Nisan, March 25, 515 BC (Ezra 6:19).

After the near-genocide of the Jews in Persia (averted by Esther and Mordecai between 482 and 472 BC), and after the assassination of Xerxes (465 BC), Rehum and Shimshai persuaded Artaxerxes to stop the work of restoring Jerusalem's walls and foundations (Ezra 4:17). However, in 457 BC, Artaxerxes overrode this and granted Ezra permission to lead a second return expedition to Jerusalem (Ezra 7:11). Ezra set out from Babylon on 1 Nisan, Thursday, March 4 (a date that intriguingly means "march forth" in English), 457 BC.

Nehemiah, in distinctly troubled times, built its street (רְחֹב, *rechob*, broad open place, plaza, town square) and wall (which, interestingly, does not mean simply "wall," but חָרוּץ, *charuwts*, which is an adjective, meaning, "sharp, diligent"). Nehemiah began his work on 3 Av, Friday, July 6, 444 BC (Neh 3, 6:15) and completed it in fifty-two days, on 25 Elul, Monday, August 27, 444 BC.

So there are four possible decrees which could mark the starting point of Daniel's 490 years: (1) Cyrus: 539 BC. Adding 483 years to this date reaches 57 BC, and the final "week" then runs from 56 to 50 BC. This is far too early for the coming of Messiah, the prince; (2) Darius: 522 BC. Adding 483 years to this date reaches 40 BC, and the final "week" then runs from 39 to 33 BC. This is also too early for the coming of Messiah, the prince; (3) Artaxerxes: 457 BC. Adding 483 years to this date reaches AD 26, and the final "week" then runs from AD 27 to 33. The week ends exactly in the year of the cross; (4) Artaxerxes: 444 BC. Adding 483 years to this date reaches AD

39, and the final "week" then runs from AD 40 to 46 BC. This overshoots the coming of Messiah, the prince. Only the first decree of Artaxerxes works.

Now let us see how well it works. Daniel says that within 490 years there would be an end to sin, atonement for iniquity, the incoming of everlasting righteousness, sealing of both vision of prophet and the anointing of a most holy place (Dan 9:24). If we use Artaxerxes's first decree, the seventieth week runs from AD 27 to AD 33, encompassing all of Jesus' ministry, which ran from AD 29 to AD 33. Did Jesus do all these thing? Yes, either explicitly or figuratively. (For example, he did not end sin, but he saved us from being condemned to sin.)

Daniel says that from the date of the decree, within 483 years, Jerusalem would be built again, in a troubled time (Dan 9:25). The 483 years run from 457 BC to AD 26. Jerusalem was restored and rebuilt between 538 and 444 BC, which is within the 483 years.

Daniel says that after the 483 years, the Messiah would be cut of and have nothing (Dan 9:26). The 483 years run from 457 BC to AD 26. Jesus was crucified in AD 33, the last year of the seventieth seven, or the 490th year, which is certainly after the 483 years.

Daniel says that the people of a prince who is to come would destroy Jerusalem and the temple (Dan 9:26). He doesn't say exactly when that would happen, but he may be referring back to the phrase "after the sixty-two weeks," which means, in context, after the 62 + 7 weeks, or after the 483 years. Titus destroyed the temple in AD 70, certainly after the 483 years.

Daniel says "he" shall make a strong covenant with many for one week (Dan 9:27). In context "he" could refer either to the prince of the people to come or to the Messiah. The word covenant here is בְּרִית, *berith*. According to Strong's *Concordance* (s.v. 1285), this word occurs 284 times in the Old Testament. In every case, it refers to a covenant made by God. To claim, as some do, that this covenant is a false promise by an antichrist is to take this word out of its firmly established context. So use of the word *berith* suggests that "he" is the Messiah, not the prince of the people to come. This is further supported by the timeline; the covenant with many would be made in one "week." The final week of Daniel's 490 years runs from AD 27 to 33. Jesus' ministry ran from AD 29 to 33. Did Jesus make a covenant with many in this interval? Yes, he did so in AD 33 (Mark 14:14; Matt 26:28; Luke 22:20). The word for covenant in Greek is διαθήκη, *diathíki*, which, according to Strong (*Concordance*, s.v. 1242) means "a set-agreement having complete terms determined by the initiating party, which also are fully affirmed by the one entering the agreement." This definition tightly aligns with that of *berith*.

Daniel says that for half of the week "he" shall put an end to sacrifice and offering (Dan 9:27). The final week runs from AD 27 to 33. Jesus' ministry ran from the fall of AD 29 to the summer of AD 33 (the ascension). There were 1,350 days from Jesus' baptism to the ascension. In the seventieth week there were 2,555 days (Gregorian) and 2,583 days (Hebrew).³ The 1,350 days of Jesus' ministry thus equal 52.840% of the Gregorian term and 52.226% of the Hebrew term in the seventieth week. Therefore, Jesus' ministry took roughly half of the seventieth week, just as Daniel foretold, and in it Jesus indeed put an end to sacrifice and offering. Jesus cleansed the temple three times in his ministry: (1) before the Passover of AD 30 (John 2), (2) on Palm Sunday (Matt 21; Luke 19), and (3) on the Monday after Palm Sunday (Mark 11).

Finally, Daniel says that "on the wing of abominations shall come one who makes desolate, until the decreed end is poured out on the desolator" (Dan 9:27). The word for abomination is שִׁקּוּץ, *shiqquts*, a detested thing. The word for "the desolator" is actually "the desolate," from the verb שָׁמֵם, *shamem*, "to be desolated, appalled, ruined, astounded, horrified, laid waste, ravaged." The abomination, logically, was the conscious rejection and murder of the Messiah by the Jewish elite. Jesus foretold that they would suffer a terrible end for doing this (Matt 24:2; Luke 19:44), and the OT is full of God's promises of Israel's destruction if they persisted in disobedience (Deut 28:15–68). A fair interpretation of Daniel might therefore read, "After rejecting the Messiah, Titus will come and desolate Jerusalem, laying waste to the disobedient, defeated, and horrified Jews."

PAGAN ECHOES

There were also pagan prophecies swirling about at this time. Suetonius wrote:

> A firm persuasion had long prevailed through all the East that it was fated of the empire of the world, at that time, to devolve on someone who should go forth from Judea. This prediction referred to a Roman emperor, as the event showed; but the Jews, applying it to themselves, broke out into rebellion.⁴

Contrary to Suetonius's belief, this prophecy nicely fits not a Roman emperor, but Jesus, King of the Jews.

READY FOR THE CHRIST

Since Micah's prophecy about the Messiah's birth in Bethlehem, over four centuries before Christ (Mic 5:2), the Jews had seen the years go by with no sign of the Messiah. With the ascension of Herod the Great, the scepter had passed from Judah in 37 BC, and Shiloh had not come (Gen 49:10). Contemporaries were acutely aware that the remaining possible years for the coming of the Messiah fit in a narrow window between AD 27 and AD 33, Daniel's last seven. This knowledge inspired great anticipation. From the death of Herod to the ministry of John the Baptist, people knew that Messiah the Prince had to be already in the world. Somewhere, he walked among them as

---

3. Using an average of 365 days for Gregorian years and 369 days for Hebrew years.
4. Suetonius, *Lives of the Twelve Caesars*, "Vespasian."

an adult, Jewish man. That meant he must have been born around the turn of the first century. In the final seven years, prophecy affirmed that he would change the world. Anticipation was high. And, indeed, Jesus was born in 2 BC, began his public ministry in AD 29, and accomplished all that Daniel prophesied the Messiah would accomplish by AD 33, the year of the cross, the last year of Daniel's seventieth seven.

This is why Simeon rejoiced on seeing the infant Jesus presented at the temple, for the Holy Spirit had told him that he would not die before seeing the Lord's anointed. This is why Anna, the prophetess of Asher, at once recognized the baby Jesus as Israel's redeemer (Luke 2:36). This is why the magi, who came from the East, interpreted the Bethlehem star as the sign of the king of the Jews. (Since the magi were a Babylonian tribe, they would certainly have been familiar with the prophecies of Babylon's most famous official, Daniel, who served under Nebuchadnezzar and Cyrus the Great.) This is why Herod was more than usually troubled. He, too, expected the coming of a powerful rival prince. This is why the chief priests and scribes could instantly inform Herod that the Messiah would be born in Bethlehem; his coming was much on everyone's minds. This is why, when John the Baptist appeared, the Pharisees asked if he was the Messiah; John began preaching at exactly the height of their anticipation. This is why John, Andrew, Philip, Nathanael, and others were immediately ready to see who Jesus was: the Messiah, whom all Israel expected at exactly that time. This is what makes the rejection of Jesus by the Sanhedrin so remarkable. The Jewish elite did not overlook Jesus by mistake. They were fully informed of his credentials. They knew he fit the Messianic prophecies exactly. They rejected the Messiah not out of ignorance but by choice.

Pinpointing the Date of Jesus' Birth

THE EARLY CHURCH AUTHORITIES, including Irenaeus, Clement of Alexandria, Tertullian, Africanus, Hippolytus of Rome, Hippolytus of Thebes, Origen, Eusebius, Epiphanius, and Paulus Orosius, consistently placed the birth of Jesus in 3–2 BC.[1] This was correct. The faulty thesis that Jesus' was born in 4 BC arose with an erroneous dating of Herod the Great's death.

DATING HEROD'S DEATH

Jesus was born while Herod the Great was still alive (Matt 2:1). For years, scholars have held that Herod the Great died in 4 BC based on the following argument: Herod Philip II became tetrarch of Gaulanitis, Trachonitis, Batanea, and Paneas in the year of Herod's death. Josephus states that Philip died in the twentieth year of Tiberius (AD 34) after ruling thirty-seven years.[2] Therefore, AD 34 minus 37 years = 4 BC. (In the BC-AD system, there is no year 0). Thus, Philip became tetrarch in 4 BC, and so Herod must have died in 4 BC. That is the prevailing argument. It is, however, wrong.

All copies of Josephus dated prior to AD 1544 say that Philip died in the twenty-second year of Tiberius (AD 36).[3] In sixteenth-century Europe a new and valuable invention arose—the printing press. With it came another new phenomenon—the printer's error. A printer's error after AD 1544 made the text of Josephus read "the twentieth year of Tiberius." Since all the pre-AD 1544 manuscripts say, "the twenty-second year of Tiberius," they are nearer to the source and thus more reliable. The year AD 36 minus the 37 years of Herod's reign = 1 BC.[4] Therefore, Philip's reign began in 1 BC, and Herod died in 1 BC.

---

1. Finegan, *Handbook*, 291.
2. Josephus, *Ant.* 18:4:6.
3. Josephus, *Ant.* 86; and Steinmann, "When Did Herod the Great Reign?"
4. Beyer, "Josephus Reexamined: Unraveling the Twenty-Second Year of Tiberius," 85.

Josephus also relates that Herod died after a lunar eclipse[5] and before Passover.[6] In what year did these phenomena occur? Only in 1 BC. A total lunar eclipse was visible in Jerusalem the night of 9–10 January, 1 BC.[7] And in 1 BC, Passover (14 Nisan) occurred on Wednesday, March 17. So, Herod not only died in 1 BC; he died between January 10 and March 16 of 1 BC. And we can refine the date even better.

Josephus relates that Herod was agonizingly sick in his declining days. His physicians tried many remedies to cure him, including bathing in the mineral waters at Callirrhoe near the Dead Sea. When he realized he was dying, Herod summoned all the Jewish leaders and arrested them. He ordered them executed on his death, so that there would be mourning in Israel, not celebration, upon his passing. He knew how much his subjects hated him. Then he sent for and received permission from Caesar Augustus to execute his son, Antipater, who had poisoned Herod's brother, Pheroras. He carried out the execution and died five days later. After his death came his funeral (which was extravagant), seven days of mourning, a feast in his honor, and the assumption of the throne of Judea by Archelaus, his son. Then came Passover. We can estimate the time required for these events to transpire. For Herod to have made a trip to Callirrhoe, have tried a cure, and to have acknowledged its failure must have taken at least a week. To have summoned all the Jewish leaders and to have placed them under arrest must have taken at least a week. To send to Rome for permission to execute Antipater and to receive the answer of the busy Augustus must have taken at least a month.[8] The execution of Antipater might have taken one day only. Five days later, Herod died. Then came Passover. All these events equal at least fifty days. Fifty days after the eclipse of January 10 is Monday, March 1, 1 BC. Herod thus died very close to this date.

THE MAGI

The Bible says that magi from the east saw the star (Matt 2:2). The magi (from which we derive our word "magic") were a caste among the Medes. The Medes were a people group from western Persia, whose capital was Ecbatana (modern Hamadan, Iran). They are the Kurdish people of today. The Medes were one of the six noble families who chose the Persian king. They were suppressed when Darius the Great took the throne.

The Medes, like the Chaldeans of Ur under Nebuchadnezzar, were known for their wisdom and love of science, which meant the study of natural phenomena, especially the stars. Herodotus reported their conspiracy to control the throne in the saga of Darius the Great's rise to power. Xenophon, who had firsthand experience at the Persian court, reported that they were responsible for educating the Persian crown

---

5. Josephus, *Ant.* 17:6:4.
6. Josephus, *Ant.* 17:9:3.
7. Nollet, "Astronomical and Historical Evidence for Dating the Nativity in 2 BC," 214.
8. Casson, *Speed under Sail of Ancient Ships*.

prince. Philo, the Jew of Alexandria, praised their efforts to find truth through the study of natural history. Matthew reported their wisdom and reverence in following the star of Bethlehem and worshiping Jesus.[9]

As wise men in Persia, the magi were almost certainly well acquainted with the book of Daniel. Daniel's tomb is still an object of pilgrimage in Iran today. Since Daniel was a Jew, but also the second most powerful man in Nebuchadnezzar's government and the third most powerful man in Babylon in the Persian government of Cyrus the Great, the magi would have respected him. Since Daniel's prophecies were astonishingly accurate during his lifetime, the magi would have been deeply curious about the fulfillment of his future prophecies, which focused on the Jews and the coming of Messiah the Prince (Dan 9).

Anyone familiar with the books of Ezra and Nehemiah, Persian history, and Daniel could easily calculate that the years 3 and 2 BC were in the sixty-fourth heptad (period of seven years) in Daniel's prophetic seventy heptads (490 years). Daniel 9 said that Messiah the Prince would be cut off and have nothing at the end of the seventieth heptad. The year AD 33, the year of the cross, fell within the seventieth heptad.

There were only thirty-four years from 2 BC to AD 33. Everyone knew, when the magi reached Jerusalem, that (1) the Messiah was either already born and would be more than thirty-four years old when he was cut off, or (2) that he was about to be born and would be thirty-four years or younger when he was cut off.

Herod had taken the scepter from Antigonus, the last Hasmonean king (of Judah), in 37 BC, and he had murdered the last Hasmonean royal heir, Hyrcanus II, in 30 BC. By 2 BC, Herod was old and sick, and the Messiah had not yet come. The prophetic window was closing. If Messiah the Prince did not come now, the validity of all the Hebrew prophets would be in doubt.

THE STAR OF BETHLEHEM

The work of Frederick A. Larson[10] shows, using astronomy software, that the star of Bethlehem was a real celestial event and pinpoints Jesus' advent. Reviewing his work inspired this author to conduct his own primary research on the subject, and this research retracing Larson's steps produces a thesis almost entirely aligned with his.[11]

The Bible lists eight characteristics about the Bethlehem star:

1. It was a sign of birth (Matt 2:2).

2. It was a sign of a king (Matt 2:2).

3. It was connected to the Jews (Matt 2:2).

---

9. Simon "the magus" in Acts 8:9 is not really a Median magus. The Bible says he practiced Magic (μαγεύων), not that he was a magus from the east like those in Matthew 2.

10. Larson, "The Star of Bethlehem."

11. Moseley, "Bethlehem Star."

4. It rose in the east (Matt 2:1–2).

5. It appeared at a specific time (Matt 2:7).

6. It endured over time (Matt 2:9–10).

7. It was ahead of the magi as they traveled south from Jerusalem to Bethlehem (Matt 2:9).

8. It stopped over Bethlehem (Matt 2:9).

A meteor, comet, or supernova could not fulfill all these conditions. Moreover, "in the years 3 and 2 BC there were no comets and no novae."[12] The ancients called planets "wandering stars" because they seemed to behave erratically. While other stars observed fixed trajectories, planets appeared to wander throughout the starry field, sometimes even going backwards. Today's astronomers call this "retrograde motion." It is analogous to a car, which is really going forward on the highway, appearing to go backward when your car passes it at a greater speed. When the earth travels on its orbit faster than a planet traveling on its orbit alongside the earth, the other planet seems to fall behind or "go backward." This is planetary retrograde motion.

In the seventeenth century, Johannes Kepler discovered the laws of planetary motion. Using them we can calculate the former or future positions and appearances of celestial bodies with precision. With astronomy software, such as Starry Night Pro, we can recreate the appearance of the sky from any place on earth at any time, and we can animate or freeze that view.

ROYALTY IN THE SKY

Between September of 3 BC and May of 2 BC, Jupiter, viewed from Babylon, the king of planets, made three conjunctions with Regulus, the star that the Romans called *rex* and the Persians called *sharu*, king. Jupiter approached Regulus and conjoined with it in the night sky, creating a bright light. This was unusual, but not unique, since Jupiter conjoins with Regulus about every twelve years. But this time, after passing Regulus, Jupiter turned around (entered retrograde motion), and conjoined with Regulus again. Then it turned around again (entered retrograde motion) and repeated the performance a third time. Three crossings of the king planet and the king star, with three brilliant flashes in the night sky, were startling and unique.

THE LION OF JUDAH IN THE SKY

All this activity occurred against the backdrop of the constellation Leo, the lion, the constellation in which Regulus sits. Since Jacob called Judah a lion and said that the scepter would not pass from Judah until Messiah came (Gen 49:9–10), this celestial

12. Finegan, *Handbook*, 319.

activity connected royalty (the king planet and the king star) with Judah, the lion. To the magi, this must have looked very like the birth of a new and triple-crowned king of the Jews. Was Jesus triple crowned? Yes. Like Melchizedek, Jesus was both king and priest (two crowns). But unlike anyone else, he was Messiah the Prince, the Savior (the ultimate crown).

CONCEPTION IN THE SKY

The conjunction of Jupiter and Venus, which occurred on June 17, 2 BC, was probably the birth star, the star of Bethlehem. The conjunction was so close that without a modern telescope the two planets would have looked like a single star. From the point of view of astrological symbolism,[13] Jupiter is the king planet and Venus (Ishtar in Babylonia), a female; so their conjunction can suggest a coming birth. The average time of human gestation is 277 days. Counting 277 days backwards from the date of the Jupiter-Venus conjunction yields September 13, 3 BC which was the date of the first conjunction of Jupiter and Regulus and which was probably the first phase of the star of Bethlehem phenomena that that Matthew described, marking Jesus' conception. The Sabbath, Saturday, September 13, 3 BC, is therefore the likely date of Jesus' conception, and this is a good date not only because it fits the observed activity of the "star" but because in synchronizes well with all the other chronological markers in Matthew and Luke.

BIRTH IN THE SKY

On Wednesday, June 17, 2 BC, after completing its triple conjunction with Regulus, Jupiter, the king planet, continued through the heavens to another spectacular rendezvous, this time with Venus, the mother planet. They appeared to touch, and each contributed its full brightness to what seemed like the most brilliant "star" anyone had ever seen. The conjunction reached its apex as the two planets set in the west, right over Judea from the perspective of the Babylonian magi. This is probably the date of Jesus' birth not only because it fits the celestial activity described in Matthew but because it fits all the other time markers in Matthew and Luke very well.

POINTING TO BETHLEHEM

Later that year, in late November to early December, 2 BC, Jupiter's position in the sky, when viewed from Jerusalem, was to the south, in the direction of Bethlehem. This was the appearance of the "star" that "led" the magi to the city of David. This was six

---

13. The ancients regarded astrological symbols as significant, although astrology is not a religious or scientific discipline.

months after the brilliant conjunction of Jupiter and Venus which occurred on Jesus' birthday. The travel time from Babylon to Jerusalem was about four months (Ezra 7).[14] This allowed two months for the magi to confer, decide the meaning of what they had seen, plan for their trip, possibly get political approval to pass from Parthian territory into enemy Roman territory, and gather their precious gifts for the Messiah (which may have involved some fundraising).

STOPPING OVER THE CITY OF DAVID

On December 2, 2 BC, Jupiter entered retrograde motion. It continued in this state till December 25 (by the Julian calendar, December 23 by our Gregorian calendar). During this time, Jupiter appeared to travel horizontally above Bethlehem, when viewed from Jerusalem, while the other planets visible, Mercury and Venus, dipped toward the horizon as they crossed the night sky. Jupiter's horizontal stasis throughout December, right above Bethlehem when viewed from Jerusalem, made it appear to come to rest above Jerusalem. After December 25, Jupiter again appeared to behave like other planets, breaking out of its horizontal lock and dipping toward the horizon as it traversed the sky.

Since Bethlehem is only five miles south of Jerusalem, the magi did not the need a star to show them how to get there. But seeing the star confirm their goal caused them to rejoice "exceedingly with great joy" (Matt 2:10). They presented gifts to Jesus, who was then about six months old, and, according to Matthew, was living in a house, not a stable (Matt 2:11). This makes sense, because Luke says the angel told the shepherds to look for a βρέφος (*bréphos*, newborn) wrapped in swaddling clothes and lying in a manger (Luke 2:12, 16). Later, Matthew says the magi found a παιδίον (*paidíon*, little child, usually under seven years old in Greek culture, Matt 2:11).

Thus, December 25 was probably the date of the adoration of the magi and of the first giving of gifts to celebrate Christ's advent, the first Christmas. But it was not Jesus' birthday.

THE STAR

In summary, the star was not a single star, but a series of celestial events that would appear to be a single star from a terrestrial point of view. First, Jupiter conjoined with Regulus on Saturday/Sunday September 13–14, 3 BC, and passed back over Regulus twice on Thursday, February 19, 2 BC, and on Saturday, May 9, 2 BC. Right after this kingly pageant finished in May, on Wednesday, June 17, 2 BC, Jupiter and Venus conjoined, creating the brightest "star" anyone alive had ever seen. The star reached maximum brightness as it set in the west over Jerusalem. Then, just when the magi arrived

---

14. The exiles took three months and twenty-seven days to make the return.

in Judea, Jupiter appeared to the south of Jerusalem in November or December, 2 BC in the direction of Bethlehem. Jupiter entered retrograde motion and appeared to stop over Bethlehem from December 2 to 25, 2 BC. Matthew's account of the star of Bethlehem is an exact description of the true celestial events that accompanied Jesus' advent.

JESUS' BIRTH

Since Herod died in 1 BC, there is no reason to dispute the early church's assertion that Jesus was born in 2 BC and that Herod tried to kill him by slaughtering the innocents of Bethlehem in late 2 BC or early 1 BC. The date of Jesus' birth that best fits with all chronological markers in the Gospels is Wednesday, June 17, 2 BC. The date of December 25 is associated with Jesus' advent, because the adoration of the magi occurred on December 23, 2 BC, which, in the Julian calendar then used by the Romans, was December 25.

Pinpointing the Start of Jesus' Ministry

JESUS' MINISTRY BEGAN AFTER that of John the Baptist. John began his ministry in the fifteenth year of the reign of Tiberius Caesar (Luke 3:1). Tiberius's first year as emperor ran from Tuesday, August 19, AD 14, to Tuesday, August 18, AD 15. Therefore, Tiberius's fifteenth year as emperor ran from Saturday, August 19, AD 28, to Saturday, August 18, AD 29.[1] For John the Baptist to begin his ministry in Tiberius's fifteenth year, he would have had to begin no later than August 18, AD 29.

The Gospel of John helps us bracket the dates of Jesus' ministry. It mentions that Jesus' ministry included three Passover feasts: (1) John 2:23, (2) John 6:4, and (3) John 11:55. The last Passover of Jesus' adult ministry was in AD 33, the year of the cross. The first Passover of Jesus' adult ministry came after his baptism in AD 29. Thus, Jesus' ministry spanned five calendar years (AD 29, 30, 31, 32, and 33) and therefore it encompassed four Passovers (in AD 30, 31, 32, and 33).

The Gospel of John gives a very specific sequence of dates following Jesus' return from his sojourn in the wilderness. On the first day after the Pharisees questioned John the Baptist about his identity (John 1:19), Jesus walked by the place where John was baptizing, and John proclaimed Jesus the Lamb of God (John 1:29). The next day this occurred again (John 1:35), and John the son of Zebedee and Andrew the brother of Simon Peter went to stay with Jesus.

The fact that they asked where Jesus was staying is a clue. During the Feast of Tabernacles, everyone who had come to Jerusalem for the High Holy Days would be staying for a week in makeshift tents (tabernacles), commemorating Israel's sojourn in the wilderness after the Exodus. Naturally, they would assume that Jesus had been staying somewhere with someone, but assuredly not at a fixed, predictable address.

The next day (John 1:43), Jesus proposed to return to Galilee, which would be expected if this day were after the last day of Tabernacles (*Isru Chag Sukkot*). This fixes the day Jesus decided to return to Galilee and go to the wedding at Cana: Thursday, October 18, AD 29. This also fixes the date for the wedding of Cana, which was on the third day after Jesus proposed to return to Galilee (John 2:1): Sunday, October 21, AD 29. Jesus proposed to leave Judea on Thursday; it took him till Sunday to arrive

---

1. Bromberg, "Kalendis Calendar Calculator"; Finegan, *Handbook*, 339.

Pinpointing the Start of Jesus' Ministry

(because the Sabbath on October 20 would have broken his journey); and then the wedding occurred on Sunday.

All these dates fit together like a puzzle very precisely. Jesus was baptized around Sunday, September 2, AD 29. On the day John baptized Jesus in the Jordan River, John, Andrew, Peter, Nathanael, and Philip were all at hand. At any other time of year, this would have been unusual for them, because they all lived in Galilee. But it would be understandable if they were all in Jerusalem for some major event. One event that would bring them all to Jerusalem together would be Passover, as when Jesus was twelve years old (Luke 2:42). But the believing Jews also gathered in Jerusalem for the High Holy Days of AD 29, Rosh Hashanah (New Year) and Yom Kippur (Day of Atonement). This would fit well with John's call to "repent, for the Kingdom of Heaven is at hand" (Matt 3:2).

In AD 29, the Jewish New Year fell on September 24. The Day of Atonement fell on October 4. The Jordan River, between the Sea of Galilee and the Dead Sea, is below sea level, and the weather there is warm year-round, so Jesus could have been baptized comfortably in the fall. "When all the people were being baptized, Jesus was baptized too" (Luke 3:21).

John's Gospel describes Jesus' baptism and the dove descending on Jesus (John 1:32). After Jesus' baptism, he went into the wilderness for forty days (Matt 4:1–11; Mark 1:12–13; Luke 4:1–2). This sojourn started around Monday, September 3, AD 29. Before Jesus returned from the wilderness, the priests and Levites went to John the Baptist to question his identity. They would have been rather busy in Jerusalem before Rosh Hashanah, Yom Kippur, and the Feast of Tabernacles, which ended on Sunday October 14. They might easily have made the day's trip to the Jordan on Monday, October 15, AD 29.

After Jesus' time in the wilderness, he again appeared to John the Baptist, around Tuesday, October 16, AD 29. John then proclaimed Jesus the Lamb of God. The next day, Wednesday, October 17, Jesus again passed by the place where John was baptizing, and John again hailed him as the Lamb of God. John the son of Zebedee and Andrew, who were disciples of the Baptist, left John and began following Jesus (John 1:35–37). On Thursday, October 18, *Isru Chag Sukkot,* the farewell day of the Feast of Tabernacles, Jesus naturally decided to return to Galilee (John 1:43). At this time, Jesus was thirty-one years old (Luke 3:23). On Sunday, October 21, Jesus attended the wedding at Cana and performed his first miracle (John 2:1).

AN END TO SACRIFICE AND OFFERING

For forty years prior to the fall of the Second Temple, the priests of Israel found the sacrifice of Yom Kippur (the day of national atonement) unacceptable to God.[2] What happened forty years before AD 70 in Israel?

In August of AD 29, John the Baptist began his mission. On Sunday, September 2, AD 29, John baptized Jesus, publicly recognizing him as Messiah. On Thursday, October 4, AD 29, Yom Kippur, the first of forty unacceptable sacrifices were presented in the temple. This was the thirty-second day of Jesus' forty-day fast in the wilderness. After the Feast of Tabernacles, the priests and Levites traveled to Bethany on the Jordan to question John the Baptist. Perhaps the disturbing presentation of an unacceptable sacrifice on Yom Kippur motivated them to enquire. On Tuesday, October 16, AD 29, Jesus returned from his sojourn in the wilderness, reached the banks of the Jordan River, and John the Baptist proclaimed him the Lamb of God. Every sacrifice for the next thirty-nine years would prove unacceptable. The national sins of Israel were unforgiven. Yet the Lamb of God who takes away the sins of the world walked among them from AD 29 to AD 33. The curses of Deuteronomy 28, Leviticus 26 and the prophecy of Daniel 9 fell on Jerusalem and the temple, destroying both, in AD 70.

---

2. Jewish Babylonian treatise *Yoma* 39b.

Pinpointing the Date of Jesus' Crucifixion

PONTIUS PILATE, THE ROMAN procurator who presided over Jesus' trial and crucifixion, governed from AD 26 to 36. The latest possible year of Jesus' crucifixion, resurrection, and ascension is therefore AD 36, Pontius Pilate's last year in office. In AD 36, the emperor Tiberius recalled Pilate to Rome to account for his harsh treatment of the Jews. While it is conceivable that all the events of the crucifixion and resurrection might have happened in AD 36, the only year in the tenure of Pontius Pilate that fits the whole biblical account is AD 33.

The Gospel of John mentions three Passover Feasts that happened during Jesus' ministry, as follows. John 2:13 records the first Passover, when Jesus first cleansed the temple, which was on Friday, March 29 (9 Nisan), AD 30. John 6:3-4 records the second Passover Feast, before which Jesus went up on a mountainside with his disciples and fed the five thousand. This Passover was on Monday, April 24, AD 31. No Gospel records the Passover in AD 32. Perhaps nothing noteworthy happened in the Passover of that year. But Passover came and went, whether any Gospel mentioned it or not. Jesus' passion occurred on Passover (Matt 26:2; Mark 14:1; Luke 22:1; John 11:55; 12:1, 13:1, 18:28, 39). This final Passover was on Friday (Matt 27:62,15:42; Luke 23:54; John 19:31), which was April 1 in AD 33, the year of the cross. This last Passover had to be in AD 33. Passover fell on the following days during the years of Jesus' ministry. The only year that fits is AD 33.[1]

Year AD	Passover
29	Saturday, April 14
30	Wednesday, April 3
31	Monday, March 24
32	Monday, April 12
33	Friday, April 1

The events of Jesus' ministry fit perfectly into the time frame from September 2, AD 29 (his baptism), through May 13, AD 33, (his ascension), a total of 1,350 days or a little over fifty calendar months or about 4.17 years. Lacking such tools as Kalendis and Microsoft Excel, Eusebius was close, but not quite right, when he wrote that "the

1. Bromberg, "Kalendis Calendar Calculator."

whole time of our Savior's ministry is shown to have been not quite four full years."[2] Finegan also presents a life of Jesus that spanned the years AD 29–33, including four Passovers (although he is wrong about specific dates within those years, which can be verified by using Kalendis).[3]

WHY JESUS' PASSOVER WAS ON THURSDAY

In ancient times, Jews who were residents of Jerusalem observed a single Passover on the evening of 14 Nisan, as the law of Moses required. However, Jews who lived outside of Jerusalem or who were visiting Jerusalem observed two Passover meals in succession. The reason for this double-Passover tradition was that ancient Jews did not have modern calendars or clocks. Since the Hebrew year is complex, including months with twenty-nine or thirty days and intercalary (extra) months in certain years, fixing the exact date of the Passover or the date of any pilgrimage holiday (Exod 23:14–17; Deut 16:5–6), was the responsibility of the priests in Jerusalem. They reached their decision by observing "the appearance of the new moon and the state of the crops . . . [and] "announced their decision to the outlying districts by means of fire-signals and messengers."[4] Such messages, however, did not always reach cities outside of Judea in time to observe the holiday. And Jewish communities "took it upon themselves to inflict punishment" on anyone who violated the second-day holy day. "Excommunication, even beating, was frequently the lot of such a transgressor."[5] Therefore, Jewish communities outside the land of Israel adopted the practice of observing an extra day of the pilgrimage holidays to ensure that they made no error.[6] This led to Jews in the diaspora (living outside Judea) holding two Passovers, a practice some Jews have continued until the present day.[7]

Jesus and his disciples ate the Passover supper a day before Jerusalem residents did because they were from Galilee and they wished to avoid the error that might occur if their calendar was unaligned with the official one in Jerusalem. Thus, the Last Supper occurred on Thursday, and Jesus died on Friday, the same day when the Jews of Jerusalem were killing their Passover lambs, between 2 and 3 p.m. on 14 Nisan or April 1, AD 33. Christ became the ultimate Passover Lamb.

2. Eusebius, *Church History* 1:10:4.
3. Finegan, *Handbook*, 367.
4. Hirsch, "Festivals."
5. Schechter et al., "Holy Days."
6. "Hirsch, "Festivals."
7. Appell, "Why Do Some Jews Have One Seder and Others Have Two Seders?"

Relationships in Jesus' Community

JESUS' IMMEDIATE FAMILY

In the household of Joseph and Mary (mother of Jesus) there were at least seven children other than Jesus: James, Joseph, Simon, Judas, and at least three unnamed daughters (Matt 13:55–56; Mark 6:3). The Catholic view is that all these children were older than Jesus and were the offspring of Joseph and a first wife who died before Joseph was betrothed to Mary. The Protestant view is that Jesus was the older brother of all these half-siblings, who were born to Joseph and Mary after the immaculate conception of Jesus. Readers should consider both views and come to their own conclusions.

THE PATRISTIC VIEW

The early church father Tertullian taught that Mary was a virgin when she conceived Jesus but that she had normal marital relations with Joseph thereafter. Other early church fathers, namely Origen, Hilary of Poitiers, Athanasius, Epiphanius of Salamis, Jerome, Didymus the Blind, Ambrose, and Augustine believed in Mary's perpetual virginity. Even though learned and worthy of respect, the church fathers did not speak with the authority of Scripture. They formulated theological opinions which have been both right and wrong. This is evident because the church fathers sometimes disagreed with each other, so they cannot always all have been right. Since believers are a nation of priests (1 Pet 2:9), they have the right, the duty, and the power through the Holy Spirit to search the Scriptures (Acts 17:11) and test the spirits (1 John 4:1) in pursuit of truth.

THE PERPETUAL VIEW

Catholic doctrine maintains that Jesus was Mary's only child and that Jesus' half-siblings were from a previous marriage of Joseph. The Bible last mentions Joseph in AD 11, when Jesus was twelve years old (Luke 2:42). Mary appeared without Joseph at the cross, in AD 33. This suggests that Joseph had died before Mary, since, at the cross, Jesus placed his mother in the care of his disciple, John. Had Joseph still been alive, Joseph doubtless would have continued to care for his wife. Joseph may therefore have been older than Mary and may have predeceased her, and if so, perhaps he had a previous marriage and children by a deceased wife. It is thus possible that these were Jesus' older half-siblings. Irenaeus, bishop of Lyons, France, taught that Mary was a perpetual virgin. Later Catholic scholars and popes, along with Luther, Zwingli, and Wesley, embraced Irenaeus's perpetual virginity doctrine.

THE PROTESTANT VIEW

It is possible that Joseph simply died before growing very old. So, perhaps Joseph and Mary had seven or more children after Mary bore Jesus. Mary's response to the angel Gabriel's annunciation, that she would conceive a child, was: "How will this be, since I am a virgin?" (Luke 1:34). Since she was betrothed to Joseph, this seems to be an odd question. She might have assumed that when married to Joseph, God would cause her to conceive and have a special child. That is what God did for Sarah and Abraham, Isaac's parents, and for Elizabeth and Zacharias, John the Baptist's parents. Perhaps Mary had already taken a vow of lifelong virginity. But if she had done that, why would she be betrothed to Joseph? Mary's confusion was not that she doubted that she would ever have a child; she seems not to have known how she could have one yet, since she was only betrothed, but not yet living with Joseph. Gabriel explained that the Holy Spirit would conceive in her.

JESUS' CARE FOR MARY FROM THE CROSS

Jesus on the cross consigned Mary to John because there was no one else to care for her. The Catholic thesis is that Jesus' half-siblings were not her biological children and therefore would not have taken her in. This is a possible, but not necessary, explanation. Twice, in AD 30, Mary and Jesus' half-siblings tried to take him into custody or temper his ministry, because they thought he was "out of his mind" (Matt 12:46–50; Mark 3:21, 31–35; Luke 8:19–21). Consider the implication of this. Mary knew Jesus was special, but she joined his half-siblings in thinking that he had gone mad. So, Mary had not, at this point, become a full believer; she did not yet place full faith and trust in Jesus as Messiah.

At the cross, Mary was a follower, but was she yet a full believer? Or was she simply mourning her son? In late April or early May of AD 33, the risen Jesus appeared to James, his half-brother, and James became a believer (1 Cor 15:7). By the day of the ascension, Mary was definitely a believer. That was Friday, May 13, AD 33. So, Mary was not a believer as late as the fall of AD 30. She was a believer by May AD 33. But when, in those two years, she went from disbelief to full belief in Jesus as Lord and God, Scripture does not say.

It is possible that James became a believer before his mother. What is certain is that on the day of the cross, April 1, AD 33, James was not a believer. Therefore, James was not present at the cross. Why would he expose himself to such danger and shame? Mary may have been a believer or may have been simply grieving. For either reason, she was present at the cross. Naturally, therefore, Jesus consigned his mother to John, who was a believer and was probably Mary's nephew. John was wealthy; he possessed a house in Jerusalem into which he could immediately take her; and he was an apostle destined to die a natural death and to live long enough to care for Mary for the rest of her life. James, Jesus' sibling, was murdered by Ananias (Annas), the defrocked high priest of Jerusalem, in AD 62.[1] If Mary had been in James's care when Ananias murdered him, her life, as an ageing widow, would have been at risk.

If Mary were, as many think, only fourteen to sixteen years old when she conceived Jesus in 3 BC, she would have been born between 17 and 19 BC. Mary would thus have been fifty to fifty-two years old at the Cross. She would have been seventy-nine to eighty-two years old when her second-oldest son, James the Just, died. Tradition says that John died in his nineties in AD 98. So John was a safe person to whom Jesus could entrust his mother, if, as tradition suggests, she also lived a long life.

MATTHEW'S DESCRIPTION OF MARY'S VIRGINITY

As an apostle writing by the Holy Spirit, Matthew's testimony is trustworthy. Matthew wrote that Joseph took Mary as his wife and "kept her a virgin until she gave birth" to Jesus (Matt 1:25). Matthew's statement that Joseph kept Mary a virgin until she gave birth suggests that after Jesus' birth, Joseph no longer kept her a virgin. If Matthew had wished to state that Mary remained a virgin forever, he could easily have written, "and he kept her a virgin forever" or simply "he kept her a virgin." Saying that he "kept her a virgin until she gave birth" implies a time limit to her virginity. Mary's marital relationship after Jesus' birth neither supports nor undermines the claim of Jesus' immaculate conception by the Holy Spirit. Only the contention (which first-century Jews made without evidence) that Mary was sexually active before Jesus' conception would challenge this doctrine. But Scripture is emphatically clear: Mary was a virgin when the Holy Spirit conceived Jesus in her (Matt 1:20). So the immaculate conception of Jesus is a biblical truth. Mary's perpetual virginity is a thesis that believers must evaluate in light of Scripture, prayer, and tradition.

---

1. Josephus, *Ant.* 20:9:1.

APPENDICES

KING AND PRIEST

Jesus was a king and priest, like Melchizedek (Matt 2:2; Heb 7:17; Rev 19:16). The problem is that the kings of Judah were Jews (that is, of the tribe of Judah), but the priests were of the tribe of Levi. So, the question is: how could Jesus, who was a Jew, also have been a priest? It was possible because in Jesus' lineage the royal and priestly authorities combined.

God told Aaron (a Levite): "You and your sons with you shall guard your priesthood for all that concerns the altar and that is within the veil; and you shall serve. I give your priesthood as a gift, and any outsider who comes near shall be put to death" (Num 18:7). King David was of the tribe of Judah, yet David's sons were priests (2 Sam 8:18), and David sometimes wore the priestly ephod and presented sacrifices to Yahweh (2 Sam 6:14, 18, 24:25). The Bible recorded these facts but did not record any displeasure by God about them. They somehow did not invoke the death penalty required in Numbers. By contrast, when King Saul, who was of the tribe of Benjamin, dared to perform a priestly sacrifice in place of the Levite priest and prophet Samuel, God tore the kingdom from him (1 Sam 13:8–14). The inescapable conclusion is that God made an exception for David and his descendants, especially Jesus.

In addition, Luke records that Elizabeth, the mother of John the Baptist, was a relative of Mary, the mother of Jesus. Elizabeth was descended from Aaron of the tribe of Levi, and she was married to Zechariah, a priest who was also a Levite (Luke 1:5). This means that at least one of Mary's parents, if not both, had Levite blood by marriage. Therefore, Jesus was descended both from Aaron and King David. Like Melchizedek and David, Jesus was both priest and king.

JAMES AND JUDE

Jesus' half-siblings James and Judas both became followers of Christ after the Lord's resurrection, when he appeared to James in late April or early May of AD 33 (1 Cor 15:7). Jesus' half-brother James, nicknamed "the Just," wrote the book of James in the Bible. He became leader of the Jerusalem church. The Jews martyred him. (He was not James the son of Zebedee or James the Less.) Jesus' other half-brother, Judas, wrote the New Testament book of Jude. (He was not the person commonly called Saint Jude; he was the apostle Judas Thaddaeus Lebbaeus).

OTHER POSSIBLE FAMILY TIES

Mary's relative, Elizabeth, and Zacharias, both Levites, were the parents of John the Baptist. Jesus and John the Baptist were therefore second cousins.

Mary's sister may have been the wife of Zebedee (Mary Salome), and their sons, James and John, may have been Jesus' first cousins. It seems odd that two sisters, Mary the mother of Jesus and Mary Salome, would have the same first name (Mary), but that is probably why the wife of Zebedee is commonly called by her second name, Salome. Matthew Levi and James the Less were both sons of Alphaeus; if this Alphaeus was the same person, they were brothers. If Alphaeus was the same person as Clopas or Cleophas (having both a Greek and Aramaic name, as was common), and if Cleophas (Clopas) was the brother of Joseph, stepfather of Jesus, then Matthew and James the Less were also first cousins of Jesus. Let us examine these theories.

WERE THE SONS OF ZEBEDEE JESUS' COUSINS?

The answer to this question may be solved by examining the identities of the women who watched Jesus die on the cross. The Gospels of John, Mark, and Matthew record them.

Table of the Women at the Cross

John	Mark	Matthew
Jesus' mother (Mary)		
Sister of Mary (Jesus' Mother)	Mary Salome	The Mother of the Sons of Zebedee
Mary wife of Cleophas (Clopas)	Mary the mother of James the Less and Joses	Mary the mother of James and Joseph
Mary Magdalene	Mary Magdalene	Mary Magdalene

From John's Gospel we see that there were four women at the cross, Jesus' mother Mary, her sister, and two other Marys. "Standing by the Cross of Jesus were his mother and his mother's sister, Mary the wife of Cleophas (Clopas), and Mary Magdalene" (John 19:25).

From Mark's account we see the two Marys and the identity of the other women, the sister of Mary, Mary Salome. "There were also women looking on from a distance, among whom were Mary Magdalene, and Mary the mother of James the younger and of Joses, and Mary Salome" (Mark 15:40).

From Matthew's account we see this list of women at the cross: "There were also many women there, looking on from a distance, who had followed Jesus from Galilee, ministering to him, among whom were Mary Magdalene and Mary the mother of James and Joseph and the mother of the sons of Zebedee" (Matt 27:55–56).

All four Gospels indicate there were women followers at the cross. Luke names none, Mark and Matthew name three, and John names four. The sister of Mary (Jesus' mother), Mary Salome, and the mother of the sons of Zebedee may be the same woman. If so, James and John were first cousins of Jesus and probably knew Jesus from childhood.

But to be fair, there are counter-arguments. Mark says that "many other women came up with him to Jerusalem" (Mark 15:41), although he only specifies three at the cross, and Matthew also says there were also many women at the cross. If the sister of Mary, Mary Salome, and the mother of the sons of Zebedee are three different women, and if Mary the wife of Cleophas (Clopas) and Mary the wife of James the Less and Joses (or of James and Joseph) are two different women, and if there were therefore seven women at the cross, of which John names four, Mark names another two, and Matthew includes one more, then the sons of Zebedee are not necessarily the cousins of Jesus.

WERE MATTHEW LEVI AND JAMES THE LESS BROTHERS?

James the Less and Matthew may have been brothers, the sons of Mary the wife of Cleophas (Clopas), who was the brother of Joseph, the husband of Mary, Jesus' mother. Eusebius wrote, "Cleophas (Clopas), of whom the Gospel also makes mention . . . was a cousin, as they say, of the Savior. For Hegesippus records that Cleophas (Clopas) was a brother of Joseph."[2] According to the apostolic father Papias of Hierapolis, Cleophas (Clopas) and Alphaeus were the same person. Papias also reported that, according to some, Cleophas's wife, Mary, had two husbands, and she was the mother of "James the bishop and apostle, and of Simon and Thaddaeus, and of one Joseph."[3]

The first knot to untangle is who Papias meant by "James the bishop and apostle." This cannot have been James the son of Zebedee, because Papias says in the same fragment that the mother of James the son of Zebedee was "Mary Salome." This could not have been the mother of James the Just, the half-brother of Christ, because his mother was Mary, the mother of Jesus, unless Catholic doctrine is correct, and Mary the wife of Cleophas was the first wife of Joseph; but that is improbable, because, if so, she likely would have been known by her more prominent and famous husband, Joseph, not by her more obscure spouse, Cleophas. So Papias must have been referring to the tenth apostle, James the Younger or the Less, and this is tightly confirmed because Matthew 10, Mark 3, Luke 6, and Acts 1 all identify James the Less as the "son of Alphaeus."

So if Mary, the wife of Cleophas (Clopas), is the same person as Mary the mother of James the Less, and if the father of James the Less was Alphaeus, and if Alphaeus and Cleophas (Clopas) were the same person, and if Cleophas (Clopas) was the brother of Joseph, husband of Mary, mother of Jesus, and if Alphaeus the father of James the Less was the same person as Alphaeus the father of Matthew Levi, then Matthew and James the Less were brothers and were therefore Jesus' cousins.

---

2. Eusebius, *Church History* 3:11:2.

3. Papias of Hierapolis, "Fragment X." He lived from about AD 70–163, very near to the events in the New Testament.

Now, if Matthew and James the Less were brothers, why do the Gospel writers never list them as such? After all, they always list Peter and Andrew as brothers and James and John as brothers. Perhaps Matthew, the despised tax collector, was never listed with James the Less as his brother because his Levitical family had cast him out for being a tax collector and collaborator with Rome. Perhaps Matthew felt his sinful vocation made him unworthy to claim his Levitical heritage. Matthew himself never mentioned his family name, Levi; only Mark and Luke did (Mark 2:14; Luke 5:27). Matthew simply called himself "the tax collector" (Matt 10:3).

Still, how could Matthew Levi and James the Less be brothers and cousins of Jesus? Joseph was descended from David, of the tribe of Judah. Matthew was of Levi, and so must his father have been. Could Cleophas (Clopas) have been a Levite and yet have been the brother of Joseph, who was of the tribe of Judah? Yes. Cleophas (Clopas) might have been Joseph's half-brother. This is not a far-fetched thesis.

Joseph had two fathers, Jacob, his biological father, and Heli, his legal stepfather.[4] Joseph's mother, a woman whose name history has not recorded, was the widow of Heli. Jacob, his brother, became her second husband, according to the Levirate commandment in Mosaic law (Deut 25:5–10). Joseph's mother might have outlived her second husband, Jacob, and she might have married a third time to a Levite. She and her third husband might have had a son, Cleophas (Clopas), who would have then been both a Levite and a half-brother of Joseph, the stepfather of Jesus. Cleophas (Clopas) then might have grown up and taken a woman named Mary for a wife, and she might have born him Matthew Levi, James the Less, and, according to Papias, three other boys named Simon, Thaddaeus, and Joseph. Thaddaeus is not the tenth disciple, Judas Thaddaeus Lebbaeus, because Scripture identifies him as the son of James, not of Cleophas (Clopas). The last son, Joseph, seems simply to be a person with a common name, but not identified clearly with anyone else in Scripture. But Simon is probably the eleventh disciple, Simon the Zealot, the Cananean. If James, John, Matthew, Simon the Zealot, and James the Less were Jesus' first cousins, such relationships help explain why these disciples readily responded to Jesus' call. He was far from a rank stranger. He was family.

Of course, to be fair and take the contrary view, it is possible that Matthew and James the Less were never grouped together to emphasize that, despite their father having the same name, they were sons of two different men called Alphaeus and were not brothers.

WAS JUDAS THADDAEUS LEBBAEUS JESUS' SECOND COUSIN?

Judas Thaddaeus Lebbaeus, commonly known as Saint Jude (not the author of the book of Jude) may have been the son of James the son of Zebedee. He may therefore

---

4. Eusebius, *Church History* 1:7.

have been Jesus' second cousin. Here is the reasoning: Luke identified Judas Thaddaeus as Judas of James (Luke 6:16). Many translations interpolate the word Judas "son" of James, which probably is correct. The question is, son of which James? Since Luke mentions James without further qualification, he must mean a prominent, easily recognizable James. The three famous men named James in the New Testament were:

1. James the Elder, the son of Zebedee,
2. James, the son of Alphaeus, the Less, and
3. James the Just, the younger half-brother of Jesus.

Judas Thaddaeus Lebbaeus probably was not the son of James the Just or James the son of Alphaeus because neither of these men would likely have been old enough to have had a son who was old enough to be a disciple. Let us do the math. James the Just was the younger half-brother of Jesus.[5] Jesus died in AD 33, and he was born in 2 BC;[6] that would make him thirty-one years old at the start of his ministry in AD 29.[7] If his younger half-brother were thirty, and if James had a son at the age of eighteen, that son would have been born in AD 17 and would only have been thirteen years old when Jesus called the Twelve in August of AD 30. Since Jewish boys come of age at thirteen, it is just barely possible, but rather unlikely, that Jesus would have called so young a person to be one of the Twelve.

James the son of Alphaeus probably was called the Less because he was younger than James the son of Zebedee. If James the Less was also the brother of Matthew, he probably was the younger of the two brothers, based on the fact that he comes after Matthew in the Bible lists of disciples. If Judas Thaddaeus Lebbaeus were the son of James the Less, he probably would be no older than if he were the son of James the Just, probably too young to be a disciple.

There is no reason, however, why James the son of Zebedee may not have been five or ten years older than the other two men named James, in which case, if Judas Thaddaeus were his son, he would be old enough for Jesus to call him among the Twelve, eighteen or nineteen years old in August AD 30. This further makes sense because, if Luke names any James without further qualification, the first James who followed Jesus, the son of Zebedee, would be the obvious man implied. By this reasoning, Judas Thaddaeus may have been the grandson of Zebedee and therefore the second cousin of Jesus.

---

5. Unless you hold, with Catholics, that James the Just and all Jesus' other half-siblings were from a previous marriage of Joseph.

6. Probably around June 17, 2 BC, since the adoration of the magi was on December 23, 2 BC (December 25 in the Julian calendar, which the Roman Empire used in the first century).

7. Luke 3:1 says that John the Baptist began his ministry in the fifteenth year of Tiberius Caesar, which ended on August 18, AD 29; so Jesus' ministry also began in AD 29. At the cross, Jesus was not yet thirty-five.

SIMON THE ZEALOT

Hippolytus, an early church father who lived from AD 170 to 235, wrote, "Simon the Zealot, the son of Cleophas (Clopas), who is also called Jude, became bishop of Jerusalem after James the Just, and fell asleep and was buried there at the age of 120 years."[8] By identifying Cleophas (Clopas) as the father of Simon the Zealot, Hippolytus agrees with another ancient writer, Papias. He wrote, "Mary the wife of Cleophas or Alphaeus . . . was the mother of James the bishop and apostle and of Simon and Thaddaeus and of one Joseph."[9] Two witnesses make the testimony probable, and so it is likely that Simon the Zealot was also the brother of Matthew Levi and of James the Less and was also a cousin of Jesus. Simon the Zealot, the Cananean, may have been from the village of Cana.[10] Uncertain tradition holds that he was the bridegroom of the famous wedding in that town. If Simon were Jesus' cousin and Mary's nephew, Mary's domineering role in the wedding at Cana would be understandable.

OTHER CONNECTIONS

Simon Peter and Andrew, sons of Jonah, were partners in the fishing business with James and John, the sons of Zebedee (Luke 5:7, 10). They were born in Bethsaida in Galilee (John 1:44). Andrew and John were disciples of John the Baptist, Jesus' second cousin (John 1:35–42). Although Peter and Andrew were not apparently related to Jesus, they may have been boyhood friends. Philip was a Galilean, also born in Bethsaida (John 1:44). He was Nathanael Bartholomew's friend; Philip introduced Nathanael Bartholomew to Jesus. Nathanael Bartholomew was from Cana in Galilee (John 21:2), the village where Jesus turned water into wine. Judas Thomas Didymus ("the Twin") may have been close to John, since only John's Gospel records specifics about his life. The Bible never tells us whose twin Thomas was. Some say he was the twin of Jesus, but this is, of course, impossible. Jesus had no twin; his birth was unique, and even if by twin the Scripture meant a half-brother of Jesus who looked very much like him, the problem is that Scripture lists all of Jesus' half-brothers by name (Matt 13:55–56; Mark 6:3) but never includes anyone named Thomas in that roster. Some say Thomas was Judas Iscariot's twin, but there is no biblical basis for that, either. So, whose twin he was, this side of heaven, we shall probably never know.

GALILEAN TIES

However the relationships in Jesus' spiritual family sort out, what we can infer is that in a small region like Galilee, family and business relationships were closely intertwined.

8. Hippolytus, "List of the Apostles and Disciples."
9. Papias of Hierapolis, "Fragment X."
10. Hippolytus, "List of the Apostles and Disciples."

All of the Eleven were family, business partners, or neighbors. Only Judas Iscariot (from Kerioth in Judea, southwest of Jerusalem), the son of Simon, may not have grown up in Galilee. Perhaps he fell in with Jesus in Jerusalem, or perhaps his family was originally from Judea and had migrated to Galilee. In that case, he may have grown up there with the other Eleven.

If James, John, James the Less, Matthew, Judas Thaddaeus, and Simon the Zealot were Jesus' cousins, it is interesting that they recognized Jesus' divine authority and followed him before the other children of Joseph and Mary did. Although Jesus' half-brothers, James the Just and Judas, later acknowledged Jesus as Lord and wrote the New Testament books of James and Jude, neither of them ever "pulled rank" among the apostles by promoting themselves as Jesus' relatives. Perhaps they were embarrassed that they were so late coming to recognize the deity of their half-brother. Followers of Christ who were his relatives would hardly dare to feel undue pride in their blood relationship, remembering Jesus' words:

> "Who are my mother and my brothers?" And looking about at those who sat around him, he said, "Here are my mother and my brothers! For whoever does the will of God, he is my brother and sister and mother." (Mark 3:33–35)

The Genealogies of Matthew and Luke

TABLE OF THE GENEALOGIES OF MATTHEW AND LUKE.

Luke's Genealogy (Luke 3:23–38)	
1	Adam
2	Seth
3	Enosh
4	Kenan
5	Mahalalel
6	Jared
7	Enoch
8	Methuselah
9	Lamech
10	Noah
11	Shem
12	Arphaxad
13	Cainan
14	Shelah
15	Eber
16	Peleg
17	Reu
18	Serug
19	Nahor
20	Terah

Appendices

	Matthew's Genealogy (Matt 1:1-17)		Luke's Genealogy (Luke 3:23-38)	
1	Abraham		22	Abraham
2	Isaac		23	Isaac
3	Jacob		24	Jacob
4	Judah & Tamar		25	Judah
5	Pharez		26	Pharez
6	Hezron		27	Hezron
7	Ram		28	Ram
8	Amminadab		29	Amminadab
9	Nahshon		30	Nahshon
10	Salman & Rahab		31	Salmon
11	Boaz & Ruth		32	Boaz
12	Obed		33	Obed
13	Jesse		34	Jesse
14	David		35	David
1	Solomon		36	Nathan
2	Rehoboam (first king of Judah—good to bad)		37	Mattatha
3	Abijam (second king of Judah—bad)		38	Menna
4	Asa (third king of Judah—good to bad)		39	Melea
5	Jehosaphat (fourth king of Judah—good)		40	Eliakim
6	Jehoram (fifth king of Judah—bad)		41	Jonam
Illegitimate, uncounted monarchs 1. Ahaziah (Jehoahaz) 2. Queen Athaliah 3. Jehoash 4. Amaziah				
7	Uzziah (tenth king of Judah—good)		42	Joseph
8	Jotham (eleventh king of Judah—good)		43	Judah
9	Ahaz (twelfth king of Judah—bad)		44	Simeon
10	Hezekiah (thirteenth king of Judah—good)		45	Levi
11	Manasseh (fourteenth king of Judah—bad to good)		46	Matthat
12	Amon (fifteenth king of Judah—bad)		47	Jorim
13	Josiah (sixteenth king of Judah—good)		48	Eliezer
14	Jeconiah, uncrowned son of King Josiah		49	Joshua
			50	Er
	51	Elmadam		
	52	Cosam		
	53	Addi		
	54	Melchi		
	55	Neri		

	Matthew's Genealogy (Matt 1:1–17)		Luke's Genealogy (Luke 3:23–38)
1	Jeconiah, uncrowned son of King Josiah		
2	Shealtiel	56	Shealtiel
3	Zerubbabel (governor of Judah after Babylon)	57	Zerubbabel (governor of Judah after Babylon)
4	Abiud	58	Rhesa
5	Eliakim	59	Joanan
6	Azor	60	Joda
7	Zadok	61	Josech
8	Achim	62	Semein
9	Eliud	63	Mattathias
10	Eleazar	64	Maath
11	Matthan	65	Naggai
12	Jacob (Joseph's biological father)	66	Hesli
		67	Nahum
		68	Amos
		69	Mattathias
		70	Joseph
		71	Jannai
		72	Melchi
		73	Levi
		74	Matthat
		75	Heli (Joseph's legal or levirate father)
13	Joseph (and Mary)	76	Joseph (and Mary)
14	Jesus	77	Jesus

COMPARISON OF THE GENEALOGIES OF MATTHEW AND LUKE.

Luke, a rational Greek, recorded Jesus' genealogy with factual precision. Matthew, a Hebrew of priestly heritage (his other name was Levi), embedded rich symbolism in Jesus' identity.

Matthew opened his Gospel emphasizing Jesus as Christ—the Greek word for Messiah—meaning anointed, in the sense of an anointed king. Matthew began by calling Jesus son of David, through whose royal line God promised the Messiah (2 Sam 7:12–16; Isa 11:1), and also son of Abraham, through whose offspring God promised the Messiah (Gen 18:18, 22:18). Matthew's genealogy identified Joseph not as the father of Jesus, but as the husband of Mary. The Greek text is explicit in making Jesus born to Mary, rather than to Joseph. Matthew's careful wording is meant to affirm the virgin birth, stating that Jesus was begotten not by Joseph but by God.

As a man of numbers, Matthew organized his genealogy in a clever mathematical array, arranged in three sets of fourteen, as he explicitly stated, each of a distinct character. The first set includes four mothers: (1) Tamar, (2) Rahab, (3) Ruth, and (4) Bathsheba. The second set spans Judah's royal line, but omits four generations, ending with "Jeconiah and his brothers at the time of the exile to Babylon." The last set connects Joseph to Zerubbabel, the governor of Judah after the return from the Babylonian exile, through a series of otherwise unknown names.

The total of forty-two generations is achieved only by omitting four names, further suggesting that the choice of three sets of fourteen was deliberate. Fourteen is seven doubled. Seven is the number symbolizing perfection and completion in Hebrew. Twice seven means doubly perfect. And fourteen is also the gemetria (Hebrew numerical equivalent) of David's name. In classical Hebrew, there were once no vowels, so David is rendered by the (transliterated into English) consonants DVD. In Hebrew gemetria $D = 4$, $V = 6$, and $D = 4$, the sum of which equals 14. Matthew was embedding a message into his genealogy. By grouping Jesus' ancestors into three sets of fourteen, Matthew was branding the Messiah's lineage with the "watermark"—"David, David, David."

Of course, three sets of fourteen equals forty-two ($3 \times 14 = 42$), and yet there are only forty-one names in Matthew's lineage. The last set of fourteen contains only thirteen names. As a professional bean counter, it is unlikely that Matthew made an obvious math error. Furthermore, since Matthew deliberately left names out of Jesus' lineage, he could easily have added one more to perfect his trilogy of fourteens, had he wished to do so.

The explanation becomes obvious by reading Matthew's text carefully: "So, all the generations from Abraham to David were fourteen generations, and from David to the deportation to Babylon fourteen generations, and from the deportation to Babylon to the Christ fourteen generations." Matthew counted David to Jeconiah (who was exiled to Babylon) as the second set of fourteen. Then he counted Jeconiah twice as the beginning of the third set of fourteen that ended with Jesus. This made sense, because Jeconiah lived in Judah before the exile and lived in Babylon at the start of the exile. He bridged both sides of the line.

Matthew's message was expressed in the important events embedded in each set of fourteen, as follows. The first set of fourteen represents God's promise to Abraham that found fulfillment in God's promise to David. The second set of fourteen represents God's promise to David, whose royal descendants survived the ups and downs of Judah's turbulent history and of its ultimate exile to Babylon. The third set of fourteen represents God's promise to restore the exiled Jews to Judah after seventy years of banishment in Babylon (Jer 29:10); Zerubbabel led the survivors home in 539 BC (Ezra 2:2). The three sets cumulatively point to the coming of the long-expected Messiah, Jesus.

WOMEN IN JESUS' ANCESTRY

Luke recorded only one female ancestor of Jesus: Mary. Matthew recorded five women: Tamar, Rahab, Ruth, Bathsheba, and Mary. Genealogies in the first century usually named only men. The meaning of these women in Jesus' ancestry is therefore significant.

Tamar

Tamar was the daughter-in-law of Judah, fourth son of Jacob and Leah. Tamar married Judah's son Er, who displeased God and died without giving Tamar children. Judah gave Tamar to his other son, Onan,[1] who refused to impregnate Tamar, and who also displeased God and died without giving Tamar children. Judah promised to give Tamar to another son, Shelah, when he became old enough. But Judah did not make good his promise. Desperate and disgraced, Tamar disguised herself as a prostitute and waited by the roadside in Timnah for her father-in-law, Judah, to pass. Judah shamelessly slept with her, thinking she was a harlot. When he offered to pay for her services, she asked only for his staff and seal. Three months later, her pregnancy became obvious. Tamar was accused of prostitution. But she produced Judah's staff and seal, clearing her name and proving Judah's guilt. She escaped punishment and gave birth to twins, Perez and Zerah (Gen 38:29). Judah had no further intimate relations with Tamar, and Perez became the ancestor of King David (Ruth 4:18–22), and he was also the ancestor of Jesus (Matt 1:3).

Rahab

Was Rahab, the ancestor of Jesus, the harlot of Jericho? Boaz, a main character in Ruth, was the son of Salman (Ruth 4:21; 1 Chron 2:11) and Rahab (Matt 1:5). Ruth 4:18–22 provides a ten-generation genealogy from Perez (born in 1676 BC), the son of Judah, through Boaz, the husband of Ruth, to King David (born 1040 BC). From the birth of Perez to the birth of David is 637 years. Since there are ten generations in this interval, each generation could span an average of seventy-one years (counting nine generations, since David only needs to be born within this interval, not live his entire life in the interval). This is reasonable.

There is, however, a problem with identifying the Rahab who was Salman's wife with Rahab, the harlot of Jericho. Jericho fell in 1406 BC. If Rahab the harlot, and not some other Rahab, was Salman's wife, then the events in Ruth occurred almost or literally within living memory of Jericho's fall. This would mean that there would

---

1. Deuteronomy 25:5–10 said that if a man died childless, his brother should marry his widow and the first-born son must carry on the dead man's name so that it would not die out in the community of Israel. This is called a levirate marriage, from the Latin word *levir*, meaning "husband's brother."

be an interval from Salman and Ruth to David of 367 years, which would include five generations. That would work out to an average lifespan of ninety-two years (considering four generations, not including David, who only needs to have been born in this interval). Ruth 4:18–21 thus requires uncomfortably long lifespans. Rahab must have borne Boaz to Salman at an age young enough to be pre-menopausal unless God worked a miracle for her as he did for Sarah. But this is an awkwardly eisegetical presumption. Still, such long lifespans need not be impossibly long by Old Testament standards. First Samuel 17:12 may support unusual longevity in David's ancestry, since it says that Jesse, David's father, was "very old" in Saul's time. Whoever wrote the postscript to Joshua (24:29), noting that Joshua lived to 110 years old, made no comment on Joshua's age, so perhaps such longevity around the time of Jericho's fall was not yet uncommon.

The many theories of gaps in Bible genealogies might solve the puzzle, but they are speculative, and they are problematic if the chronological markers in the Bible are able to hang together without the use of this hermeneutical *deus ex machina*.

Perhaps a better solution arises when examining the Greek of the New Testament. James 2:25 and Hebrews 11:31 both refer to Rahab the prostitute. Matthew 1:5 refers to Rahab, the mother of Boaz and the ancestor of Jesus. The books of James and Hebrews spell Rahab's name Ραάβ, *Raab*, while Matthew spelled it Ραχάβ, *Rachab*. If the two Rahabs were different women, no chronological problem exists.

So, either the Rahab in Jesus' ancestry was the harlot of Jericho, and David's forbears lived unusually long (but not impossibly long) lives, or Rahab, Jesus' ancestor, was another woman with a similar name. Assuming that the two Rahabs were different women does no violence to the text of Scripture, and it has the advantage of not stretching credulity by having to assume improbably long lives among David's ancestors. The preponderance of evidence, therefore, favors the conclusion that Rahab, Jesus' ancestor and Salman's wife, was not the harlot of Jericho.

Bathsheba

Bathsheba was the daughter of Eliam (Ammiel), one of David's thirty warriors (2 Sam 23:34; 1 Chron 3:5). She married Uriah the Hittite, a gentile convert to Judaism. She was possibly also a Hittite, but there is no direct evidence of this. David committed adultery with her and murdered her husband (2 Sam 11). The Bible does not make it clear whether Bathsheba willingly slept with David or whether she was an unwilling victim. The law required putting both King David and Bathsheba to death for the sin of adultery (Lev 20:10). Interestingly, the Bible records no example of the Israelites ever carrying this punishment out. The only time when the Jews appeared willing to carry out this sentence was in the case of the woman caught in adultery, whom the scribes and Pharisees brought before Jesus on the Sabbath at the Feast of Tabernacles in AD 32 (John 8:3–11). In any case, David compounded the sin of adultery with murdering Bathsheba's husband. He repented profoundly (Ps 51). His first child died by Bathsheba died shortly after childbirth. Their second son, Solomon, became Israel's most powerful king. Yet because of his sin, the sword never left David's house. His son Absalom died in a bitter civil war against his father. Another son, Adonijah, was executed after trying to usurp the throne from David and Solomon.

Ruth

Ruth was a Moabite, therefore a gentile. The land of Moab was named after Moab the son of Lot, conceived through incest with his elder daughter, who got him drunk and slept with him after the death of Lot's wife in the destruction of Sodom. Lot's younger daughter did the same and conceived a son named Ben Ammi, who became the ancestor of the Ammonites, who lived in what is modern-day Jordan (Gen 19:30–38). Ruth was faithful and good. She married Boaz, a Jew. Their son, Obed, was the father of Jesse, who was the father of King David.

Characteristics of Women in Jesus' Lineage

Woman	Ancestry	Character
Tamar	Unknown, possibly Canaanite, possibly Israelite	Lonely, victim of Judah's neglect and lust, incestuous
Rahab	Unknown	Unknown
Ruth	Gentile, Moabite, descendant of Lot's incest	Good
Bathsheba	Possibly Hittite, but probably Jewish	Possibly sexually immoral, possibly an innocent victim of David's lust
Mary	Jewish	Good

Male, female, Jew, gentile, sinner, and victims of sin are all represented in the Messiah's bloodline. All are valuable enough for Christ to die on a cross for their sake.

THE GENEALOGIES OF MATTHEW AND LUKE

Matthew recorded Jesus' genealogy from his stepfather, Joseph, through the line of the kings of Judah, including David, and back to Abraham, the patriarch of the Hebrews. Luke gave a different genealogy, starting with Adam and following Adam's descendants down to Jesus. Both Matthew and Luke state that Jesus was not the biological son of Joseph, the husband of his mother, Mary, but was begotten miraculously by the Holy Spirit, born to Mary through a virgin birth.

While the genealogies of Matthew and Luke are different, they are not contradictory. Matthew did not mention every one of Jesus' ancestors. He only mentioned the ones he deemed legitimate. He omitted King Ahaziah (Jehoahaz), the evil son of Queen Athaliah; he reigned for only one year. He omitted Queen Athaliah, who usurped the throne of Judah and killed almost all of Judah's royal house. He omitted her son, King Jehoash, and he omitted his son, King Amaziah. Matthew's reason for omitting Queen Athaliah is obvious. She was illegitimate. His reason for omitting the other three kings is probably found in Exodus 20:5: "I the LORD your God am a jealous God, visiting the iniquity of the fathers on the children to the third and the fourth generation of those who hate me." King Ahab certainly qualified to be called one who hated God, so omitting these four generations of Judah's rulers associated with and following Ahab may have seemed justifiable to Matthew.

In any case, Matthew touched on the mountain peaks in Jesus' ancestry and omitted the valleys. He did this because he wanted to group Jesus' ancestors into three batches of fourteen. Luke's genealogy of Jesus, on the other hand, threw everybody in. And Luke traced Jesus' family to King David not through King Solomon, but through Nathan, another of King David's sons. This leads to a puzzling, apparent contradiction.

THE MYSTERY OF TWO FATHERS

Matthew and Luke seem to give different ancestors for Joseph, the husband of Mary. If the Gospels were made up years after the events, why would the Gospel authors not just copy each other's genealogies and avoid an obvious error? Rather, Matthew and Luke were so painstakingly accurate that they recorded the complex details of Jesus' lineage with infinite care, even though they might easily have skipped them to produce tidier books.

Matthew said that Joseph's grandfather was Matthan, and his father was Jacob. Luke said that Joseph's grandfather was Matthat, and his father was Heli. John of Damascus (a Syrian Christian monk in the eighth century AD), thought Luke's words "as was supposed of Joseph" to be a parenthetical note, meaning that Luke was calling Heli the maternal grandfather of Jesus.[2] John Wesley thought that the expression "Joseph of Heli," without the word "son" being present in the Greek, indicated that "Joseph of Heli" should be read "Joseph [son-in-law] of Heli," which would be a common enough way of writing in the first century.[3] Both of these proposed solutions suggest that Luke was tracing the ancestry of Jesus through Mary.

But the fourth-century historian Eusebius offered a better solution. Since Eusebius was nearer to Jesus' day than John of Damascus or John Wesley, he was able to draw on more ancient sources that perhaps have since been lost to us. Also, Eusebius's solution, although complex, requires no "stretching" of the original language, such as presuming that "of Heli" means "the son-in-law of Heli."

Eusebius stated that both genealogies are correct ancestries of Joseph, explaining as follows: Matthew named Matthan as Joseph's grandfather. He descended from

2. Jones, "The Two Genealogies of Jesus."
3. Wesley, "Luke 3: Wesley's Notes on the Bible."

King David through King Solomon. Luke named Melchi as Joseph's grandfather. He descended from King David through a minor son, Nathan.

Matthan married a woman named Estha. Matthan and Estha had a son named Jacob. Then Matthan died. Estha remarried, and her second husband was Melchi. Melchi and Estha had a son named Heli. So, Estha had two sons, Jacob by her first husband, Matthan, and Heli by her second husband, Melchi.

The Biological and Legal Grandparents and Parents of Joseph

Matthan	married	Estha	married	Melchi
	parents of		parents of	
	Jacob (biological father of Joseph)		Heli (legal father of Joseph)	

Jacob and Heli were brothers from the same mother, Estha, but had different fathers. When he grew up, Heli got married, but before he and his wife could have a child, Heli died. Heli's widow married Jacob, Heli's half-brother. Under Mosaic law, this was Jacob's duty. Deuteronomy 25:5 said that if a man died childless, his brother should marry his widow and the firstborn son must carry on the dead man's name so that it would not die out in the community of Israel. This is called a levirate marriage, from the Latin word *levir*, meaning "husband's brother." So Jacob, Heli's half-brother, married Heli's widow, and she bore Jacob a son, whom they named Joseph. Joseph was the stepfather of Jesus. As the law required, Joseph carried on Heli's name. As Luke correctly said, Joseph was thus "of Heli." And Matthew also correctly said that Jacob "begot" Joseph; he was Joseph's biological father.

The Biological and Legal Parents of Joseph

Jacob	married	Unnamed Wife	married	Heli (died childless)
	parents of		no children	
	Joseph (stepfather of Jesus)			

As usual, there are no contradictions between the Gospels. Jesus descended legally from King David and King Solomon through his step-grandfather, Heli, and legally from King David and another of King David's sons, Nathan, through his other step-grandfather, Jacob.

THE CURSE OF JECONIAH

Skeptics say that since Matthew said Jesus descended from the cursed King Jeconiah, he cannot have been the Messiah. Scripture said of King Jeconiah, the son of King Josiah:

> Thus says the LORD: "Write this man down as childless, a man who shall not succeed in his days, for none of his offspring shall succeed in sitting on the throne of David and ruling again in Judah." (Jer 22:30)

This curse disqualified any of Jeconiah's descendants from being king of the Jews. Some scholars argue that since Jesus was not the biological son of Joseph, the curse does not apply to him. However, if Jesus inherited the royalty of King David through the ancestry of Joseph, his legal, adoptive father, it stands to reason Jesus would also inherit the curse of Jeconiah through him. The solution is that the Jeconiah cursed in Jeremiah 22 is a different man from the Jeconiah named by Matthew in Jesus' genealogy, which says:

> And Josiah the father of Jechoniah and his brothers, at the time of the deportation to Babylon. And after the deportation to Babylon: Jechoniah was the father of Shealtiel, and Shealtiel the father of Zerubbabel, and Zerubbabel the father of Abiud. (Matt 1:11–13)

Note the plural word "brothers" (Matt 1:11). According to 1 Chronicles 13:15, King Josiah had four sons, in this order: (1) Johanan, who never became king although he was the firstborn; (2) Eliakim, whose name changed to Jehoiakim when he became king (2 Kgs 23:34); (3) Mattaniah, whose name changed to Zedekiah when he became king (2 Kgs 24:17); and (4) Shallum, whose name changed to Jehoahaz when he became king (Jer 22:11, 2 Kgs 23:30).

Matthew said that Jeconiah had brothers (plural) who were carried away to Babylon. But 1 Chronicles 3:16 said that King Jehoiakim had only two sons, Jeconiah and Zedekiah. Therefore, King Jeconiah had only one brother, Zedekiah, who was carried away to Babylon, not brothers, plural, as Matthew 1:11 said. So the Jeconiah in Matthew 1:11 is a different man from King Jeconiah.

Who then was Matthew's Jeconiah? He could have been Johanan, the son of King Josiah. This fits the obvious statement in Matthew 1:11 that King Josiah begot Jeconiah (Johanan) and the statement in 1 Chronicles 3:15 that Johanan was King Josiah's firstborn son. All that this requires us to believe is that Johanan had a second name: Jeconiah. Since all three of Johanan's brothers had second names, it is reasonably likely that Johanan had a second name, too.

Here are the names and second names (royal names) of King Josiah's sons: (1) Johanan, second name: Jeconiah (probably his planned royal name, although he never became king); (2) Eliakim, second name: Jehoiakim (his royal name when he became king); (3) Mattaniah, second name: Zedekiah (his royal name when he became king); and (4) Shallum, second name: Jehoahaz (his royal name when he became king).

One might object that Eliakim, Mattaniah, and Shallum had second names because they became kings, and that Johanan would not have had a second name because he did not become a king. But not everyone in the Bible who had dual names became a king. Jesus gave Simon the nickname of Peter ("rock"). Nebuchadnezzar changed the name of Daniel to Belteshazzar, and Daniel's three colleagues, Hananiah, Mishael, and Azariah, had their names changed to Shadrach, Meshach, and Abednego. None of these people became kings.

Yet it is odd that Johanan, the firstborn son of Josiah, did not become king, even though all three of his younger brothers did so. King Josiah died in battle against Pharaoh Necho II in the great war when Egypt and Assyria fought and lost against Babylon. After King Josiah's death, Jehoahaz (also known as Shallum) became king at the age of twenty-three, even though he was two years younger than Eliakim, his brother. He reigned only three months, after which Pharaoh Necho took him captive into Egypt. Pharaoh Necho made Eliakim, the second son of King Josiah, the king of Judah, changing his name to Jehoiakim. He reigned for eleven years. In 598 BC, Nebuchadnezzar took Jehoiakim bound in fetters to Babylon and installed Jehoiakim's son, Jeconiah (also known as Coniah and Jehoiachin), the cursed one, on Judah's throne. After three months and ten days, Nebuchadnezzar deposed Jeconiah, took him captive to Babylon, and installed Jeconiah's uncle, Mattaniah, on the throne of Judah, changing his name to Zedekiah. He was Judah's last king. When Nebuchadnezzar finally destroyed Jerusalem in 586 BC, he blinded Zedekiah and took him captive into Babylon. Thus, two of Johanan's brothers, Jehoiakim and Zedekiah, were taken captive into Babylon, just as Matthew 1:11 said.

It is possible that Johanan was given a regal name, like his brothers, in preparation for his becoming king of Judah. It is possible that the name he received was Jeconiah, which means "God has established" or "established by God." In these turbulent times, when Josiah's sons and grandson took the throne not in order of their birth but in compliance with the dictates of the warlords of Egypt and Babylon, Johanan never got the chance to rule Judah, as should have been his right as the firstborn of King Josiah. Or perhaps he died in battle before he could wear the crown. Or perhaps Pharaoh Necho or Nebuchadnezzar disapproved of him.

We can further verify that Johanan was really the uncursed Jeconiah in Jesus' lineage. First Chronicles 3:17–19 says that Jeconiah (who was cursed) had a son named Shealtiel, who had a son named Pedaiah, who had a son named Zerubbabel, whose sons were Meshullam, Hananiah, Hashubah, Ohel, Berechiah, Hasadiah, Jushabhesed, and whose daughter was Shelomith. Matthew 1:12 said that the Jeconiah in Jesus' ancestry had a son named Shealtiel, who had a son named Zerubbabel, who had a son named Abiud. Matthew's Jeconiah had brothers (plural) who were deported to Babylon (Matt 1:11), but the Jeconiah of 1 Chronicles had only one brother, Zedekiah, who was deported to Babylon (1 Chron 3:16; 2 Kgs 25:7; Jer 39:7, 52:11). Both Jeconiahs had descendants named Shealtiel and Zerubbabel, but their genealogies make it clear that they were different men. The Zerubbabel in Jesus' lineage was not the Zerubbabel of 1 Chronicles 3:19. Jacob, Joseph's biological father, descended from Abiud, the son of the different Zerubbabel in Matthew's genealogy (Matt 1:12).

The only person named Jeconiah who could have: (1) been a son of Josiah (Matt 1:11), (2) had plural brothers who were carried off to Babylon (Matt 1:11), and (3) had a son named Shealtiel (Matt 1:12), who had a son named Zerubbabel (Matt 1:12), who had a son named Abiud (Matt 1:13), is Johanan, the firstborn son of King Josiah. Therefore, Johanan, although never crowned, must have received a regal name, Jeconiah, and Jesus descended from him, not from the cursed King Jeconiah.

ZERUBBABEL

Zerubbabel led the Jews back from Babylon to Jerusalem, along with Jeshua the priest (Ezra 2:2). He became the governor of Judah under the Persian king, Artaxerxes I. He is identified only as Zerubbabel, the son of Shealtiel (Ezra 3:2, 5:2; Neh 12:1; Hag 1:1, 12, 14, 2:2, 23). Neither Ezra 3 nor Nehemiah 7, when recording the number of Jews returning from Babylonian exile to Judah, name any sons of Zerubbabel. Therefore, the Zerubbabel who led the Jews back from Babylon need not be the Zerubbabel of 1 Chronicles 3:19. This makes sense, because the Zerubbabel of 1 Chronicles 3:19 was cursed and would thus not have been qualified to become the ruler of Judah. So the Zerubbabel who led the return from Babylon was a descendant of King David (Matt 1:5–12) but was not of King Jeconiah's cursed line. He was a descendant of Johanan (Jeconiah), who was never king and was never cursed.

There is a further, telling difference between the cursed line of Jeconiah and the uncursed Zerubbabel. Of King Jeconiah, God said:

> As I live, declares the LORD, though Coniah the son of Jehoiakim, king of Judah, were the signet ring on my right hand, yet I would tear you off and give you into the hand of those who seek your life, into the hand of those of whom you are afraid, even into the hand of Nebuchadnezzar king of Babylon and into the hand of the Chaldeans. (Jeremiah 22:24–25)

God likened King Jeconiah to a signet ring that he tore off his right hand. By contrast, of the uncursed Zerubbabel, God said: "I will take you, O Zerubbabel my servant, the son of Shealtiel, declares the LORD, and make you like a signet ring, for I have chosen you, declares the LORD of hosts" (Hag 2:23). God likened Zerubbabel to a signet ring that he had chosen. In Zechariah, God said:

> Not by might, nor by power, but by my Spirit, says the LORD of hosts. Who are you, O great mountain? Before Zerubbabel you shall become a plain. And he shall bring forward the top stone amid shouts of "Grace, grace to it!" Then the word of the LORD came to me, saying, "The hands of Zerubbabel have laid the foundation of this house; his hands shall also complete it. Then you will know that the LORD of hosts has sent me to you. For whoever has despised the day of small things shall rejoice and shall see the plumb line in the hand of Zerubbabel. (Zec 4:6–10)

This Zerubbabel, clearly not cursed, was the leader of the Jews who returned from Babylon back to Jerusalem. His mission was to restore the worship in the temple that Nebuchadnezzar destroyed. He was the descendant of righteous King Josiah and acted in the role of Judah's king, even though he was a governor under the overlordship of King Cyrus of Persia. The righteous Zerubbabel,[4] chosen and blessed by God, brought forth the literal capstone, used to rebuild the temple, and the figurative capstone of the living temple, God's people, in the person of Jesus Christ.

This is the only possible and correct ancestry of Jesus that is consistent with the texts of 1 Chronicles, 2 Kings, Jeremiah, Haggai, Zechariah, and Matthew. Jesus descends from King David not through the cursed King Jeconiah but through the uncursed Prince Jeconiah (Johanan) and therefore is not barred from being King of the Jews (Matt 2:2; Rev 19:16).

---

4. The name Zerubbabel is not Hebrew, but Aramaic. It means "the seed of Babylon." Since both men of this name would have been born in the Babylonian exile, this is hardly a strange name for them. It may even have been a kind of a title.

Did Matthew Misquote Scripture?

MATTHEW 27:9 QUOTES THIS Scripture regarding the prophecy of Judas's death:

> Then was fulfilled what had been spoken by the prophet Jeremiah, saying, "And they took the thirty pieces of silver, the price of him on whom a price had been set by some of the sons of Israel, and they gave them for the potter's field, as the Lord directed me." (Matt 27:9–10)

The problem is that Jeremiah did not make this precise prophecy. But Zechariah wrote:

> Then I said to them, "If it seems good to you, give me my wages; but if not, keep them." And they weighed out as my wages thirty pieces of silver. Then the Lord said to me, "Throw it to the potter"—the lordly price at which I was priced by them. So, I took the thirty pieces of silver and threw them into the house of the Lord, to the potter. (Zech 11:12–13)

Zechariah mentioned setting a price on God at an insulting thirty pieces of silver but did not mention a field. Jeremiah mentioned buying a field in a doomed land to show that God promised to redeem the land through a future Messiah.

> Jeremiah said, "The word of the Lord came to me: Behold, Hanamel the son of Shallum your uncle will come to you and say, 'Buy my field that is at Anathoth, for the right of redemption by purchase is yours.' Then Hanamel my cousin came to me in the court of the guard, in accordance with the word of the Lord, and said to me, 'Buy my field that is at Anathoth in the land of Benjamin, for the right of possession and redemption is yours; buy it for yourself.' Then I knew that this was the word of the Lord. And I bought the field at Anathoth from Hanamel my cousin, and weighed out the money to him, seventeen shekels of silver. I signed the deed, sealed it, got witnesses, and weighed the money on scales. Then I took the sealed deed of purchase, containing the terms and conditions and the open copy. And I gave the deed of purchase to Baruch the son of Neriah son of Mahseiah, in the presence of Hanamel my cousin, in the presence of the witnesses who signed the deed of purchase, and in the presence of all the Judeans who were sitting in the court

of the guard. I charged Baruch in their presence, saying, "Thus says the Lord of hosts, the God of Israel: 'Take these deeds, both this sealed deed of purchase and this open deed, and put them in an earthenware vessel, that they may last for a long time.' For thus says the Lord of hosts, the God of Israel: 'Houses and fields and vineyards shall again be bought in this land.'" (Jer 32:6–15)

Matthew drew his ideas from the prophecies of both Jeremiah and Zechariah, citing only the more ancient and famous prophet, Jeremiah, while adding Zechariah's thoughts without citation.

Matthew was making a "conflated reference" of prophetic sayings, something he did elsewhere in his Gospel (Matt 1:23, 2:15–18, 4:15–16, 8:17, and 12:18–21). Aramaic paraphrases or interpretations of the Hebrew Bible were called "targums," and they were used commonly for teaching in the first century AD, when Hebrew was declining as a spoken tongue. This was a common practice, and in this tradition whenever referring to more than one prophet, an author might cite the more famous of the two and blend their two prophecies into one.

Zechariah did not mention the field, but Jeremiah did. So Matthew simply followed the practice of referring to the more famous author, Jeremiah, when referencing the field. The same thing occurred in Mark 1:2–3, where Mark quoted both Malachi and Isaiah, but referred only to Isaiah. Matthew's Greek text refers not to a prophecy "by" Jeremiah, but a prophecy "through" Jeremiah. This is shorthand, similar to Jesus referring to all of Psalm 22 by quoting only its first line on the Cross: "My God, my God, why have you forsaken me?"

Jeremiah's theme was that, although Babylon would utterly destroy apostate Israel, God would restore the promised land after seventy years of exile. Zechariah's theme was that Rome would destroy apostate Israel a second time. He also foretold an end to God's covenant with Israel and foretold a transfer of his covenant to a people who would love God sincerely (the church, consisting of both Jewish and non-Jewish Christians). He prophesied that the Messiah would establish this new covenant. Matthew traced the thread of Messianic promise from (1) Nebuchadnezzar's destruction of Judah to (2) the Jewish exile in Babylon to (3) the return under Jeshua, Zerubbabel, Ezra, and Nehemiah to (4) the Sanhedrin's rejection of Jesus as Messiah to (5) the establishment of the new covenant with all believers, and to (6) the coming destruction of the temple and the old covenant by pagan Rome.

Zechariah prophesied to post-exilic Judah from 520 to 519 BC. In the context of this prophecy, God was saying to Israel that they had insulted God's prophet, Zechariah, by giving him wages of a mere thirty pieces of silver. In making reference to this, Matthew was establishing that the thirty pieces of silver Judas received was symbolic of rejecting and insulting God[1]. Probably the Jewish elite, who paid this price, were ironically aware of the unholy connotation of thirty pieces of silver. They were perhaps

---

1. Thirty pieces of silver is the price of a mere slave (Exod 21:32).

APPENDICES

implying, with a smirk, that Judas was at last ready to reject Jesus, the "false God." Back in Zechariah's day, God said he would break his relationship with the unfaithful Jews and destroy their kingdom. That same doom would come to pass in the Apostolic Age when Titus destroyed Jerusalem in AD 70.

By saying "throw it to the potter," Zechariah was hearkening back to Jeremiah, who wrote, "Behold, like the clay in the potter's hand, so are you in my hand, O Israel" (Jer 18:6). This was reminiscent of God's words in Isaiah: "We are the clay; you are the potter; we are all the work of your hand. Be not so terribly angry, O LORD, and remember not iniquity forever" (Isa 64:9).

Extracting his desired meaning from the prophecies of Jeremiah and Zechariah, Matthew was saying, "Some of the sons of Israel insulted God by setting price of thirty pieces of silver upon him, and, as the LORD directed, they threw it to the potter, that is, to God, the Creator, who crushed Israel and make a new pot of her; now this is happening again."

Paul's View on Women in Church

THE VERSES THAT SUPPORT the view that women should be silent in church come from the apostle Paul, and they are as follows.

> I do not permit a woman to teach or to exercise authority over a man; rather, she is to remain quiet. (1 Tim 2:12)

> Let two or three prophets speak, and let the others weigh what is said. If a revelation is made to another sitting there, let the first be silent. For you can all prophesy one by one, so that all may learn and all be encouraged, and the spirits of prophets are subject to prophets. For God is not a God of confusion but of peace. As in all the churches of the saints, the women should keep silent in the churches. For they are not permitted to speak, but should be in submission, as the Law also says. If there is anything they desire to learn, let them ask their husbands at home. For it is shameful for a woman to speak in church. Or was it from you that the word of God came? Or are you the only ones it has reached? If anyone thinks that he is a prophet, or spiritual, he should acknowledge that the things I am writing to you are a command of the Lord. (1 Cor 14:29–37)

These seem pretty clear statements. The problem is that if these statements by Paul are absolute, meaning that they apply under all circumstances, then Paul contradicted what he wrote elsewhere and also contradicted other passages in the Old and New Testament. So, there are five possibilities:

1. Paul was wrong.
2. These verses by Paul are right, but other verses by Paul are wrong.
3. Paul was right but many other passages in the Bible are wrong.
4. Paul never wrote these verses.
5. Paul meant these verses to apply only under specific circumstances, but not universally.

APPENDICES

PARSING 1 CORINTHIANS 14

First, let us do a little surgery on these verses. First Corinthians 14:33–34 says, "For God is not a God of confusion but of peace. As in all the churches of the saints, the women should keep silent in the churches."

In the original Greek manuscripts of the New Testament there was no punctuation and no verse numbers. These are the products of much later editors. So, the way we would find these words in Paul's original (using English as an example) would be:

> forgodisnotagodofconfusionbutofpeaceasinallthechurchesofthesaintsthewomenshouldkeepsilentinthechurches

We have to provide all the spaces between words, the capital letters, the commas, and the periods. Therefore, it is legitimate to think that what Paul wrote was

> For God is not a God of confusion but of peace, as in all the churches of the saints. Women should keep silent in the churches.

That is, if Paul was saying that women should keep silent in the churches, he was not necessarily saying that this is what they already did in all the churches of the saints. In fact, the phrase "as in all the churches of the saints" makes much more sense if attached to the previous phrase than if it is attached to the phrase about women keeping silent, for if the women already kept silent in all the churches of the saints, why did Paul bother to tell them to do what they were already doing? Or, if they were doing it everywhere else, but not in Corinth, that supports the argument that this passage was directed to Corinth only, not to churches universally. A fair reading of the text (in Greek or in English) suggests that this phrase really should attach to the previous phrase, meaning that God is the God of peace in all the churches of the saints. That is uncontroversially true.

WOMEN IN AUTHORITY

In Galatians 3:28, Paul wrote: "There is neither Jew nor Greek, there is neither slave nor free, there is no male and female, for you are all one in Christ Jesus." If Jesus does not make a distinction between men and women, according to Paul, why would Paul do so?

Paul established the church in Philippi in the house of Lydia, apparently a single woman (Acts 16:15, 40). In Laodicea, the church met in the house of a woman named Nympha (Col 4:15). Is it likely that these women refrained from speaking in the churches that met in their own houses? Paul also endorsed Priscilla, wife of Aquila, as his coworker in Christ, not his assistant. Acts 18:26 says that Aquila and Priscilla took Apollos into their home and that they, not Aquila alone, expounded the way of God to him more accurately. Phoebe was a deacon (διάκονον) of the church in Cenchreae, near Corinth. She was at least one of the couriers who took Paul's epistle to the Romans to Rome (Rom 16:1). Is it likely that a deacon of the church never spoke in the church, even if she was a female?

There are other examples in the Bible of women speaking in the assembly of the faithful (because all "church" means in the original Greek is "those who have been called, the chosen people"). Examples are:

- Deborah, who was a prophetess and Judge of Israel,
- Huldah, a prophetess who instructed King Josiah and the high priest,
- Anna, the prophetess who proclaimed in the Jerusalem temple that the infant Jesus was the Messiah,
- The Samaritan woman at the well, who recognized Jesus as the Messiah and led her entire village to Christ, and
- The four unmarried daughters of Philip the Evangelist, who not only were prophetesses, but were prophesying while the apostle Paul was visiting their assembly in Caesarea! (Acts 21:9).

Peter, in his sermon on Pentecost, at the birth of the church, quoted the prophet Joel (Joel 2:28), saying:

> And in the last days it shall be, God declares, that I will pour out my Spirit on all flesh, and your sons and your daughters shall prophesy, and your young men shall see visions, and your old men shall dream dreams; even on my male servants and female servants in those days I will pour out my Spirit, and they shall prophesy. (Acts 2:17–18)

Joel and Peter said that daughters would prophesy and that the Holy Spirit would be poured out on his female servants. When God sends a divine message to a prophet, the prophet is obligated to share that word with the community of God. Paul actually made this point in 1 Corinthians 14:29: "Let two or three prophets speak, and let the others weigh what is said." If God himself said that he would ordain women as prophets, who was Paul to tell them that they should be silent in church and have no authority over men? The prophetesses Deborah (Judg 4:9) and Huldah (2 Chron 34:23–28) spoke out and had authority over men, with God's blessing.

Paul was well-versed in Scripture. The Holy Spirit also inspired him to communicate God's word. So it is highly unlikely that Paul was too stupid to recognize these apparent contradictions or that he just did not care about them. Nor is it plausible to argue that Paul was right and all these other Bible passages are wrong.

THE INTERPOLATION OF 1 CORINTHIANS 14:34–35

One possibility is that Paul may not have written 1 Corinthians 14:34–35. Some scholars theorize that these verses were added by copyists and are not Paul's original writing. There is some merit to this argument. Verses 34 and 35 do not appear in the same place in all ancient manuscripts of 1 Corinthians, suggesting that copyists may have found them in the margins of older manuscripts and did not quite know where to put them. Also, verses 34 and 35 seem to interrupt Paul's train of thought. If we cut these verses out, consider how much better the whole passage flows. Please read the passage and imagine that verses 34–35, the verses in brackets, are not in it.

> Let two or three prophets speak, and let the others weigh what is said. If a revelation is made to another sitting there, let the first be silent. For you can all prophesy one by one, so that all may learn and all be encouraged, and the spirits of prophets are subject to prophets. For God is not a God of confusion but of peace, as in all the churches of the saints,
>
> [the women should keep silent in the churches. For they are not permitted to speak, but should be in submission, as the Law also says. If there is anything they desire to learn, let them ask their husbands at home. For it is shameful for a woman to speak in church.]
>
> Or was it from you that the word of God came? Or are you the only ones it has reached? If anyone thinks that he is a prophet, or spiritual, he should acknowledge that the things I am writing to you are a command of the Lord.

This passage really makes a lot more sense without verses 34 and 35 than with them. After all, why would Paul rebuke the women for thinking that the word of God had come only to them? Did any women say that? Or is it not more likely that someone who received a prophecy might be carried away and think too much of his divine gift—and might need to realize that true prophecies may also come to other believers, not only to them?

Also, in verse 34, Paul writes: "For they are not permitted to speak, but should be in submission, as the Law also says." But the law of Moses never said that. So, was Paul ignorant of the law? Not likely. He was a star student under Gamaliel. Was Paul therefore referring to some other law, like Greek law? There is no scriptural support for that.

Also, was it logical for Paul to tell women that if they wanted to learn, they should ask their husbands to teach them at home? In this very letter, 1 Corinthians 7:8, Paul wrote, "To the unmarried and the widows I say that it is good for them to remain single, as I am." How would unmarried or widowed women learn from their husbands at home? Paul further wrote:

> If any woman has a husband who is an unbeliever, and he consents to live with her, she should not divorce him. For the unbelieving husband is made holy because of his wife, and the unbelieving wife is made holy because of her husband. Otherwise your children would be unclean, but as it is, they are holy. But if the unbelieving partner separates, let it be so. In such cases the brother

or sister is not enslaved. God has called you to peace. For how do you know, wife, whether you will save your husband? Or how do you know, husband, whether you will save your wife? (1 Cor 7:13–16)

If a woman cannot teach a man or have any authority over a man, how could a believing wife save an unbelieving husband? Notice that Paul put a believing wife and husband on the same footing, writing, "For how do you know, wife, whether you will save your husband? Or how do you know, husband, whether you will save your wife?"

So, given the possible logical flaws in these verses, the idea that they might not be Paul's original writing could be true. But then we have to deal with 1 Timothy 2:12: "I do not permit a woman to teach or to exercise authority over a man; rather, she is to remain quiet." Is this also a copyist's interpolation? First Timothy 2:12 has the same problems as the other verses. Did Paul forbid Priscilla to teach Apollos? Apparently not. Would Paul have chastised Huldah for telling King Josiah and the high priest what to do when God did not reprimand her? Would Paul rebuke God for pouring out his Spirit on female servants and authorizing daughters to prophesy? Paul would have had to lack self-awareness, intelligence, and humility to take such a stance, and the whole testimony of Scripture about Paul simply cannot line up with his being blinkered, stupid, or arrogant.

THE CIRCUMSTANCES OF CORINTH AND EPHESUS

Probably Paul meant 1 Corinthians 14:34–35 and 2 Timothy 2:12 to apply to certain churches planted in Corinth and Ephesus, where specific conditions prevailed, requiring specific remedies. If this is correct, the women in the Corinthian and Ephesian churches were to keep silent in church, because these women, not all women, found it hard to keep order. Apparently these women, not all women, were unruly and needed to respect discreet manners and customs. Apparently these women, not all women, had believing husbands at home who would be willing to teach them. And with respect to 2 Timothy 2:12, Paul did not permit the women of Ephesus to have authority over the men in the church at Ephesus but exhorted them to keep silent, because apparently these women, not all women, tried to exercise authority inappropriately over men and were unruly in their speaking out. It is likely that in these controversial verses Paul was delivering instructions to certain women whose unruly behavior called for specific discipline. And since "the Lord disciplines the one he loves" (Heb 12:6), it is safe to believe that Paul offered this discipline in love, not in anger. If this conclusion is true, the prohibition against women speaking out or having authority in church is conditional, not universal.

APPENDICES

FEMALE COWORKERS

When Paul wrote his letter to the Philippian church (from house arrest in Nero's Rome), the church had become larger, replete with deacons and overseers. Yet he asked the Philippians to help the women Euodia and Syntyche "who have labored side by side with me in the gospel together with Clement and the rest of my coworkers, whose names are in the book of life" (Phil 4:3). Here were two other women, who, like Priscilla, Paul grouped together with himself, Aquila, Clement, and others as coworkers, women who did the same work that these men did. And what did these women do? They taught the gospel. They did not serve meals or wash clothes; at least that wasn't their main mission. Yet Paul did not call these women "deacons" (servants). He called them "coworkers."

Paul told Timothy and Titus that "he" did not allow women to teach. But he did not say that God didn't allow it. And he cannot have meant he never allowed it, because in the case of Prisca, Lydia, Euodia, and Syntyche, he obviously did allow it. Not all of Paul's opinions are God's opinions. In 1 Corinthians 7:10 and 12, Paul clearly stated that he, not the Lord, endorsed certain views.

WOMEN IN THE HELLENIC WORLD

Timothy and Titus were ministering in ancient Greece. In the Hellenistic world, women generally did not read, write, or participate in any educated endeavor. The few who did were exceptional, if not scandalous. Sappho, the poetess of Lesbos, was apparently sexually promiscuous and perhaps homosexual. The rich and beautiful Phryne of Athens had many lovers; essentially, she was a cultured prostitute. Decent women in the Hellenistic world could not go out of the house, could not go shopping, could not take their children to school, lived in a small attic on the top floor of their house, ate alone, and focused on sewing, cleaning, and meal preparation for their husbands and sons. Their lives were as bad as slaves or worse and were exceptionally lonely and depressing.

When Christianity suddenly sprung women from this prison and made them (along with the other underclasses of antiquity, such as children and slaves) as valuable as any other human, they suddenly found themselves accepted at dinners (the Lord's Supper) and in congregations where they could learn, serve, sing, and receive special support (if they were widows or orphans). Nothing like this had happened to women for thousands of years. They must absolutely have exploded, like children suddenly being released onto a playground. No wonder Paul told them to dress modestly, to be quiet in the assembly, and not to teach. They were probably full of chatter, opinions, excitement, and quite out of control. How could they teach? They really knew almost nothing. They had a lot of learning to do.

Lydia and Prisca were different. They were Jewish, not Greek. Jewish women were probably the most liberated in antiquity. They could read. They could study.

They could travel. They traveled four times per year on pilgrimages to Jerusalem if they could afford it. They could own property. They could run businesses. They could counsel kings (as Abigail, Deborah, Huldah, and Esther did). They could even become the monarch of Israel (as Athaliah and Salome Alexandra did). And, of course, some of them had been God's prophetesses. With God's permission these women could and did teach, prophesy, and have authority over men. It is a matter of biblical record.

CONCLUSION

Paul's injunction against women teaching was for certain times and places. Paul himself enrolled women as teachers and coworkers when the circumstances were favorable. Women can certainly teach men in church if they are equipped to do so, and men should not teach anyone in church if they are unequipped to do so.

Calendar Tool

IN CONVERTING JEWISH, JULIAN, Gregorian, Persian, and other calendars, the tool used in this study is "Kalendis Calendar Calculator," version 9.837(1557) by Dr. Irvin L. Bromberg, University of Toronto, Canada, http://www.sym454.org. This is a very useful tool, and readers are encouraged to use it to cross-check the chronologies in this book. Like all calendars, however, it presents some difficulties. Dr. Bromberg appears to use Tishri as the first month of the Jewish year, rather than Nisan. The northern Kingdom of Israel used Tishri as the first month in its calendar. Judah used Nisan. Judah was more faithful than apostate Israel, whose first king, Jeroboam I, even invented new holy days, which God condemned. In Exodus 12:2, Moses recorded God's statement that Nisan, the month of the Passover, was "the first month of the year." In Leviticus 16:29, Moses recorded God's statement that Tishri (the month of the Day of Atonement or Yom Kippur) was the "seventh month." It is preferable to adopt the calendar decreed by God rather than one invented by men.

Months of the Hebrew Calendar

English	Number	Days	Gregorian Equivalent
Nisan (alternate name Aviv or Abib, literally "barley")	1	30	March–April
Iyar (alternate name Ziv, literally "light")	2	29	April–May
Sivan	3	30	May–June
Tammuz	4	29	June–July
Av	5	30	July–August
Elul	6	29	August–September
Tishri (alternate name Ethanim, literally "strong" plural)	7	30	September–October
Cheshvan (alternate Bul)	8	29 or 30	October–November
Kislev	9	30 or 29	November–December
Tevet	10	29	December–January
Shevat	11	30	January–February
Adar I (called Adar Rishon in leap years)	12	30	February–March
Adar II (called Adar Sheini in leap years)	12 (13 in leap years)	29	February–March

The Hebrew Year

The Hebrew months are roughly lunar, but the Hebrew years, like ours, are solar. Hebrew years contain both intercalary days and months to compensate for the disparity between lunar and solar time-keeping. There are, therefore, six types of Hebrew year that rotate in regular succession. Their lengths are: 353 days, 354 days, 355 days, 383 days, 384 days, and 385 days. The average length of a Hebrew year is thus 369 days, and no Hebrew year ever equals 360 days. The Hebrew system keeps pace well with our Gregorian years, and the disparity between the Hebrew and Gregorian calendars is therefore surprisingly slight.

The AD-BC Calendar

THE AD-BC SYSTEM WAS invented by a Romanian monk named Dionysus Exiguus (Dennis the Short) in AD 525. Pope John I gave him the task of producing a calendar to show the dates on which future Easters would fall. This was not as easy as it might seem. The abbreviation "AD" stands for *anno domini*, Latin for "in the year of our Lord." Christian-era history counts forward from AD 1, so 2022 is 2,022 years after the supposed year of Jesus' birth. The abbreviation "BC" stands for "Before Christ." Historians with an anti-Christian bias replace the terms BC and AD with BCE and CE, "Before the Common Era" and "Common Era." However, since the "Common Era" dates history according to the birth of Jesus, this scheme fails to erase the centrality of Christ in human events. This is pointless political correctness.

Dionysus concluded that he was living 525 years since the incarnation of Jesus Christ. How he arrived at that calculation is questionable. In Dennis's system, there is no year 0. Year 1 is the supposed birth year of Jesus. Pre-Christian history counts backward from that year. So, 500 BC is five hundred years before Christ and is earlier than 100 BC, which is only one hundred years before Christ.

The Jewish calendar measures time according to the moon's rotation around the earth. The Roman (Julian) and our current (Gregorian) calendars measure time according to the earth's rotation around the sun. Our calendar year and the Jewish calendar year are of different lengths. Some Bible commentators try to reconcile our calendar with the Jewish calendar simply by assuming that one Jewish year = 12 months x 30 days = 360 days. But this calculation is always wrong.

The true solar year is 365.25 days. Our calendar (the Gregorian calendar) has 365 days in a year. We have a "leap year" every four years, in which we have twenty-nine, rather than twenty-eight, days in February to catch up with the missing one-quarter day in the non-leap years. The Jewish calendar has years of six different lengths: 353, 354, 355, 383, 384, and 385 days. The variances occur by sometimes adding an extra day to one or more months and sometimes by adding an extra month at the end of the year and sometimes by doing both. The result is that synchronizing the Jewish and the Gregorian calendar is a complex exercise. With computer programs today it is easy, if the program is properly written, which is not always the case. But in the pre-computer

APPENDICES

world, this was a challenge. The fact that authors of the Bible always got their dates precisely right is a strong indicator of the Bible's divine inspiration.

Julius Caesar proposed the Julian calendar in 46 BC. It had a 365-day year. The previous Roman calendar had twelve months and a 355-day year, with an intercalary (extra) month of twenty-seven or twenty-eight days, sometimes added between February and March. Its purpose was to keep the calendar aligned with the seasons. But it was a flawed calendar that did not keep up. This was obvious even to casual observers when it snowed in what was supposed to be the month of July.

In AD 1582, Pope Gregory XIII endorsed a revised Julian calendar named the Gregorian calendar after him. It reduced minor errors in the Julian calendar. But even with the Gregorian, or our more exact ISO, calendar, the churches still do not always manage to get the dates of Easter, or Resurrection Sunday, right. For example, in 2016, the Catholic and Protestant churches celebrated Easter on Sunday, March 27. In the same year, the Greek Orthodox Church celebrated it on Sunday, May 1. But in that year, 16 Nisan in the Hebrew calendar, the actual date of Jesus' resurrection, was on April 24.

About the Author

I GREW UP EXPOSED to Christianity, but in my late teens I concluded that the Bible was a compilation of myths, and, compared to the *Mahabharata* and *Arabian Nights*, rather inferior ones. I felt too smart to be a Christian. So I sought truth elsewhere. But, after traveling the world and diving deeply into the great religions, I grew tired being a seeker after truth. I wanted to be a finder of it. My family urged me to read the Bible and visit a church. I did so gingerly. I visited a megachurch in Southern California with chorus lyrics projected on a big screen. The meandering tunes and euphoric devotees made me want to reach for a pinch of salt.

The pastor, however, preached salvation through Christ alone. He promised that if I would walk to the altar and repent before God in Jesus' name, I would receive the Holy Spirit. I doubted him, but I was rational. Faith is the daughter of doubt. I had crossed the Himalayas and met the Dalai Lama. I had trekked through steaming Java jungles to a Sufi shrine. I could walk down this air-conditioned aisle and prove or disprove the pastor's claim.

At the altar, I prayed a rather impudent prayer. "God, I know you exist. If this is the way to know you personally, I accept it." If I had been God (which fortunately for all of us I am not), I would have responded to my impertinence by reducing me instantly to a grease spot. Instead, a light flickered on in my heart. I had been in the occasional midnight chant in Asia, and I attributed this sensation to mere ambience. But it lasted. It lasted until today and will last beyond the horizon of time. I was saved. The problem was that my mind was far behind my heart. My overly "educated" brain possessed clear and convincing proofs that the Bible was philosophically and scientifically wrong. Either the Bible or my brain had to give. So, I began to devote myself to disproving the Bible.

To my ongoing humiliation, the battering rams of "enlightenment" kept splintering against the impervious gates of Scripture. Everywhere I turned—archaeology, paleontology, astronomy, history, physics, mathematics, and philosophy—the Bible proved right, and I proved wrong. I burned with shame to think how many Christians I had "defeated" in debate and how smugly superior I had felt to them. How could God have any desire to love me, who had been such an arrogant fool? The answer came when I realized I could witness comfortably to Muslims, Hindus, Buddhists, and skeptics because I had once embraced their positions.

In the summer of 2008, Grace Church of Glendora, California, asked me to teach an adult theology class for three Sundays. I was extremely nervous. I simply did not know the Bible well enough to teach it. During those first three Sunday lessons, I was bathed in sweat. By the third, I learned that no substitute teacher had been found, and I ended up teaching the Bible, verse by verse, repeatedly, from then until Sunday, May 29, 2016. In the course of doing this, I grappled with every problem and seeming contradiction in the Bible that I could find. From apparent discrepancies in chronology and with science, to the arcane mystery of Solomon's Sea, I discovered, through eight thousand hours of research and teaching and by writing 1,005 GB of original course material, that the Bible is totally inerrant.

I was blessed to have a class of devoted and highly educated adults. Among them were a trained and professional theologian, philosophers, educators, mathematicians, physical scientists, a rocket scientist (literally), and Bible students of many decades. They were of inestimable help in correcting and guiding me as I presented and tested my lessons. As iron sharpens iron, so we sharpened each other. I turned my original course material into many books on theology, of which this is one.

In May 2022, I earned a master's degree in theology with high distinction at Liberty University's Rawlings School of Divinity, Lynchburg, Virginia. I am pursuing a Ph.D. in theology at the same university. I live in rural Massachusetts and own a parcel delivery company with sixty-five employees and thirty-four vans.

Bibliography

"The Acts of Andrew." Translated by M. R. James. *Early Christian Writings*. http://www.earlychristianwritings.com/text/actsandrew.html.

"The Acts of Andrew and Matthias." *New Advent*. https://www.newadvent.org/fathers/0820.htm.

"The Acts of John." Translated by M. R. James. *Gnostic Society Library*. http://gnosis.org/library/actjohn.htm.

"The Acts of Philip." *Gnostic Society Library*. http://gnosis.org/library/actphil.htm.

"The Acts of Timothy." *The North American Society for the Study of Christian Apocryphal Literature*. https://www.nasscal.com/e-clavis-christian-apocrypha/acts-of-timothy.

Allen, David L. *Lukan Authorship of Hebrews*. Nashville: B&H Academic, 2010.

Antiochian Orthodox Christian Archdiocese of North America. "The Patriarchate of Antioch: Founded by Saints Peter and Paul." http://ww1.antiochian.org/patofant.

Appell, Victor S. "Why Do Some Jews Have One Seder and Others Have Two Seders?" *ReformJudaism.org: Jewish Life in Your Life*. https://reformjudaism.org/learning/answers-jewish-questions/why-do-some-jews-have-one-seder-and-others-have-two-seders.

Augustine of Hippo. "De Adulterinis Conjugiis 2:6–7." *Evidence Unseen*. https://www.evidenceunseen.com/bible-difficulties-2/nt-difficulties/john-acts/jn-753–811-does-this-belong-in-the-bible/#_ftn13.

Bereford, James. *The Ancient Sailing Season*. Boston: Brill, 2013.

Beyer, David W. "Josephus Reexamined: Unraveling the Twenty-Second Year of Tiberius." In *Chronos, Kairos, Christos II*, edited by Ray Summers and Jerry Vardaman, 85–96. Macon, GA: Mercer University Press, 1998.

"Biography of Saint Luke." *New Advent*. https://www.newadvent.org/cathen/09420a.htm.

Bromberg, Irving L. "Kalendis Calendar Calculator." http://individual.utoronto.ca/kalendis/kalendis.htm.

Bruce, F. F. "Christianity under Claudius." *Bulletin of the John Rylands Library* 44 (March 1962) 309–26.

Caldwell, Zelda. "Three of the Oldest Images of Jesus Portray Him as the 'Good Shepherd.'" *Aleteia*, March 27, 2019. https://aleteia.org/2019/05/12/three-of-the-oldest-images-of-jesus-portrays-him-as-the-good-shepherd/.

Cassius Dio. *Roman History*. https://penelope.uchicago.edu/Thayer/e/roman/texts/cassius_dio/home.html.

Casson, Lionel. *Speed under Sail of Ancient Ships*. https://penelope.uchicago.edu/Thayer/E/Journals/TAPA/82/Speed_under_Sail_of_Ancient_Ships*.html.

Cheetham, S. "The Province of Galatia." *The Classical Review* 8.9.(1894) 396.

Cholmondeley, Helen H. "Betrayal." *Poetry Explorer.* https://www.poetryexplorer.net/poem.php?id=10024418.

Cicero, *Against Verres,* 2:5:161-163.

Clement of Alexandria. *Stromata ("Miscellanies").* https://www.newadvent.org/fathers/0210.htm.

Davies, W.D. and D.C. Allison. *Matthew 1-7.* International Critical Commentary. New York: T & T Clark, 1988, 146 no. 125.

De Montor, Artaud. *Lives and Times of the Roman Pontiffs, from St. Peter to Pius IX,* vol. 1. Paris: D & J Sadlier, 1869.

De Voragine, Jacobus. *The Golden Legend.* New York: Fordham University Press. https://sourcebooks.fordham.edu/basis/goldenlegend/index.asp.

Elwell, Walter A. *Encountering the New Testament: A historical and Theological Survey.* 3rd ed. Grand Rapids: Baker Academic, 2013.

Encyclopedia Britannica. "Aksum." https://www.britannica.com/place/Aksum-Ethiopia.

Encyclopedia Britannica. "What Was Hadrian's Relatinship with His Jewish Subjects?" https://www.britannica.com/story/what-was-hadrians-relationship-with-his-jewish-subjects.

Ephraim, Saint. "On Thomas the Apostle." *NSC Network,* October 10, 2014. nasrani.net/2008/05/20/hymns-of-saint-ephraem-ephrem-the-syrian-on-apostle-thomas-and-india/.

Eusebius. *Church History.* https://www.newadvent.org/fathers/2501.htm.

Finegan, Jack. *Handbook of Biblical Chronology.* Rev. ed. Peabody, MA: Hendrickson, 1998.

Gottheil, Richard, et al. "Captivity, or Exile, Babylonian." *Jewish Encyclopedia.* https://www.jewishencyclopedia.com/articles/4012-captivity.

Gospel of Barnabas. https://barnabas.sabr.com/.

Gregg, Steven. *Revelation: Four Views, A Parallel Commentary.* Nashville: Thomas Nelson, 1997.

Herodotus. *The History of Herodotus, Book IV.* Translated by George Rawlinson. http://classics.mit.edu/Herodotus/history.4.iv.html.

Hippolytus. "List of the Apostles and Disciples." *North American Society for the Study of Christian Apocryphal Literature.* https://www.nasscal.com/e-clavis-christian-apocrypha/list-of-the-apostles-and-disciples-by-pseudo-hippolytus-of-thebes/.

Hirsch, Emil G. "Festivals." *Jewish Encyclopedia.* https://jewishencyclopedia.com/articles/6099-festivals.

Irenaeus. *Against Heresies.* https://www.newadvent.org/fathers/0103.htm.

James, M. R., trans. "The Acts of Thomas." The Gnostic Society Library. http://gnosis.org/library/actthom.htm.

Jerome. *Commentary on Galatians.* Washington, DC: Catholic University of America Press, 2010. https://books.google.com/books?id=vwbtWmJYyIUC&q=.

———. *On Illustrious Men.* https://www.newadvent.org/fathers/2708.htm.

Jones, Victoria Emily. "The Two Genealogies of Jesus, the Curse of Jeconiah, and the Royal Line of David." *The Jesus Question,* December 21, 2015. https://thejesusquestion.org/2015/12/21/the-two-genealogies-of-jesus-the-curse-of-jeconiah-and-the-royal-line-of-david/.

Josephus. *Antiquities of the Jews.* https://www.biblestudytools.com/history/flavius-josephus/antiquities-jews/.

———. *War of the Jews.* https://www.biblestudytools.com/history/flavius-josephus/war-of-the-jews/.

Justin Martyr. "Dialogue with Trypho." *Early Christian Writings*. https://www.newadvent.org/fathers/0128.htm.

———. "First Apology." *Early Christian Writings*. https://www.newadvent.org/fathers/0126.htm.

Kaneda, Toshiko, and Carl Haub. "How Many People Have Ever Lived on Earth?" *Population Reference Bureau*, May 18, 2021. https://www.prb.org/articles/how-many-people-have-ever-lived-on-earth/.

Keller, Timothy. *The Reason for God: Belief in an Age of Skepticism*. New York: Penguin Books, 2018.

Kitto, John, et al. *The Journal of Sacred Literature and Biblical Record*, vol. 11. London: John Crockford, 1860.

Larson, Frederick E. "Star of Bethlehem." http://www.bethlehemstar.net.

Mattison, Mark M., trans. *Gospel of Judas*. https://www.gospels.net/judas.

Mattison, Mark M., ed. "Gospel of Thomas." gospels.net/thomas.

Meinardus, Otto F. A. "St. Paul Shipwrecked in Dalmatia." *The Biblical Archaeologist* 39.4 (Dec. 1976) 145–47.

Merrill, Elmer Truesdell. "The Expulsion of Jews from Rome under Tiberius." *Classical Philology* 14.4 (1919) 365–72.

Moseley, James Allen. "Bethlehem Star." https://www.youtube.com/watch?v=5Z-hZWAvpIE.

———. *The History of Daniel: Truth in Exile*. Petersham, MA: Winterwood, 2019.

———. *The History of Jesus, the Son of Man*. Petersham, MA: Winterwood, 2019.

———. *The History of Revelation: Beyond the Veil*. Petersham, MA: Winterwood, 2019.

"The Muratorian Canon, Fragment III, Robert-Donaldson Translation." *Early Christian Writings*. http://www.earlychristianwritings.com/text/muratorian.html.

New Advent Catholic Encyclopedia. "Gospel of Saint Luke." https://www.newadvent.org/cathen/09420a.htm.

Nollet, James A. "Astronomical and Historical Evidence for Dating the Nativity in 2 BC." In *Perspectives on Science and Christian Faith*. 64.4 (December 2012) 211–19.

O'Kane, Murray. *Little Lives of the Great Saints*. Charlotte, NC: TAN, 2009.

Orosius, Paulus. *Histories against the Pagans*. http://attalus.org/info/orosius.html.

Papias of Hierapolis. "Fragments of Papias." *Early Christian Writings*. http://www.earlychristianwritings.com/text/papias.html.

Pew Research Center. "The Global Religious Landscape." *Pew Research Center*, December 18, 2012. https://www.pewresearch.org/religion/2012/12/18/global-religious-landscape-exec/.

Plutarch. *Lives*. https://penelope.uchicago.edu/Thayer/e/roman/texts/plutarch/lives/home.html.

"Roman Empire Population." *UNRV Roman History*. http://www.unrv.com/empire/roman-population.php.

"Saints Thaddaeus and Bartholomew." *The Armenian Prelacy*. https://armenianprelacy.org/2020/11/25/saints-thaddeus-and-bartholomew/.

Schechter, Solomon, et al. "Holy Days." *Jewish Encyclopedia*. https://www.jewishencyclopedia.com/articles/7814-holidays.

Schnabel, Eckhard J., et al. *Revelation: An Introduction and Commentary*. Downers Grove: InterVarsity, 2018.

Schnelle, Udo. *Apostle Paul: His Life and Theology*. Nashville: Baker Academic, 2012.

Shelton, W. Brian. *Quest for the Historical Apostles: Tracing Their Lives and Legacies*. Grand Rapids: Baker Academic, 2018.

Smith, William. *A New Classical Dictionary of Greek and Roman Biography, Mythology, and Geography.* New York: Harper & Brothers, 1851. https://quod.lib.umich.edu/m/moa/acl3132.0001.001/3.

Steinman, Andrew. "When Did Herod the Great Reign?" *Novum Testamentum* 51.1 (2009) 1–29.

Strong, James. *Strong's Exhaustive Concordance to the Bible.* Peabody: Hendrickson, 2009.

Suetonius. *Lives of the Twelve Caesars.* https://www.gutenberg.org/files/6400/6400-h/6400-h.htm.

Tacitus. *Annals.* https://penelope.uchicago.edu/Thayer/e/roman/texts/tacitus/home.html.

———. *Histories.* https://penelope.uchicago.edu/Thayer/e/roman/texts/tacitus/home.html.

Tertullian. *The Acts and Martyrdom of the Holy Apostle Andrew.* https://www.tertullian.org/fathers2/ANF-08/anf08-95.htm.

———. *Prescription against Heresies.* https://www.newadvent.org/fathers/0311.htm.

"Walking Englishman's Walk Time Calculator." https://www.walkingenglishman.com/walktime.aspx.

Wesley, John. "Luke 3: Wesley's Notes on the Bible." *BibleHub Commentaries.* https://biblehub.com/commentaries/wes/luke/3.htm.

"*Yoma* 39b." *Talmud.* https://www.sefaria.org/Yoma.39b.5?lang=bi.

ZA Blog. "What Language Did Jesus Speak?" *Zondervan Academic Blog*, September 7, 2016. https://zondervanacademic.com/blog/what-language-did-jesus-speak.

www.ingramcontent.com/pod-product-compliance
Lightning Source LLC
Chambersburg PA
CBHW081414230426
43668CB00016B/2237